# PRINCETON SEMINARY

*Faith and Learning*

# PRINCETON SEMINARY

David B. Calhoun

*Volume 1*
*Faith and Learning*
*1812–1868*

THE BANNER OF TRUTH TRUST

THE BANNER OF TRUTH TRUST
*3 Murrayfield Road, Edinburgh EH12 6EL*
*P.O. Box 621, Carlisle, Pennsylvania 17013, USA*

❉

© David B. Calhoun 1994
First Published 1994
ISBN 0 85151 670 X

❉

*Typeset in 11/12pt New Baskerville*
*Printed and bound in the USA*

To Anne, Allen and Isabel

An Old University town . . .
Kirk and College keeping time,
Faith and Learning, chime for chime

*Princetoniana*

# CONTENTS

APPENDICES

The Index to both volumes of this work
will be found at the end of Volume 2.

# ILLUSTRATIONS

# ABBREVIATIONS

| | |
|---|---|
| *AP* | *American Presbyterians: Journal of Presbyterian History* (1985—) (Philadelphia: Presbyterian Historical Society) |
| *JPH* | *Journal of Presbyterian History (1962-1984)* (Philadelphia: Presbyterian Historical Society) |
| *JPHS* | *Journal of the Presbyterian Historical Society* (1901-1961) (Philadelphia: Presbyterian Historical Society) |
| *LAA* | *The Life of Archibald Alexander, D.D., First Professor in the Theological Seminary, at Princeton, New Jersey,* James W. Alexander (New York: Charles Scribner), 1854 |
| *LAG* | *The Life of Ashbel Green, V.D.M.,* ed. Joseph H. Jones (New York: Robert Carter & Bros.), 1849 |
| *LCH* | *The Life of Charles Hodge, D.D., LL.D., Professor in the Theological Seminary, Princeton, N. J.,* Archibald Alexander Hodge (New York: Charles Scribner's Sons), 1880 |
| *LJAA* 1, 2 | *The Life of Joseph Addison Alexander,* Henry Carrington Alexander (New York: Charles Scribner's), 1870 |
| *LJWA* 1, 2 | *Forty Years' Familiar Letters of James W. Alexander,* ed. John Hall (New York: Charles Scribner), 1860 |
| *LSM* 1, 2 | *The Life of Samuel Miller,* Samuel Miller, Jr. (Philadelphia: Claxton, Remsen & Haffelfinger), 1869 |
| *PSB* | *Princeton Seminary Bulletin* |
| *SSW* 1, 2 | *Selected Shorter Writings of Benjamin B. Warfield,* ed. John E. Meeter (Nutley, N.J.: Presbyterian and Reformed Publishing Company), 1973 |

PRINCETON JOURNALS

## ACKNOWLEDGEMENTS

We are indebted to the following sources for use of the pictures which they have kindly provided for this volume:

The portrait of the young Charles Hodge is reproduced courtesy of the Frick Art Reference Library, New York.

William P. Alexander preaching in Kauai, Hawaiian Islands, from HMCS Library, Mission Houses Museum, Hawaii.

Diary of Lewis Miller (1796–1882), courtesy of The Historical Society of York County, Pennsylvania.

# FOREWORD

Having read this first volume of Dr. Calhoun's history of Princeton Theological Seminary twice, prior to its publication, I am deeply thankful that its inspiring story can now be taken up by so many around the world. Of course, the general Christian reader does not commonly go to the records of theological institutions to find inspiration. Perhaps not many such places have had a history calculated to produce that effect, and if they had they seldom have found authors worthy of the theme. Whether that be so or not, for outstanding spiritual value Princeton Seminary has a story which ought never to have been forgotten. Here that story is recovered and told with a wealth of colour and detail as it has never been told before. Backed by years of careful research, by his own long experience in the training of men for the ministry, and, above all, by his spiritual commitment to the message these pages convey, David Calhoun has given us a record which must find a permanent place in the Christian literature of the English-speaking world.

For most of us, Princeton Seminary has been known chiefly for the truths and the ideas which successive generations of its faculty and its graduates put into print. What we lacked was a sense of these authors as people, as they were once known in everyday life. The human element was too much hidden from us. But, as Dr. Calhoun says in his Preface, the primary answer to the question, "What is Princeton?" has to be given in terms of *men*, and it is only as we come to know them that we can begin to understand the immense influence of the work which began in their secluded New Jersey village in 1812. The Seminary came into existence to prepare heralds of the gospel, to teach them not only what to think but what to believe, and to enforce the lesson that "Preaching Christ is the best, hardest, sweetest work, on this side of beholding him." This volume tells us how that endeavour took shape. And beyond Princeton, it shows us why these men came to stand at the forefront of world evangelization. Of the students of the first fifty years—2,422 in number—no less than a third were to be found in mission fields, and we read that W. B. Sprague could say in 1862, "You can scarcely pause in any country, and look around you, without finding yourself in contact with an evangelizing influence that has emanated from Princeton."

We admire the balance of Dr Calhoun's treatment of his subject. Events, people and thought are all given their place. If Presbyterian interests are here so also is the presentation of things yet more fundamental—the emphases which led such Baptists as Francis Wayland and C. H. Spurgeon to speak of the Seminary as they did. Controversy is here also but with that same wisdom and moderation which Princeton ever urged on its men. Into the narrative first-hand quotations from the Princetonians are skillfully woven, and this is done sufficiently to bring us into the presence of the men themselves. When it is possible for women to receive their place in this story the opportunity is not missed, whether it be to tell us of Betsey Stockton, a black convert in the revival of 1815 who became a missionary in the Sandwich Islands and then a school-teacher in Princeton, or of the wife of one of the professors. The glimpses we have of such people as Sarah Hodge tell us much both about her husband and her sons. Perhaps there is scarcely an anecdote which shows the spirit of the supporters of old Princeton Seminary better than the one concerning Marian Hall on page 319. Her outlook is exactly the outlook which these pages are calculated to inspire afresh.

There is a great deal about this volume which is especially timely. A mood of doubt and uncertainty has seized many churches with respect to all things old or traditional. Not a few would tend to regard it as axiomatic that the history of a seminary for the years 1812-1868 can have little relevance to needs which face us at the end of the twentieth century. A serious reading of these pages will lead to a different conclusion. The trouble with too much contemporary Christianity is not that it has hung on too long to the lessons of the past and has found them to fail. It is rather that those lessons are so very little known. In my earlier ministry I had the privilege of the friendship of two preachers who were trained at Princeton before 1929. When one of them, W. J. Grier of Belfast, lent me the rare *Life of Archibald Alexander* it was the means of opening my eyes to a new world with respect to the church in America. I do not doubt that these pages will have the very same effect for others.

Thankfully the *Life of Alexander* is no longer rare[1] and that is a second reason why this book is timely. Never in the last hundred years have the works of the teachers of Princeton Theological Seminary been as available as they are today. The Alexanders and the Hodges, fathers and sons, are in print again. Some of Samuel Miller has also been republished, as have works by such graduates of the seminary as William S. Plumer, W. B. Sprague, Samuel I. Prime, and John Nevius. It is improbable that any group of authors from a single institution has ever exercised such influence so long after their deaths as these men are presently doing. This process of recovery can only be given further impetus by Dr Calhoun's work and no one will be able to put this volume down without understanding why their words and memories remain fresh and powerful at this point in time.

Some years ago I had the opportunity to wander round the Seminary one summer's afternoon. It was vacation time and all was quiet. On entering the chapel it appeared to be empty of all save memories, but then, unseen, an organist began to play. The music was the Genevan tune, the Old Hundredth, and who could hear it without thinking of the words which had so often resounded within those walls,

> Because the Lord our God is good,
> His mercy is for ever sure;
> His truth at all times firmly stood.
> And shall from age to age endure.

In these pages the sound of that music will continue.

Iain H. Murray
December 21, 1993

# PREFACE

*The Log College, founded by William Tennent of Neshaminy, Pennsylvania, trained men for the Presbyterian ministry during the 1730s and 1740s.*

I N the beginning of his book *The Log College,* Archibald
Alexander wrote:

By association, objects which have nothing interesting in themselves
acquire an importance, by reason of the persons or things which
they constantly suggest to our minds. . . . And the more intimately
these associations are related to religion, the deeper and more
permanent the feeling becomes. By the abuse of this principle
much superstition has been generated; but the moderate and
judicious use of it may, undoubtedly, be conducive to piety.[1]

With this goal in mind, Alexander told the story of the Log
College of Neshaminy, Pennsylvania, and its contribution to
the First Great Awakening in America. Because of the doctrinal orthodoxy and evangelical piety of William Tennent, Sr.,
and his students, the Log College was an important symbol
for Archibald Alexander and those who joined with him in
the first American Presbyterian seminary in Princeton, New
Jersey. Back of Princeton Seminary was Princeton College,
John Grier Hibben said at the seminary's centennial in 1912,
and back of Princeton College was "the Log College, and
back of the Log College, the school house on the hills of
Scotland and of Ulster in Ireland."[2]

The Log College had long disappeared when Princeton
Seminary was founded in 1812. But the Presbyterian minister
of the church at Neshaminy rescued part of one of the decay-
ing logs and made a walking stick, which he gave as a token
of respect to Archibald Alexander's colleague Samuel Miller.
Years later, when Miller was an old man, he gave the
Princeton students this "venerable cane, the last remnant of
the Log College." By then the name "Princeton" also had

acquired symbolic significance.

This book is the story of the first 117 years of the Presbyterian seminary in the small New Jersey town described by Princeton's third professor, Charles Hodge, as "this little favored spot." Almost immediately Princeton Seminary became an intellectual and theological school of great importance, but it was also a notable center of Christian discipleship and missionary outreach. It was the home not only of sturdy Calvinistic theology, but also of the spirituality and evangelistic zeal which was the strength of such institutions as the Sunday Afternoon Conference and the Society of Inquiry on Missions. Above all, Princeton was the place of a remarkable group of people who shared a common vision— a seminary dedicated equally to "piety of the heart" and "solid learning." This book is about these people, especially the two dozen professors who, with the students, made Princeton Seminary what it was. It is more, however, than the story of a school and the teachers and students who gave it life. Princeton Seminary was one of the centers—in its earlier years, perhaps *the* center—of American evangelicalism during the nineteenth century. And as William McLoughlin has written, "The story of American evangelicalism is the story of America itself in the years 1800-1900."[3]

Samuel Miller, B. B. Warfield, and Lefferts A. Loetscher were each encouraged to write a history of Princeton Theological Seminary.[4] None accomplished that task, but Dr. Loetscher produced an admirable beginning in his *Facing the Enlightenment and Pietism: Archibald Alexander and the Founding of Princeton Theological Seminary.*[5] The rest of the story must be gathered from nineteenth- and early twentieth-century biographies, letters, sermons, and records, and from a growing collection of scholarly articles, dissertations, and books. Books by and about the Princeton professors are abundant and, often, voluminous. Published biographical data for some—such as Archibald Alexander, Samuel Miller, and Charles Hodge—is adequate; but for others—such as A. A. Hodge and B. B. Warfield—it is slight. For still others— especially the women of Princeton (mainly the wives of the college and seminary professors)—it is, unfortunately, almost nonexistent.

An early Princeton graduate, Benjamin B. Wisner, became pastor of the Old South Church of Boston. When he was working on a history of his church, he wrote to his former teacher Samuel Miller for information concerning one of his predecessors, Samuel Blair. Dr. Miller replied:

Truly, when I first read your letter, I could hardly have imagined what a complicated and difficult thing it would prove to collect facts concerning a man so much distinguished as Dr. Blair was. But so it is;—and, if any one, sixty or seventy years hence, or even thirty or forty, should wish to know some facts concerning you or me, they will, perhaps, have to hunt for them very laboriously, and, it may be, unsuccessfully. Oh, how poor a thing is posthumous reputation! And, on the other hand, how infinitely, how absorbingly important that honour which cometh from God![6]

I too have searched—very laboriously and sometimes unsuccessfully—for information about the Princetonians. And I take comfort in the fact that if I have slighted or misrepresented anyone, God has not.

Not only must information be discovered, it must be interpreted. The biography of Samuel Miller, Princeton's second professor, was written by his son, who stated in the preface:

There are two extremes into which biographers are apt to fall. The one is adopting a continued strain of eulogy, and endeavoring either wholly to keep out of view, or ingeniously to varnish over, the errors and weaknesses of those whose lives they record. . . . The other, and a more mischievous extreme is, recording against departed worth, with studied amplitude, and disgusting minuteness, the momentary mistakes of forgetfulness, the occasional vagaries of levity, and the false opinions, expressed not as the result of sober reflection, but thrown out either in a mirthful hour, or in the heat of disputation.[7]

I have avoided the second extreme, and I have tried to avoid the first. It will be no secret to the reader that I like the Old Princetonians. They were Christians of godliness and learning who faithfully taught the Bible and the Reformed faith to generations of seminarians. Through their writings, they have taught thousands around the world—down to the present day. I have searched for "the occasional vagaries of levity," and I have not ignored their flaws and defects. They were not perfect; but colleagues, friends, and opponents all agree that the Princetonians were Christians of intelligence, culture, and compassion.

After the 1929 reorganization of the seminary by the General Assembly of the Presbyterian Church, interest in Princeton's history was limited largely to the dwindling number of those who shared its theological convictions and followed its traditions. In recent years, however, a larger number of scholars have recognized Princeton Seminary's significance for its time—and for ours—and have investigated the Princetonians with greatly differing conclusions. Most of the recent literature concentrates on the Princeton theology—its philosophical commitments; its apologetics; its views on Scripture, slavery, evolution; and its role in the Presbyterian controversy of the early twentieth century. Mark Noll, one of the major forces in the renewed interest in the Princeton Theology, has noted that "for all their acknowledged significance, the Princetonians have been the subject of relatively scant *historical* scrutiny."[8] Princeton was more than its theology. Its story includes theology and piety, faculty and students, college and seminary, town and nation, Presbyterian Church and parachurch organizations, home and foreign missions. While focusing on the personalities and life of the seminary, I have glanced from time to time across the street, across the nation, and across the ocean. I have not treated adequately everything of importance in the Princeton history. But I have, I hope, set forth something of its size, its scope, and its significance.

This book is a chronicle of the Princeton history, but it is also a story—with a point. From 1812 to 1929, Princeton Theological Seminary represented a coherent, continual effort to teach and practice what the Princetonians believed was historic Reformed Christianity. In this they were, in my opinion, successful. They taught theology as they found it in the Bible, and as they received it from Augustine, Calvin, Turretin, and, especially, the Westminster Standards. Their lives proved that they were not only scholars teaching the faith—they were Christians living it. The Princetonians were not always right in everything they taught or wrote, but they stood squarely in the great stream of historic Christianity and orthodox Calvinism. They faithfully, sometimes powerfully, and often winsomely, preached, taught, wrote, argued, and lived the truth as they saw it.

At the seminary's centennial, Francis Landey Patton said of Princeton's teachers: "These men of course were not alike; but they all spoke the same thing and there were no divisions among them."[9] Part of the reason for their unity was, undoubtedly, the closeness of the faculty—spiritually, confessionally, and even physically. Archibald Alexander's "spiritual" son, Charles Hodge, became the seminary's third professor and first graduate to teach at Princeton. Then there were two of Dr. Alexander's sons, and two of Dr. Hodge's sons and a grandson—giving rise to "the Princeton puzzle." "What is Princeton?" "An everlasting succession of Alexanders and Hodges!" Of Princeton's thirty-one professors until 1929, twenty-three were graduates of the seminary. Some may see this as a weakness, but it did bring to Princeton a long line of men devoted to the Princeton tradition and to each other. How strong that devotion was becomes evident in the pages of this book.

On two occasions I have lived in Princeton and studied at Princeton Seminary. Alexander Hall, Miller Chapel, and Hodge Hall are constant reminders of the great men of the nineteenth century. An impressive portrait of B. B. Warfield hangs in the Campus Center. Across the university campus and a block down Witherspoon Street is the town cemetery, where—along with Jonathan Edwards and other college presidents—many of the Princeton professors are buried.

For the past decade it has been my privilege to serve as a member of the faculty of Covenant Theological Seminary, a school which sees itself as a spiritual and theological descendant of Princeton. Earlier, when I studied at Covenant, one of the major textbooks was Charles Hodge's *Systematic Theology*. At Covenant the names of Archibald Alexander, Samuel Miller, Charles Hodge, A. A. Hodge, B. B. Warfield, and Gresham Machen continue to be held in high honor and their works read and valued as faithful expositions of the Reformed faith.

I am grateful to many who have helped and encouraged

me in this work. Both the text and the endnotes of this book bear ample evidence to the host of scholars upon whom I have depended. John M. Mulder, now president of Louisville Presbyterian Theological Seminary, guided me through my Princeton dissertation. William Harris, Princeton archivist, has provided books, articles, photographs, and good advice. The trustees of Covenant Theological Seminary granted me a sabbatical to work on this project, and my Covenant colleagues have supported me in it. Concordia Theological Seminary in St. Louis provided me with a room for writing and the resources of its fine library. My wife, Anne, has encouraged me with love and read my manuscript with skill. Iain Murray, editor of the Banner of Truth Trust, provided invaluable guidance and assistance—on many occasions sharing with me his considerable knowledge of Old Princeton and his astute interpretations of American church history.

It will not be out of place, I trust, to record here that the study of the history of Old Princeton Seminary has been to me an intellectual challenge and spiritual blessing. And it is my hope that this book may challenge those who read it to seek "solid learning" in the truth of God and that it may be— in the words of Princeton's first professor in his book on the Log College—"conducive to piety."

David B. Calhoun
Covenant Theological Seminary
St. Louis, Missouri
September, 1993

# Nassau Hall

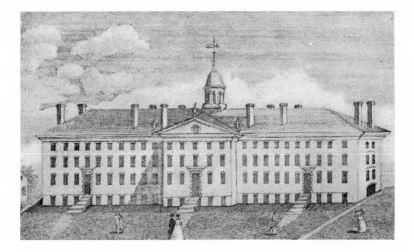

*Nassau Hall, built in 1756 as the home of Princeton College.*

Our Aim in the Undertaking is to promote the Interests of the Redeemer's Kingdom; and to raise up qualified Candidates for the Ministry.

JONATHAN DICKINSON

IN the closing years of the seventeenth century, a few families settled in western New Jersey at a place they called Stony Brook. Located on an old Indian path between the Raritan and the Delaware rivers, the village was just over two hundred feet above sea level on the first of the foothills of the Allegheny Mountains. In 1724 it was renamed *Princeton* in memory of William III, Prince of Orange-Nassau and King of England. Composed mainly of Quakers, French Huguenots, and Presbyterians of English, Scottish, and Scotch-Irish backgrounds, the little town grew slowly. A wooden Quaker Meeting House was built in 1709, and by 1755 there was a Presbyterian congregation.

By then the Middle Colonies had become the center of Presbyterianism in America. Some Presbyterians in New England migrated south beyond the territory of Congregationalism and organized churches on Long Island and in New Jersey. Other Presbyterians, in Virginia, Maryland, Pennsylvania, and Delaware, struggled to plant churches, often facing hostility and persecution from intolerant officials. In 1706, in Philadelphia, seven ministers formed the first American presbytery, bringing together Puritan graduates of Harvard and Yale, and Scotch-Irish ministers who had won their degrees at Glasgow and Edinburgh. The church grew, and ten years later the first synod of three presbyteries was established.

Early in American history, prospective ministers had been trained in European universities or at Harvard and, later, at

Yale. Further specialized theological and pastoral preparation usually followed college graduation. Some students
returned home or taught school while pursuing their studies
privately and meeting, when possible, with other ministerial
candidates for discussion and encouragement. Others
remained in residence at Harvard or Yale to use the library,
attend the president's divinity lectures, and confer with him
from time to time. Most students, however, received their
training by living and studying with an experienced pastor—
a practice with a long English and New England Puritan
tradition.

Pastors directed students in their reading and gave them
opportunities for practical experience in the various duties of
the ministry; while the pastors' wives provided food, lodging,
and sympathetic and valuable counsel. Prospective students
sometimes arrived unannounced at a pastor's door, as did
Samuel Hopkins at Jonathan Edwards's home in Northamp-
ton, Massachusetts. Some pastors became noted as teachers
and directed the study and training of several young men at
the same time in what came to be called "schools of the
prophets."

One such school was the academy founded by William
Tennent, Sr., on the Little Neshaminy Creek in Bucks
County, Pennsylvania, in 1727. Students spent their days
studying in the college and lodged at night with their teacher
and with nearby families. In the fall of 1739, during his
second visit to America, the twenty-four-year-old George
Whitefield visited Neshaminy and wrote in his journal that
Tennent was there preparing:

gracious youths, and sending them out into our Lord's vineyard.
The place wherein the young men study now is, in contempt, called
*the College.* It is a log-house, about twenty feet long, and nearly as
many broad; and, to me, it seemed to resemble the school of the
old prophets. . . . From this despised place, seven or eight worthy
ministers of Jesus have lately been sent forth; more are almost ready
to be sent; and a foundation is now being laid for the instruction of
many others. The devil will certainly rage against them; but the
work, I am persuaded, is of God, and will not come to nought.[1]

The Log College closed in 1742, but its graduates had

begun similar academies in such places as Londonderry (Faggs Manor), Pennsylvania, and Nottingham, Maryland. After Yale College proved unfriendly to the Great Awakening by expelling David Brainerd for his "intemperate, indiscreet zeal," a group of New Jersey and New York Presbyterians discussed the founding of an institution in their area for the training of ministers. When efforts of Jonathan Edwards and others to have Brainerd reinstated at Yale failed, they "concocted the plan and foundation of the college." "If it had not been for the treatment received by Mr. Brainerd at Yale," one of the founders, Aaron Burr, Sr., later declared, "New Jersey College would never have been erected."

New Jersey College received its first charter from acting governor John Hamilton on October 22, 1746. It was granted to seven men who became the first trustees—four ministers and three laymen of the Presbyterian Church, and all but one graduates of Yale. These seven chose five others—Gilbert Tennent, William Tennent, Jr., Samuel Blair, Samuel Finley, all of the Log College, and Richard Trent, a graduate of Yale. The new college was the fourth to be founded in America—after Harvard, Yale, and William and Mary—and the first in the Middle Colonies. It was modeled after the English dissenting academies, emphasizing religion, mathematics, and English, and encouraging scientific research—which, it firmly believed, could only confirm revealed truth. While not officially sponsored by the Presbyterian Church, it was, in the eyes of its founders, closely connected with the church, serving both it and the nation. The purpose of the new school, they said, was not only to educate ministers of the gospel but also to raise up "men that will be useful in other learned professions—ornaments of the State as well as the Church." [2]

The college began in Elizabethtown, New Jersey, in the manse of the first president, the Reverend Jonathan Dickinson—a man Archibald Alexander held to be "in the foremost rank among the fathers of the Presbyterian Church" in the United States. The eight or ten students who came to the new school used Dickinson's library, met classes in his parlour, and ate in his dining room. Four and a half months later, they sorrowfully accompanied the body of their president to his grave. Fortunately, young Aaron Burr consented to take over "the charge of the college"; so the students had only to pack their chests, bid goodbye to the mourning Dickinson family, and ride the six miles to Burr's Newark church. They were pleased with their learned and devout teacher and happy when he married fair Esther Edwards, daughter of the famous New England preacher and theologian, Jonathan Edwards—although one of the students worried that she was "rather too young for the president." As the new wife of a pastor and college president, Esther's days were "spent in a hurry of business"—as she wrote in her journal—"dining ten ministers" on one occasion and cooking "mynce-pyes and Cocoa-nut tarts" for presbytery on another. She entertained her husband's friend George Whitefield, writing that she much enjoyed "his company and conversation, as well as [his] preaching." Esther was especially glad when her father stayed with them. One entry in her journal noted the return of her husband and father from a meeting in Philadelphia late one Saturday night. The men were ill—Burr with a cold and Edwards with exhaustion—but Esther "got something for their refreshment and . . . put 'em both to Bed." She reported that although Mr. Burr was still very sick, "he went out all [the next] day." Her father seemed much better, and Esther believed his Sunday sermons to be "charming."[3]

The first class of six graduated on November 9, 1748, after hearing a final address in Latin from President Burr, who reminded them of "manifold advantages of the liberal arts and sciences . . . rendering them useful members of Church and State." Five went on to become Presbyterian ministers; and the sixth, Richard Stockton, became a lawyer and signer of the Declaration of Independence.

The college prospered under Burr, who served for three years without salary. The curriculum was organized and a permanent location was secured in Princeton. When funds were needed for a building, Presbyterian ministers Gilbert Tennent and Samuel Davies crossed the stormy Atlantic to spend part of 1754 in Great Britain appealing for aid. They were well-received by Presbyterian and Independent ministers of England and by the General Assembly of the Church of Scotland. In London they were hospitably entertained and encouraged by George Whitefield "to come out boldly" for the new college. Tennent visited his native Ireland and brought the matter of the American college to the attention of the Synod of Ulster. When news came back that the ministers had several thousand pounds in hand, the trustees busied themselves with selecting the site and drawing up plans for a permanent building. The distinguished architect, Robert Smith of Philadelphia, in collaboration with Dr. William Shippen, decided upon a Georgian structure of rough stone, with a hipped roof, and a cupola design borrowed from St. Mary-le-Strand in London.

Esther Edwards Burr made several trips to Princeton to view the progress on the new building. She and her husband were on such a visit in August of 1756 when she wrote:

About 3 o'Clock it seemed a little cooler so set forward came safe to Princeton before sun set then walked to take a little view of the College for we had not patience to tarry till morning—Just looked at the Presidents House which is under cover—then returned to our Lodgings, ate supper and tired almost to Death we were glad to go to Bed.

She described getting up very early the next morning to take a "more particular view" of the college and their house:

the College is a Famous building I assure you and the most commodious of any of the Colleges as well as much the largest of any upon the Continent. There is something very striking in it and a grandure and yet a simplicity that cant well be expressed—I am well pleased with the House they have begun for us.[4]

In November 1756, during the fall vacation, the Burrs and the seventy students moved from Newark to Princeton. Esther was pleased that "not a china thing so much as cracked" in the move.[5] The new college building provided space for all the needs of the school—classrooms, dormitory, chapel, library, and refectory. The trustees wanted to call the new building Belcher Hall in honor of the governor of New Jersey, a staunch and much-needed champion of the infant college, but the governor forbade it. May I ask "the favor of your naming the present building Nassau Hall," he said, "as expressing the honor we retain in this remote part of the

[7]

globe to the immortal memory of the glorious King William III, who was a branch of the illustrious House of Nassau."

There was not yet a Presbyterian church building in Princeton; and townspeople, faculty and students worshiped together in the chapel of Nassau Hall.[6] Its fine pipe organ was the first such instrument used in Presbyterian services in America. Even though there was regular preaching in Princeton, some of the students, from time to time, would walk the twenty miles to Freehold, New Jersey, to hear the famous William Tennent, Jr., preach in his own pulpit.

A year after the college moved into Nassau Hall, Aaron Burr—burdened by the multiple duties of administrator, teacher, and fund-raiser—died at the age of forty-one.[7] Four days later, twenty-two students graduated in the commencement of 1757, the first at Princeton. The next day the trustees, "after earnest prayers," elected Burr's father-in-law, Jonathan Edwards, as their new president. John Brainerd, a brother of David Brainerd and a trustee of the college, was one of two deputized to bring Edwards word of his election. "It was with great reluctance" that the famous preacher and scholar received the news. It seemed to him to threaten what he had hoped to make his life's work—the preparation of a series of volumes on the Arminian controversy. "But the college at Princeton, which had been founded and thus far carried on by men whose sympathies were with the warm-hearted, revivalistic piety to which his own life had been dedicated, had claims upon him which he could not disown."[8] After repeated requests from the Princeton representatives, he accepted the call on the advice of a council of his friends and took up his duties in January 1758.

Edwards preached a few times in the college chapel—including a two-hour sermon on "The Unchangeableness of Christ"—"to the great delight and profit of his hearers"; and he met several times with the senior class, who spoke of the "light and instruction" he brought to their discussions. Smallpox was prevalent in the area, and Edwards was inoculated in the hope of rendering him immune to a violent infection. The treatment proved fatal, however, and "the greatest American theologian of the eighteenth century fell a victim to the new science."[9] *The Pennsylvania Journal and*

*Weekly Advertiser* reported the sad news on March 30, 1758, and paid tribute to Princeton's president:

On Wednesday the 22nd Inst. died at Nassau-Hall, an eminent Servant of God, the Rev. and pious Mr. Jonathan Edwards, President of the College of New Jersey; a Gentleman of distinguished Abilities, of an heavenly Temper of Mind; a most rational, generous, catholick, and exemplary Christian, admired by all that knew him, for his uncommon Candour and disinterested Benevolence: A Pattern of Temperance, Prudence, Meekness, Patience and Charity; always steady, calm and serene, a very judicious and instructive Preacher, and a most excellent Divine; And he lived chearfully, resigned in all things to the will of heaven, so he died, or rather as the Scripture emphatically expresses it, with respect to good men, he fell asleep in Jesus, without the least appearance of pain.[10]

The search for a new president focused on two men, Samuel Davies and Samuel Finley. One had graduated from the school of Samuel Blair, a son of the Log College, the other from the Log College itself. One was eminent as a preacher, the other as a classical scholar and teacher. One lived in Virginia, the other in Maryland, colonies to which the college was looking for students. Davies was chosen. At first he declined absolutely, partly because the Virginia Presbyterians were unwilling to give him up, and partly because he believed that Mr. Finley would make the better president. Finally, in May 1759, the trustees persuaded Davies to accept the presidency. The modest, scholarly, eloquent preacher was described by one trustee as a man upon whom the God of heaven had bestowed "prodigious, uncommon gifts."[11] Despite poor health, he had faithfully served his scattered Virginia congregations, riding through forests and fields in his five-hundred-mile circuit. At Princeton, he drove himself mercilessly to remedy fancied defects in scholarship, rising at dawn and seldom retiring before midnight. Samuel Davies died of pneumonia in February 1761 at the age of thirty-seven, after having been bled for "a bad cold." His death dismayed the college and "spread a gloom all over the country."

All eyes now turned to Samuel Finley, a Scots-Irishman who had come to the colonies with his parents when he was nineteen. He became a minister and was known to be "a very accurate scholar and a very great and good man." During his pastorate in Nottingham, Maryland, he headed an academy renowned for its standards of scholarship. When the University of Glasgow recognized his work with the Doctor of Divinity degree, he became the second American minister and the first Presbyterian to receive an honorary degree abroad. Finley was unanimously elected president on May 21, 1761. Although his preaching gifts did not match those of Davies, he became a popular, energetic, able president and a teacher to whom, according to one of his students, "every branch of study taught in the college appeared to be familiar." The college's commencement exercises in the fall of 1764 were held in the newly built Presbyterian church. The preacher was none other than George Whitefield, who preached in Princeton several times in November 1763, and who now returned at the unanimous request of president, tutors, and students. His text was Philippians 3:8—"Yea doubtless, and I count all things but loss for the excellency of the knowledge of Christ Jesus my Lord: for whom I have suffered the loss of all things, and I do count them but dung, that I may win Christ." At the close of the sermon, according to the *New York Mercury*, the great evangelist "gave a very striking and animated Exhortation to the young Gentlemen who were candidates for the Honours of the College." Samuel Finley was president for five years before he died on July 17, 1766. The college's first five leaders, only two of whom served for more than two years, died before Princeton was twenty years old. Migrants from New England, or Scotch-Irish ministers of the Middle Colonies, they all wholeheartedly supported the Great Awakening and held to the New England Calvinistic theology and piety of Jonathan Edwards.

When Samuel Davies was in Scotland in 1754 soliciting funds for the college, he mentioned in one of his letters a young minister of much promise, by name "Weatherspoon or Witherspoon." John Witherspoon's book *Ecclesiastical Characteristics, or the Arcana of Church Polity* (1753) was a satire on the moderate party of the Church of Scotland. It had been printed five times in two years and was creating a sensation. Witherspoon caustically described the moderates as men "moderate in ability, showing a moderate amount of zeal and doing a very moderate amount of work." Thirteen "maxims" offered advice to ministerial candidates on how to get along in a "moderate" world. "All ecclesiastical persons suspected of heresy," it stated, "are to be esteemed men of great genius, vast learning, and uncommon worth." In the pulpit, a moderate's "authorities must be drawn from heathen writers . . . as few as possible from Scripture." Also a moderate "must be very unacceptable to the common people." In his conclusion, entitled an "Athenian Creed," Witherspoon suggested, with heavy sarcasm, that all moderates subscribed to the following dogma: "I believe in the divinity of Lord Shaftesbury, the saintship of Marcus Antoninus, the perspicuity and sublimity of Aristotle, and the perpetual duration of Mr. [Francis] Hutcheson's works, notwithstanding their present tendency to oblivion. Amen."

Born in the manse of Yester in the East Lothian village of Gifford, Scotland, on February 5, 1723, John Witherspoon was descended from a long line of Calvinist divines. His great-grandfather had signed the Solemn League and Covenant, and a distant ancestor on his mother's side was none other than John Knox. John Witherspoon enrolled in the University of Edinburgh at the age of thirteen. On February 23, 1739, he defended his Latin thesis in the university common hall and, three days later, was awarded the master of arts degree. He continued his studies at Edinburgh in the faculty of divinity and in January 1745, having been licensed to preach, began to serve the kirk in Beith, Ayrshire. A year later, after raising militia to repel the invasion of Charles Stuart, "the Young Pretender," Witherspoon was captured by rebel forces and suffered a brief but severe imprisonment.

John Witherspoon emerged as a leader of the Scottish evangelicals with the publication of his *Ecclesiastical Characteristics*. His reputation as a forceful, orthodox Presbyterian was confirmed by his *Essay on Justification* (1756) and *Treatise on Regeneration* (1764). In his books and sermons, he stressed the authority of Scripture and held up the old doctrines of the sovereignty of God, the depravity of man, and substitutionary atonement. Witherspoon's views did not prevail in Scotland, but his reputation grew both at home and abroad. In 1757 he became pastor of the Laigh Kirk in Paisley, a flourishing industrial town on the outskirts of Glasgow. He declined invitations from prestigious Reformed pulpits in Dublin and Rotterdam. Witherspoon's orthodox Calvinism and his gifts of leadership appealed to the trustees of the College of New Jersey as they searched for the college's sixth president. Futhermore, he was a Scot and so was identified with neither the Old Side nor the New Side of American Presbyterianism. The two parties had divided in 1741 and reunited in 1758; but tensions remained, and the trustees had the difficult task of finding a man acceptable to both sides. John Witherspoon was ideal, and when he turned down the invitation the trustees did not give up. For two years they sought to persuade him to accept the presidency, and then he attempted to convince his reluctant wife to move to America. The new professor of divinity and Log College graduate, John Blair, held the college together until the matter could be resolved. Finally the Witherspoons agreed to come.

On August 7, 1768, the *Peggy* from Glasgow sailed up the Delaware to one of the Philadelphia wharves. John Witherspoon stepped ashore, a heavy-set man of forty-six, with brown hair, a strong face with large nose and ears, and blue eyes which looked out from beneath bushy brows. With him were his wife, Elizabeth, their five children, and three hundred books for the college library. After a hearty welcome in Philadelphia, the Witherspoons set out by horse and carriage for Princeton. About a mile from town, the faculty and the entire student body greeted them and escorted them on. Tallow dips were lit in every window of Nassau Hall that night as the college community celebrated the arrival of its new first family. At Princeton's commencement on September 28, an unusually large crowd gathered to hear the new president give his inaugural address in Latin on "the Connection & mutual influences of Learning & Piety."

John Witherspoon found, in the place of the little group of eight or ten students who had congregated around the scholarly Dickinson in May 1747, a fully-fledged college of 120 students from every part of the country. Among the American colleges of Witherspoon's day, only Princeton was intercolonial, primarily because of the widespread distribution of Ulster Scots. As these immigrants moved out into western Pennsylvania, pushed into the Valley of Virginia between the Blue Ridge and the Alleghenies, took up their little farms in the Carolina Piedmont, or crossed the mountains into Tennessee and Kentucky, they turned to Nassau Hall for their ministers and teachers. Princeton became the educational and religious capital of all Scotch-Irish America and the college's influence reached from the Atlantic to the distant frontier communities of the West.

The financial condition of the college, however, was in a precarious state; bankruptcy had been a genuine threat in 1768. Witherspoon dealt with the crisis by making a series of highly successful trips throughout the colonies. He preached to packed churches from Boston to Charleston, South Carolina, recruiting students and gathering funds. Under his determined leadership, the college's finances, faculty, and student body steadily increased.

John Witherspoon worked hard to improve the teaching at Princeton. He introduced the lecture method (previously, instructors had assigned reading material to the students and then quizzed them in class). He purchased the famous Rittenhouse Orrery, a mechanical model of the solar system, and promoted the study of mathematics and natural sciences. The president taught classes in moral philosophy, divinity, rhetoric, history, Hebrew, Greek, Latin, and French—which he spoke with a decided Scottish accent. Of these subjects, none was more important than moral philosophy—a combination of ethics, epistemology, theology, and political theory. Year after year, Witherspoon taught this required course to the seniors—an appropriate culmination to their college work.[12] The president stressed the importance of reason in ethical and moral decisions and argued that its proper use served to support revelation. His lectures incorporated some of the features of Common Sense Realism, a philosophy that had emerged in mid–eighteenth-century Scotland. He appealed to "certain first principles or dictates of common sense" as "the foundations of all reasoning," including the principle that our senses can be trusted with the information they give us.[13] "It is always safer in our reasonings," John

Witherspoon told his students, "to trace true facts upward, than to reason downward from metaphysical principle"— another tenet of the Scottish philosophy.[14]

John Witherspoon's vision for Princeton College was for an educational institution that would produce consecrated Christian students with an integrated and thoroughly biblical world view. "Religion," he said, "is the grand concern to us all . . . whatever be our calling and profession." He implored his students "to keep clear views of the importance of both piety and literature, and never suffer them to be divided." He insisted that "piety, without literature, is but little profitable; and learning, without piety, is pernicious to others, and ruinous to the possessor." Therefore, Witherspoon told his students, "the great and leading view which you ought to have in your studies, and which I desire to have still before my eyes in teaching . . . may be expressed in one sentence—to unite together piety and literature—to show their relation to, and their influence upon one another—and to guard against anything that may tend to separate them, and set them in opposition."[15] Accordingly, the president set out to create a "Christian Enlightenment" at Princeton, combining the best of modern learning with biblical orthodoxy. He rejoiced when George Whitefield returned to Princeton in 1770. Whitefield preached to the students on Sunday, June 17, and to the Presbyterian congregation the following morning. Princeton was always Whitefield's favorite American college because of its revered connections with the Log College and the Great Awakening.

John Witherspoon had found a volatile political situation when he arrived at Princeton in 1768. Revolutionary ideas dominated both the college and the town. At the college commencement of 1765, graduating seniors had protested the Stamp Act by receiving their degrees dressed in homespun clothes of colonial manufacture. In January 1774, just one month after the Boston Tea Party, students burned the college's supply of tea. Witherspoon did nothing to check the patriotic fervor, but allowed, even encouraged, the college to become a "hotbed of radical sentiment."[16] The transplanted Scot had become "as high a son of liberty as any man in America," according to John Adams. Adams, traveling from

Boston to Philadelphia to attend the First Continental Congress, arrived in Princeton at noon on Saturday, August 24, 1774. He attended prayers in Nassau Hall, toured the campus, and drank a glass of wine with Witherspoon in the president's house, where the two men discussed national events. Adams remained for Sunday in Princeton. His terse remark—"Heard Dr. Witherspoon all Day, a clear, sensible Preacher"—suggests that he spent most of his time at divine services!

Armed with John Locke, Samuel Rutherford, and the Puritans, Witherspoon defended the patriot cause in speeches, sermons, essays, and letters. He joined religious and civil freedoms, observing that "there is not a single instance in history in which civil liberty was lost and religious liberty preserved entirely."[17] In the spring of 1776, Witherspoon helped to form the new state legislature, which then elected five delegates from New Jersey to the Continental Congress—three of whom were connected with the college at Princeton: Richard Stockton of the class of 1748, Francis Hopkinson, an honorary alumnus, and President Witherspoon. In Philadelphia, Witherspoon took part in the independence debates in late June and early July; and, on July 4, 1776, he joined fifty-five other delegates in signing his name to the Declaration of Independence. He served as a member of congress until December 1779 and again from December 1780 to May 1782. He sat on more than one hundred committees, working with Thomas Jefferson, Benjamin Franklin, John Adams, and other prominent Americans to plan the laws and direct the affairs of the new nation.

John Witherspoon's role in the colonial cause was not overlooked by the British. Horace Walpole is said to have informed the parliament that "Cousin America" had "run off with a Presbyterian parson"; and King George III called the American Revolution "that Presbyterian parson's war." In July 1776, British soldiers quartered on Long Island burned Witherspoon in effigy. British troops occupied Princeton from December 7, 1776, to January 3, 1777. They used Nassau Hall as a barracks and stable and stripped the chapel and the church for firewood. They plundered the libraries of the president and the college. During the Battle of Princeton, on January 3, 1777, the British broke the windows of Nassau Hall to fire out, but American artillery aimed at the building did greater damage. After the British abandoned the town, it looked as if "it had been desolated with the plague and an earthquake." The college and the church were "heaps of ruins."

At least 230 Princeton graduates and students offered some kind of military service to their country before 1783; the college produced only thirteen known Loyalists. In the membership of the Drafting Committee for the Constitution of the United States, there were as many graduates of Witherspoon's Princeton as there were from Harvard, Yale, Columbia, and Pennsylvania combined.

Not only was John Witherspoon an American statesman and the president of Nassau Hall, but he also became a leader in the Presbyterian church. On August 10, 1768, three days after his arrival in America, he preached at Second Presbyterian Church in Philadelphia. On the following Sunday he delivered his first sermon in the Presbyterian church at Princeton, a pulpit he occupied until his death. Witherspoon led the movement for the national organization of the Presbyterian church. He composed the denomination's first Form of Government, stating, in words which would become foundational for Princeton Seminary, that "truth is in order to goodness, and the great touchstone of truth, its tendency to promote holiness." The synod selected John Witherspoon to preach the opening sermon at the first General Assembly of the Presbyterian Church, which met in Philadelphia's Second Presbyterian Church in May 1789, and then elected him as the first moderator. A committee, with Witherspoon as chairman, drafted an address to the first Congress of the United States then meeting in New York City.

While John Witherspoon attended sessions of the Continental Congress and later the New Jersey Legislature, Samuel Stanhope Smith managed the affairs of the struggling college—with its damaged buildings, depleted funds, and plummeting enrollment. In 1779 Witherspoon left the president's house to Smith and moved a mile away to his farm, which he named Tusculum. There he had built "a small but neat house," located, according to Witherspoon, "in a pleasant, retired situation, surrounded with woods, in all the simple majesty of their uncultivated state."[18] Witherspoon took great pride in his kitchen garden. One day a visitor remarked, "Why, doctor, I see no flowers in your garden." "No, madam," was the reply, "no flowers in my garden, nor in my discourses either."[19] Witherspoon returned full time to his college duties in 1782 but, lacking his earlier energy, he was content to leave administrative matters more and more to Smith. His presence and his teaching and preaching, however, continued to dominate the college. The leading men from every section of the country—many of whom had served with him in the Continental Congress and had learned to know and revere him—sent their sons to Nassau Hall to be under Dr. Witherspoon's instruction.

A visitor in 1787 described John Witherspoon as an "intolerably homely old Scotchman," but one of his pupils insisted that Witherspoon had "more of the quality called presence" than any other man of his generation except General Washington. Archibald Alexander, who first saw Witherspoon at the General Assembly of 1791, wrote that "all he said and everything about him bore the marks of importance and authority" and that "his pointed remarks" in the assembly "commonly put an end to the discussion."[20] It was often said that Dr. Witherspoon spoke with more "authority" than almost any other preacher—a quality one hearer attributed to the fact that there was not "a single argument, or important assertion, or exhortation" which was "not sustained by a pertinent quotation from the holy oracles."[21]

Through his own reputation and that of the Princeton graduates serving in church and state, John Witherspoon's influence was unique. No fewer than 114 of his students became clergymen. He once told a friend at a meeting of the General Assembly, "You can scarcely imagine the pleasure it has given me in taking a survey of this Assembly to observe that a decided majority of all the ministerial members have not only been sons of our college, but my own pupils."[22] Witherspoon also worked hard to provide leadership for the new nation by making Princeton a "school for statesmen."[23] Soon his students were filling important positions in education and government. They founded at least ten colleges; thirteen of them became college presidents. Many others were teachers, who helped spread Princeton's thought and prestige across the land. Among the Princetonians in government and law with Witherspoon's signature on their diplomas were a president and vice-president of the United States, nine cabinet officers, twenty-one United States senators, thirty-nine congressmen, three justices of the Supreme Court, one attorney general, twelve state governors, and thirty-nine judges. The president was James Madison, who graduated in 1771, and remained for several months more to study a number of subjects under the guidance of Witherspoon. His teacher was the major influence in shaping the thought of the young statesman, one of the primary authors of the Constitution of the United States.

\*　　\*　　\*

From late June 1783 until early November, the American Congress shared Nassau Hall, only partially rehabilitated from wartime damage, with the Princeton faculty and fifty students then in residence in the college. "From a little obscure village," Ashbel Green wrote his father, "we have become the capital of America. Instead of almost silence in the town, nothing is to be seen or heard but the passing and rattling of wagons, coaches, and chairs, the crying about of pine apples, oranges, lemons, and every luxurious article both foreign and domestic."[24] Ashbel Green was one of the most promising students at the college. His father, Jacob Green, had been converted through the preaching of George Whitefield and Gilbert Tennent in Boston in 1740 and 1741. He became a Presbyterian minister in Hanover, New Jersey, and had served as interim president of Princeton between Edwards and Davies. Ashbel's grandfather was one of the seven founders of Princeton, and his maternal great-grandfather was the first president of Yale.

As a youth serving with the American army, Ashbel Green had found his faith shaken by the deism of some of its officers. Reading Samuel Clarke's *Demonstration of the Being and Attributes of God* and other apologetical works convinced him that the deists were wrong but left him spiritually un-satisfied. He turned to the Bible with the prayer that God would help him "form a just opinion of the truth or fallacy of that book." Late in life he recalled the results. "Proceeding in this way," he wrote, "I had not gone through the four evangelists, till all my skepticism left me; and to this day it has never returned."[25] Apologetical books have their value, stated Green:

and yet I am firmly of the opinion, that to a really anxious inquirer after the truth, the way I took will be more likely to issue in a full and solid satisfaction of his own mind, than a knowledge of all the controversial writings that the advocates of revelation have ever given to the world. These advocates show us what are the dictates and legitimate conclusions of human reason, but when we become satisfied that we find God himself impressing his signet on his own word, there is an end at once of all doubt and distrust.[26]

Moved now to seek personal fellowship with God, the young man found a place for private devotions "in a copse of wood, on a piece of rising ground," a short distance from the house in which he was living. There was a large rock and next to it a young chestnut tree, on the bark of which Green cut the words, "Holiness to the Lord."

Ashbel Green planned to study at Yale but enrolled in Princeton instead, because a letter from Yale went astray and remained in a nearby post office for six weeks. Looking back many years later on this circumstance, Green wrote to his son:

Had I received it seasonably, (and I never could tell why I did not) I should certainly have gone to Yale, and not to Nassau Hall. . . . the whole of my subsequent life has taken its completion and its course from the college with which I then became connected. Thus, my son, the overruling providence of God often assigns us our allotment in this world, not only without our contrivance, but in opposition to it, and the disappointment of our fondest wishes.[27]

At Princeton, Ashbel Green studied under Witherspoon and Smith. He valued the friendship and confidence of both men and was indebted to Dr. Witherspoon, he always said, for "whatever of influence or success" he attained in life. At his graduation from Princeton College in 1783, he gave the valedictory address to a distinguished audience. "We had," wrote Green, "on the stage, with the trustees and graduating class, the whole of the congress, the ministers of France and Holland, and commander-in-chief of the American army. The valedictory oration had been assigned to me, and it concluded with an address to General Washington. I need not tell you, that both in preparing and delivering it, I put forth all my powers."[28] For two years Green served as a successful tutor at the college while he tried to decide between a career in law or theology. The issue was finally settled when Dr. Smith, on a walk back to the college from Dr. Witherspoon's house, urged Green to become a minister. "Theology," said Smith, "is not the road either to fame or wealth. The law, in this country, leads to those objects. But if you wish to do good, and prefer an approving conscience before all other considerations, I have no hesitation in saying that you ought to preach the gospel."[29]

\*　　\*　　\*

In 1789 John Witherspoon was saddened by the death of Elizabeth, his wife of forty-one years. Two years later considerable comment was engendered by his marriage to Anne Dill, a twenty-four-year-old widow. Witherspoon was so enthusiastic about the occasion that he granted the Princeton students a three-day holiday. Two daughters were born to Witherspoon and his new wife. In 1792 Witherspoon became totally blind; but he continued to ride into town, where he preached in his Princeton pulpit with "unabated fervor and solemnity." He met the college students in his home for informal instruction in the classics. On September 23, 1794, he presided at commencement. Eight weeks later he died quietly in his chair while waiting to hear news from the day's last newspaper.

John Witherspoon served Princeton for twenty-six years, longer than his five predecessors together. He successfully led the college through a difficult period and defined its direction for at least the next century, although his admiring successors struggled to balance his ideals and maintain an educational program combining "Christianity, patriotism, and science."[30] He was a successful educator, the most important Presbyterian clergyman of his time, and a considerable force in American political developments. Edmund S. Morgan has written that "in 1740 America's leading intellectuals were clergymen and thought about theology; in 1790 they were statesmen and thought about politics."[31] John Witherspoon was both and did both.[32]

Samuel Stanhope Smith, a member of John Witherspoon's first graduating class and his son-in-law, became Witherspoon's successor in 1795—the first alumnus of the college to become its president. After graduation from Princeton in 1769, Smith had served faithfully as a missionary and pastor in his native Virginia. There he founded Prince Edward Academy, later called Hampden-Sydney College, six months before the signing of the Declaration of Independence. One hundred and ten students gathered around him and his three assistants, all Princeton men. They recited in unfinished buildings and lived in log cabin dormitories which they built themselves.

With a solid reputation as an able educator, Smith returned to Princeton in 1779 as professor of moral philosophy. Dr. Witherspoon was busy in Congress and Smith capably handled the instruction and government of the college, assuming the role of vice-president in 1786. Smith was a tall, handsome man, with penetrating blue eyes and quiet dignity. George Washington described him as "both learned and good," and Archibald Alexander thought he had "never seen his equal in elegance of person and manners."

Dr. Smith greatly strengthened the Princeton faculty with impressive appointments. Walter Minto was named to the professorship of mathematics and natural philosophy in September 1787. A native Scot, trained at Edinburgh and Pisa, Minto was Princeton's first professional scientist. In 1795 another Scot with wide training in Europe, John Maclean, became the first professor of chemistry to teach on a college campus in the United States. When Archibald Alexander visited Princeton College in 1801, he wrote that Maclean was "at home, almost equally in all branches of science."[33] In 1787 Smith displayed his own scholarly ability in his impressive *Essay on the Causes of the Variety of Complexion and Figure in the Human Species*.[34] Against writers like Voltaire who held that the different races testified to the multiple origins of humanity, Smith argued that the different races descended from one human pair; he showed how climate and social conditions are fully adequate to explain the current differences between human races. With Smith, Minto, and Maclean, the college—for the first time in its history—had three genuinely professional teachers.

In 1803 the campus (an expression created by John Witherspoon for the college's pastoral setting) was expanded by the addition of the Library and Philosophical Hall, built to the west and east of Nassau Hall. The Library housed not only the college's books but also the American Whig Society and Cliosophic Society, the nation's oldest college literary and debating clubs. Philosophical Hall was the college's dining room.

Despite his success, Smith found himself in trouble with many of the college's supporters and with a growing number of the trustees. The 1806 student body of nearly two hundred no longer included many ministerial students. The president's promotion of the study of modern languages and natural sciences created concern that the college was advancing a new curriculum at the expense of theology and those subjects necessary to prepare candidates adequately for the ministry. Student unrest and disorder, common to American colleges at the time, and Smith's inability to deal with the problem worried those who saw Princeton as no longer fit to nurture the piety required in ministers. In February 1800, three seniors were suspended for disrupting morning chapel. Two years later, during a period of disorder among the students, a great fire devastated Nassau Hall. A general student rebellion in April 1807 further discredited Smith's leadership. The number of students dropped to little more than half, and the college was forced to cut back its faculty, leaving only Smith and John Maclean. Many trustees saw the rebellion as a dangerous expression of anti-Christian dissipation and blamed Smith for being unable to handle the situation.

President Smith's easy-going tolerance of divergent views

and several of his scholarly opinions led to the growing suspicion that his own orthodoxy was not above question. It was reported in 1804 that he taught that "polygamy and concubinage are not moral evils" but only violations of civil law. Smith saw himself as continuing both the emphases of John Witherspoon—Christianity and Enlightenment; his letters, however, revealed a considerable degree of dissatisfaction with the strictness of Presbyterian orthodoxy. His sermons contained much of the old evangelical fervor, but at the same time "themes from the Enlightenment were leavening the old gospel of revivalistic Calvinism." Compared with his predecessors, Smith gave less attention to the person, revelation, and sovereign activity of God. Rather, he was inclined to stress human free will and happiness and, without denying miracles, offered scientific explanations of the supernatural. The perception was growing that Smith "was wavering in his Calvinism, weak on the sovereignty of God in salvation, and shaky in defending original sin."[35] It was obvious to many Presbyterians that something had to be done.

# 2

# The Seminary

*Alexander Hall. The cornerstone for the Seminary's first building was laid on September 26, 1815. Called "Seminary" and "Old Seminary," In 1893 the building was named Alexander Hall in honor of the Seminary's first Professor.*

I admonish you again and again, that you read the sacred Scriptures in a far different manner from that in which you read any other book: that you approach them with the highest reverence and the most intense application of your mind; not as the words of a man, nor an angel, but as the words of the Divine majesty, the least of which should have more weight with us, than the writings of the wisest and most learned men in the world.

HIERONYMUS WELLER VON MOLSDORF
*Colleague of Martin Luther, quoted by Archibald Alexander*
*in his Inaugural Address, August 12, 1812*

CONCERNED about President Smith and Princeton College and with the alarming need for more ministers, the Presbyterian church moved toward the establishment of a separate theological seminary. There was precedent for such an undertaking in the Log College of William Tennent and in the schools of several American denominations. In 1784 the Dutch Reformed church began a seminary in New York City. Ten years later the Scottish Associate Presbyterian Synod established its theological school in a log building in Beaver County, Pennsylvania.[1] In 1802 the Moravian seminary was founded in Nazareth, Pennsylvania; and two years later John M. Mason began the Associate Reformed Seminary in New York City. These schools—with a single teacher and a few students— were little more than modifications of the old apprentice arrangement; but a new pattern was set in 1808. New England Congregationalists, alarmed by the loss of the Hollis professorship at Harvard to the Unitarians, joined to begin a new school at Andover, Massachusetts. By the end of its first year, Andover Seminary had admitted the astounding number of thirty-six students.

In the post–Revolutionary War period, Princeton College was no longer producing significant numbers of candidates for the ministry. During most of its history, about half of the Princeton graduates had become ministers; but now the college was turning out far more men interested in careers in law, politics, and education. In 1803 President Smith

[27]

attempted to revive Princeton's leadership in ministerial training by adding a professor of theology whose primary responsibility was to supervise postgraduate ministerial education. He chose the Reverend Henry Kollock, pastor of the Elizabethtown Presbyterian Church. The brilliant young preacher had graduated from Princeton in 1794 at the age of fifteen. He now returned to Princeton as professor in the college and pastor of the Presbyterian church. Kollock's sermons were so successful, it was said, that visitors in town often stayed for the Sabbath just to hear him preach. The General Assembly of 1806 recommended to the favorable consideration of the presbyteries a letter from Smith which set forth the advantages offered in theological instruction at Princeton College. Paying only one dollar a week for board, students could enjoy "the assistance of the President and Professor of Theology, without any fee for instruction." They would receive lectures in divinity, ecclesiastical history, church government, Christian and Jewish antiquities, and the duties of the pastoral office. For those who desired it, there were classes in the Hebrew language, "so useful and almost indispensable to a good divine." A weekly "Theological Society," the availability of classes in science, a varied student body, and "a large and well-selected theological library" were set forth as added attractions. Students were slow in responding, however, and Kollock resigned his professorship in 1806. [2] Smith's efforts to persuade Presbyterian leaders to support the college's theological program had failed. Sentiment was building for a separate theological school.

As early as 1800, Ashbel Green, now pastor of Philadelphia's Second Presbyterian Church, was quietly putting forth the idea of a theological seminary independent of Princeton College. Samuel Miller, one of the pastors of the Presbyterian church in New York City, supported Green's plan. He pointed to the example of other denominations that were establishing seminaries and stressed the shortage of ministers in the Presbyterian church, with its "near four hundred vacant congregations." In May 1805, Green made a stirring speech to the General Assembly of the Presbyterian Church. He did not mention theological seminaries but underscored the shortage of ministers. "It is a melancholy fact," he reported, that Presbyterian interests, as well as "the Redeemer's kingdom," suffered for want of a greater number of able and faithful ministers of the gospel. He added, "'Give us ministers' is the cry of the missionary regions;—'Give us ministers,' is the importunate entreaty of our numerous and increasing vacancies;—'Give us ministers,' is the demand of many large and important congregations in our most populous cities and towns."[3]

The General Assembly responded to Ashbel Green's appeal with a call for presbyteries to work to increase the number of candidates for the ministry and to support them adequately. During the next several years the discussion concerning a seminary continued, both privately and publicly. Samuel Miller wrote to Ashbel Green: ". . . if it be desired to have the divinity-school uncontaminated by the college, to have its government unfettered, and its orthodoxy and purity perpetual, it appears to me that a separate establishment will be on many accounts desirable." At the 1808 General Assembly, Archibald Alexander, pastor of the Third Presbyterian Church in Philadelphia and the retiring moderator, preached the opening sermon on I Corinthians 14:12—"Seek that ye may excel to the edifying of the church." In his sermon, Alexander made the first proposal to the General Assembly that the church should found theological seminaries. There would not be "a regular and sufficient supply of well-qualified ministers of the Gospel," he stated, "until every Presbytery, or at least every Synod, [should] have under its direction a seminary established for the single purpose of educating youth for the ministry."

Challenged by Alexander's sermon, the Presbytery of Philadelphia, under Ashbel Green's leadership, sent an overture to the next General Assembly proposing the establishment of "a theological school." The assembly appointed a committee of eight ministers and three laymen, with Congregational delegate President Timothy Dwight of Yale as chairman, to consider the overture. Four days later the committee reported that it had considered three plans:

The first is to establish *one great school* in some convenient place near the centre of the bounds of our Church. The second is, to establish *two* schools in such places as may best accommodate the northern and southern divisions of the Church. The third is, to establish such a school within the bounds of *each of the Synods.*

The committee presented arguments for each of these plans but stressed the advantage of "one great school."

It would be furnished with larger funds, and therefore with a more extensive library and a greater number of professors. The system of education pursued in it would, therefore, be more extensive and more perfect; the youths educated in it would also be united in the same views and contract an early and lasting friendship for each other,—circumstances which could not fail of promoting harmony and prosperity in the Church.

The three plans were sent to the presbyteries for their consideration. Ten presbyteries favored one school, one voted for two schools, ten favored synodical schools, six were opposed to establishing any seminary, and the remaining presbyteries gave no answer! At the 1810 General Assembly, a committee, with Samuel Miller as chairman, decided that a majority of the presbyteries had voted for the establishment of a theological school or schools and that, when misconceptions were removed, the greater number had favored a single school. The committee urged the church to move at once to establish "a seminary for securing to candidates for the ministry more extensive and efficient theological instruction than they have heretofore enjoyed."

The committee called for a school that would provide not only "learned and able" ministers but also men of "real piety." It committed the Presbyterian General Assembly to a "promise and pledge" to the churches. In forming a seminary, it would "endeavor to make it, under the blessing of God, a nursery of vital piety as well as of sound theological learning, and to train up persons for the ministry who shall be lovers as well as defenders of the truth as it is in Jesus, friends of revivals of religion, and a blessing to the church of God." The committee's report was approved; and the General Assembly sent a pastoral letter to the churches, calling their attention to the proposal and earnestly soliciting their patronage and support in the establishment of the seminary. It also appointed a committee—composed of

Green, Miller, Alexander, and four other ministers—to draw up a "Plan of the Seminary."[4] Chairman Ashbel Green, who largely wrote the "Plan," commented that he worked without "any other guide than the nature of the subject." "If I ever taxed my faculties to their best effort," he said, "it was on this occasion."[5]

By the time of the 1811 General Assembly, $14,000 had been contributed by the presbyteries for the proposed seminary. A group of Princeton College trustees proposed joining the new seminary to the college, with "the principal direction of the college" gradually adjusted "to promote the objects of the theological institution."[6] The ministers of the church, however, were not anxious to relinquish the authority over the seminary to the college which many of them had come to distrust; and so the General Assembly of 1811 rejected the proposal. The assembly then adopted, with small changes, Ashbel Green's "Plan" and voted to establish the new seminary between the Raritan and Potomac rivers.

The "Plan" stated that the purpose of the seminary was to provide "an adequate supply and succession of able and faithful ministers" who "truly believe, and cordially love" the Confession of Faith, catechisms, and polity of the Presbyterian church. The new school, the "Plan" added, would

unite, in those who shall sustain the ministerial office, religion and literature; that piety of the heart which is the fruit only of the renewing and sanctifying grace of God, with solid learning; believing that religion without learning, or learning without religion, in the ministers of the Gospel, must ultimately prove injurious to the Church.[7]

The General Assembly, as the "patron" of the seminary and the "fountain of its powers," would elect the professors and govern the school through a board of directors. The directors would oversee the instruction, inaugurate the professors, and guard the purity of their teaching. The professors would be required to subscribe to the Westminster Confession of Faith, the Catechisms, and the Form of Church Government of the Presbyterian Church, according to a prescribed and strictly worded formula. They would report regularly to the directors concerning the content of their classes and their method of teaching and to make "such alterations or additions" as the board should direct. The students would be examined "at every stated meeting" of the board, with a final examination conducted by the directors and the faculty. Successful students would receive a certificate of graduation, recommending them to their presbyteries.

The 1812 General Assembly voted to locate the seminary in Princeton and elected the Board of Directors, consisting of twenty-one ministers and nine elders. Of the thirty men chosen, fourteen were trustees of the College of New Jersey, and the others were alumni or recipients of honorary degrees from the college. The assembly then turned to the important task of electing the first professor for the new school. An eyewitness described the solemn scene:

It was unanimously resolved to spend some time in prayer previously to the election, and that not a single remark should be made by any member, with reference to any candidate, before or after the balloting. Silently and prayerfully these guardians of the Church began to prepare their votes. . . . Not a word was spoken, not a whisper heard, as the teller passed around to collect the result. The votes were counted . . . and the Rev. Dr. Alexander was pronounced elected.[8]

Although he felt himself "altogether unqualified" and regretted leaving his Philadelphia congregation, Archibald Alexander was compelled to accept "the call of the whole Church by their representatives."

On August 12, 1812, the usual traffic between New York and Philadelphia—the young nation's two largest cities—passed through Princeton on the old King's Highway. Handsome three-seated coaches, holding nine passengers inside and three on top, arrived and departed regularly. A hundred horses were waiting to take the places of the tired ones. The town's inns—the old Hudibras, King's Arms, and Sign of the College, as well as the newer Thirteen Stars and Washington Arms—were crowded with guests. Groups of men stood in the shade discussing the hot, humid weather or talking excitedly about politics. Earlier in the summer, the American Congress had followed the request of President John Madison, a graduate of Princeton College, and declared war against Great Britain.

Many people packed the town's Presbyterian church—a simple two-story brick meeting house built in the 1760s and containing fifty-seven pews and galleries on three sides—for the inauguration of Dr. Archibald Alexander as the first professor of the new theological seminary. Distinguished pastors and teachers, college faculty and students, and townspeople were present, as well as the three new seminary students— William Blain, John Covert, and Henry Blatchford. Blain and Covert were from New York; and Blatchford, who was born in England, had attended Union College in New York State. In the crowded church, it would have been easy not to notice a boy watching the proceedings from the gallery; but Charles Hodge would never forget that day. Writing over sixty years later, Hodge reported that he could "well remember, then a boy of fourteen . . . listening to the doctor's inaugural address and watching the ceremony of investiture."[9]

The sermon of the day was given by Samuel Miller.[10] Taking II Timothy 2:2 as his text, the scholarly New York City pastor preached on "the duty of the Church to take measures for providing an able and faithful ministry." The congregation listened carefully as he pointed to the example of the Dutch Reformed Church, the Scottish Associate Reformed Church, and the New England Congregationalists in founding seminaries. He stressed the need for more ministers in the Presbyterian church. "We have slumbered," Miller reminded his fellow Presbyterians, "until the scarcity of labourers in our harvest has become truly alarming!" Samuel Miller believed that the new seminary would provide orthodox, learned, and godly ministers who would strengthen the unity and peace of the church. He continued:

Yes, brethren, we have more reason to rejoice, and to felicitate one another, on the establishment of this seminary, than on the achievement of a great national victory, or on making a splendid addition to our national territory. It is the beginning, as we trust, of an extensive and permanent system, from which blessings may flow to millions while we are sleeping in the dust.

The War of 1812 had started just two months before. The Louisiana Purchase, nine years earlier, had more than doubled the size of the infant nation. But, to Samuel Miller, a far greater achievement was the establishment of the seminary. We are almost staggered by his faith and courage. Addressing one professor and the three students who made up the first class, he dared to hope that from the work there being started "blessings [would] flow to millions"! Miller ended his sermon with a searching appeal for support for the new venture. "The eyes of the Church are upon us," he said. "The eyes of angels and, above all, the eyes of the King of Zion, are upon us."

At that moment the eyes of the congregation were on the short, slight man with fine features and "lively countenance," who rose to speak. Archibald Alexander began by telling of his deep sense of "insufficiency for the work." He then added, "If the design be of God, he will prosper the undertaking, notwithstanding the weakness of the instruments employed in carrying it on; and will crown our feeble efforts with success." Then followed a lengthy address on John 5:39—"Search the Scriptures." Alexander stated that two distinct duties faced the person who responded to that command: "first, to ascertain that the Scriptures contain the truths of God: and, secondly, to ascertain what those truths are."

Dr. Alexander took his hearers through an investigation of the canon of the Old and New Testaments, the integrity of the text, and the authenticity and inspiration of the Scriptures. He argued, against the Roman Catholics, that the Scriptures are the only rule for faith and practice and, against "rationalists" and "enthusiasts," that they are a sufficient rule. He discussed how the Scriptures should be interpreted in order to find their true and full meaning and listed the helps which the Bible student needs in order to "search the Scriptures." Since the expounder of the Bible should be well acquainted with the very "words by which the Holy Ghost teacheth," knowledge of the Hebrew and Greek languages, he said, is a "necessary prerequisite." Other helps, Alexander added, include the early translations, Bible commentaries, and books on general and biblical history, geography, and science.

Alexander then described "a help which, though put in the

last place in this discourse, is of more real importance than all the rest": "the illumination and assistance of the Holy Spirit." He stressed that the student of the Bible must:

be possessed of sincere and ardent piety. He should be a man "taught of God," conscious of his own insufficiency, but confident of the help of the Almighty . . . . He, who would understand the Scriptures, therefore, ought not to "lean to his own understanding," but by continual and earnest prayer should look unto the "Father of lights," from whom proceedeth every good and every perfect gift; and who hath promised to give wisdom to those who lack it, and ask for it.

Alexander added, "There is no person who needs more to be in the constant exercise of prayer than the Theological student: not only at stated periods, but continually in the midst of his studies, his heart should be raised to heaven for help and direction."

The new professor then turned to "a few leading points, on which the Scriptures furnish us with information of the most important kind"—the true character of God, the origin of evil, the doctrine of redemption, the work of the Spirit in uniting the redeemed soul to Jesus Christ, the will of God as stated in the law and displayed in the character of Christ, and heaven and hell.

Despite the heat of the day, the congregation listened intently as Archibald Alexander spoke with great feeling:

How delightful must it be to sit as a disciple at the feet of Jesus, and with a child-like docility imbibe precious instruction from his Word and Spirit! . . . When at any time it pleases God to shine upon his Word, whilst the believer reads its sacred contents, what a divine glory illuminates the holy page! What attractive beauty draws forth the best affections of his heart! What wonders do his opened eyes behold in the cross! He seems to be translated into a new world, and is ready to exclaim, "I have heard of thee by the hearing of the ear; but now mine eye seeth thee." . . . O! Could the pious reader of the Scriptures constantly retain these spiritual views and these holy impressions, heaven would be begun. . . . But whilst we are on our pilgrimage to this promised land, the Scriptures will be "a light to our feet and a lamp to our paths." They will answer the same purpose to us which the pillar of cloud and of fire did to the

Israelites. They will guide us in the right way through all our journey. Let us, then, be persuaded diligently "to search the Scriptures."

After Alexander's hour-and-a-half discourse, Philip Milledoler came to the pulpit to give the charge to the professor and students. Milledoler had been Archibald Alexander's predecessor at Third Presbyterian Church in Philadelphia and Samuel Miller's colleague in the "collegiate" churches in New York City. Echoing the faith of Samuel Miller, he told the little group that on their faithfulness under God might "depend the future peace and prosperity of the church, and the salvation of thousands, perhaps, millions, yet unborn." He expressed the hope that one day students from the seminary would be scattered across the United States and vie with the British "in carrying the lamp of eternal truth, and planting the standard of the cross, on the remotest shores of heathen lands."

Archibald Alexander then took the vow required by the General Assembly. Carefully he repeated the words in his high, clear voice:

In the presence of God and of the Directors of this Seminary, I do solemnly, and *ex animo* adopt, receive, and subscribe the Confession of Faith, and the Catechisms of the Presbyterian Church in the United States of America, as the confession of my faith; or as a summary and just exhibition of that system of doctrine and religious belief which is contained in the Holy Scripture, and therein revealed by God to man for his salvation; and I do solemnly, *ex animo* profess to receive the Form of Government of said Church, as agreeable to the inspired oracles. And I do solemnly promise and engage, not to inculcate, teach, or insinuate any thing which shall appear to me to contradict or contravene, either directly or impliedly, any thing taught in the said Confession of Faith or Catechisms; nor to oppose any of the fundamental principles of Presbyterian Church Government, while I shall continue a Professor in this Seminary.[11]

The service was over. People filed by to congratulate the new professor and to shake the hands of the three students.

*     *     *

[36]

Two days later, Samuel Stanhope Smith resigned as president of Princeton College, after what he described as "the fatiguing and, I hope, faithful service of thirty three years." The trustees unanimously elected Ashbel Green as his successor. Some had wanted Samuel Miller to replace Smith; but the evening before their meeting, Miller pressed every trustee to vote for Green. Miller was pleased with Dr. Green's acceptance, which, he wrote, "gladdened the hearts of the friends of religion and of the College." On October 1, 1812—the day of Dr. Smith's actual retirement—the college board as a body visited him to express "their highly respectful and grateful sentiments, towards him, for his long and faithful services."[12]

After Ashbel Green's graduation and marriage to Elizabeth Stockton, who was the daughter of a prominent Princeton family, he had served the college first as a tutor and then as professor of mathematics and natural philosophy. He was licensed to preach by the Presbytery of New Brunswick in February 1786. When Dr. Witherspoon heard Green's first sermon in the church in Princeton, he tapped him on the shoulder and said, "Well, well, continue to do as well as that, and we'll be satisfied"—"the only praise," commented Green, "that he ever gave me to my face."[13]

Ashbel Green declined an invitation to become pastor of the Independent Church in Charleston, South Carolina, but in May 1787 he accepted the call of the strategic Second Presbyterian Church of Philadelphia. He soon became the most popular preacher in the city, drawing capacity crowds to hear his sermons. He was an able and faithful pastor, especially keen in catechizing the children and youth of his congregation. He fought slavery and deism, promoted the missionary movement, and worked tirelessly to build up the many new Christian enterprises of the time. With courtly manners and important family connections, Green was a well-respected citizen of the city. In 1792 he was awarded the Doctor of Divinity degree by the University of Pennsylvania. That same year, he was elected chaplain to the United States Congress, which met in Philadelphia prior to its move to Washington in 1800. When Nassau Hall burned on March 6, 1802, Green raised money in Philadelphia for its restoration and served as interim president during the winter session of

1802-03, when Dr. Smith was away on a fund-raising trip to the South.

In October 1812, Ashbel Green left the Philadelphia church which he had served for twenty-five years and moved into the president's house on Nassau Street in Princeton. His inaugural address in November dealt with "The Union of Piety and Science." Green had become firmly convinced that education, in itself, could be dangerous if it were not securely rooted in Christian orthodoxy and piety.[14] Like Smith, Ashbel Green was loyal to John Witherspoon's legacy; but, unlike Smith, he believed that the heart of Witherspoon's commitment was his doctrinal views and his concern for revivals and Christian conduct.[15] Green gathered the three faculty members for a day of prayer on November 16 and wrote down a list of goals for himself. The first three of his resolutions were:

1st . . . to endeavour to be a father to the institution. . . . 2d. To pray for the institution as I do for my family . . . and especially that [God] may pour out his Spirit upon it, and make it what its pious founders intended it to be. 3d. To watch against the declension of religion in my own soul . . . to which the pursuits of science themselves may prove a temptation.[16]

Dr. Green began systematic Bible teaching on Sunday afternoons—the first time in Princeton's history that the Bible was a part of formal study. One of the college students described those Bible classes, attended by teachers and students:

Upon the ringing of the bell we assembled, and waited to receive the President as he entered, at the appointed moment, with the book of God under his arm. The lesson from the Scriptures was always connected with singing and prayer. It was the object of the Doctor to give us, as far as possible, some connected view of revealed truth. For this purpose, we studied the historical, devotional, and preceptive parts of the Bible somewhat in turn, thus bringing both the Old and New Testaments under review. Often we were expected simply to answer questions on the chapters previously assigned; but it was deemed far better for us to give a synopsis of their contents, either in our own language, or in that of the inspired writers themselves, as we might prefer. A considerable portion of the Psalms we committed almost entirely to memory, especially the more striking passages.[17]

Many of the students appreciated these classes. One recalled that on Sunday afternoons "the Doctor laid aside whatever was stiff and formal in manner, and seemed like a tender, warm-hearted father in the midst of a group of children." "We retired to our rooms," he wrote, "with the conviction that there was one who felt an interest in our eternal welfare."

With a new seminary in Princeton, Presbyterians anticipated a larger number of able ministers for their churches and missions. With Ashbel Green at their college, they hoped for well-trained and spiritually minded leaders for the nation.

# 3

# Archibald Alexander

*The house into which Archibald Alexander and his family moved on July 29, 1812. Here Princeton Seminary began the next month.*

To love him with all the heart and with all the soul and with all the strength is more than all whole burnt offerings and sacrifices.

I dwell with him that is of a contrite and humble spirit.

But to do good and to communicate forget not.

The Lord is nigh unto them which are of broken heart and saveth such as be of a contrite spirit.

Verses pasted in the cover of
Archibald Alexander's Bible

I N 1812 Archibald Alexander was forty years old. He had
already served as a preacher, college president, and
pastor. His preparation for leading the first Presbyterian
seminary had been enriched by his experience of American
life in the South, the Middle States, and New England; on the
frontier, in the country, and in a major city.

Alexander's grandfather came to America from Londonderry, Northern Ireland, in about 1736. He settled in
Pennsylvania, where he was converted in the Great Awakening. A few years later, with other Scotch-Irish neighbors, he
migrated south to the Valley of Virginia, a scenic area west of
the Blue Ridge Mountains and east of the Alleghenies. His
son William was a thrifty merchant-farmer, who married
the daughter of a wealthy landowner. William, the father of
Archibald, was a Presbyterian elder, although he did not
exhibit the personal faith and earnest piety of his father.

Archibald Alexander was born in 1772 in a log house some
seven miles east of Lexington beside a branch of the James
River. When he was a boy, the area was barely a generation
beyond the frontier. His grandmother had been killed by
Indians not too many years earlier. Alexander reminisced in
his old age that it had been his lot "to draw the first breath
of life at the foot of a lofty mountain, and on the bank of a
roaring mountain torrent; where the reveillé was often the
hideous howling of hungry wolves."[1] Life on the small farms
in the valley was simple, hard, and sometimes crude. Survival
meant rugged discipline, so little Archibald learned to ride a

horse, swim, and shoot. On his eleventh birthday he received his own rifle.

Archibald attended five different schools before he was ten years old. By the time he was five he was reading the New Testament, and by seven years of age he had learned the Westminster Shorter Catechism and was working on the Larger. His education, however, began in earnest when he came under the teaching of William Graham at Liberty Hall Academy. In 1774, Hanover Presbytery authorized a "seminary" for Augusta County and invited William Graham of the Princeton class of 1773 to be its teacher. In a "hewed log-house, twenty-eight feet by twenty-four, one story and a half high," Graham placed his little library and his air pump, "electric machine," sextant, microscope, telescope, maps, and two twelve-inch globes. There he taught his students Greek, Latin, science, and, his first love, philosophy—handing on to Alexander and his colleagues many of John Witherspoon's lecture notes. Archibald Alexander always believed he received from Graham the equivalent of a Princeton College education. Assisting Graham was the remarkable James Priestly, who had the school classics so completely memorized that he never used a book when hearing his classes recite Ovid, Virgil, Horace, or Homer. He often took his pupils to some sequestered, romantic spot, to "spout before them the orations of Demosthenes, in the original, with all the fire of the Grecian orator himself." Later in his school career, Alexander was taught by Archibald Roane, afterwards governor of Tennessee.

Young Archibald won high standing at every public examination and was reported to his father to be a boy of great promise. Only two of the students at Liberty Hall were professing Christians, but William Graham stood firm both in doctrine and discipline. The teachings of Hume and Voltaire had reached this distant outpost of learning, although—Archibald Alexander wrote—most students "cared as little about infidelity as they did about religion."[2] Archibald was not interested either. He laughed at those who were devout Christians and was little moved by gospel preaching. He spent his time when he was not studying in dancing and playing cards.

[44]

When he was sixteen, Archibald Alexander left Graham's school to become a private tutor in the family of General John Posey, who lived near Fredericksburg 140 miles away across the Blue Ridge Mountains. Working nights to keep ahead of his three pupils, he acquired a more accurate knowledge of Latin, the key that would later unlock for him the theological literature of Western Christianity. Late in life, Alexander could say that "during the half century then past, he had read more Latin than English."[3]

In the extended household of General Posey, the young tutor found lively discussions—often about religion. A revival in the area, one of the beginnings of the Second Great Awakening, was winning converts. One day a Baptist carpenter suddenly asked Alexander whether he believed in the second birth. Taken aback, Alexander answered that he did. Asked then if he had experienced it, Alexander answered frankly, "Not that I know of." The conversation ended with the disturbing words, "Oh, if you had experienced this change you would know something about it!" Alexander began seriously to consider the subject: "It seemed to be in the Bible; but I thought there must be some method of explaining it away; for among the Presbyterians I had never heard of anyone who had experienced the new birth, nor could I recollect ever to have heard it mentioned." Before this time, Alexander's "only notion of religion was that it consisted in becoming better."[4]

In a trunkful of books sent to him from home, Alexander found *A View of the Internal Evidences of the Christian Religion* by Soame Jenyns. He was moved by "bright and overwhelming evidence" that led him to further reading and prayer, but "all this was without a radical transformation of character."[5] Mrs. Tyler, part of the group at General Posey's and an Episcopalian who was converted under Baptist preaching, deeply impressed him. She often asked her young friend to read to her from the writings of John Flavel, an English Puritan who was ejected from his church by the Uniformity Act of 1662.[6] An event occurred one Sunday night which must be described in Alexander's own words:

My services as a reader were frequently in requisition, not only to save the eyes of old Mrs. Tyler, but on Sundays for the benefit of the whole family. On one of these Sabbath evenings, I was requested to read out of Flavel. The part on which I had been regularly engaged was the "Method of Grace"; but now, by some means, I was led to select one of the sermons on Revelation 3:20, "Behold I stand at the door and knock," etc. The discourse was upon the patience, forbearance and kindness of the Lord Jesus Christ to impenitent and obstinate sinners. As I proceeded to read aloud, the truth took effect on my feelings, and every word I read seemed applicable to my own case. Before I finished the discourse, these emotions became too strong for restraint, and my voice began to falter. I laid down the book, rose hastily, and went out with a full heart, and hastened to my place of retirement. No sooner had I reached the spot than I dropped upon my knees, and attempted to pour out my feelings in prayer; but I had not continued many minutes in this exercise before I was overwhelmed with a flood of joy.[7]

By the end of his year as tutor, Archibald Alexander had achieved an improved working knowledge of Latin, had acquired a hasty overview of history and philosophy, and had made a modest beginning in biblical study and theology. Most importantly, he had become deeply concerned about the meaning of the Christian gospel. It was no small accomplishment for one year or less in the life of a boy only recently turned seventeen.

Alexander was now reading avidly the Christian books which he could find in western Virginia. He turned especially to the seventeenth-century Puritans and the Scottish Presbyterians and their successors of the next century. Not surprisingly, John Flavel became his favorite writer. He later declared that to Flavel he owed more than to "any uninspired author."[8] He also read John Owen, Richard Baxter, Joseph Alleine, Thomas Halyburton, Thomas Boston, Ebenezer Erskine, Philip Doddridge, and George Whitefield. He read Benjamin Jenks's *Submission to the Righteousness of God*—a vigorous presentation of justification by faith from a Church of England clergyman who confessed that he had preached for a long time without knowing the true method of salvation. Alexander carefully studied the New Testament commentary by the evangelical Anglican William Burkitt.

After Archibald Alexander returned home in 1789, he

visited with William Graham the scenes of the revival which was now spreading among the Presbyterians in southern Virginia. He saw large crowds gathered for communion services in the open air and listened to powerful revival preaching. Even William Graham's sermons (which Alexander once thought the worst he had ever heard) were now eloquent and moving. He saw evidences of people converted from sin, but still he was troubled with nagging doubts and fears concerning his own relationship to God. Conversations with William Graham and John Blair Smith— brother of Samuel Stanhope Smith and his successor as president of Hampden-Sydney College—heightened his confusion. Finally another minister, James Mitchell, sought out young Alexander and ascertained that his trouble was that he thought that he had not "experienced those convictions without which he could not expect to be saved." Mitchell told him that no degree of conviction was required and that the only purpose which conviction served was to show our need of Christ, "and this," he added, "you have." Alexander later wrote:

He then represented Christ as an Advocate before the throne of God, ready to undertake my cause, and able to save to the uttermost all who come unto God by him. A new view opened before me at this moment. I did feel that I needed a Saviour, and I knew Christ as an Advocate was able to save me.[9]

Soon the struggle was over, and in the autumn of 1789 Alexander made a profession of faith which remained from then on unshaken by doubts. He later looked back on his experience as an example of "how seldom believers can designate with exactness the time of their renewal." He wrote: "Now, at the age of seventy-seven, I am of opinion, that my regeneration took place while I resided at General Posey's, in the year 1788."[10]

After a time of serious illness during the winter and early spring of 1790, Alexander chose, with characteristic misgivings concerning his own qualifications, to study for the ministry under William Graham. With ten or twelve other students, he gathered around their teacher at Liberty Hall. Since Graham was also a pastor, his program of training was a blend of the two methods of ministerial education: "apprenticing" with a pastor and studying for a year or so under a professor or president of a college.

Graham devoted one day a week to hearing the students' papers on assigned topics and discussing theological subjects with them. Alexander and his colleagues studied the theology of Francis Turretin in Latin and read the works of John Owen, Joseph Butler, Thomas Boston, and Jonathan Edwards. Graham stressed, however, the importance of thinking for oneself. Quite early in their relationship, the teacher told the students something that Alexander never forgot. "If you mean ever to be a theologian," he said, "you must come at it not by reading but by thinking." Alexander wrestled with the great issues of theology and came to love clear, biblical doctrines rather than elaborate, speculative formulations. Graham's students read John Locke and studied Scottish Common Sense Realism, which their teacher had learned from John Witherspoon at Princeton College. This tough-minded inductive philosophy became part of Alexander's intellectual equipment and would leave its mark on the entire history of "Old Princeton" Seminary.

William Graham also gave his students opportunities to put into practice what they were learning. In the autumn of 1790 Alexander was shocked when Graham suddenly asked him to "exhort" the people during a church service. The reserved and shy boy surprised himself and astonished the congregation with a fluency which, fifty years later, he described as "equal to any I have enjoyed to this day." Archibald Alexander's time at Liberty Hall brought great intellectual and spiritual growth, and he always felt that he owed more to William Graham than to anyone else "in regard to the direction of his studies and the moulding of his character."[11]

In October 1790, Alexander was received under care of Lexington Presbytery. He was assigned a paper (in Latin) on the subject of justification by faith alone and a sermon on "the difference betwixt a dead and living faith." The next April he read both paper and sermon and was examined by presbytery in Latin, Greek, and the liberal arts. He was now assigned Hebrews 6:1-6 for a lecture and Jeremiah 1:7 for a "popular sermon." Alexander, who was physically small and very boyish in appearance, "disliked exceedingly" the text— "But the Lord said to me, Do not say, I am only a youth, for to all to whom I send you you shall go, and whatever I command you you shall speak." Nonetheless, he accepted it obediently.[12]

The presbytery also elected Alexander, already a ruling elder, as a commissioner to the General Assembly. He rode to Philadelphia on horseback, accompanied by William Graham. Along the way, they were joined by John Blair Smith, president of Hampden-Sydney College. When they reached Philadelphia, Alexander, almost like Luther entering Rome, felt "a great awe" at the thought of the large city. He wrote, "My impression was that all eyes would be directed towards me." He was soon relieved, however, that "they took no notice of us." The young Virginian watched with great interest and amazement the proceedings of the assembly. The opening sermon was delivered by Dr. Robert Smith, the father of Samuel Stanhope Smith and John Blair Smith. He met the dignified and lofty Ashbel Green, the elegant Samuel Stanhope Smith, and the plain but imposing John Witherspoon. He was frequently at the home of Mrs. Hodge, grandmother of Charles Hodge, who in future days would become his beloved junior colleague at Princeton Seminary.

During the fall meeting of presbytery in 1791, Alexander completed his examinations. Up to the last minute he was reluctant to take this step toward ordination, but he was encouraged by William Graham. On October 1, 1791, he was licensed at the age of nineteen. He later wrote, "During the service I was almost overwhelmed with an awful feeling of responsibility and unfitness for the sacred office." Immediately Alexander started off on a preaching tour, like the Methodist circuit-riders—his saddlebags filled with tracts and Bibles, his preaching warm and evangelical. In the next fifteen months, he preached 132 sermons, sometimes two hours or more in length. For three years he was continually traveling, often preaching to little groups of six or eight, and sometimes to large gatherings of hundreds.

Alexander's whole ministry was shaped by the experiences of these years. He learned to preach simple sermons in plain language, combining the great doctrines and themes of the Bible with searching application. He regarded it as a high compliment when told of someone who had heard him in an out-of-the-way place and commented, "I guess he aint a very *larned* man." He always carried his pocket Bible with him and composed his sermons while in the saddle. Seldom satisfied, Alexander revised his sermons after preaching them. Occasionally he believed that a sermon was very good, but, when he preached it, he was "greatly humbled" and sometimes so discouraged that he felt that he "could never venture into the pulpit again." He learned to preach effectively without notes. Early in his itinerant ministry a puff of wind blew his notes into the congregation, and he determined "to take no more paper into the pulpit."

Archibald Alexander met old converts of George Whitefield and Samuel Davies and came to value highly the simple, heartfelt piety of ordinary Christians. During a preaching tour in eastern Virginia, he was astonished that an uneducated Baptist carpenter was a preacher. He questioned him concerning his call to the ministry, and "when the old millwright had finished his narrative," Alexander wrote, "I felt much more inclined to doubt my own call to the ministry, than that of James Shelburne."[13]

During these missionary years when he was preaching almost every day, Alexander continued to study. There was no major subject which did not interest him. Deism was rampant in Virginia, so he undertook an answer to Thomas Paine's *Age of Reason* and read as widely as he could on the evidences of Christianity. He studied church government and read Edward Stillingfleet's *Irenicum* and Martin Chemnitz on the Council of Trent. He loved mathematics and geometry and was interested in physics. He studied theology and, most of all, the Bible, reading his Greek New Testament with ease.

All his life Archibald Alexander retained a vivid awareness of frontier life and of the importance of "domestic missions," and he would often urge his seminary students to spend "a few years in itinerant preaching."[14] He knew firsthand the needs and opportunities. He remembered visiting an elderly, illiterate couple who had spent most of a night trying to spell out portions of the New Testament. Alexander wrote, "Here was a family of whom the heads had grown gray without having ever attended public worship; and who until now knew no more of a Saviour than the heathen." When they heard the gospel, they were "like persons come into a new world."[15]

Hanover Presbytery ordained Archibald Alexander on June 7, 1794. He now concentrated his ministry in serving several churches of southern Virginia, where the young pastor experienced gracious hospitality. Slaves were more numerous here than in the Valley, and Alexander preached to them and collected books for them to read. He described the Christian slaves as "eminent for piety" and wrote of the members of his Cub Creek Church, "It was a lovely sight to see these seventy blacks surrounding the table of the Lord."[16]

In 1797 Alexander, now twenty-four, added to his pastoral duties the presidency of a struggling young college. Hampden-Sydney College had been opened in 1776 by the Presbytery of Hanover, primarily to train ministers. The two brothers, Samuel Stanhope Smith and John Blair Smith, had served as its first two presidents. The college suffered during the Revolutionary War, the full enrollments of its early years dwindling drastically. For eight years it survived without a president; when Archibald Alexander took charge, it was, as he said, "as low as it could be to have an existence."[17] In the teaching he joined John Holt Rice and Conrad Speece, two men who became noted figures in the Presbyterian church.[18] Though he had a house of his own, the young president normally took his meals with the students.

When he became president of Hampden-Sydney College, Archibald Alexander resigned from the Cub Creek Church but continued as co-pastor of the Briery Church for another year and a half. He frequently preached elsewhere and found time for some of the most intensive study of his life. Alexander always credited "whatever accuracy he had in classical and scientific knowledge" to the first years of his presidency of the college—acquired, he said, "under spur of necessity." Careful investigation of the book of Romans confirmed his Calvinism after he was temporarily attracted to the Arminianism of a Methodist preacher. The arguments against infant baptism which he found in the writings of John Gill so unsettled him that for two years he refused to administer it. An extensive study, however, convinced him that infant baptism was indeed biblical. He later observed that his doubts on the subject were caused by "too rigid notions as to the purity of the church."[19]

In April 1801 Alexander resigned from the presidency of Hampden-Sydney College and the next month attended the General Assembly in Philadelphia. It was a busy week for the commissioner from Hanover Presbytery. He saw old friends and met new ones, including the young New York City pastor, Samuel Miller. He served on committees drafting the General Assembly's view of the current "state of religion" and studying the missionary opportunities facing the church. He assisted in drawing up a plan for the work of John Chavis, a black missionary to the slaves in Virginia and North Carolina. He was instructed by the assembly to convey the Presbyterians' desire for united missionary action to the Congregationalist General Association soon to meet in Connecticut.

Alexander traveled on horseback through Princeton and New York City to Litchfield, Connecticut, to report the General Assembly's action to the Congregationalists. The first item of business, he later recalled, was "the distribution of long pipes and papers of tobacco, so that the room was soon filled with smoke." Alexander admired the hospitality of New England, criticized the lack of congregational singing in the churches, and for the first time preached in a robe. Mounting the high pulpit stairs, he became, as he said, entangled in his "own train." In another place, Alexander and a companion noticed a church crowded with people. Leaving their horses at a tavern, they entered the building covered with dust from their journey. Though the service was already in progress, the minister, suspecting that the two strangers were preachers, descended from the pulpit and, informing them that an extensive revival was in progress among his people, pled with them to preach. So, said Alexander, "up I went with all my dust unbrushed, and gave an extempore lecture on the Parable of the Sower." The exhausted minister was delighted and declared that the sermon was "exactly adapted to his people's present condition." Alexander found that he was a matter of curiosity in New England—an orthodox Christian from a state which was supposed to be given over to deism and a preacher who spoke without notes!

The New England trip put Archibald Alexander in touch with the currents of theological thought in America. In the early nineteenth century, New England was the center of perplexing theological ferment. When Alexander visited Newburyport, Massachusetts, he was told that no two ministers in town agreed. There was an old-fashioned Calvinist, an antinomian, a moderate Calvinist, an ultra-Hopkinsian, an Arminian, and a high Arian. "I preached for them all," Alexander wrote![20] He met Jonathan Edwards, Jr., Samuel Hopkins, and Nathan Strong. An acquaintance took him to Franklin, Massachusetts, for a visit with Nathanael Emmons—believing, Alexander surmised, "that by his conversation I should be brought over [to the New Divinity], for I was already quite a follower of Edwards." Alexander attended commencement at Harvard and found the professors all for making "little of doctrinal differences." At Dartmouth College, he heard young Daniel Webster speak on the recent discoveries in chemistry. Webster was present when Alexander preached in Hanover and predicted that the Virginia minister would become a man of eminence in the church. In Hartford, at the church of a graduate of Princeton College, Alexander was thrilled to discover that "a glorious revival" had taken place the previous year—"more considerable [in that town] than any which had occurred since the great awakening in the time of President Edwards." In the Old South Church in Boston, he met an octogenarian convert of George Whitefield's preaching.

Alexander returned home by way of Princeton, arriving at the time of the college's graduation. He had difficulty finding a place to stay until his friend Henry Kollock, the professor of theology at the college and pastor of the Presbyterian church, took him "to the house of old Mrs. Knox, where the students of divinity had their abode."[21] Alexander was invited to sit on the platform during the commencement exercises. He witnessed the awarding of nine honorary degrees, and then observed the trustees hurriedly convening. When their meeting was over, Alexander was given the honorary degree of Master of Arts! He then returned to Virginia and, turning down offers of a professorship at Dartmouth and a pastorate in Baltimore, accepted, in May 1802, the invitation of the trustees to resume the presidency of Hampden-Sydney.

On his way north in 1801, Archibald Alexander reined up his horse at a Virginia crossroads and deliberated as to whether he should take the road leading to the home of the Reverend John Todd or the one to the Reverend James Waddel's house. He chose the road that led him to the door of Waddel, the famous blind preacher.[22] James Waddel, who was born in the north of Ireland, had studied at Nottingham Academy under Samuel Finley, later president of Princeton College. En route to Charleston, South Carolina, where he planned to become a teacher, young Waddel heard Samuel Davies preach in Hanover County, Virginia. Davies forbade Waddel to leave Virginia and urged him to devote himself at once to the ministry! He was licensed to preach on April 2, 1761, and turned down calls from Upper Falling and Peaks of Otter, from Nutbush and Grapy Creek, from Brown's Meeting House and Jennings' Gap, from the Fork of James River in Augusta, and from Halifax to go to the churches of Lancaster and Northumberland in the lower part of the Great Northern Neck of Virginia! While there he was visited by George Whitefield, who spent a week preaching with his usual power and effectiveness. His congregations, however, preferred the preaching of their pastor to the impressive oratory of the great evangelist. Later Waddel served churches at Opaken and Cedar Creek until the Revolutionary War forced his move to Tinkling Spring Presbyterian Church in the Shenandoah Valley. Seven years later he was in Louisa County on the east slope of the Blue Ridge, where, despite his blindness, he preached to a small congregation in a rough meeting house. Waddel was noted for his "glowing evangelical eloquence."[23] Under his preaching, it was said, "audiences were moved simultaneously and irresistibly, as the trees of the wood are shaken by a tempest."[24] Patrick Henry knew his preaching well and thought that James Waddel and Samuel Davies were the greatest orators of the day. Archibald Alexander heard Waddel preach only once—a sermon on the parable of the Pharisee and the publican—but years later Alexander still remembered his vivid words. James Waddel's wife, Mary Harrison Waddel, was the daughter of Colonel Nathaniel Harrison and the first cousin of William Henry Harrison, who became the ninth president of the United States in 1841.[25]

When Archibald Alexander visited the Waddels' home that summer day in 1801, he found their daughter Janetta reading to her blind father. To help him in the preparation of his sermons, she read Scripture passages from Cruden's concordance and notes from various commentaries, some of which were in Latin. Archibald had seen Janetta before and had been struck by her beauty but now he "learned more fully the excellencies of her character." He proposed to her and was accepted before proceeding on his journey northward! The following April, Janetta and Archibald were married.

Archibald Alexander never felt completely happy as the head of a college. In 1806, he said, "the conduct of the students became very irregular," and he "grew weary of governing them."[26] He accepted an invitation to preach at the Third Presbyterian Church in Philadelphia and was called as pastor. Later he came to believe that his departure from Virginia was somewhat hasty and impatient; but "what I did rashly," he said, "Providence ordered for good." If he was glad to leave the college, he was not happy to leave his native state. He loved Virginia—the beauty of its mountains and valleys, its people, and especially the "warm and impulsive religion which the revivals of Virginia had made dear to him."[27] His son would later write that "until his last breath" his father was "intensely a Virginian."[28] Although for some time he suffered from homesickness, his years in Philadelphia enabled the Presbyterian church to get to know him and him, the church.

Philadelphia was the largest city of the nation, with its population of fifty thousand (and metropolitan area of over a hundred thousand). Cosmopolitan and stately, it boasted of being the cultural center of America—the city of science, literature, and art. It stood between the North and the South and shared the outlooks of both. Its fine houses and grand design, laid out by William Penn in 1682, greatly impressed visitors. As the greatest commercial and manufacturing center in the country, it had played an important role in the shaping of the new nation. Philadelphia had served also as the "capital" of American Presbyterianism. The first presbytery was organized there in 1706; and the first General Assembly met there, as did almost all succeeding assemblies.

First Presbyterian Church, "mother church" of the denomination, had occupied a prominent place in the city's life from its founding in 1698. In 1794 First Church erected an imposing new building with a broad porch and four massive columns fronting on Market Street. Second Presbyterian Church, at Third and Arch Streets, had grown out of the New Building, or Tabernacle, erected for the preaching of George Whitefield during the Great Awakening. Later Gilbert Tennent gathered his New Side congregation there.[29] Ashbel Green was now pastor of Second Church, remarkable for its prodigious steeple which jutted up over the quaint roofs of Arch Street. Pine Street Church (later called Third Presbyterian Church), located at Fourth and Pine Streets, had been established in 1768 by First Presbyterian Church, to serve the residents of the fast-growing Society Hill neighborhood and to preserve "peace and harmony" at First Church since these people were New Side in their sympathy. At first served by the pastors of the mother church, the new congregation in 1771 called George Duffield, a pronounced New Side Presbyterian. Pine Street Church was a plain, two-story structure, surrounded on three sides by its graveyard and facing the fourth side onto Pine Street.[30] A Fourth Presbyterian Church was organized in 1799 in a rented house at Third and Lombard Streets and quickly grew large enough to require a regular pastor and, in 1802, a new building.

Archibald Alexander was installed as pastor of Pine Street Church on May 20, 1807. It was a middle class congregation—a large number of its members were associated with shipping and traffic on the Delaware River several blocks away—and was known for its old-fashioned Scotch-Irish

Presbyterianism. Communion was received from long tables placed in the aisles, and tokens were used.[31] The people were suspicious of evangelistic fervor, although Alexander found to his great delight that there was "not a person in the congregation who is not friendly to warm evangelical preaching; and this they must have fresh from the mint, for they are greater enemies to the reading of sermons than the Virginians themselves."[32]

Dr. Alexander was a successful pastor and a popular and effective preacher. After one very long sermon he announced the conclusion of the service with a hymn, but not a person moved. The whole congregation was stirred with deepest feeling, and he arose and spoke forty-five minutes longer. He held regular catechism classes for the children of the church. One student remembered those sessions years later:

We assembled on Saturday afternoon in the main aisle of the church. Our seats were the baize-covered benches used by communicants when sitting at the Lord's table. The aisle was paved with bricks. . . . A large tin-plate stove in the main aisle was the only heater. Near it the pastor took his seat and put the class through the Shorter Catechism. The older children were required to bring written proofs of certain points assigned.[33]

Soon Alexander's ministry extended beyond Third Church. He helped found the Philadelphia Bible Society, the first in the United States, and organized the inter-denominational "Evangelical Society," a ministry of lay people which reached the city's poor. The society gathered children and adults into services for teaching and prayer and conducted evangelistic street meetings. This practice was so novel that police were sent to protect the outdoor preachers. The society's work led to flourishing Sunday schools, popular Sunday evening church services, and even the founding of new churches, including the nation's first Presbyterian church for African Americans. Alexander took special interest in the establishment of the First African Presbyterian Church and raised funds to help support the pastor, former slave John Gloucester.

The busy city pastor did not neglect his study. He added

to his knowledge of textual criticism and biblical interpretation and continued to read the Greek New Testament
and the Septuagint. He began serious study of Hebrew
under the guidance of a "learned Jew," and developed the
lifelong practice of reading at least one chapter a day in the
Hebrew Old Testament. His shelves began to be filled with
vellum-bound folios and quartos of the Latin writings of the
sixteenth- and seventeenth-century Catholic, Lutheran, and
Reformed theologians.[34] During his Philadelphia years,
Alexander acquired a "reputation as a theologian of original
and clear views and strict adherence to Reformed tenets."[35]
His theological views, which had been somewhat influenced
by William Graham's New England ideas, now began "to fix
themselves more definitely in the direction of the common
Westminster theology."[36]

Archibald Alexander had an active, successful ministry in
Philadelphia. During his six years as pastor, he baptized
306 people. The membership of Third Church increased by
more than fifty per cent. Evangelical work throughout the
city felt the impact of his presence and ideas. He kept up
with his studies, making significant progress in Hebrew and
clarifying his theological position. But, missing the open
country life of Virginia, he disliked the crowded ways of the
city and, despite his successes, regarded his Philadelphia
years "as the least agreeable portion of his life."

Alexander's election by the General Assembly of 1812
as the first professor of the church's seminary at Princeton
marked a new beginning in his ministry. He delivered a
farewell sermon to his Philadelphia congregation and, with
his wife and four children, moved into a small, tree-shaded
house on Mercer Street in Princeton.[37] The Alexanders
found the little town "remarkably pleasant"—although
Alexander noted that "every place . . . has its inconveniences
and difficulties" and added wisely that "heaven is not to be
expected in this world."[38]

Dr. Alexander set about the task of creating a theological
seminary for the Presbyterian church. He acknowledged
that his education had lacked "the rigour and method of
the schools" and that there were a good many gaps in his
learning. But he, as the only professor, was expected to

begin with "an attempt in every department of theological study."[39] "We are appalled," a later Princetonian wrote, "at the burden that was laid upon one pair of shoulders."[40]

Although the seminary's "Plan" provided for the academic year to begin in November, Archibald Alexander began immediately after his inauguration in August to meet his little class of three students once a day. They worked their way through a long list of subjects which included Hebrew, Old Testament, Bible history and geography, Greek, and English Bible. Six more students arrived by the next spring, and another five joined the first-year class in the summer. Alexander's modest home was the library, chapel, and classroom. The students studied there and shared meals and family worship. They were almost members of his family—"not merely learning of him but living with him." And so Princeton Seminary began its work "with but a single professor, though this single professor had great things in his heart."[41]

Even though Archibald Alexander was busy with the new seminary, he missed preaching and wrote, "As I have been so long accustomed to preach, it does not seem pleasant to be altogether silent."[42] Soon he began Sunday evening services in his home for the seminary students and a few invited guests—as many as could find space. Later, the meeting was moved to the refectory, the largest room in the college, to accommodate the growing congregation. Young Charles Hodge never missed; and years later he recalled those "memorable days" when Princeton was "brought under the influence of a man who as an 'experimental' preacher was unequalled and unapproached."[43]

The year 1812 had been very important for Archibald Alexander. He was happily settled in Princeton with his wife and four children. The seminary had made a beginning, and God was using his preaching in the college and town. As he worked hard on drafting a plan of study for the three-year course, he became more aware every day of the critical need for a second professor.

# 4

# Samuel Miller

*Arch Street, Philadelphia. The Second Presbyterian Church (on the left),
served by Ashbel Green, was the church Miller attended in his youth.*

[I] set apart a day of fasting and prayer for the divine direction in my choice of a profession. Before the day was closed, after much serious deliberation, and, I hope, some humble looking for divine guidance, I felt so strongly inclined to devote myself to the work of the ministry, that I resolved, in the Lord's name, on this choice. How solemn the undertaking. May the Lord help me to make a suitable estimate of its character, and to enter upon it with the deepest humility, and at the same time with confidence in the riches of his gracious aid.

Samuel Miller's Diary
August 20, 1789

IN 1813 the General Assembly elected Samuel Miller professor of Ecclesiastical History and Church Government at Princeton Seminary. The New York City minister, who had declined calls to prominent churches and invitations to the presidency of three colleges, resigned his pastorate and made his way to Princeton to join his friend and new colleague, Archibald Alexander.

Miller, about three years older than Alexander, was a successful pastor and an accomplished author who was at home in the cultured circles of city life. For some time he had been impressed with a deepening concern for the usefulness of his life and ministry. After his older brother Edward had died in the typhoid epidemic of 1812, he wrote, "I am now the only surviving son of seven born to my parents. One sister and myself are all that remain of nine children. . . . Solemn situation! When shall I be called to give an account of my stewardship? Lord God, thou knowest. Oh, prepare me for all thy will."[1] Samuel himself was stricken with typhoid early in 1813. During his illness he prayed, "The Lord make me thankful for this privilege [of life]; and grant that, if I should be restored to my wonted health, my life—my all—may be consecrated unreservedly to his glory! Oh for grace to improve this solemn dispensation of his providence."[2]

Samuel Miller was born on October 31, 1769. His father, the son of a Scot who migrated to Boston in 1710, was a Presbyterian pastor in Delaware, where he married the daughter of an English sea captain who had become a planter in

Maryland. Through his great-grandmother, Samuel Miller was descended from John Alden and Priscilla Mullins of the *Mayflower* and Plymouth Colony, the hero and heroine of Longfellow's "Courtship of Miles Standish." Samuel remembered his mother as "one of the most pious women" that he ever knew.

The eighth of nine children, Samuel Miller studied at home with his father and two older brothers until he entered the University of Pennsylvania in 1788. The great city was an exciting place for the small-town boy. The Constitutional Congress had begun its sessions there in May 1787. Two years later the first General Assembly of the Presbyterian Church met in the city. "Sammy" lived with his sister and brother-in-law, Colonel and Mrs. Samuel McLane, and went to Ashbel Green's Second Presbyterian Church. Worried about Samuel, John Miller wrote his daughter:

You will endeavor to guard him against the dangerous snare of vain and trifling company; against imbibing the spirit, and following the maxims and habits of a degenerate world; against all those things, which, in your devoutest hours, you will judge are inconsistent with a spiritual and holy life.[3]

After only one year, Samuel graduated with the "first honor" of his class and gave the "Salutatory Oration" in Latin—a speech "against the neglect of female education." His brother Edward received a medical degree at the same commencement. At first inclined toward a business career, Samuel was now unsure of his future. Returning home, he set apart a day for fasting and prayer, and before night he had decided to prepare for the ministry. He wrote Ashbel Green requesting advice about theology books and set out on a course of study with his father, a competent Latin and Greek scholar who had also an unusually good knowledge of Hebrew for that time.

On April 19, 1791, Samuel appeared before the Presbytery of Lewes in Maryland. He wrote:

After an examination respecting my experimental acquaintance with religion, and my views in seeking the holy ministry, the Presbytery declared themselves fully satisfied, and agreed unanimously to receive me on trials. After this I was examined on the Latin and Greek languages and preached a homily to the Presbytery on 1 Corinthians 15:22.

Two months later he met with the presbytery again. He read a lecture on Luke 10:30-38 and an exegetical paper in Latin on the descent of Christ into hell. After further examination in rhetoric and logic, he was "approved." Samuel wrote on that day:

O my God, whose I am and whom I am bound to serve, I entreat thee, as I advance in this pursuit, and whilst I am endeavoring to prepare myself to serve thee in the ministry of reconciliation, be pleased to add thy blessing to the whole. Oh grant me that "preparation of the heart," and that "answer of the tongue," which thou alone art able to give. O Lord, suffer me not to undertake to dispense the bread of life to others, in Christ's name, without being fed and nourished by it myself; without knowing, experimentally, "what I say and whereof I affirm."[4]

Samuel Miller's mother had died in 1789 and on July 22, 1791, his father died. Samuel received a legacy of $186.66 and his father's large library. On October 13, he met with the presbytery for the third time. After preaching his assigned sermon on Romans 8:14, he passed a "long and strict" examination on college studies and theology and was finally licensed to preach the gospel. He continued his studies, living during the winter of 1791 in Carlisle, Pennsylvania, with the family of Charles Nisbet. The Scottish Nisbet, noted for his learning and preaching, had become president of Dickinson College in 1785. Dr. Nisbet received the young theological student "with all the condescension and kindness of a parent," Samuel wrote. Miller spent his days reading in Nisbet's library and his evenings with the family, asking questions and listening to Dr. Nisbet's marvelous flow of conversation.[5]

In the spring of 1792 Miller returned to Delaware, where he preached in his father's churches. The young preacher's reputation soon reached New York City, and he received a call from the Presbyterian church to join John Rodgers and his associate, John McKnight, as one of the pastors of what was probably the wealthiest and most influential Presbyterian church in the country. In January 1793 Samuel Miller began a ministry of twenty years in New York City—a captivating place for any ambitious young man at the end of the eighteenth century. It was a rapidly growing city of forty-one thousand people. Hundreds of ships passed through its harbor each year, and a dozen languages were spoken in its streets. Gentlemen with powdered wigs and ladies in elegant French fashions were entertained at balls, garden teas, and at the John Street Theatre.

The Presbyterian church, organized in 1716, was one of the oldest and most prestigious in town. Its Wall Street congregation across from Federal Hall was the only church to open its building to George Whitefield during his first visit to the city in 1740. John Rodgers, the senior pastor, was converted as a boy under the preaching of Whitefield.[6] He studied for the ministry in Samuel Blair's academy at Faggs Manor, Pennsylvania, and served a Presbyterian church in Delaware for fifteen years before coming in 1765 to the struggling New York church. Almost immediately a revival stirred the church, and the congregation grew rapidly. A second building, known as the Brick Church, was erected and dedicated on the first day of 1768. Rodgers was not a powerful preacher or impressive scholar, but Samuel Miller appreciated his "solid and respectable talents."[7]

Miller was examined by the Presbytery of New York in Latin, Greek, geography, logic, rhetoric, philosophy, astronomy, ethics, ecclesiastical history, and church government. He preached an assigned sermon on Romans 3:24, presented a Latin exegesis, and on June 5, 1793, he was ordained. Deeply moved by this experience, he wrote:

O Lord, I have this day renewedly, and, I hope, with some sincerity, given myself away to thee! I am now emphatically not my own. I am doubly thine—peculiarly thine! O Lord, accept of my dedication! Fill me with thy love; prepare me for thy service; help me to be more and more like Christ, and more and more to glorify Christ![8]

The "boy minister" appeared even more youthful than his twenty-five years. Dressed in full canonicals including the three-cornered hat, Miller soon became a familiar figure on the streets of New York. He proved to be a popular preacher in a city accustomed to the able sermons of men such as John

Livingston of the Dutch Reformed church and John Mason of the Associate Reformed church. He faithfully visited the families of his congregation and won their respect and love when he preached every Sunday during the city's raging yellow fever epidemics. The work was too much, however, and in 1796 Samuel Miller was forced to take some time away. After a one-thousand-mile journey on horseback through Delaware, southeastern Pennsylvania, and Virginia, he returned refreshed to the city. In May 1798, a third building, the Rutgers Street Presbyterian Church, was opened to accommodate the growing New York City congregation.

Samuel prevailed on his physician-brother, Edward, to join him in New York. A number of doctors had died in the yellow fever epidemic of 1795, and Edward Miller's skill was needed in the city. The two brothers lived together until Samuel married. Edward remained a bachelor. The ladies of New York called him "the divine Doctor Miller" to distinguish him from "Doctor Miller, the divine"! In 1798, yellow fever again devastated the city. Charles Brockden Brown, the Philadelphia novelist, wrote on September 20, "The number of Physicians is rapidly declining, while that of the sick is as rapidly increasing. Dr. Miller, whose practice, as his skill, exceeds that of any other physician, is almost weary of a scene of such complicated horrors."[9] At least half of the city's fifty thousand people fled. Two thousand of those who remained died within three months. While his brother cared for the sick, Samuel comforted the families of the 186 people from his church who died.

On October 24, 1801, Samuel Miller, now thirty-two, married Sarah Sergeant. Forty-five years later, on his anniversary, Miller wrote:

It was not my own wisdom that selected this precious companion. I was led to make the choice by what we are accustomed to call "pure accident." The circumstance of hearing her strongly recommended to another, in a confidential conversation, not intended to reach my ear, determined me to seek her hand. . . . The Lord chose for me far better than I could have chosen for myself.[10]

Sarah was the great-granddaughter of Jonathan Dickinson,

the first president of Princeton College, and the daughter of Jonathan Dickinson Sergeant. Her father—a graduate of the College of New Jersey, member of the Continental Congress, and the first attorney general of the Commonwealth of Pennsylvania—was, as Sarah once wrote, "from both sides of his house a Puritan child."[11] Her mother's father was a Presbyterian minister and related to the famous missionaries David and John Brainerd. A lively young woman who enjoyed the theater and fashionable French writers, Sarah rebelled against her parents' Christianity and went through a period of mental distress that took her, she wrote, to "the borders of insanity." It is surprising that Samuel married Sarah before she was a professing Christian. He did not seem to be completely aware of the depths of her spiritual depression but did recognize her "profound reverence for religion." At times he seemed perplexed over her painful pilgrimage but prayed for her steadily and joyfully noted any signs of progress. Sarah continued to struggle but, during a period of severe depression in 1802, she gained "a hope that she [had] given herself to Christ." On December 5, Samuel wrote:

This day my beloved wife sat down, for the first time, at a sacramental table, and placed herself among the professing people of God. She has been, ever since our marriage, becoming more and more serious. . . . God grant, that her dedication may have been sincere, and the work of grace in her heart genuine and deep! She is not wholly without doubt concerning herself; but, on the whole, thought it her duty to go forward. May the Lord bless and help her!

Doubts continued to plague Sarah Miller, however, until 1805 when she came to rest "on a firm gospel foundation." The next year a sermon on the resurrection of Christ, preached in the Wall Street Church by the president of Union College, Dr. Eliphalet Nott, confirmed her faith. She wrote, "I was as well convinced, when the sermon closed, that this wonderful event had taken place, as that any one had in my own life; and that, if this was true, Christ must be the Sent of God, he in whom we were to believe; and I was willing to place all my dependence on him."[12]

As a promising young minister, Samuel easily found a place among the social and intellectual elite of the city. He knew the important people in education, politics, and the arts, and developed an amazing breadth of interest. He carried on a steady correspondence with many of the religious and political leaders of his day, both in America and in Europe, and attracted attention by his writings on such topics as slavery, the French Revolution, and the Masons.[13] He had a special love for history and helped to found the New York Historical Society in 1804, when he began work on a history of the state. In 1803 his *Retrospect of the Eighteenth Century* was published in two volumes.[14] Reprinted in London about eighteen months later, it was widely acclaimed on both sides of the Atlantic and earned Samuel Miller honorary degrees from two American colleges and membership in several foreign learned societies. Described by a modern scholar as "one of the most important American productions of the early nineteenth century," Miller's book gave an appreciative but critical review of the accomplishments of the eighteenth century in science, medicine, geography, the visual arts, language, history, biography, literature, and education.[15]   (He planned additional volumes on politics, theology, and ethics.)

In ecclesiastical circles, also, Samuel Miller became well known. He helped form the New York Missionary Society in 1796—along with "a few of the ministers of this city, who cordially agree in the doctrines of grace"—to send and support missionaries "among the heathen." In 1801 he attended the General Assembly in Philadelphia, his first as a commissioner, where he met Archibald Alexander. Miller was again a commissioner in 1803 and in 1806, when he was elected moderator. He was one of the founders of the New York Bible Society in 1809.

Samuel Miller became the major defender of Presbyterianism against the high church views of Episcopalian John Henry Hobart, who in 1800 attacked the legitimacy of Presbyterian ordination by stating that "there is no authorized ministry, no true church, no valid ordinances" where episcopally-ordained bishops are missing.[16] Hobart, a Princeton graduate and friend of President Smith's, went on to argue that "where the gospel is proclaimed, communion with the church by the participation of its ordinances, at the hands of the duly authorized priesthood, is the indispensable condition of salvation." In 1805 Miller wrote to Ashbel Green that he had decided to answer this attack—"to defend our Presbyterian opinions, and to put our people on their guard." In 1807, in his *Letters Concerning the Constitution and Order of the Christian Ministry,* Miller reasserted Presbyterian church polity against Hobart's "clerical encroachment" on the rights and liberties of the people. He argued that Christ commissioned one ministry and that the titles of bishop, elder, and presbyter are used interchangeably in the Bible. He found a scriptural basis for the parity yet distinction of the offices of teaching and ruling elders from I Timothy 5:17. He asserted that the emergence of episcopacy in the fourth century—with the neglect or suppression of the office of the ruling elder—was due to clerical ambition. In 1808 Miller published *A Continuation of Letters Concerning the Constitution and Order of the Christian Ministry* to answer Episcopalian responses to his earlier *Letters.* Here he devoted an entire chapter to the office of ruling elder, repeating his thesis that the order of ruling elder was a biblical office which disappeared in the fourth century because the clergy wanted to "get rid of a bench of officers, of *equal power* with themselves in the *government* of the church."[17]

On January 10, 1809, Miller was invited to ordain ruling elders in a church in New Jersey. In doing so, he acted on his conviction that this was truly an ordained office of equal importance with that of the teaching elder or minister. He later wrote:

The fact, so far as I know, is indubitable, that from the commencement of the Reformation to this hour, in the Reformed Churches of Scotland, France, Holland, Geneva and Germany— all of which were Presbyterian—in short, throughout the whole Presbyterian world of Europe, the ordination of ruling elders by the imposition of hands has been altogether unknown.

Despite the fact that there was no precedent for his action, his conviction was so deep that "both scriptural principle and scriptural example called for this method of setting them apart [and] he could no longer forbear to adopt it."[18] In May 1809, he preached a sermon entitled "The Divine Appointment, the Duties and the Qualifications of Ruling

Elders"—eventually published in 1811, as a forty-seven page booklet. Miller argued from I Timothy 5:17 for "two kinds of elders"—one whose duty it was to labor in the word and doctrine and another who joined with the teaching elders in the rule of the church. Miller showed how the Jewish synagogue practice was the model for the early church. Finally he urged the practical necessity for the office of ruling elder in order to attend to the details of everyday church life.

From his early days in New York, Samuel Miller became convinced that the collegiate arrangement of the Presbyterian church was unwise and should be abandoned. As John Rodgers, senior pastor of the united congregations, approached retirement, Miller pressed for the separation of the four churches. This led to a clash with John McKnight, who accused Miller of maneuvering to take the more prestigious Wall Street congregation for himself and then of planning to force McKnight out altogether. A board of ruling elders appointed to arbitrate the dispute exonerated Miller, but the experience left him deeply ashamed and hurt. The congregations, however, were formally separated; and in 1809 Miller became the sole pastor of the Wall Street Church.

On September 29, 1813, Samuel Miller was inaugurated as professor of Ecclesiastical History and Church Government at Princeton Seminary. He publicly professed his adherence to the standards of the Presbyterian church by subscribing to the required statement and then signed his name below the signature of Archibald Alexander. For his inaugural address, Miller presented lessons from "Witnesses for the Truth during the Dark Ages." He showed that all these "witnesses" were "zealous trinitarians" who held to the doctrines of grace and stressed the importance of "sound learning." He closed with the "practical thoughts"

that their history gave powerful evidence of the reality of vital religion, and striking proof that the doctrines of grace were the genuine doctrines of God's Word; that it presented important examples for our imitation, and beacons for our warning; that it suggested, as very important, that men substantially united in zeal for the truth should know and love one another; and taught us never to despair of the Church, or even allow ourselves to be discouraged, in even her most troublous and perilous times.

"Paul," concluded Samuel Miller, "is no more! . . . Wickliffe, Luther, Calvin, are all gone! But the kingdom of Christ did not die with them! It still lives; and it will live forever!"[19]

Since his election by the General Assembly in the spring, Miller had had a deep impression of the "importance and awful weight of this undertaking." On the day of his inauguration he wrote:

Today I could not help *trembling* under a sense of its unspeakable solemnity! Yes, this is an office which an *Owen*, or an *Edwards* would undoubtedly undertake with trembling. How, then, ought *I* to feel, with all my want of the requisite qualifications! God of all grace!— Thou with whom is the residue of the Spirit—I cast myself on thy care! I implore light, and guidance, and strength from thee! Oh that my deficiencies may not be permitted to disgrace me, and, above all, to disgrace the *precious cause* in which I profess and hope that I am engaged! Oh that I may have grace given me to be wise and faithful, and thus to be made a blessing to the youth whom I may be called to instruct.[20]

Just after his return to New York from his inauguration at Princeton, Samuel Miller was stricken with typhoid fever and almost died. He recovered to write, "the Lord had mercy on me, and raised me up again, I hope with the purpose of employing me for his glory." Finally on December 3, 1813, Miller and his family moved to Princeton in a heavy stagecoach. At the town of New Brunswick, because of the poor condition of the road it was necessary to change from the heavy coach to a lighter vehicle. After some delay they set out again; a farm wagon followed with their baggage.

The slow journey gave Miller time to reflect on the past forty-four years of his life. He saw his move from the city church to the little seminary in the village of Princeton as a new beginning. He looked back on his years in New York with mixed feelings. He had accomplished many things, but perhaps he had not escaped entirely the worldly influences of the city. The carriage passed through spacious orchards of peach and apple trees, bare in the winter cold, and neared Nassau Hall. To prepare himself for his new life and work, Samuel Miller had written out seven resolutions. Perhaps he read them over again.

I.     I will endeavor hereafter, by God's help, to remember more deeply and solemnly than I have ever yet done, that *I am not my own*, but Christ's servant; and, of course, bound to seek, not my own things, but the things which are Jesus Christ's.

II.    I will endeavor, by the grace of God, to set such an example before the candidates for the ministry committed to my care, as shall convince them, that, though I esteem theological knowledge and all its auxiliary branches of science *very highly*, I esteem *genuine* and *deep piety* as a still more vital and important qualification.

III.   I will endeavor, by the grace of God, so to conduct myself toward my *colleague* in the seminary, as never to give the least reasonable ground of offence. It shall be my aim, by divine help, ever to treat him with the most scrupulous *respect* and *delicacy*, and never to wound his feelings, if I know how to avoid it.

IV.    And, whereas, during my residence in New York, a very painful part of my trouble arose from disagreement and collision with a colleague, I desire to set a *double guard* on myself in regard to this point. Resolved, therefore, that, by the grace of God, while I will carefully avoid *giving offence* to my colleague, I will, in *no case, take offence* at his treatment of me. I have come hither resolving, that *whatever may be the sacrifice of my personal feelings*—whatever may be the consequence—I will not take offence, unless I am called upon to relinquish truth or duty. I not only will never, the Lord helping me, indulge a *jealous, envious,* or *suspicious* temper toward him; but I will, in *no case,* allow myself to be wounded by any *slight,* or appearance of *disrespect.* I will *give up all my own* claims, rather than let the cause of Christ suffer by *animosity* or *contest.* What am *I*, that I should prefer my own honor or exaltation to the cause of my blessed Master?

V.     By the grace of God, I will not merge my office as a *minister of the Gospel,* in that of *professor.* I will still preach as often as my Master gives me opportunity and strength. I am persuaded that no minister of the Gospel, to whatever office he may be called, ought to give up preaching. He owes it to his *ordination vows,* to his *office,* to his *Master,* to the *Church of God,* to *his own character,* to the benefit of *his own soul,* to go on preaching to his last hour. Lord, give me grace to act on this principle!

VI.    As indulgence in *jesting* and *levity* is one of my *besetting sins,* I will endeavor, by the grace of God, to set a *double guard* on this point. The example of a professor before a body of theological students, in regard to such a matter, is all important.

VII.   Where *so many clergymen* are collected in one village, clerical character is apt to become *cheap* ; and it seems to me, that a peculiar guard ought to be set, by each one, to prevent this, by a careful, dignified, and sacredly holy example. Resolved, that I will endeavor, by the grace of God, to exercise special and prayerful attention to this matter.[21]

Archibald Alexander welcomed his friend most cordially. He believed that the church, in electing Samuel Miller, had made the wisest possible choice. Miller was a pastor with skills in homiletics and practical theology. He had defended the scriptural character of Presbyterian church government with marked ability. His love for historical studies complemented Alexander's exegetical and theological bent. Three weeks after arriving in Princeton, Samuel Miller wrote to a friend:

I know it will give you pleasure to be told that the most perfect harmony and cordiality reign between [Dr. Alexander] and myself; that the number of our pupils is twenty-four; that they generally discover an excellent spirit; that my health is gradually improving; that my labors here prove more pleasant than I had ventured to anticipate; that my Sarah seems happy in Princeton; and that the general aspect of things is promising.[22]

In the summer of 1814, construction began on the Millers' handsome new house.[23] It was located near the seminary on the site of Sarah's father's house, which had been destroyed by fire during the British occupancy of Princeton in December 1776. Dr. Miller happily set out trees and planted a garden which soon became a show place in the town. There was, however, much work to be done in helping Archibald Alexander develop the seminary and teach the growing number of students.

# 5

# Faith and Energy

*Ashbel Green, one of the founders of Princeton
Seminary and President of Princeton College,
1812-1822.*

Thus it was that with no buildings and but slender resources, save the Church's faith and energy, Princeton Seminary was established.

GEORGE TYBOUT PURVES

THE second year of the seminary had already begun when Samuel Miller arrived in December 1813. The War of 1812 was occupying the nation's attention, and General Winfield Scott had recently passed through Princeton with five hundred soldiers. Dr. Alexander, privately lamenting the policy which had involved the nation in this conflict, worried that the seminary students might be conscripted for military service.

By the third year there were thirty-nine students, including New Englander Sylvester Larned. "Princeton is on a hill, the only hill I have seen in the State," he wrote to his sister on November 20, 1814. The professors, he continued, were Doctors Alexander and Miller. "So far as I have had opportunity to judge," he wrote, "I should pronounce them men 'full of faith and the Holy Ghost.' The young men under their care are generally genteel, friendly, and pious. Indeed, one of the traits almost everyone here possesses is, particularly, politeness."[1] The students lived in the professors' homes, at the college, or in rooms in town. Thomas Coleman Searle wrote to his parents on December 15, 1814, "I believe I have told you that I was to be in Dr. Miller's family. Such a favor I had *no* hope of enjoying; but I am accommodated with an excellent separate room. I teach two of the children a little each day, I find my own wood & light, & then they will take nothing but my instruction for my board."[2]

The seminary students shared the Nassau Hall classrooms

and library with the college students, by whom they were "uniformly treated with the respect due to their station," the directors reported to the General Assembly of 1813. The seminarians often ate with the college students in their dining room and joined in the college Bible society and literary society meetings. One of the early seminary students said, "When the Seminary was born, the College threw a protecting arm around her, as if she had been an adopted child. The College Library was our library. Our recitation room was in one of the College buildings. Our place of worship was the College Hall."[3] The college, too, benefited. President Ashbel Green reported to the trustees that the theological students had influenced the college "all in favour of religion, morals, order and industry."

Before long Dr. Green had much more to be happy about. When he arrived at Princeton College in October 1812, Christian commitment and zeal were rarely seen. Only a handful of the college's hundred students were even professing Christians. Green was shocked to discover that the majority of the students "seemed to be bent on mischief." Religious services were conducted regularly, but students misbehaved or stayed away. Real enthusiasm was displayed not for the Sabbath and other Christian observances but for patriotic celebrations. On Independence Day in 1813 the whole front of Nassau Hall and all the public rooms were decorated with green boughs and flowers. In the morning the faculty and students assembled in the chapel for the reading of the Declaration of Independence, patriotic orations, and music. After a sumptuous dinner there were more speeches. In the evening Nassau Hall was brilliantly illuminated until nine o'clock, when at the stroke of the bell every light was extinguished. Fearing that the excitement might end in disorder, President Green patrolled the college until a late hour; but to his great relief all remained quiet.

During the fall of 1813, however, there were numerous incidents of misconduct; and on January 9, 1814, students set off "the big cracker"—two pounds of gunpowder in a log placed against one of the doorways in the main entrance of Nassau Hall. The explosion cracked the walls of the old building from top to bottom. Continuing disorder troubled the college until spring vacation gave the president some relief after a tortuous term.

It was Ashbel Green's great hope that Princeton might experience a religious revival that would restore the atmosphere of piety which had once prevailed. During the fall of 1814, Daniel Baker, of Liberty County, Georgia, and three other students began a daily meeting for "family prayers." They prayed earnestly for revival and spoke "privately and tenderly" to their fellow students on the subject of religion. To Dr. Green's great joy, revival soon spread through the college. On January 9, 1815, President Madison proclaimed a national day of prayer. Baker and his three friends—"four warm-hearted missionaries"—spent the day going from room to room talking about spiritual things. There was growing interest, and in the middle of January it became apparent that something unusual was taking place. "The divine influence seemed to descend like the silent dew of heaven," Dr. Green wrote to the trustees, "and in about four weeks there were very few individuals in the College edifice who were not deeply impressed with a sense of the importance of spiritual and eternal things." [4] Mischievous youths who had plotted to burn an outhouse or set off fire crackers in the lecture rooms now prayed and anxiously discussed religious matters. "For a time," wrote Green, "it appeared as if the whole of our charge was pressing into the kingdom of God."

Almost the entire college attended the prayer meetings held every evening at eight o'clock. Green, Alexander, and Miller took turns preaching to the students on Sunday mornings, and the seminary professors also preached during the Friday evening prayer meetings. Dr. Green was stricken with "such an affection of dizziness" that he gave up regular preaching for a time. By remaining seated, he was able to address the students on Tuesday evenings and to talk to them briefly on Saturdays after prayers and on Sundays following their afternoon Bible recitations. He welcomed students to his study, and many came to talk and pray with him. Seminary students ministered with sermons, exhortations, and private counsel. The preaching centered on God's grace in the gospel but included "the various topics of practical religion." "There was considerable variety in the manner in which different individuals were exercised," wrote Green. "Some had more terror and some less. But in general, it was rather a weighty sense of sin than awful terrors, that took possession of the minds of the awakened."[5] Green reported that more than forty students apparently had become "the subjects of renewing grace" and that twelve or fifteen more retained such "promising impressions of religion as to authorize a hope that the issue, in regard to most of them, may be favourable." Almost all the other students showed a hopeful "tenderness of conscience" and a "very desirable regard to religious duties." "I believe there were never such times in Nassau Hall before," wrote a visitor; "the old college is literally a Bethel."[6]

Dr. Green listed four "instrumental causes" of the revival in his report to the trustees. First, the study and preaching of the Bible, with practical applications, made a powerful impact. Also, the corporate worship of the college and seminary students in the chapel following the burning of the Presbyterian church gave Green and the seminary professors the opportunity to preach very carefully chosen messages adapted to the interest and needs of the students. Then, the vigorous and vigilant discipline of the college resulted in greater attention to religious matters. Finally, the prayer and witness of the Christian students and the regular Christian services of the college were used by God to bring revival to the campus, "without any unusual occurrence in providence."

Ashbel Green drew up a short paper entitled "Questions and Counsel for the Students of Nassau Hall who hope that a work of saving grace has been wrought upon their hearts." Thirteen sets of questions explored the students' understanding of the gospel and their response to it. Green encouraged them to work through the entire exercise once a week for several months. "When you find yourself doubtful or deficient in any point, let it not discourage you," he explained, "but note down that point in writing, and bend the attention of your mind to it, and labour and pray till you shall have made the attainment which will enable you to answer clearly." Green counselled the students to "remember that secret prayer, reading the Word of God, watchfulness, and self-examination, are the great means of preserving comfort in religion, and of growing in grace." He also urged them to read "some author of known piety and excellence," recommending the works of Owen, Baxter, Doddridge, Watts, Witherspoon, Newton, Scott, and Venn. He instructed the students to "be careful to avoid a gloomy, and to cherish a cheerful, temper" and reminded them that Christianity "goes into every duty, relation, station, and situation of life." "If you have true religion," he wrote, "you will have a better spirit, you will be better sons, better scholars, better friends, better members of society, and more exemplary in the discharge of every duty."[7]

The seminary students were actively involved in promoting the revival at the college, in Princeton, and elsewhere. During 1814 a number of seminarians visited Wilmington, Delaware, to assist in the work of a revival in that city. Back in Princeton, Betsey Stockton, a young black woman attached to Dr. Green's family, was converted through the preaching of seminary student Eliphalet Gilbert. Betsey, a slave owned by Robert Stockton, came to Green through his marriage to Stockton's daughter. He freed her when she was twenty, but she chose to remain as a hired servant. She was educated by Green's family, especially by his son James, and eagerly read the books in the president's library. On September 20, 1816, she joined the Presbyterian church. Betsey Stockton taught a class for black children in Princeton and soon began to feel a desire to go to Africa as a missionary.

※　　　※　　　※

Meanwhile, the seminary was active in its new work. John McDowell, pastor of the Presbyterian church in Elizabethtown, New Jersey, and a seminary director, took long journeys to different parts of the country to collect funds for the school. The directors received the first students. They continued to act in admitting students until 1815, when the task was delegated to the faculty. Students arrived at various times during the school year, producing a confusing jumble of men of differing attainments in one class. By the end of the summer session of 1815, four students—John Covert,

Henry Weed, Halsey Wood, and Leverett Huntington—completed their work and left the seminary.[8] These students must have received in some way or other the "certificate of approbation" which the "Plan" required and which the directors reported to the General Assembly had been given to them. But there does not seem to be any record of the certificates being given. Perhaps they were put under the graduates' plates at breakfast time, or Dr. Alexander handed them informally to each student when he called to say good-bye—or Dr. Miller, because he was the clerk of the faculty.

In September 1815 the cornerstone was laid for the first seminary building. Four acres of land several blocks from Princeton College, on the turnpike to Trenton, had been donated by college trustee Richard Stockton, son of the signer of the Declaration of Independence. Ashbel Green, always generous in his support of the seminary, purchased two more acres. The board of trustees of the College of New Jersey met on September 26. A little before five o'clock in the afternoon, a procession formed on the college campus to march the several blocks to the site of the seminary building. President Green led the way followed by professors and students of the seminary; then trustees, officers, and students of the college; next clergy and "strangers" who were in town; and, finally, the townspeople of Princeton. Dr. Green introduced the service with a few remarks, and Dr. Alexander read the introduction of the "Plan of the Seminary." Green, standing on the cornerstone, prayed that the new building "might be the educational home of many generations of Christ's ministers who should carry the everlasting Gospel to all nations."

The directors' minutes called for a building of "usefulness with plainness and simplicity." Architect John McComb received one hundred dollars for his plans and five dollars plus traveling expenses for each day he came from New York City to inspect progress on the building.[9] The workmen, supervised by Peter Bogart (who was to become the seminary's first steward), labored from dawn until sundown six days a week. Their daily wage was $1.50 to $2.00, plus "one gill and a half of ardent spirits."[10] By the fall of 1817, the seminary was using the handsome and dignified structure of gray sandstone that closely resembled its larger neighbor, Nassau Hall.[11]

James W. Alexander, the son of Archibald Alexander, remembered the great benefits which came from the new building:

All concerned felt the cheering influence of this change to premises which they could call their own, and which had an air of comfort and permanency. The students were brought near to one another and to their teachers. The result was seen in greater diligence and punctuality, increased fellowship in religion and zeal in the pursuit of knowledge; so that we suppose there has never been a period in the history of the Seminary, during which there was more animation or delight.[12]

The four-story building contained rooms for a hundred students and a dining hall. Members of each class sat together during meals; senior students presided and asked the blessing. The new building also housed the library and the oratory, or prayer hall, which was used for lectures, chapel services, and for the meetings of various student societies. Students sat on graceful wooden benches with straight backs, three or four to a bench. Long after they left Princeton they remembered that "dear old room, plain and Presbyterian in its aspects, with the countenance of John Calvin looking down on us from the walls."[13]

In 1819, the Alexanders moved into their new house next door to the still unfinished seminary building. Classes met in Dr. Alexander's study until the new building was complete. The kitchen of the Alexander house was not ready for use until 1821, and all the cooking had to be done in the basement.

\*    \*    \*

During these early years Archibald Alexander, assisted by Samuel Miller, worked hard to develop the seminary's curriculum. The "Plan" set forth the desired goal. It stated that in order to receive the seminary's certificate, the student must be able to demonstrate in oral exam that he had "laid the foundation for becoming" an effective minister. He must be "a sound biblical critic," with skill in the original languages of the Bible and knowledge of Bible content, history, and geography. He must be "a defender of the Christian faith," with knowledge especially of the issues relating to deism. He must support the doctrines of the Confession of Faith and Catechisms by "a ready, pertinent, and abundant quotation of Scripture texts." He must, by his study of theology and church history, become "an able and sound divine." He must have read "a considerable number of the best practical writers on the subject of religion." He must be skilled in sermon preparation and know the duties of pastoral care in order to become "a useful preacher and a faithful pastor." He must study the Form of Government of the Presbyterian Church so that he would be "qualified to exercise discipline and to take part in the government of the Church." This ambitious goal necessitated establishing courses in biblical studies, apologetics, church history, theology, ethics, and pastoral subjects.

At first Dr. Alexander and the students were hindered by the lack of suitable texts in their various fields of study. "The knowledge sought," they reported to the directors, "was often contained in massy folios, and mostly in foreign languages." Alexander did his best to supply texts "by collecting scraps, and making translations and abridgments from every work" which he found suitable to his purpose.

After three years, as the first students completed their program, the seminary curriculum was fully organized. The entire first year was devoted to Bible. In addition to much analytical study of the English Bible, students took courses in Hebrew and Greek, Biblical Criticism (including both textual criticism and interpretation), and Bible history (described as "Sacred Chronology," "Sacred Geography," "Jewish Antiquities," and "Oriental Customs"). Dr. Alexander told an applicant for admission in 1818 that Humphrey Prideaux (*The Old and New Testament Connected in the History of the Jews and Neighboring Nations,* 2 volumes) and Samuel Shuckford (*The Sacred and Profane History of the World Connected from the Creation of the World to the Dissolution of the Assyrian Empire at the Death of Sardanapalus, and to the Declension of the Kingdoms of Judah and Israel under the Reigns of Ahaz and Pekah,*

2 volumes) were required textbooks for first-year students. Students should also have, he said, a Hebrew Bible and lexicon, a Greek New Testament and lexicon, and—perhaps as a concession to the weakness of the flesh—an English Bible and concordance! Second-year students continued to study the original languages of Scripture and added systematic (didactic) theology and biblical and church history. The third-year curriculum included systematic (didactic and polemic) theology, church history, church government, pastoral care, and homiletics.

Dr. Alexander taught the biblical languages for a few years until he could hand them over to the third professor anticipated in the seminary's "Plan." Alexander's excellent knowledge of Greek made his daily reading of the Greek New Testament a delight. In Philadelphia he had made his first successful attempt to learn Hebrew. At least two years before coming to Princeton, he had acquired a Syriac New Testament and had made enough progress in this language to teach it to a student during the second year of the seminary's existence. This was the first "elective" offered at Princeton and indicated the seminary founders' serious commitment to languages.

Dr. Alexander also taught the course in biblical criticism. He believed that the higher critical methods being developed in Germany were destructive; he favored an approach to the Scripture which he called "the English ground of faith and common sense instead of the German ground of skepticism and nonsense."[14] In 1826 he wrote, "There is something reprehensible, not to say impious, in that bold spirit of modern criticism, which has led many eminent Biblical scholars in Germany, first to attack the authority of particular books of Scripture, and next to call in question the inspiration of the whole volume."[15] Alexander was eager, however, to consider and test honestly any claim to truth. In 1833 he declared, quite characteristically,

But we are persuaded, that if the church consents to close her eyes upon the increasing facilities for biblical investigation which are possessed in Germany, and to turn away from the controversies which are there waged, she will find herself in a field of battle without armour, or, if armed, with the mail and greaves and heavy weapons of a former age, wholly unsuited to the emergency, and the new modes of attack.[16]

Samuel Miller had three distinct areas of teaching: ecclesiastical history, church government, and homiletics. Bible history was part of ecclesiastical history and included a brief series of lectures on "Sacred Chronology" and "Sacred Geography." In 1834, after twenty years of teaching, Miller explained to a professor at the new seminary at East Windsor, Connecticut, his approach to his classes. He wrote:

I make the Bible my only text-book in the commencement of my course of Ecclesiastical History; and as far as the Old Testament narrative reaches. I consider the visible church as having been founded in the family of *Adam,* and as beginning as soon as man was placed under a dispensation of mercy.

My plan is to begin with a *Lecture* preliminary to my course of instruction, announcing my plan;—showing the importance of studying the Bible, and being familiar with its history as well as its doctrines;—and labouring to impress the minds of the students with the necessity of their being at home in the Bible, —both as Christians and as Ministers. I then give out a certain number of chapters, on the history of which the class is to be examined at the next interview. When we come together the next time, I spend about twenty or thirty minutes in examining them on the portion specified, and having done so, deliver a lecture on the most prominent and interesting points embraced in the narrative. I have delivered Lectures on the following subjects. 1. The Creation, including the question whether the days of creation were natural, or demiurgic. I reject the New Haven doctrine that the days of creation were demiurgic, and cannot doubt that they were six natural days. 2. The Divine Origin and Purpose of Sacrifices. 3. The Origin of Language. 4. The Character of the Antediluvian Period. Etc. On all these subjects I recommend particular books, as they occur to me; such as I suppose contain the best views, either for or against the doctrine which appears to me to be right: such as Shuckford; Prideaux; Winder's *History of Knowledge,* Faber's *Three Dispensations,* Faber's *Horae Mosaicae,* Farmer on Miracles; Ancient Universal History; Warburton's *Divine Legation of Moses,* several works on Atonement and Sacrifice, such as Magee's, Outram's, etc.; Commentators; particular Essays, etc., etc.; Josephus; Stackhouse's *History of the Bible,* Bedford's *Chronology,* Buddeus' *Historia Ecclesiastica Veteris Testamenti,* etc., etc.; Jahn's *Hebrew Commonwealth,* etc.; Russell's work, intended to fill the place between Schuckford and Prideaux, etc. All, or as many as possible, of the foregoing works, I should wish to have in my study, when I entered on my duties, together with as good maps of the places and countries mentioned in Scripture, as can be procured.[17]

For church history Samuel Miller used his own lectures to supplement class readings in Johann Mosheim's history. His students first read Maclaine's translation and, later, Murdoch's, whose notes Miller found "rich and instructive" and whose bibliographical material was of great value to the students.[18]

Archibald Alexander was called to the seminary as professor of theology, and it was in this area that he primarily concentrated his efforts. He gave introductory lectures on "mental and moral science" (epistemology and ethics) to the first-year students. The young men were introduced to the prevalent Scottish common sense philosophy of Francis Hutcheson, Thomas Reid, and Dugald Stewart. This philosophical system attempted to rescue the English "moderate" enlightenment from the idealism of George Berkeley and the skepticism of David Hume. Many thinkers, especially since Locke, had interposed between people and the real world the concept of ideas. These ideas, they said, were the real object of our thought; hence we do not know anything at a distance, but only in our minds. The Scottish philosophy responded that the doctrine of ideas would only lead to skepticism (as it had for Hume) and taught that normal people, responsibly using the information provided by their senses, actually grasped the real world. All people, wrote Reid, unless "blinded or misguided by prejudice or pernicious philosophical views," actually hold in common propositions about themselves and the external world. Human beings, then, are capable of real knowledge; and truth is much the same for everyone, everywhere. Common sense philosophy also taught that people can know something about the past, just as they can know true things about the present world. Based on reliable evidence, we can establish strong probabilities about what happened in the past. If the evidence is good enough, we are justified in believing these facts with virtual certainty.

As already noted, Alexander learned the Scottish philosophy from William Graham, who taught John Witherspoon's ideas. Like a great number of American thinkers, they believed that the inductive scientific method of seventeenth-century philosopher Francis Bacon was the one sure way to build on this common sense foundation. Careful and objective investigation of the facts and scrupulous avoidance of speculative hypotheses would lead, Bacon believed, to the same kind of success in ethics and theology as the scientists were having in studying the physical world. Common sense philosophy and the Baconian scientific method seemed to support many of the basic assumptions of the Christian faith; and churchmen—from Calvinists to Unitarians—claimed them as allies.

In his lectures on ethics, Alexander stressed the basic importance of natural law (which contains in essence biblical moral law), argued for an ethic of "intentions" (against the result-oriented utilitarians), and discussed the complex relationship between conscience, intuition, and reason.[19] Conscience interpreted by reason is the best light we have at any given moment, Dr. Alexander told his students, and we have the moral obligation to obey it. If because of faulty reason our consciences lead us into error, we are nonetheless guilty of sin, because we are morally accountable for the evil of our nature which has corrupted our reason. Archibald Alexander's moral philosophy, in its wrestlings with some of the deepest contemporary aspects of ethics, was a distinguished effort in this field.

Dr. Alexander treated apologetics in the curriculum under "studies preliminary of theology." The students read the writings of the Anglicans Samuel Clarke and William Paley. Alexander often followed Joseph Butler's famous *Analogy* in seeking to show that the arguments used by deists against "revealed religion" applied also against their own "natural religion." He recommended Watson's *Apology for Christianity,* Jenyns's *View of the Internal Evidence of the Christian Religion,* Leslie's *Short and Easy Method with Deists,* and Paley's *View of the Evidences of Christianity.*[20] He wrote a preface to Isaac Watts's *Rational Defense of the Gospel,* in which he contended that Watts's arguments were distinguished from many others in "the vein of evangelical piety which runs through them."[21]

When in 1823 a little group of rationalist students became active at Princeton College, Dr. Alexander was invited to answer them in a sermon in the college chapel. He enlarged this sermon into a book, that appeared in 1825 with the title *A Brief Outline of the Evidences of the Christian Religion.*[22] Besides dealing with the "evidences" for the authenticity, inspiration, and canonical authority of the Bible, Alexander presented the arguments for Christianity from miracles and prophecy. His book was widely used; and, according to his son, Dr. Alexander received "innumerable letters from persons converted as well as convinced by his 'Evidences.'"[23]

Alexander argued strongly for the "reasonableness" of Christianity. "It is reasonable to believe, what by our senses we perceive to exist," he wrote; "and it is reasonable to believe whatever God declares to be true."[24] He believed that "a just and impartial consideration of the universe cannot fail to lead the sincere seeker of truth to the opinion, that there must exist a great first cause, powerful and intelligent, who has made the world for some particular end." Alexander knew, however, that the "human intellect is prone to wander from the truth" and that "reason is liable to be perverted." Following the argument of John Calvin in the *Institutes of the Christian Religion,* Alexander held that truth "which reason often missed, or mistook, and at best spelled out with hesitation, the voice of revelation declares with decisive authority." He wrote, "The universe, which to the atheist is full of darkness and confusion, to the Christian is resplendent with light and glory.... Without the book of revelation, the book of nature would be as a volume sealed; but with this key, we can open its wonderful pages, and receive instruction from every creature of God."[25]

Alexander continued to urge the importance of "evidences," however, to support the truthfulness of Christianity and the authority of the Bible. James W. Alexander wrote that while his father was far from being a rationalist, "he was never satisfied with the tactics of those reasoners who under the pretext of exalting revelation, dismiss with contempt all arguments derived from the light of nature."[26]

It proved to be an important event in American Presbyterian history when, during his Philadelphia period, Archibald Alexander rejected the New England theological "innovations" for the older Calvinism of the Westminster Confession of Faith. His study of theology led him to the conclusion that the Reformed theologians of the sixteenth and seventeenth centuries had "pushed theological investigation to its greatest length, and compacted its conclusions into the most symmetrical method."[27]

Alexander told the students, "Theology is not taught systematically in the sacred scriptures of the Old & New Testament." He traced its rise—as a system—in the sixth century, and its decline in the following centuries until the Protestant Reformation, when "theology was purged from the filth & errors of the Schoolmen." He saw the *Common Places* of Philip Melanchthon as "the commencement of systematic theology among the Protestants." Alexander pointed to Zwingli, Bullinger, Calvin, and Beza, as representative Reformed theologians. He noted the work of the Americans Samuel Willard and Samuel Hopkins and praised the sermons of Timothy Dwight as containing a system of theology "written with elegance & good sense."[28] Alexander had great sympathy with the theological method and evangelical spirit of Johann Cocceius and Herman Witsius and the other "covenant" theologians, and he was aware of Thomas Chalmers's effort to create a new approach to theology by organizing it around the plan of redemption. He preferred to arrange his course in systematic theology, however, in the logical order "pursued by the schoolmen and . . . by most systematic writers among Protestants."

For the Princeton theology text, Alexander chose the *Institutio Theologiae Elencticae* of Francis Turretin, the seventeenth-century theologian of Geneva.[29] Turretin was a student in Calvin's Academy, where he later taught theology for some thirty years. He was "a stalwart but in many ways moderate representative of Geneva orthodoxy during what was virtually its last generation."[30] Alexander was impressed with the piety of Turretin, who wrote, "When God is set forth as the object of theology, he is not to be regarded simply as God in himself (for thus he is incomprehensible to us), but as revealed and as he has been pleased to manifest himself to us in his word. . . . He is our God. . . not only as the object of knowledge, but also of worship." Alexander also saw in Turretin's polemical emphasis—directed mainly against Amyraldianism (with its attempts to soften the doctrine of God's decrees)—a useful tool in the contemporary American theological situation.[31]

Turretin's theology was not easy; it was "ponderous, scholastic and in a dead language," but Dr. Alexander had observed that those who worked through its twenty loci and their subdivided questions "were apt to be strong and logical divines."[32] Students read sections of the Latin text and then "recited" in class on that material. Charles Hodge once recalled that when he was a seminary student, his friend John Johns was always prepared: he "would day after day be able to give the State of the Question—all the arguments in its support in their order, all the objections and answers to them, through the whole thirty or forty pages, without the professor saying a word to him." Hodge added, "Whatever may be thought of this method of instruction, it was certainly effective. A man who had passed through that drill never got over it."[33]

In class Dr. Alexander added stimulating comments, sometimes dissenting from Turretin, and gave lectures of his own to update and modify the text. These lectures became more numerous from year to year, until they constituted an important part of the course. Alexander encouraged the students to do original study and thinking, and he assigned topics for papers. He created a Theological Society, where students, teacher, and neighborhood ministers could discuss topics of theology more informally.

Dr. Alexander's deep spirituality pervaded his teaching of theology. Elisha Swift remembered how Dr. Alexander would explain some theological topic and then "he would seem to pause, and painful anxiety to be stamped upon his countenance, as though he were ready to say, I fear the Heavenly Father is not here! let us lay aside our helps and repair to him."[34]

Polemic theology, which concentrated on refuting "erroneous" religious beliefs, was set forth in the seminary's "Plan" as a separate discipline from didactic theology; and

Alexander treated it so from his early days at Princeton. In his lectures he made extensive use of the *Institutes of Comprehensive Polemic Theology* of Johann Friedrich Stapfer, a Swiss Reformed theologian. Alexander attempted to arm the students against ancient heresies in whatever guise they might reappear, as well as to equip them against newer error. He dealt with atheism, pantheism, "indifferentism," deism, paganism, Judaism, Islam, "humanitarianism," Socinianism, Roman Catholicism, Arminianism, "fanaticism," and Campbellism. Each student in the class was assigned a paper on one of these "false systems."

Dr. Alexander taught the students to be fair and moderate in controversy. "Consider," he urged them, "whether the danger & importance of error justifies public controversy." We must be "satisfied of the purity of our motives" and "avoid whatever is apt to create prejudice in opponents or auditors." "Attribute to an antagonist no opinion he does not own, though it be a necessary consequence," he told the students. Strive "for truth, not victory. If you are convinced of error confess it." He stressed that one must "know when to put a stop to controversy. It is a great evil in keeping it up, after the controversy is exhausted."[35] Archibald Alexander's own life reveals that though he had strong convictions, he kept his involvement in active controversy to a minimum—stating, when he felt it necessary, his own views with uncompromising clarity and thereafter remaining silent. He lived out his own advice to the students—"Do your whole duty, and quietly leave to God the defense of your reputation."[36]

Archibald Alexander and Samuel Miller lectured not only on philosophical, theological, historical, and biblical subjects, but also on the application of faith and knowledge to the concrete problems and duties of the pastor's work.

In his lectures on pastoral theology, Dr. Alexander discussed the nature of the pastoral office, the minister's call and qualifications, his marriage and financial affairs, his responsibilities to home and foreign missions, pastoral visitation and religious instruction, revivals, preaching, and public worship. He stressed the need for ministers to serve the frontier, the slaves, and children. He told the students that if he were a young man, he would, God willing, choose to preach to children—"a rich uncultivated missionary field."[37] For Alexander, pastoral visitation was a combination of piety, authority, compassion, and common sense—each of which he possessed in generous measure. Yearly pastoral visits to each family should be "devoted entirely to religious instruction and devotional exercises." He commended to his students the early Calvinistic practice of dividing a congregation into districts for catechizing children. On these topics the versatile professor was especially impressive. One of his students wrote, "We well remember that his class went to his lectures on pastoral theology as if going to the sanctuary. It was a season of worship."[38]

In their homiletics class, the students read *Lectures on Rhetoric and Belles Lettres* by the Scottish Hugh Blair. Overshadowing the text, however, was Alexander's own less formal style. An effective and sought-after preacher, he stressed naturalness and simplicity. William Sprague, who entered the seminary in the fall of 1816, remembered that when Alexander preached he felt rather as if he "had been talked to than preached to."[39] Theodore Cuyler compared Dr. Alexander's sermons to "the waters of Lake George, so pellucid that you could see every bright pebble far down in the depths; a child could comprehend him, yet a sage be instructed by him."[40] According to Charles Hodge, Dr. Alexander's sermons were "generally a stream," following "'their own sweet will,' always keeping in their course, but still free." Hodge explained, "We have often sat in admiration and witnessed this process of spontaneous evolution, no one knowing what was to come next, and yet something always did come making a real advance on what had preceded, awakening attention and exciting expectation."[41]

Dr. Alexander's voice was clear and high pitched and his gestures restrained. He had the habit of placing his forefinger under his chin, and sometimes against his nose in a peculiar manner. He always began quietly, avoiding "all that brings the speaker's personality before the hearer." When he got into his sermon, however, "his eye kindled, his face was radiant," as he was carried along by "the operation of the Holy Spirit" working through his thoughts and words. Listeners often commented that Dr. Alexander preached as though he were speaking to each person in the audience individually. In commenting on the fact that the best sermons can never be exactly reproduced—much less written—J. W. Alexander remembered his father's example and stated that "the best written discourse" of Dr. Alexander is "no more to his best preaching, than a black candle is to a burning flame."[42]

At the 1816 meeting of the Synod of Virginia in Fredericksburg, Dr. Alexander preached on the text "For even Christ our Passover is sacrificed for us" (*I Cor.* 5:7). He began with his characteristic humility and modesty; and one eminent lawyer, greatly disappointed in the performance of the famous preacher, rose from his seat and left the church. Samuel B. Wilson, later professor of theology in Virginia's Union Seminary, described the rest of the sermon. As Alexander

passed from the description of the Jewish passover, to the sacrifice of Christ, he said, bending forward and looking intently on the communion table spread before him, where the bread and wine lay covered, *"But where is our lamb?"* At these words, so impressively uttered, and accompanied by a gesture so significant, an old French dancing master, who scarcely ever entered the church, rose from his seat near the pulpit, and gazed intently, to see if there was not something on the communion table, which he had not seen.[43]

Dr. Alexander's sermons were always instructive and moving, but he was at his best in certain places. Francis Wayland, Baptist preacher and president of Brown University, heard Dr. Alexander preach twice one Sunday at Gardiner Spring's New York City church. He wrote to J. W. Alexander:

He preached a sermon to Christians, admirable throughout, but not, that I recollect, marked by any of those bursts of eloquence of which he was so capable. A high pulpit and a city audience is not the place for those things. An old Virginia church, or court-house, crowded around the windows, is the place for such eloquence. Those magic bursts of feeling must be rare among the conventionalities and respectabilities of a city congregation. The sound of a bell depends as much on the quality of the metal as on the vigor of the blow.

James replied that Wayland was entirely correct in his evaluation of his father's preaching. "In the pulpit he was two different men," he wrote, "and least of all was he himself when he came into the cities to preach."[44]

Archibald Alexander's doctrinal sermons were "replete with truth and wisdom," Charles Hodge commented; but he was more impressive when he took some biblical story or scene and described it, or when he preached an "experimental" sermon drawn from personal experience, observation, and the Bible. After Dr. Alexander's death, Hodge recalled three of his most memorable sermons—on Abraham's offering up Isaac, on the transfiguration, and on the last three days in Christ's life. "The only way in which I can give an idea of the impression produced by these discourses," Hodge said, "is by saying that his hearers felt, in a measure, as they would have done had they been present at the scenes described. We left [the] Chapel after his sermon on the transfiguration, feeling that we had seen the Lord in his glory, at least as through a glass darkly."[45] Not only Dr. Alexander's preaching but his reading of Scripture impressed the students. John S. Hart, who studied at the seminary from 1831 to 1834, wrote:

Who that ever heard that almost despairing wail with which the venerable Dr. Archibald Alexander used to utter the cry, "Eloi, eloi, lama sabacthani!" but felt that he had received a new revelation of the meaning of that mysterious utterance? It was not that Dr. Alexander understood Hebrew better than thousands of others have done. It was because he had meditated on the subject until he had the whole dreadful scene fully before him.[46]

Dr. Alexander told his students that they should not wait to begin preparation for preaching until they were "in the vein." "Begin, however you feel," he said, "and write until you get in the vein—however long it be. 'Tis thus men do in mining."[47] He urged the students to avoid a show of scholarship in their sermons.[48] "Sometimes a preacher becomes so enveloped in criticism or metaphysics," he told them, "that plain people cannot understand him. The minister should be a critic and metaphysician, but carry only the result to the pulpit." But neither should preachers be careless in the construction and delivery of their sermons. He told the students that one of the best sermons he ever heard violated many rules of grammar, rhetoric, and elocution, "but it was not its violation of rules that made it excellent."[49] "Preaching the Gospel is not to gratify a refined taste," Dr. Alexander said, "but the preacher should avoid disgusting men of taste. It is a grievous fault to speak nonsense in the name of the Lord. The main object is to make preaching useful to the souls of men."

"Avoid generalities," continued Alexander; "they convey no instruction. Do not preach on subjects that you don't understand." He suggested concentrating on the "greatest truths" because people are "generally lamentably deficient as to even these." In fact, the preacher should "go over the whole system of theology and natural religion and evidences." He then listed doctrines that were central in his theology course as appropriate for the core of preaching. Alexander held before the students the "doctrine of election . . . as a ground of joy." Morality should be taught by pointing out the "injury to society" of wrongdoing and not by "denunciation." "Party politics is not admissible. But discussion of duties or rulers is appropriate." "Constant preaching of moral duties alone tends to harden people," Alexander said. The minister should preach on "Christian experience, afflictions, and temptations" and "should know how to deal with awakened souls."

Alexander offered some pointed caveats. "Want of variety will weary anybody," he said. "Have enough subjects, and preserve the peculiar dress given to each text." He warned against a "cold" or "formal-pompous manner," "ranting, noisy preaching," and an "angry" or a "timid method." "There are no discourses," said this able preacher, "heard with so little attention as sermons." It is not easy "to propose truth clearly, level to the meanest capacity; yet to preserve dignity of style."[50]

One evening a week, Dr. Alexander met with the first two classes to hear and evaluate their sermons. He was sympathetic and kind in his criticism, which only gave a keener edge to occasional caustic comments. He listened once to a student preaching on the words "Let there be light and there was light." The student launched, with great eloquence and forceful delivery, into a lengthy description of the creation of light. "You're a very smart young man," Dr. Alexander said when the sermon was over, "but you can't beat Moses." Another student preached "a grand discourse upon the religious instincts." When he finished, Dr. Alexander commented, "My instincts are not sufficient to comprehend, much less to criticise, that discourse."[51] Some doubt emerges as to the thoroughness of Dr. Alexander's sermon critiques from the fact that he dismissed one student preacher with the single sentence "a very fine specimen of public speaking: call the next." But the student, who later had a distinguished career, commented appreciatively, "He encouraged me by making only one remark, and that a compliment."[52]

Samuel Miller supervised the weekly preaching of the senior class and met with them in their Society for Improvement in the Composition and Delivery of Sermons. He valued learning and eloquence but urged his students "to lay much more stress, and to place unspeakably more reliance, on the efficacy of pure truth" and "the promise" of God.[53] Miller set forth his own ideal when he described the sermons of John Henry Livingstone as "plain, simple Bible truth in Bible language." He thought that this approach to preaching was "the final result of the most enlightened wisdom, and the richest experience of the best ministers the Christian Church has ever seen."[54] Dr. Miller counseled the students to "always have a sermon upon the anvil." "The first you write will seem to yourself very meagre and defective," Miller said. "Never mind that. Do not be discouraged. Practice makes perfect. Lay this one aside and try again. Thus go on. Keep all you write, for you will find a satisfaction in comparing the earlier ones with what you produce in after years." Miller advised, "Let your paper be of medium size, of strong texture and white. Use black ink, and write with a bold, large hand. You may not see the need of all this *now*, but you will by and by."[55] One of Dr. Miller's students, Leroy J. Halsey—later professor at McCormick Seminary—commented that

as a critic, he was acute, skillful, and faithful to the last degree in detecting everything like an error or a blemish; and yet his keenest criticisms were given with all the gentle kindness of a father. Full of interesting and appropriate illustrations and anecdotes, drawn from his extended reading, and his wide range of observation and experience, he was accustomed to enrich and enliven his critical remarks, on these occasions, from this fund, in a manner which rendered the service to the students one of the most attractive and profitable in the whole seminary curriculum. In presiding on these occasions, with consummate skill drawing the balance between the merits and the defects of each performance, tempering to each speaker the word of condemnation with the word of encouragement, repressing the forward, bringing forward the timid, polishing the rough edges of self-confident ignorance, and eliciting the latent excellencies of the modest and retiring; interspersing his remark with apt incidents recited in his vivacious and inimitable manner, he was the perfection of dignity, benignity, and grace. He blended in equal proportions the wisdom and authority of the instructor, with the wit and genial freedom of the friend. In nothing perhaps did he more surely and deeply impress his own genial spirit, and his fine scholarly taste, upon the successive classes of students under his care, and through them upon the whole ministry of the church, than in these informal and delightful homiletical critiques of the Oratory.[56]

Miller's own sermons were substantial, clear, and well ordered rather than sparkling. At least one acquaintance was sorry to see Samuel Miller's style of preaching change from "vehement and fervid" in Delaware to a "deliberate mode of speaking" in New York. His New York sermons were fully written but preached from memory or with only the briefest notes. At a later period, especially after he went to Princeton, he generally read his sermons. His voice was not strong, but his speech was deliberate and dignified. He was "always instructive, always calm, always accurate," according to J. W. Alexander.[57] William Sprague commented that there was "the same symmetry" about Miller's sermons as there was about his character—"everything was in its right place."[58]

Dr. Miller also taught church government. In 1836 he wrote to a professional colleague who had requested information concerning his course:

I always make the study of Church Government a separate matter from that of Ecclesiastical History. In pursuing the former study, I have ever most painfully felt the want of a suitable textbook. I know of none, and consider the formation of one as a great desideratum for our theological seminaries.

My method of proceeding is to deliver a course of lectures on the subject of Church Government, referring as I go along to the best books that I can find, on the following points:—I. The Nature and Design of the Church. II. The Head of the Church. III. The Members of the Church. IV. The general Necessity of the Ministry, as an Ordinance of Christ. V. Lay Preaching, etc. VI. The different simple Forms of Church Government. (1) Popery. (2) Prelacy. (3) Independency. (4) Presbyterianism—considering Congregationalism as not a simple form, but as something between the two last. VII. Ruling Elders. VIII. Deacons. IX. Licentiates. X. Discipline: its Nature, Design and essential Principles, etc. In the latter part of the course, I just take our Form of Government and Discipline, and go over its chapters in order, explaining and commenting on each at some length.[59]

Princeton Seminary's first two professors were spiritually minded and competent men who worked together effectively to teach the broad curriculum. Archibald Alexander wrote to a minister in West Jersey on March 4, 1819, "Our duties occupy our time to a degree that you can hardly conceive of . . . a recitation or lecture every day—sixty compositions to hear and correct each month—as many speeches—advice to some one or other almost every day." No wonder, then, that in January 1819 Dr. Alexander declined the call of the First Presbyterian Church of Princeton to be its pastor.

By 1822, there were eighty students who, during the seminary's two semesters (November to May and July to October), listened to their professors' lectures and, when addressed, politely rose to answer. Adequate financial support was a continuing problem. Yearly operating costs had increased to $4,500, and funds were sometimes insufficient to pay the professors' salaries. Samuel Miller wrote in 1822 that "by pursuing a constant system of importunate *begging* . . . the seminary has been just *kept from sinking*, ever since it was organized."[60] There was, however, a permanent fund of some $18,000, from which only interest could be used. Hoping to improve the financial situation of the seminary, the General Assembly adopted a resolution recommending that the school be incorporated with a board of trustees to consist of twenty-one members, twelve of whom would be laymen.

The daily routine of the college, seminary, and little town was enlivened by the grand celebrations of the Fourth of July and the college commencements—abounding with crowds, speeches, rows of wagons, booths, and tents, and with huge piles of melons and barrels of cider. A thrill went through the town in September 1824 when the Marquis de Lafayette visited Princeton on his triumphal tour of the United States. Near the central gate of the front campus of the college, and before a great crowd of students, villagers, and country people, Richard Stockton delivered an address of welcome. President Carnahan presented the Marquis with the doctor-of-laws diploma, signed by John Witherspoon, which the college had conferred upon him *in absentia* in 1790. Lafayette replied, and the guests retired to the gaily decorated refectory for a bountiful breakfast.[61]

*       *       *

By 1822, Princeton Seminary had trained over a hundred students. They were now pastors and "domestic" missionaries; and a few had gone overseas as the first of a great stream of Princeton's foreign missionaries. John Monteith went as a missionary to the new settlement of Detroit in 1817. Sylvester Larned, whose youthful preaching was often compared to George Whitefield's, went to the Presbyterian church in New Orleans. Yellow fever struck that city during August 1820. On Sunday, August 27, Larned preached from Philippians 1:21—"For me to live is Christ, and to die is gain." The following Thursday, on his twenty-fifth birthday, "he fell asleep in Jesus, or rather awoke to the glory and joy of his Lord."[62] Zebulon Butler graduated in 1826. During his senior year, Dr. Alexander passed on to him a letter written by the citizens of Vicksburg, Mississippi, asking for a preacher. Butler rode on horseback to Mississippi, where he became one of the pioneers of the Presbyterian church in the old Southwest.

Henry Woodward, Princeton's first foreign missionary, went in 1820 to Ceylon, where he served for fourteen years with the American Board of Commissioners for Foreign Missions. Woodward— grandson of Eleazar Wheelock, the Great Awakening preacher and founder of Dartmouth College—decided to become a missionary during his student days at the seminary. He later wrote, "When I looked upon the millions perishing, my eye effected my heart and I felt woe be to me, if I do not preach the Gospel in some dark Corner of the earth."[63] Episcopalian John Newbold, to whom his fellow students attributed far more influence than any other man in the seminary, planned to go as a missionary to Persia or India; but he died soon after completing his studies.[64] Several of Newbold's classmates became missionaries—L. D. Hatch to the slaves of Alabama; Epaphras Chapman to the Osage Indians along the Arkansas River; and Baptist Jonathan Rice, a medical doctor, to Burma. The American Board of Commissioners for Foreign Missions sent Charles Stewart and Artemas Bishop to the Sandwich Islands in 1823. They were accompanied by Betsey Stockton, the young black woman who was converted in the Princeton revival of 1815. She was described as "an humble Christian friend" who was to help the Stewarts with domestic matters and begin a school for the native children. Ashbel Green encouraged Miss Stockton in her mission and published her letters to him in the *Christian Advocate.* The first single woman sent overseas by an American mission board, Betsey Stockton quickly learned the Hawaiian language and became an effective missionary teacher.[65]

In its first decade, Princeton Seminary trained Presbyterian missionary statesmen John Breckinridge and Elisha Swift; William B. Sprague, editor of *Annals of the American Pulpit* and author of other important books; Albert Barnes, pastor and New School Presbyterian leader; Jeremiah Chamberlain, the founder of Centre College in Kentucky, and George Washington Gale, the founder of Knox College in Illinois; fifteen college presidents, including John Maclean of Princeton and Theodore Dwight Woolsey of Yale; Robert Baird, author and founder of the American and Foreign Christian Union; and preacher and professor of theology at Union Theological Seminary in Virginia, Benjamin F. Stanton. The infant Presbyterian seminary also trained influential leaders of other denominations: John W. Nevin, who joined the German Reformed Church; Samuel Schmucker, Lutheran churchman and educator; and Episcopal bishops John Johns of Virginia and Charles P. McIlvaine of Ohio. But of the many outstanding students during those early years, none was more important to Princeton Seminary and American Presbyterianism than the man to whose early life we now turn.

# Charles Hodge

*Young Charles Hodge became instructor
in languages at Princeton Seminary
in 1820 and Professor of Oriental and
Biblical Literature two years later.*

May I be taught of God that I may be able to teach others also. It is only the heart that has been deeply exercised in divine things which can enable us to preach experimentally to others. Piety is the life of a minister.

Charles Hodge's Diary
February 13, 1820

EIGHTEEN-year-old Charles Hodge graduated from Princeton College in 1815. His pale, worn look as he gave the valedictory address testified to long, hard hours of study. Suffering from "a weak chest," Charles returned home to Philadelphia for a year of rest and unpressured study and reading. He visited relatives in their country homes and, in October, accompanied Archibald Alexander on a tour through Virginia. During that journey—in stage coaches and on horseback—young Charles enjoyed his experiences with Dr. Alexander. He was moved by Alexander's sermon on the sacrifice of Isaac. He watched in wonder on another occasion when "the doctor" so graphically described the coming of "the Son of Man" that "the entire congregation, by one impulse, rose, and bent to the windows, that they might see Him, and take their places among the multitudes thronging to meet Him."[1]

When he was a child, Charles Hodge had lost his own father; and Archibald Alexander became, in a special sense, his father. Charles first met Dr. Alexander in August 1812, when the seminary professor visited the Princeton Academy and asked the young student about a Greek word in the lesson before him. This was the first thread of a cord, as Hodge later said, which bound him to Dr. Alexander—"a cord never broken."[2] Hodge always affirmed that he was "moulded more by the character and instructions of Dr. Archibald Alexander, than by all other external influences combined."[3]

[105]

Charles Hodge was born in Philadelphia on December 27, 1797. He was always proud that his ancestors had been "Presbyterians and patriots."[4] His grandfather Andrew Hodge came from Northern Ireland in about 1730 and settled in Philadelphia, where he became a successful merchant and active churchman. He withdrew from the First Presbyterian Church because of its opposition to the Great Awakening and helped organize Second Presbyterian, which called as its pastor the famous revival preacher Gilbert Tennent. Hodge's father, Hugh Hodge, graduated from Princeton College and became a surgeon and business man. In 1790 he married Mary Blanchard, a Boston beauty of French Huguenot descent. After three of their children died during Philadelphia's great yellow fever epidemics of 1793 and 1795, Hugh, Jr., was born in 1796 and Charles in 1797. The next July, Hugh Hodge died of yellow fever, leaving his widow in very limited circumstances with two infants.

Mary Hodge made the rearing and training of her sons her single and absorbing life work. She kept boarders in her home to support the family and took her boys to Second Presbyterian Church, carefully drilling them in the Westminster Shorter Catechism. The pastor, Dr. Ashbel Green, systematically taught the children of his congregation. When they learned the answers to the Shorter Catechism, they joined a Bible class which met weekly in the pastor's study; later the children received instruction from Dr. Green's series of lectures on the Shorter Catechism.[5]

Charles Hodge claimed that there was nothing unusual about his Christian life "unless it be that it began very early." "As far back as I can remember," he wrote years later, "I had the habit of thanking God for everything I received, and asking him for everything I wanted. If I lost a book, or any of my playthings, I prayed that I might find it. I prayed walking along the streets, in school and out of school, whether playing or studying." Charles was a quiet, well-behaved boy, who conscientiously obeyed what he had been taught. He wrote, "I cannot recollect that I ever uttered a profane word, except once. It was when I was thirteen or fourteen years old. I was walking with my brother, and struck my foot against a stone, and said: 'D—n it.' My brother was shocked and exclaimed, 'Why Charles!!' I cannot tell why I said it . . . . I felt like a very, very small Paul, when he said: 'It was not I who did it, but something dwelling in me.'"[6]

Charles attended school in the house of "an old lady in Arch Street," next with a Presbyterian elder whose classroom looked out on Independence Hall, and then with a Sweden-borgian schoolmaster. Mrs. Hodge sent Charles and Hugh to the classical academy in Somerville, New Jersey. In the summer of 1812, Mary Hodge moved the family to Princeton to continue her sons' education. She rented a small frame house on Guinea Lane (later called Witherspoon Street), where she kept as boarders seven Hodge relatives who were students at Princeton College. Hugh began premedical studies at the college and Charles was off to the little town academy. After a few months, he was ready for college and was admitted to the sophomore class in September 1812.

Charles Hodge's Philadelphia pastor soon arrived to become Princeton College's eighth president. Dr. Ashbel Green taught mathematics, literature, ethics, philosophy, and Bible. In Bible class one day, Charles was called on to recite. "Was Paul ever at Malta?" Green asked. "Y—yes sir," Charles ventured, "He—touched there on his voyage to Rome." His friend John Johns murmured, "Hm—m—m. Pretty hard touch!" As Hodge suddenly recalled the violent shipwreck, he exploded with laughter—to be "justly reprimanded" by the nonplussed professor. Greek was taught by the brilliant and popular Philip Lindsley. "He told our class," Hodge later recalled, "that we would find that one of the best prepa-rations for death was a thorough knowledge of the Greek grammar. This was his way of telling us that we ought to do our duty."[7]

Like other college students and townspeople, young Hodge was deeply affected by the Sunday evening preaching of Dr. Alexander. Sixty-two years later he recalled one of those sermons which he had heard as he sat on a shelf in the back part of the room—his feet dangling half way to the floor. Alexander had suddenly paused in his address. Then, stretching out his arm to attract attention, he very deliberately uttered the sentence, "I don't believe a praying soul ever enters hell." "That bolt," Hodge said, "I suspect, pierced more hearts than one."[8]

When revival came to the college in the winter of 1814-15, Charles Hodge made a public profession of Christ. With a college friend, he joined the Presbyterian church on January 13, 1815. College teacher John Maclean remembered the Saturday when he was startled by a student rushing up to him in the street with the abrupt announcement that "Hodge had enlisted." The war with England was still going on, and a sergeant with a drummer was in town enlisting recruits. "Is it possible," Maclean asked, "that Hodge has enlisted?" "Yes," came the reply, "he has enlisted under the banner of King Jesus!" Maclean and President Green believed that the public stand taken by the young student contributed significantly to the revival which was already underway. Charles's mother was surprised by his decision; but, she wrote to his brother, she would not "throw a straw in his way" when she saw his determination. Charles's experience was genuine and sincere but he came to appreciate that it was the culmination of his early Christian training and environment.

Charles Hodge was now deeply excited about his Christian faith and eager to tell others about it. He lost no time in writing his brother, Hugh, to urge him to seek "the one thing needful."[9] He talked about the gospel with his college mates. One dejected student, who was expelled for gambling, met Charles and was converted before he left Princeton. He gratefully reported his change of heart to Mrs. Hodge, telling her of the role Charles had played. The revival had brought Charles Hodge's whole life into focus. He now committed himself to study for the Christian ministry.

The autumn of 1816 found Charles Hodge back in Princeton at the seminary. There were twenty-six students, including his friend John Johns. He lived in town during his first year and then moved into the new seminary building in the fall of 1817. Hodge found the seminary work demanding. He was up before sunrise and did not get to bed much before midnight. In December he wrote to his mother (once again living in Philadelphia) that Dr. Alexander had recommended nearly thirty books, with such a description of each that he felt compelled to read them. There was only another week on that topic before a new subject would be introduced with a new reading list. "One great thing, however, we learn," Hodge wrote, "that is, where information is to be found." Four evenings a week he was occupied with various seminary society meetings—informal faculty-student gatherings for the study of theology, missions, and other topics. On those nights it was nine o'clock before Hodge could begin to study. He faced the pressure with characteristic optimism. He wrote to his mother, "It is not in my nature to worry myself much about what I cannot help, as it is surely best to do as much as you can and let the rest go." He did very much want, however, "a little bag of ginger-bread" to eat after those long society-meeting evenings!

As Charles Hodge faced the close of his seminary work, he placed himself "at the disposal" of his mother and Dr. Alexander as to his future. On February 10, 1819, he wrote to his mother that he was still undecided as to what he should do on leaving seminary. "I laughingly told the Doctor he must dispose of me before a great while. He asked if I would be willing to go where he would send me. I said 'Yes.' 'Take care,' says he; 'I may shock you when I come to tell you what to do.'"[10]

The need for a third professor at the seminary was becoming acute. Dr. Alexander's first choice was Charles Hodge's close friend, John Johns. Johns decided, however, with the two professors' blessing, to enter the ministry of the Episcopal Church. On May 6, 1819, Dr. Alexander surprised Charles by asking, "How would you like to be a professor in the seminary?"[11] He wanted Charles to spend a winter "learning to read the Hebrew language with [vowel] points" and then to return to Princeton as teacher of Greek and Hebrew. By the beginning of the nineteenth century, Hebrew had fallen out of the curriculum of the colleges; and so the seminary undertook to provide instruction in that language which the General Assembly (in the seminary's "Plan") thought indispensable to the proper training of a minister. Charles Hodge was drawn to Dr. Alexander's invitation. He appreciated the influence of seminary professors like Archibald Alexander and Samuel Miller and was committed to the diligence necessary to become a teacher—even the study of "the dead languages." He wrote to his mother that he was "convinced that they are as essential to a student as tools are to workmen of a different kind."

Charles Hodge received his diploma, with six fellow students, on September 28, 1819. By November he was zealously studying Hebrew with the Reverend Joseph Banks, pastor of the Scottish Associate Presbyterian Church in Philadelphia and one of America's foremost Hebrew scholars. Hodge wrote to Dr. Alexander, "He will talk all day on any thing connected with Hebrew."[12] Alexander directed Hodge's study from Princeton, recommending Hebrew and Greek lexicons and British and German biblical works but sagely advising that "there is no advantage in accumulating too many books at once."[13] Hodge launched into the study of German and indulged a lifelong interest by attending lectures at the medical department of the University of Pennsylvania.

Hodge was licensed by the Presbytery of Philadelphia on October 20, 1819, (along with African American Samuel Cornish) and appointed to missionary work in the vicinity of the city. Through the winter and spring he preached almost every Sunday, carefully recording his efforts and his pursuit of piety in the only religious journal he ever kept. The journal's theme is captured in his prayer—"May I be taught of God that I may be able to teach others also."[14]

In May 1820 the General Assembly accepted the Princeton directors' recommendation and offered Charles Hodge a one-year appointment and a salary of four hundred dollars. He accepted the position because he believed he could continue to preach, for he was convinced that "preaching the gospel is a privilege superior to any other intrusted to men."[15] In late June, Hodge rode his horse—"the best in the world"— through blistering heat from Philadelphia to Princeton and began his work as assistant teacher of the original languages of Scripture. He roomed in town, in the house where the Alexanders had first lived, and happily boarded with Dr. Alexander and his family. He found teaching "one of the most fatiguing things in the world." Greek was difficult to teach because almost all the students had studied it for years;

but in Hebrew, Hodge wrote, "I have more the advantage of them." When some of the students complained that one so young as Hodge should not be placed over them, another responded that he did not care who was his teacher as long as he was competent to teach. From then on, Hodge's position was never questioned. To Charles Hodge, however, there were other more important qualifications. Earlier he had written to his mother, "It seems to me that the heart more than the head of an instructor in a religious seminary qualifies or unfits him for his station."[16]

In October 1820 Charles Hodge took Benjamin Wisner, who had just completed his work at the seminary, to Boston in Hodge's "old-fashioned two-wheeled gig, on springs shaped like the letter C"—a "form of conveyance," Hodge's son wrote in 1880, "now utterly extinct."[17] Samuel Miller, long concerned with the "awful degeneracy of Boston with respect to evangelical truth," had recommended Wisner to Old South Church—the only one of Boston's original nine Congregational churches not to become Unitarian. Hodge found people in New England, especially the women, "more intelligent and better informed" than in Philadelphia and New Jersey. He preached several times at Park Street Church in Boston, met with Harvard professors, and visited Nathaniel W. Taylor in New Haven and Moses Stuart at Andover Seminary. In a letter to his mother he wrote that he had stayed with Mr. Taylor, "a young minister who is the pride of the southern part of Connecticut." Hodge found this "one of the most improving incidents" in his trip, even though Taylor differed "very considerably in his theoretical opinions from the Princeton gentlemen." He described his visit with Stuart: "His talents are of the first order, and no man in the country has made any progress comparable to his in the department of Biblical Literature. He has done me great good, has marked out my road, and told me the right path, and enlarged my views as to the extent and importance of the study, more than I could have conceived it possible."[18] Benjamin Wisner stayed on in Boston, eventually to become pastor at Old South. Hodge returned home after three weeks to be present for the new session at Princeton. He brought back John Maclean, one of the college professors, in the vacant seat in his gig.

Charles Hodge was happy. He believed that he could not have planned a better life than the one he had. It was "like a silver stream," he told a friend. He was in daily contact with his beloved mentor, challenged by his seminary classes, and busy preaching in nearby churches. He was ordained on November 28, 1821, preaching before presbytery on I Corinthians 1:21—"For after that in the wisdom of God the world by wisdom knew not God, it pleased God by the foolishness of preaching to save them that believe." He organized the Society for Improvement in Biblical Literature, an organization of students, professors, and pastors, for the translation of Scripture passages and for critical analyses and essays on biblical topics. At the first session in January 1822, Hodge read a paper, later published as *A Dissertation on the Importance of Biblical Literature*. He noted that it was necessary for ministers to keep abreast of scholarly developments and, more importantly, to be prepared for a struggle with Unitarianism over the integrity and interpretation of Scripture. Although sensitive to the charge that German scholarship was destructive, he believed that it could not be ignored and called for an open attitude which would be alert to its benefits as well as its dangers.

Charles Hodge proved his value to the seminary; and on May 24, 1822, he was elected professor of Oriental and Biblical Literature—thus creating a distinct biblical department at Princeton. The increased salary was welcome; on June 17 he was married to Sarah Bache by the Right Rev. Bishop William White, the first American Episcopal bishop. He had met the vivacious Philadelphia girl—a great-granddaughter of Benjamin Franklin and a niece of Dr. Caspar Wistar (the famous physician and professor of anatomy at the University of Pennsylvania)—nine years earlier when she was a boarder in his mother's house in Princeton. Hugh Hodge wrote that Sarah was "then a girl of fourteen years of age, well-grown, in blooming health, handsome, full of imagination, and exceedingly enthusiastic, unconscious of self and absorbed in whatever claimed her attention." "It was no wonder," he added, "that she soon won the love of my brother, young as he was."[19] Sarah followed a course of private study that included religion, history, philosophy, literature, astronomy, and chemistry.[20]

During his years as a seminary student, Charles wrote often to Sarah. In one of his early letters, he deplored the fact that religion had been so neglected in their conversation and correspondence and stated that he was disappointed that he had not been able to meet the difficulties which she constantly felt in regard to Christianity. He hesitated to attempt again to convince her, thinking it best to commend her "simply to the grace of God and to the teachings of His Spirit"; but he stressed the necessity of faith. "All our ability is obtained by faith," he wrote; "nothing else will purify the heart." He told Sarah to "use Christ as though He were your own; employ His strength, His merit, and His grace in all your trials"; and he encouraged her to believe that "there is more to be learned by prayer than by study." It was through these and many similar instructions that Sarah came to Christ. She wrote to Charles on August 4, 1820, "I love to feel myself bound to you by indissoluble ties that not even the grave can change—to feel that after being cherished and guided by you through time, I shall, through your instrumentality, stand by you purified before the throne of our Heavenly Father when time shall be no more."[21]

The handsome couple—she with dark hair and a beautiful complexion and he slender and youthful, with light brown hair and blue eyes—lived in a frame house at the corner of Witherspoon and Main across from Nassau Hall. Charles wrote to his mother that he was happy to see Sarah so "cheerful and contented." He continued, "She is now singing in my ears, so that I scarcely know what I am writing. I begin to fear that many of the fond schemes I had formed will never come to much. As to studying where Sarah is, it will be out of the question, unless there be some way of charming her tongue to rest which I have not as yet discovered."[22] Soon there was another claim to his love and time, when Archibald Alexander Hodge was born on July 18, 1823.

On January 1, 1825, Sarah and Charles and their baby moved into a comfortable fifteen-room brick house, just west of the seminary building. Charles had engaged the architect John Haviland to design the house. He paid for its construction, with the understanding that at a future date the trustees would reimburse him the $5,000 that he spent. The handsome house boasted a Palladian window with a sunburst heading between the first and second stories. Hodge proudly planted elms around his new home. In December, Mary Elizabeth was born and baptized on Christmas Day. That evening Hodge wrote to his mother, "Your dear little Mary Elizabeth was baptized this afternoon in the Oratory by Dr. Alexander. Notwithstanding the rain, the place of service was so near we found it easy to take our dear little treasure out to be consecrated to God in this delightful ordinance."[23]

\*     \*     \*

With three professors and a growing student body, Princeton Seminary went about its work of training young men for the Christian ministry. Within ten years of its beginning the seminary was as national an institution as the college. Students came from New England and the South, as well as from the Middle States. There was great sorrow in the little community in February 1822 when James Turner, a Kentuckian, became the first of the Princeton students to die. Dr. Alexander, Dr. Miller, Charles Hodge, and the students crowded around his bed and, at his request, sang "How firm a foundation, ye saints of the Lord, is laid for your faith in his excellent word!" In November another student, William George Krebs of Philadelphia, was seized with a violent fever and died a few days later. Though unable to speak, "by looks and signs" he made known to Dr. Alexander "and all who surrounded him his entire resignation to the afflicting hand of God, and his joyful expectation of a happy eternity."[24]

James Waddel Alexander entered the seminary in 1822. The oldest son of Dr. and Mrs. Alexander finished his course at Princeton College before making a public profession of faith. The death of a friend turned his thoughts more urgently to God; and on March 30, 1821, he joined the Presbyterian church in Princeton. The next month he wrote in his journal:

When I look forward to future life, a dreary darkness presents itself. What am I qualified for? I never can, in conscience, embrace any other profession but the "gospel of Christ;" but, alas, where are my qualifications? I *never, never* can be a speaker.[25]

James decided to go to the seminary, however, and soon was charmed with life as a theological student. On the last day of 1822 he wrote to his closest friend that he was never more happy in his life:

I enjoy good health, good spirits, and I have a most comfortable room, and a most delightful room mate. I never had so great a variety of excellent company before: Metaphysicians, Wits, Theologians, &c., &c. I have here dearly prized friends who endear Princeton to me. Books in the greatest abundance, as I have access to six public libraries, as well as my father's. Our studies are not burdensome and far from being irksome.

I rise at half after six. Public prayers in the Oratory at 7. Breakfast at 8. From 9 to 9:30, I devote to bodily exercise. From 9:30 until 12, Study. 12-1 Exercise. Dine at one. 2-3, I usually devote to works of taste and to composing. 3-4:30 at Lecture. 4:30 Prayers. Until tea, at Exercise. After tea, until 12 (at which time I close my eyes) Societies, study, &c.[26]

James was studying Hebrew, Greek, theology, and the Confession of Faith, Biblical history, Biblical criticism, and Jewish antiquities. On Monday nights he went to Dr. Hodge's Society on Biblical Criticism. Tuesday nights he attended the Theological Society, where he gave an "original oration" every six weeks. On Thursday nights he heard a lecture at the college. The Theological Society met again on Friday nights for discussion of questions on theology and ethics. On Saturday nights there was a weekly prayer meeting, and on Sundays Alexander heard a sermon from one of the three professors or from Philip Lindsley of the college. Young Alexander found that seminary study could be demanding. He wrote, "If you have ever spent three or four weeks in thinking 'Of Providence, foreknowledge, will and fate, Fix'd fate, free-will, foreknowledge absolute, And found no end in wandering mazes lost,' you may conceive of the mental exhaustion which I now experience."[27]

On February 27, 1823, the college and seminary students and professors met to observe a day of special prayer and fasting for "a revival of religion in the colleges" of the country—the first of the yearly days of prayer for colleges. On March 9, Samuel Miller followed the exercises of the day of prayer with an appropriate sermon entitled "The Literary Fountains Healed." At the seminary the faculty was optimistic despite the continuing struggle for adequate funds. Princeton was attracting more and more students; on November 14, 1825, J. W. Alexander proudly wrote that the seminary commenced with more than a hundred students.[28] One of those students was African American Theodore Wright, "a very sensible, genteel personage," according to Alexander.[29] When Wright was recommended by the Presbytery of Albany for admission, the Princeton directors had unequivocally declared that "his color shall form no obstacle in the way of his reception."[30]

\*     \*     \*

In 1824 a new printing press was established in Princeton, and the next year Charles Hodge began the *Biblical Repertory*. The new journal, "designed to render accessible to American readers some of the fruits of the mature learning of English and German scholars," contained mainly translations and reprints of articles related to the interpretation of the Bible. Aware that some people would consider biblical studies— especially those originating in Germany—dangerous to the faith, Hodge wrote an introduction to the first issue in which he pointed out that it was not their biblical studies which led scholars to theological looseness but rather their preconceived opinions. He continued:

It is not, therefore, to the Biblical Student that this melancholy page of history furnishes its warning; it is to those who introduce the speculations of Philosophy into the study of Theology, and who avowedly or unconsciously interpret the Sacred Volume in accordance with opinions previously formed, and resting upon some other foundation than the revelation of God. And the greatest barrier to the progress of error is to be found in bringing men from other sources of theological knowledge, immediately to the Sacred Scriptures, to the strictly grammatical interpretation of the word of God, which is by no means inconsistent with the highest reverence for its character, the strongest conviction of its divine origin and consequent infallibility, and the deepest sense of our need of the aids of the Holy Spirit to remove our native prejudice to the truth, and to illuminate the mind with the knowledge of Divine things. This has been the course pursued by the wisest and best men in every age of the church. It is the plan upon which our system of doctrine is founded, and by which alone it can be defended. Danger, therefore, is not to be apprehended from the pursuit of Biblical studies, it lies in their neglect.[31]

In addition to teaching the biblical languages, Charles Hodge was now giving lectures on Romans and Corinthians and teaching hermeneutics. He worked hard in order to do justice to his demanding duties. He wrote to his brother in November 1823 that he would "find it essential to carry on the study of six languages this winter." But still he could not escape "the most painful sense of unfitness" for the work.[32] He began to feel that he needed the more precise study of the biblical languages, textual criticism, and exegesis which was to be found only in Europe. When Charles Hodge shared his plans with Archibald Alexander and Samuel Miller, the two professors reluctantly took his request to the Board of Directors. They explained that Hodge was "under a deep impression that he needed further advantages of leisurely study" and access "to those richly furnished libraries and those eminently skilled and profound masters of Oriental Literature" of France and Germany.[33] The directors gave their permission and appointed recent graduate John W. Nevin as Hodge's replacement for two years. The *Biblical Repertory* was left under the supervision of Robert Patton, professor of Greek at Princeton College. Hodge took his wife and two small children to live with his mother and brother in Philadelphia and, in October 1826, sailed from New York. After a boisterous twenty-five-day voyage, during which he learned that "the sea is no place for study," he reached France.

Charles Hodge made the most of his time in Europe. He studied in Paris, Halle, and Berlin and traveled widely. He was alert to culture, politics, philosophy, and the history and beauty of Europe. While in Dresden, Hodge regularly enjoyed the city's art gallery. "On every visit," he wrote, "I was attracted and held bound to Raphael's Madonna."[34] He attended Reformed, Lutheran, Moravian, and Catholic church services. He met famous teachers and scholars and made close friends.

Hodge studied French, Arabic, and Syriac in Paris and met Adolphe Monod, who was engaged in translating Thomas Scott's commentary into French. Hodge preached several times for the English congregation there, which included members of General Lafayette's family and Thomas Guthrie, a young Scot studying in Paris. The six-foot-two-inch Guthrie described Hodge as "a young-like, intelligent, fair, good look-ing, thin and rather little man" and praised his preaching.

While in Paris, Hodge considered his future base for study and decided on Halle over Göttingen. Halle placed more emphasis on the biblical languages and textual criticism, and several important professors taught there. In Halle, Hodge roomed in the house of Wilhelm Gesenius, the foremost Hebrew scholar of the day. Next door was Edward Robinson, student and colleague of Moses Stuart at Andover Seminary and later professor at Union Seminary in New York. Hodge was disappointed in Gesenius's "rather foppish appearance" but was impressed by his lectures on Job. Hodge met with Gesenius on a tutorial basis six times a week during the spring term of 1827. He thought Gesenius to be "by far the ablest" of the biblical critics; "he is so clear and animated," he wrote, "and so perfectly master of his subject." But because of his great ability, Hodge feared that Gesenius, a leader in the historical critical movement, was "doing the most harm."[35]

Hodge's main interest in Halle, however, was Friedrich August Gottreu Tholuck, a man "as much distinguished for his piety," he wrote, "as for his learning." At the age of twenty, Tholuck had been converted from skepticism and pantheism through the influence of the pietists. He became active in missions and Bible society work and, in 1820, began teaching theology at Berlin. His *Die Lehre von der Sünde und dem Versöhner, oder die Wahre Weiche der Zweiflers* (The Teaching on Sin and the Reconciler, or the Critical Issue for the Skeptics) was a strong evangelical statement and helped check the spread of rationalism in Germany. In 1826, over the strenuous objections of the rationalists, he was appointed professor of theology at Halle and began slowly to create a different atmosphere there. Hodge was impressed by

Tholuck's piety and admired his scholarship, which demonstrated that a valid, intelligent biblical criticism that rejected the presuppositions of modernism was possible.

Charles Hodge wrote that during one of his first meetings with Tholuck, the German theologian asked him if he did not find himself "unsettled in reading the exegetical works of the modern German school." When Hodge answered "no," Tholuck seemed surprised and asked what views he "entertained about prophecy." Hodge answered that he "considered the Prophets under the guidance of the Holy Spirit." Tholuck exclaimed, "Oh, if you are on that ground, neology never can touch you!"[36]

The two young scholars spent many hours together and became lifelong friends. When Hodge was departing for home in April 1828, Tholuck wrote, "You have been sent to me through God's mercy as a messenger of glad tidings, as a comforter in cheerless hours, as an elder brother to show me the simple way to heaven."[37] In 1872 Charles Hodge remarked that "of all the genial, lovely, and loving men whom the writer in the course of a long life has met, Tholuck stands among the very first. The writer derived more good from him than from all other sources combined during his two years sojourn in Europe."[38]

In Halle, Hodge studied German with George Müller—later well known for his orphanage in Bristol, England—and attended with great interest the scientific lectures of Alexander Humboldt. After hearing "a real evangelical sermon" on Ephesians 3:19, Hodge wrote in his journal:

My heart overflowed with joy to hear the praise of Christ and the excellence of his love. It has been very long since I enjoyed so much pleasure in hearing a sermon. For here, there are few who appear to feel the spirit of the gospel or whose hearts are warmed with the love of the blessed Saviour.[39]

In Berlin, Hodge met the conservative Protestant leaders, Ernst Wilhelm Hengstenberg and Johann August Wilhelm Neander. Hengstenberg, professor of oriental languages, had been a decided rationalist; but his confidence was shaken when he attended a Moravian church service. The simple study of the Bible led him to a firm belief in the truth of

Christianity. In one of his first lectures at Berlin, Hengstenberg stated, "It matters not whether we make a god out of stone, or out of our own understanding, it is still a false god; there is but one living God, the God of the Bible." His words were received with hissing and scraping, but he was not intimidated. Hengstenberg spent much time with the young American seminary teacher and was impressed with Hodge's Christian earnestness. "He himself is the best evidence of the truth of what he says," reported Hengstenberg.[40]

Hodge was struck that Neander—a Jewish convert to Christianity through the preaching of Schleiermacher—looked old for his thirty-five years. He wrote, "The poor man has studied himself almost to death." Hodge was pleased with Neander's lectures on Corinthians, with his clear and simple manner and his wonderful historical knowledge. Hodge had great respect for "the dear little man," although they did not always agree on points of doctrine. Neander held to the infallibility of the New Testament writers in doctrine but "not in their manner of proving" it; he opposed predestination as making God "the author of sin"; he believed in an offer of the gospel after death for those who had not heard. Neander wrote to Tholuck, "Tell our friend Hodge, that though we dispute with him, we belong to the same Lord, and are one in heart."[41]

Hodge went to hear the famous Friedrich Schleiermacher preach on "Thou shalt love the Lord thy God with all thy heart." "The words were Biblical," Hodge wrote, [but] "the ideas so vague and indefinite." Tholuck told Hodge that Schleiermacher was doing good in Germany, despite his theology, because of "the respect which he manifests for the Bible, and the reverence with which he speaks of Jesus Christ." Years later in his *Systematic Theology*, Hodge attacked Schleiermacher's "pantheism" and his rejection of the Bible as "a supernatural revelation from God" but added a famous footnote:

When in Berlin the writer often attended Schleiermacher's church. The hymns to be sung were printed on slips of paper and distributed at the doors. They were always evangelical and spiritual in an eminent degree, filled with praise and gratitude to our Redeemer. Tholuck said that Schleiermacher, when sitting in the evening with his family, would often say, "Hush, children; let us sing a hymn of praise to Christ." Can we doubt that he is singing those praises now? To whomsoever Christ is God, St. John assures us, Christ is a Saviour.[42]

In Berlin, Hodge met regularly for fellowship and discussion with a group of men and women of different churches, including Roman Catholics. At one of these he heard a "piece from an old German composer, Bach, whose works have long been neglected, but which they say are equal to almost any of the best German compositions." He developed a strong friendship with prominent German nobles, including Otto von Gerlach, "the Wesley of Berlin," and his brother Ludwig. Political discussions with the latter forced Hodge to examine the Christian basis for his views concerning government. After one lively debate, Hodge wrote, "He is a noble fellow. Though grieved with my obstinacy, he gave me *two* kisses when we went, (one, however, less than usual)."

Charles Hodge spent his thirtieth birthday in Berlin, in December 1827. He wrote:

This night thirty years ago I was born. Thirty years of love and mercy. Thirty years of sin. Thirty years and nothing done. Oh my God, from my soul I pray thee, grant me thy Holy Spirit that if permitted yet longer to live, it may be to more purpose,—that my time may be better improved in working out my own salvation and the salvation of my fellow-men.

While Hodge was in Europe, Archibald Alexander and Samuel Miller, with the help of John Nevin, carried the load of the seminary. During 1827 Dr. Miller was sick for many weeks and Dr. Alexander had to take his classes as well. The two professors prayed for their young friend in Germany and wrote regularly to him. Samuel Miller wrote to encourage him—"I do not believe, my dear colleague, that you appreciate as you ought your importance and acceptance in our Institution." Archibald Alexander's letters were full of counsel. On March 24, 1827, he wrote, "Remember that you breathe a poisoned atmosphere. If you lose the lively and deep impression of divine truth—if you fall into skepticism or even into coldness, you will lose more than you gain from all the German professors and libraries." Several months later he wrote, "I wish you to come home enriched with Biblical knowledge, but abhorring German philosophy and theology." Alexander was anxious for Hodge to return. "I wish now to begin in good earnest to prepare for another world," he wrote. "I think before very many years you will be senior Professor in this Institution, and I am afraid that you will see trouble." The next May, Alexander wrote, "Make haste and come home. There will be much for you to do. The two crazy old men that are here need some one who has vigor of nerves to put his shoulder under the burden."

In the early spring of 1828, having learned the tasks of theology under Tholuck at Halle and the methods of "believing" criticism under Hengstenberg at Berlin, Hodge departed from his German friends with real sorrow and travelled home through Switzerland, France, and England. From Switzerland he wrote to his "beloved" Sarah, "I have seen the Alps! If now I never see anything great or beautiful in nature, I am content. . . . Everything I had ever previously seen seemed absolutely nothing."[43] He was deeply moved by England—"the mother country, which, with all her faults, is the most wonderful and admirable the world has ever seen." He was unimpressed, however, by the speeches in Parliament. In Cambridge he heard, "with great delight," Charles Simeon preach. He arrived home in Princeton on September 18, 1828. Archibald Alexander, Samuel Miller, and John Maclean gathered to greet him. Watching with excitement was five-year-old Archibald Alexander Hodge, who received that day "the first abiding image of his father."[44]

Charles Hodge found the seminary growing. There were 109 students at the winter session (compared with only 65 or so at the college). More important, as Hodge wrote to Tholuck, the "spirit of piety" was strong and "perhaps more of a disposition to embark in foreign missions was manifested during the last term than usual." Missing his German friends and eager to keep up with German theological literature, Hodge wrote to Tholuck, "I look back to my sojourn in Germany with feelings of unmingled pleasure. . . . I love the German character, as exhibited in Christians, quite as much as though I were myself a German, and cannot pass a

German immigrant in the street without feelings of interest I experience for no other people." Hodge reminded his friend to be on the watch for books—"You know the kind of books I want, *valuable* works on the language, literature and exegesis of the Old and New Testaments."[45]

Hodge was home. He was broadened culturally and enriched intellectually but, as was soon clear, unmoved theologically. He gave the introductory lecture at the beginning of the 1828 school year, sharing with the seminary community some observations made during his study in Europe. He stated how much greater American "civil and religious liberty" was than that found in Europe and described how vastly superior European education was. He then discussed "the intimate connexion between speculative opinion, and moral character." How was it, Hodge asked, that in the former great centers of Protestantism—especially Germany—Christianity had ceased to be even the nominal religion? The cause was the decline of "vital religion," Hodge said. The revival of the Reformation was followed by "a period of cold orthodoxy brought about principally by perpetual controversy on unimportant subjects." After a time of partial recovery during the Pietist revival, there was almost total relapse. "It is this vital connection between piety and truth," stressed Hodge, "that is the great and solemn lesson taught by the past and present state of the German churches." Hodge claimed that "holiness is essential to the correct knowledge of divine things and the great security from error." "Wherever you find vital piety," he added, "there you find the doctrines of the fall, of depravity, of regeneration, of atonement, and of the deity of Jesus Christ." Hodge applied this lesson to the seminary students:

"Keep your hearts with all diligence, for out of them are the issues of life." Remember that it is only in God's light that you can see light. That holiness is essential to correct knowledge of divine things, and the great security from error. And as you see, that when men lose the life of religion, they can believe the most monstrous doctrines, and glory in them; and that when the clergy once fall into such errors, generations perish before the slow course of reviving piety brings back the truth; "what manner of men ought you to be in all holy conversation and godliness." Not only then for your own sake, but for the sake of your children, and your children's children, forsake not your God. . . .

Finally, lean not to your own understanding. If there be any declaration of the Bible, confirmed by the history of the church, and especially by the recent history of European churches, it is that "he that leaneth to his own understanding is a fool." When men forsake the word of God, and profess to be wise above that which is written, they inevitably and universally lose themselves in vain speculations. . . . Submit yourselves, therefore, to the teaching of him, in whom "are all the treasures of wisdom and knowledge." It is only when thus taught, that you will be able to teach others also.[46]

With these comments on the importance of one's personal walk with God, Charles Hodge touched on the most important aspect of the life of Princeton Seminary.

# 7

# The Sabbath Afternoon Conference

*James Waddell Alexander, son of Archibald
Alexander, studied at Princeton Seminary
from 1822 to 1824 and served churches in
Virginia and New Jersey before joining the
faculty of Princeton College in 1833.*

Public means of grace abound in the seminary. . . . There is our weekly Conference on Sabbath afternoon, in which we talk over together the blessed promises of our God and seek to learn better his will for the ordering of our lives.

BENJAMIN BRECKINRIDGE WARFIELD

SOUTH Carolinian John Bailey Adger, who entered Princeton Seminary in September 1829, recorded his first impressions:

My fellow-students were all devoted to the acquisition of sacred learning, and the cultivation of the spiritual life. Many of them were very godly men. Religious truth filled the very air. Our conversations were all about the Scriptures. . . . The professors, Drs. Alexander and Miller and Hodge, impressed me as no other Christian ministers had ever done. Not only their profound learning, but the saintliness of their character, filled me with awe.[1]

Like the college of John Witherspoon's vision, Princeton Seminary's stated purpose was to combine both evangelical Christianity and eminent scholarship. While the seminary's founders wanted to provide a school for the training of ministers where the spiritual would not be compromised by the academic, Witherspoon's ideal was not abandoned. "Solid learning" was just as much a goal at the seminary as it was at the college; but even more so was "piety of the heart." The first seminary teachers were profoundly aware that theological study in itself would not guarantee spiritual development. In fact, in Archibald Alexander's opinion "speculation on deep points of theology, when the mind is not under a decided spiritual influence, is always attended with evil even to those who at bottom are sincerely pious."[2]

The seminary's "Plan" had stated that it

ought to be considered as an object of primary importance by every
student in the Seminary, to be careful and vigilant not to lose that
inward sense of the power of godliness which he may have attained;
but, on the contrary, to grow continually in a spirit of enlightened
devotion and fervent piety; deeply impressed with the recollection
that without this, all his other acquisitions will be comparatively of
little worth, either to himself, or to the Church of which he is to be
a minister.

The "Plan" called for the professors to encourage godliness
among the students by "inculcating practical religion in their
lectures and recitations" and by accompanying them with
prayer "as frequently as they may judge proper." It outlined
"the path of duty" for seminary students: "devout meditation"
every morning and evening, "devotional exercises" the whole
of the Lord's Day, and a monthly day for special prayer and
self-examination.

The "Plan" required that the students, by the end of their
study, "must have read a considerable number of the best
practical writers on the subject of religion." No formal
course was provided; but the students read devotional writers
such as John Owen, Stephen Charnock, John Bunyan,
Samuel Rutherford, Thomas Boston, John Flavel, and
Thomas Halyburton. Dr. Alexander appreciated Owen's
"power, erudition, and originality" and recommended that
the students read his work on "Spiritual Mindedness" once a
year.[3] Of his father's favorite writer, J. W. Alexander wrote,
"To my taste Flavel is the most uniformly interesting, engaging, and refreshing writer on religion, ancient or modern. I
always feel that I am talking with a Christian, fresh and ruddy,
in perfect health and spirits, with no cloud or megrim, and
with every power available at the moment."[4] The sermons of
Jonathan Edwards and Samuel Davies, the journals of David
Brainerd and Henry Martyn and, later, the life of Robert
Murray McCheyne were often read and quoted. Jonathan
Edwards, the New England preacher-scholar who died
in Princeton, was much esteemed by the Princetonians.
Archibald Alexander believed that "few men ever attained
. . . higher degrees of holiness" or "made more accurate

observations on the exercises of others" than Edwards.[5] In 1824, J. W. Alexander, then a tutor at Princeton College, was reading Henry Martyn's life for the sixth time. He wrote, "If there is on earth or on record a character which I love more than that of H. Martyn, I know it not. To meet *him* in heaven is a wish that burns intensely in my heart."[6] Later, Alexander commented, "The life of McCheyne humbles me. What zeal and faith! What a proof that Old Calvinism is not insusceptible of being used" to revive the church.[7] Generations of Princeton students learned to love these and other spiritual writers. A few weeks after James Petigru Boyce arrived at Princeton in 1849, he wrote that in addition to his classes he was also "carrying on a course of reading in the biography of the great and the good who have shed lustre upon the Christian name."[8]

Thomas Halyburton (1674-1712), Presbyterian minister and professor of divinity at St. Andrews University, sought to combat the coldness and errors of deism with Christian piety and clear apologetics. A special Princeton reprint of Halyburton's *Memoirs* contained a "Recommendation" by Professors Miller and Hodge and a nine-page "Preface" by Dr. Alexander—almost an official endorsement of Halyburton as an ideal of piety for the seminary.[9] Miller and Hodge judged Halyburton's *Memoirs* to be "one of the best specimens of religious biography extant" and unsurpassed "as an exhibition of Christian experience, simple, unaffected, scriptural, and richly instructive." Archibald Alexander appreciated Halyburton's dual emphasis on piety and theology; he admired Halyburton's ability to apply the Bible "to the various conditions and exigencies of believers" and his "extraordinary insight into the deceitful windings, doublings, and complicated foldings, of the human heart."

In his preface to the Princeton edition of Halyburton's *Memoirs*, Alexander put forth his own ideas as to the "relation of sound doctrine to pious feeling and moral character." These may be compared, he wrote, to "the types used in printing, and the impression on the paper." "If there be any defect or disorder in the types, it will appear on the corresponding page." He added, "It may not be such as to destroy, or entirely obscure, the meaning of the whole passage; but still it is the cause of a defect, which mars the beauty of the impression; and often renders the sense uncertain." The lesson was apparent to Alexander—"he who trifles with the truth, trifles with his own life." "Truth is so vital, and so necessary to the existence and perfection of a pious character," Alexander wrote, "that we cannot be too solicitous to acquire correct knowledge." This "pursuit of truth" does not depend solely on one's mind; it depends on "the love of truth" which lays aside "pride, prejudice, and partiality." "Honesty and deep humility" are its "essential prerequisites." People, however, do not attain to the truth by their human abilities or attitudes. Only the Holy Spirit can make the truth effectual, thus regenerating and sanctifying the heart. The impressions that God by his truth makes on different minds will be substantially alike, Alexander stated, even though there will be "endless varieties in the minor traits," because of differences in degree of knowledge and personality. Alexander admitted that it is exceedingly difficult to ascertain "the precise nature" of the effects produced by the truth in ourselves or others. The Bible, he believed, is "our safest guide, and only unerring standard of experimental religion." He wrote, "By meditating day and night on the contents of the sacred pages, we may become so familiar with the characteristics of genuine piety, that we may find it easy to determine, that the same lineaments have, in some faint degree, been drawn on our own souls."

Alexander believed that the reading of Christian biography was also a useful way of examining the true nature of the Christian life. Alexander praised Halyburton's *Memoirs* as the best book that he knew in its descriptions of "the exercises of the human heart, both before and after regeneration." He recommended it to all professing Christians and especially "to all young ministers of the gospel, and to all candidates for the holy ministry." "Let our young Theologians be such as Halyburton was," Dr. Alexander concluded, "and error will hide its head as ashamed; and genuine piety will be inculcated and exemplified."[10]

\*     \*     \*

When the new seminary building was occupied in 1817, the directors required that the students assemble morning and evening for prayer. Morning prayers were led by senior students, and the professors took turns conducting evening prayers.[11] Every Wednesday evening Dr. Alexander led a prayer meeting in the Oratory. A. A. Hodge described the scene as he observed it toward the end of Alexander's life:

The instant the students were in their seats he came in rapidly, his cloak hanging often diagonally from his bent shoulders, his head inclined as in revery, yet flashing sudden glances on either side with piercing eyes, which seemed to penetrate all the secrets of those upon whom they fell. He sat down with his back to the windows, and his right side to the students, sitting low—almost hidden by the desk. Drawing the large Bible down before him, he seemed to lose at once all sense of human audience, and to pass alone into the presence of God. As he read, and mused and ejaculated the utterances of all the holy exercises of his soul upon the Divine Word, a solemn hush fell upon us, and we felt not as those who listen to a teacher, but as those who are admitted to approach, with shoes from off their feet, to gaze in and listen through an open window to the mysterious workings of a sanctified soul under the immediate revelations of the Holy Ghost.[12]

The seminary community worshipped with the college on Sunday mornings until 1826, when the seminary began its own services in the Oratory. Although professors and students preached and attended worship in the churches in and around Princeton, the seminary service continued. An English visitor who heard Dr. Alexander preach at Sunday worship in 1834 wrote:

The service was in the lecture room; there were from eighty to one hundred young men present. It was an interesting occasion. I was glad to worship with a body of pious youth who were devoted to the ministration of the word of life; and to hear that worship led by so good and competent a man as their revered tutor.[13]

During the earliest years of the seminary's history, Dr. Alexander had preached at the college on Sunday evenings. After a few years these evening "lectures" were discontinued in favor of a Sunday afternoon meeting at the seminary, described in a faculty report to the directors in 1816 as a "serious conference with the students on subjects relating more immediately to experimental religion." This was the beginning of the famous Sabbath Afternoon Conference, which, according to A. A. Hodge, was "in many respects the most remarkable and memorable exercise in the entire Seminary Course." B. B. Warfield stated that the conference "kept the fire burning on the altar for a hundred years."[14] After singing and prayer, a topic "in experimental or practical religion" that had been announced the week before was discussed. The conversation was led by one of the students. Then the professors spoke. More singing and prayer ended the service, which lasted about an hour and a half.

Dr. Alexander—who had the ability to talk simply, directly, and persuasively—spoke extemporaneously and without notes in the conference. He poured out "his profound personal experience of divine things" and often "left all present in a state of high emotion."[15] Alexander covered such topics as true and false sorrow for sin, spiritual joy, private devotions, dangers of a seminary life, fasting, foreign missions, the missionary spirit, religious melancholy, and the imitation of Christ.

Samuel Miller's style was more formal. He presented talks which were always "digested and methodical"; they were filled with apt, sometimes witty, anecdotes and numerous quotations from old writers. Miller often took his young sons with him to the conference. One of the sons wrote years later, "To the interesting nature of this exercise, as conducted in those days, the graduates of the institution have often borne witness; and that mere children should attend, Sabbath after Sabbath, of their own accord . . . upon such a service, was perhaps a strong testimony to the same effect."[16]

After the death of Archibald Alexander, Charles Hodge became the leading figure in the conference. He prepared careful outlines for every message he gave although he spoke without notes.[17] His son wrote that his manner was "in the highest degree earnest, fervent and tender to tears; full of conviction and full of love." Hodge's talks, more like sermons than Alexander's informal comments, covered the whole range of doctrine and personal experience and sought to demonstrate "the practical character of all doctrine" and "the doctrinal basis of all genuine religious experience and practice."[18] He never used the same message twice (even though his audience changed every three or four years) but prepared a new outline for each conference, often constructing several analyses of the same theme.[19]

William Irvin, a student at the seminary from 1859 to 1861, described Charles Hodge in the conference:

No triumph of his with tongue or pen ever so thrilled and moved human hearts as did his utterances at the Sabbath afternoon conferences in the Seminary Oratory, which will live in the immortal memory of every Princeton student. A subject would be given out on the Sunday before, generally some one which involved practical, experimental, spiritual religion—such as Christian fidelity, love of God's Word, prayer, the Lord's Supper, the great commission. After brief opening services by the students, the Professors spoke in turn; but Dr. Hodge's was the voice which all waited to hear. Sitting quietly in his chair, with a simple ease which seemed born of the moment, but was really the fruit of careful preparation, even with the pen, he would pour out a tide of thought and feeling which moved and melted all—solemn, searching, touching, tender—his eye sometimes kindling and his voice swelling or trembling with the force of sacred emotion, while thought and language at times rose to a grandeur which held us spell-bound. Few went away from those consecrated meetings without feeling in their hearts that there was nothing good and pure and noble in Christian character which he who would be a worthy minister of Christ ought not to covet for his own.[20]

\* \* \*

It was the custom for one of the seminary professors to give an "introductory lecture" to the students at the beginning of each term of study—dealing with the life of the Christian and the preparation for ministry. Many of these were presented by Dr. Alexander, who, in 1813, gave an address with twenty-five points! He admonished the students to "meditate frequently and profoundly on the imbecility of the human intellect" and to "depend entirely on God's blessing" for success in their studies. "There is reason to believe," he told them, "that though inspiration has long ceased, the Spirit of God does now, in various ways, guide, assist and elevate the minds of men." In 1818, he admonished the students to learn to think for themselves—a favorite Alexander theme—while strongly fixing their trust and hope in God. [21]

Samuel Miller's introductory lectures often dealt with the urgent need for ministers of the right kind. By the beginning of the nineteenth century, there was a general loss of respect for Christian ministers. The desperate need of the frontier and the democratization of Christianity in the Second Great Awakening led to the proliferation of preachers, especially among the Methodists and Baptists, with little or no education. Even Presbyterians were cutting short their seminary study in order to get more quickly to the field. Charles Hodge entered Princeton with twenty-five other students in 1816. Although eighteen became ordained ministers, only six of them remained in seminary for the full three years. Not only was the great need for more workers a temptation to young men to shorten their preparation, but there was the widespread idea that seminary training actually was a detriment, not a help, to the minister. Methodist circuit riders like Peter Cartwright ridiculed educated preachers, and devotional zeal and fiery preaching were regarded by many as more telling of one's call to the ministry than a trained mind.

Samuel Miller's 1825 introductory lecture was entitled "Why are there, at Present, so Few Ministers of the Gospel Really Eminent in their Profession?" He urged the students to, first of all, "cultivate deep piety" and, secondly, to study theology closely for at least three years at the seminary, with a fourth and fifth year if possible. Two years later he opened the winter session with an address on "The Importance of the Gospel Ministry," in which he told the students that "the ministerial office is the most interesting, the most responsible, the most awful under heaven."[22] His 1829 introductory lecture returned to the same theme when he dealt with "The Importance of Mature Preparatory Study for the Ministry." He deplored the fact that a large number of the seminary students failed to complete their three years of study, leaving the seminary prematurely to accept calls to churches and other ministries. He told the seminarians that the ministers who had been most effective were "those who, to fervent piety, united a competent store of literature and science, and especially an intimate acquaintance with the Bible."[23]  Five years later, Miller was still concerned that "a large majority of our theological students . . . *will* in spite of every dictate of wisdom and of scripture to the contrary . . . hasten into the pulpit with half, or less than half, an adequate training."[24]

Dr Miller insisted that the true minister must be characterized by both learning and character.  The power and authority of the office derive not from titles conferred by apostolic succession, he argued, but from "humility, meekness, purity of life and zeal for the salvation of men."  To be sure, the authenticity and value of the gospel abide and endure apart from the personal character of its ministers, but it has been given to us in earthen vessels.  As channels of gospel truth, ministers are a blessing, by the purity of both their lives and doctrine, to the church and to the world.

Samuel Miller wanted to see not only godly and well-trained men, but also cultured men, entering the ministry of the Presbyterian church.  Good manners, he believed, were no substitute for piety and sound doctrine but were important for a successful ministry.  In 1827 he wrote his *Letters on Clerical Manners and Habits, addressed to a Student in the Theological Seminary at Princeton, N.J.,* repeating what he undoubtedly told the seminary students many times.[25]  He discussed personal traits such as dignity, gentleness, and consistency, which are important in the ministry.  He gave advice on such practical matters as personal hygiene, table manners, conversation, conduct in church courts, dress, and conduct in "female society."  Miller made it clear that by proper clerical manners he did not mean "those starched, artificial, formal manners, which display constant effort and restraint; or those ostentatious, splendid, and graceful refined manners, which are formed upon more worldly principles; which qualify their possessor to make a distinguished figure in a ball-room, . . . and which manifest that he has studied *Chesterfield* more than his Bible."  In fact, Miller asserted:

many persons who pass for well-bred, and even highly bred, in such scenes, are among the most disgusting and troublesome, and, of course among the worst bred people in the world.  But my object is to recommend those manners which become the *Christian*

*Gentleman:* which flow naturally from the meekness, gentleness, purity, and benevolence of our holy Religion; and which both the precepts and examples of the Bible equally recommend.

*       *       *

The Princeton professors took seriously their responsibility to produce both learned and godly ministers. In sermons, lectures, and personal counsel they emphasized the themes of Christian living. And on Sunday afternoons in "that sacred old Oratory . . . they sought to build up Christian men rather than form accomplished scholars and to instruct them in the wisest methods of conducting their future work of saving souls and edifying the Church of Christ."[26] No single feature of seminary life was remembered by former students more often or more warmly than the conference. Reflecting on a half-century of Princeton history in an address to the alumni in 1862, William B. Sprague spoke of Archibald Alexander's "never to be forgotten Sunday afternoon talks on practical and experimental religion."[27] J. W. Alexander saw the conference as "a genuine primitive 'prophesying,'" in the tradition of the ministers' meetings for Bible study and spiritual encouragement which characterized the early Swiss and Scottish Reformations.[28] Robert Nassau remembered "those blessed conferences"; and Kenneth Grant described them as "one of the outstanding features of Princeton theological life."[29] Missionary John M. Lowrie wrote, "There are brethren in China and India, and I believe in heaven too, who will long remember room No. 29 [the Oratory], in Princeton Seminary, hallowed as it has been by conference, by tears and prayers."[30]

# 8

# The Concert for Prayer and the Society of Inquiry on Missions

*William Patterson Alexander completed his study at Princeton Seminary in 1831 and went to the Hawaiian islands where he served as a missionary until his death in 1884. An eloquent preacher and expert linguist, he established a theological school for the Hawaiians in 1863.*

We regard the missionary cause as the greatest beneath the sun.

ARCHIBALD ALEXANDER

WHEN Charles Hodge returned to Princeton from Europe in 1828, he found not only the spiritual life of the seminary prospering but also missionary interest and commitment.[1] Princeton was deeply marked by Archibald Alexander's views on missions. In his homily before Lexington Presbytery in April 1791—two decades before the founding of the American Board of Commissioners for Foreign Missions—nineteen-year-old Alexander had defined the essence of the Christian faith in terms that necessitated foreign missions: true believers "earnestly desire the whole world to come to the knowledge of [God], and it is their habitual determination to do what in them lies to bring mankind to a saving acquaintance with him."[2]

At Princeton Alexander continued to stress the importance of missions. Late in his life, in a rare criticism of the Protestant reformers, he stated that although their piety was "pure and vigorous," it was not as expansive as it might have been. He wrote, "They seem scarcely to have thought of the hundreds of millions of heathen in the world; and of course made no efforts to extend the knowledge of salvation to them."[3]

From its beginning, Princeton Seminary was a leader in the American missionary movement. In 1811 the General Assembly added a paragraph to the "Plan of the Seminary," stating a further purpose for the new school: "It is to found a nursery for missionaries to the heathen, and to such as are destitute of the stated preaching of the gospel; in which youth may receive that appropriate training which may lay a foundation for their ultimately becoming eminently qualified for missionary work."

The professors sought to increase missionary vision and to prepare effective workers for the mission fields. In 1816 they reported that "a spirit of serious enquiry and of zeal on the subject of missions appears to be gaining ground in the Seminary."[4] A member of one of the early classes, John C. Lowrie, remembered how often the first two professors moved the hearts of the students "by their impassioned appeals for the heathen."[5]

The visits of missionaries were high points in the life of the seminary. In 1821 William Ward, the distinguished English Baptist missionary and colleague of William Carey and Joshua Marshman at Serampore, came to Princeton. His visit "excited much interest," the Princeton students wrote to the Baptist Seminary in Philadelphia, and "made us more than feel the importance of making the most vigorous exertions to emancipate the heathen from their miserable subjection to sin and Satan."[6] The day after Ward's address at Princeton, Charles Hodge wrote to his brother that the missionary had "little of the graces of elocution" but "a heart alive to the importance of his cause." Hodge continued:

I never felt the importance and grandeur of missionary labors as I did last evening. I could not help looking around on the congregation and asking myself, "What are these people living for?" Granting that each should attain his most elevated object, what would it all amount to? Then looking at these men in India, giving the Bible to so many millions, which I *know* can never be in vain, I see them opening a perennial fountain, which, when they are dead for ages, will still afford eternal life to millions.[7]

One of the most powerful missionary impacts on the seminary came from the visit of young Mohawk Indian Guy Chew. When Chew died suddenly, the seminary students paid for a stone to mark his grave in the Princeton cemetery, with the words inscribed:

In memory of Guy Chew, a Mohawk Indian, who departed this life April 19th 1835, aged 21 years and 8 months. This youth continued in pagan darkness until his 18th year, when under the patronage of

U. F. M. Society he was sent to the Mission School at Cornwall, Conn. There he remained three years, experienced the renewing grace of God, and became eminent for his benevolence, piety and desire to proclaim the Gospel to his countrymen. While preparing for this blessed work, he was by a mysterious Providence called away in the morning of his days. Reader, pray for the Indians.[8]

\*    \*    \*

The Princeton missionary spirit was further nurtured by the monthly Concert for Prayer, the Brotherhood, and the Society of Inquiry. The concert had had an impressive history of almost a century of uniting Christians in specific times of prayer for the advancement of God's kingdom on earth. Beginning with shared concerns of New England and Scottish ministers, the concert was given added impetus by Jonathan Edwards's 1747 writing, *A Humble Attempt to promote Explicit Agreement and Visible Union of God's People in Extraordinary Prayer for the Revival of Religion and the Advancement of Christ's Kingdom on Earth.* Among the early fruits of the concert was the awakening in 1757 at the College of New Jersey—possibly the first revival in American history "not begun by the ordinary means of preaching."[9] Renewed interest in the monthly concert in the late eighteenth century contributed to the creation of new mission boards in England and the United States.

The Concert for Prayer was a regular part of Princeton Seminary life. At first the students attended the meeting in town, but in 1827 it was moved to the seminary "on a new and more befitting plan." It was held in the Oratory on the first Monday evening of each month. After prayer, the reading of Scripture, and the singing of a hymn, there was a missionary address by a professor, student, or guest. It was at these meetings that Dr. Alexander "poured out his stores of information" on foreign missions. On September 8, 1838, Walter Lowrie wrote to his mother, "Dr. Miller made some excellent remarks at our last Monthly Concert, on the necessity of more entire dependence on the Spirit of God in the work of missions." After the address, the missionary collection was received. Prayer, a missionary hymn, the doxology, and benediction closed the service—which Samuel Miller said should be "the most instructive, the most thrilling, the most solemn exercise during the month." The observance of the concert did not always reach Miller's high standard, but it impressed the Princeton students. Joseph Barr found "something calculated to awaken the feelings of the soul, in meeting the thousands in Christendom around the mercy-seat; having in view the one great object: the redemption of our world from sin." John Freeman's "missionary feelings were nurtured," he later wrote, "by a faithful attendance on the monthly concert of prayer."

\*　　\*　　\*

The American missionary movement grew largely out of student concerns and activities and especially out of a prayer meeting. Samuel J. Mills, son of a Connecticut Congregational minister, was converted at the age of seventeen during a revival that touched his father's church. Several years later he enrolled in Williams College in Massachusetts. He often met to pray with a few other students on the banks of the Hoosic River or in the woods near the college. Caught in a thunderstorm one day, Mills and four others took refuge behind a haystack and continued to pray while they waited out the storm—asking particularly that God would awaken a foreign missionary interest among their fellow students. Further, they personally committed themselves to the work, even though at that time no American had gone overseas as a missionary. Mills told them, "We can do this if we will."[10] These students then organized themselves as the "Society of the Brethren" and pledged their desire "to go on a mission when and where duty may call."

When several of the Williams "Brethren" enrolled in Andover Seminary in 1810, they found other students interested in foreign missions and helped organize a society there. Following Andover's lead, a "Brotherhood" was formed at Princeton Seminary as early as 1820—"for the purposes of prayer and conference on the subject of missions." The condition of membership was "an expressed determination on the part of an applicant for admission of his purpose to devote himself, should his life be spared, to labor in the foreign field."

[142]

The meetings of the Princeton society were secret—"only for the purpose of doing good, and more effectually reaching every member of the seminary," one of the "Brethren" later wrote. A glimpse of the work of the Princeton "Brotherhood" is given by John Adger, a student at the seminary from 1829 to 1833. Adger told how he first received a call to foreign missions from classmate William Thomson, who invited him to "walk down to the river and take a bath" and then spent the rest of the day until bedtime talking about missions. Adger continued:

I found out after some time that my friend Thomson belonged to a secret organization of Princeton men, all specially interested in foreign missions, who made it their business to bring that subject to the attention of individuals in their respective classes. They were thus a body of propagandists. None of those whom they approached suspected that they had been selected to be operated on. Still later I found out that within this informal association there was another more formal and more secret one, consisting only of those who had made up their mind to embark in the work. Thus there was a wheel within a wheel, and both of them worked efficiently. Old Dr. Alexander, several times, met with us in this inside organization, and we got from him a great deal of useful instruction and advice.[11]

The quiet work of the "Brotherhood" went on at the seminary through the years, encouraging commitment to the missionary cause. Walter Lowrie wrote to a friend in 1838, "The missionary brethren, of whom there are some fourteen or fifteen, include some of the best men in the seminary." Sheldon Jackson was part of "the little band of devoted men who were already committed, by covenant engagements, to go to whatever part of the world-wide mission field God in His providence should direct them." Robert Nassau told of joining the private meetings of the dozen students who had definite missionary plans. One of the requirements of the Princeton "Brotherhood" was that each member, on leaving for the mission field, send the society a written account of "his early history and religious life." John Freeman, en route to India in 1838, wrote of his life and the motives which led him to consecrate himself to missionary work. He spoke of "the cheering and inspiring influence of letters from the Brethren."

\*       \*       \*

The New England students not only began the secret "Society of the Brethren" but also worked openly and zealously to recruit others to the missionary cause. On January 8, 1811, eight seminarians organized the "Society of Inquiry on the subject of Missions" at Andover Seminary. Its purpose was "to inquire into the state of the Heathen; the duty and importance of missionary labors; the best manner of conducting missions; and the most eligible places for their establishment." The example of the Andover students led to the organization of a similar society at Princeton. In February 1814 a Princeton student wrote to Andover:

I have the pleasure of informing you, that a spirit for missions is beginning to appear, in the Theological Seminary, established in this place. A committee has been appointed to draft a Constitution, for a Society of Inquiry respecting missions, similar to the one at Andover. . . . The Lord has already disposed one of our number to go to the heathen. He has given to others, a disposition to inquire into subjects relating to them. He may raise up many from this Institution also, to carry the glad news of salvation to pagan lands.

The organization at Princeton was called the "Society of Inquiry on Missions and the General State of Religion." The constitution, adopted March 1, 1814, stated that the object of the society was to obtain "important information respecting domestick and foreign missions, with a view of ascertaining our personal duty as to engaging in them." The society did not separate "foreign missionaries abroad" from "travelling missionaries in our own country," and welcomed into full membership a third category—those preparing to be "settled pastors of congregations"—asking only that they all have a heartfelt concern for mission to the whole world. The students informed the Society of Inquiry at Andover of their action and wrote to the London Missionary Society for assistance. They invited the Andover group to join in correspondence "for our mutual support and the promotion of our common object." The Andover students gladly welcomed their Princeton brethren. "As far as public semi-naries are concerned," they wrote, "we felt ourselves almost alone" in the cause of missions. They agreed with the Prince-ton students that "personal religion" be a prominent feature in their correspondence. Six months later a reply came from the London Missionary Society. The LMS was glad for the zeal of the Princeton students in the work of missions and urged their attention both to the "new settlements" in the United States and to foreign lands.

The first regular meeting of the Society of Inquiry took place on April 1, 1814. One of the members read a report on the "Life of [John] Eliot the Missionary"; and two students debated the question "In attempting the conversion of the Western Indians, ought civilization to precede Christianiz-ation?" Thus began a forty-five-year practice of Society of Inquiry meetings on the first day of each month. The original plan for the society's meetings continued for a number of years. In 1821 the usual business included reports concerning revivals, the reading of letters addressed to the society, an essay on missions, and discussion of a question selected at the previous meeting. Even though the meetings lasted four or five hours, the day was always "hailed with gladness" by the students; for they were released by it, they wrote somewhat facetiously, from "the dull routine of studious labour."

In addition to its regular monthly meetings, the Society of Inquiry conducted annual public meetings—important affairs held in the Presbyterian church. On the evening of May 14, 1830, seminary student Charles Colcock Jones of Georgia gave the address. His topic was African slavery in the United States. The large audience included townspeople, the professors and their families, local ministers, and a number of directors of the seminary. Jones, speaking in a "warm, animated manner," set forth the duty and necessity of establishing missions to the slaves of the United States. An agent of the Board of Missions of the Presbyterian Church thanked Jones for his address and told him that he would assist him in carrying out his plan.

Beginning in 1828 the public meetings were "accompanied with appropriate singing by the Handel and Hastings

Society." Sometimes one of the student missionary volunteers sang. Robert McMullin, a few months before he left for India, thrilled the gathering with his singing of "The Missionary Chant":

> My soul is not at rest. There comes a strange
> And secret whisper to my spirit, like
> A dream of night, that tells me I am on
> Enchanted ground . . .
> . . . The voice of my departed Lord,
> Go, teach all nations, from the eastern world
> Comes on the night air, and awakes my ear.

One of the first projects of the Society of Inquiry was the establishment of a library. A friend of the students collected some money, and the first books were purchased in 1813. The next year the London Missionary Society sent some publications, especially recommending a sermon by Thomas Chalmers. The Andover students shared some of their books. The General Assembly's Committee of Missions presented about two hundred manuscripts—letters, journals, and reports dated from 1803 to 1808. Missionaries sent books. Samuel Miller presented a copy of *The Memoir of the Rev. Henry Martyn* from his own library. By 1836 the library contained 1,162 titles.

In 1823 the students formed the Reading Room Association to provide access to periodicals and newspapers. The membership subscription was seventy-five cents for the winter session and fifty cents for the summer session; the professors were given honorary memberships. The reading room was the pride of the Society of Inquiry. The standing committee's report on April 1, 1829, boasted that "the reading room . . . continues to be the chief lion of the seminary—the only place about the establishment to which anyone thinks of introducing strangers." In 1848 the reading room received seventy-one publications, including newspapers, religious magazines, and theological quarterlies from Europe.

Along with the library and reading room, the Society of Inquiry maintained a "cabinet" in a little museum on the first floor of the seminary building—containing a collection of unusual items from missionaries in various parts of the world. In writing to the theological seminary in New Brunswick, New Jersey, the Princeton students asserted the need for "real and definite knowledge" to awaken missionary effort and stated that "one god made by man's hand would make a louder appeal to our sympathies than years of abstract reasoning on total depravity." Soon there were a number of "gods" resident in the cabinet. In 1832, a member of the Society of Inquiry at Tuscaloosa, Alabama, wrote to Princeton, "I have been informed that, although you are at the chief emporium of orthodoxy in the worship of the true God that nevertheless you have a number of images of heathen deities. If this be true, surely you cannot have need of their aid, we would therefore be glad to obtain some of them." Yale students wrote in 1837 to inquire whether "two idols and a cow" promised to them by a missionary had been sent by mistake to Princeton. The students were permitted to take "the smaller idols" to add interest to their missionary services and monthly concerts in Princeton and the surrounding towns. The November 24, 1847, minutes state that certain idols "went down to Sand Hill, spent the Sabbath, returned and resumed their places in the Cabinet. No damage done."

By the 1840s, the exercises of the Society of Inquiry were elaborate and lengthy. Meetings continued to be held on the first day of the month but now included both morning and afternoon sessions. After prayer, reading of the minutes, unfinished business, and the election of new members, the various corresponding secretaries reported and then the committee on obituaries. Next followed ten-minute reports from the five committees—foreign missions; home missions; revivals; Africans and colonization; and temperance and prison reform. After a hymn, one of the committees gave its annual report.

A major activity of the Society of Inquiry was extensive correspondence with other schools. An 1845 letter from Princeton to the Society of Inquiry at Brown University described the history and purpose of this correspondence:

As it has been our custom since the year 1813, when this society was organized, to correspond with societies kindred to ours in this country and in Europe; and, through sub-committees, with missionaries in all parts of the world, for the purpose of gaining missionary intelligence, strengthening our own hearts in holy zeal for our blessed Master's cause, and promoting love and sacred unity with our Christian brethren, without regard to sect: therefore, we desire to open a correspondence with your Society, in which we will give you information regarding the state of piety and missionary spirit amongst us, and desire you may return similar intelligence.

The first letter from Princeton to another school was sent to Andover Seminary in 1814; the Princeton students acknowledged that Andover had set for them "a worthy and noble example" of missionary zeal. Andover valued Princeton's participation in the missionary cause. "We hold in our hands, to a considerable extent, under God, the destinies of the missionary cause in our land," they wrote to the Princeton students in 1821.

The Princeton Society of Inquiry joined Andover to lead the student missionary movement of the first half of the nineteenth century. In 1820 the Princetonians were in touch with college religious and missionary societies at Union, Yale, Middlebury, Williams, Dartmouth, Jefferson, Ohio, Washington, Hampden-Sydney, and Transylvania. When the society was unsure of the existence of a student organization in a college, it addressed its letter more generally—as when it wrote in 1821 to "those students in the University of Cambridge (Mass.) who profess to love our Lord Jesus Christ in sincerity." The Princeton society invited students of newly founded colleges to begin organizations that would promote the cause of missions. By the 1850s, the Princeton students were corresponding with college missionary societies from Maine to Texas to Oregon. The Society of Inquiry of the new Kenyon College wrote on June 13, 1834, about Princeton Seminary's long attention to missions. They wished to imitate Princeton's "noble example of Christian benevolence." In January 1835 the Society of Inquiry of Florence Academy, Washington County, Pennsylvania, was founded. The secretary wrote to Princeton to request the "affection and kind offices of . . . an elder brother in the great fraternity of this kind of societies in the United States." The Society of Inquiry was especially concerned to establish and maintain contact with other seminaries. In the early 1820s, Princeton began correspondence with students in the theological seminary of New Brunswick, the Baptist seminary at Philadelphia, Auburn Seminary, and the seminary of the Scottish Associate Church in Philadelphia. By 1825 the Society of Inquiry was in touch with the Moravian seminary, Bethany Theological Institute in Virginia, and the German Reformed seminary at Carlisle, Pennsylvania.

As new American seminaries sprang up, the Society of Inquiry welcomed them to the cause of missions. In 1827 Princeton initiated correspondence with the students at the Theological Seminary in Prince Edward, Virginia, and suggested that letters between the two schools serve to awaken attention to the growing debate between the North and the South concerning slavery and "its removal from our land." In 1831 Princeton began to correspond with the Society of Inquiry at the new theological seminary in Columbia, South Carolina. As early as 1829 Princeton was in touch with the Presbyterian seminary at "Allegany Town" in western Pennsylvania. Correspondence with seminaries in the west often dealt with the strategic location of these schools and the importance of their vigorous effort to evangelize the frontier.

In its early years the Society of Inquiry began correspondence with theological students in Europe. In 1821 the Princeton students wrote to the missionary seminary at Gosport, England, the missionary institution at Basle, and the Society for Advancing the Kingdom of Christ at Geneva. A letter to Geneva, written in French, expressed the joy of the Princeton students "in the advancement of the Saviour's kingdom in *cette ville chérie de Genève* after a night so long," and explained that the system of theology taught at Princeton Seminary was that of Francis Turretin of Geneva. Princeton corresponded regularly with a number of theological and missionary societies in Scotland. On February 3, 1835, Robert Murray McCheyne answered one of the letters of the Princeton students to the Student Missionary Association of the University of Edinburgh. He wrote:

We desire your animating words and your unceasing prayers for ourselves in these perilous days and at the same time we would stir up the Faith and Love which sovereign mercy hath so freely implanted in us by reminding each other that on our prayers and supplications for the heathen world depends according to God's economy of Grace the Salvation of many a soul.

On April 1, 1845, the students from the New College of the Free Church of Scotland wrote to Princeton to explain the division caused in their society by the Disruption of 1843. They were forced to vacate the university and had lost their library in a lawsuit but were more grieved, they said, by the surrender of their correspondence book. In 1827 the Princeton students wrote to the students in the Royal College in Belfast, Ireland, informing them that they were praying that Ireland would again become the "Island of Saints."

Princeton provided information about the United States, the nature of its Christianity, and the progress of its missions. In a typical letter to Scottish students in 1826, Princeton described missions to the Indians and the frontier, the union of the American Board of Commissioners for Foreign Missions and the United Foreign Missions Society, the activities of the American Bible Society, and the work of "our German Reformed Brethren" and "our Baptist brethren." The Princeton letter reported that evangelical ministers were rapidly increasing in the Episcopal church, that new colleges were springing up, and that revivals were spreading in the Northern and Middle states—especially in the colleges. There were only three unconverted students at Williams College, they wrote to the Scots, and these were "serious men."

The Princeton students also wanted information from their brethren in Europe. In an 1825 letter they asked the students in Berlin specific questions concerning the religious state of Germany, biblical criticism and theology, and the condition of the Jews in Germany. The Europeans provided a flow of news concerning events in their countries and in their churches. The students in Edinburgh reported in 1840 that interest in the cause of missions was increasing in Scotland due to the work of "our beloved Dr. [Alexander] Duff." In 1849 the students at Geneva wrote about the benefits of the Revolution of 1848 to the church but added, "We have to be upon our guard—so as not to fall under the influence of that spirit of discontent, of disgust with every-thing old. . . . " In 1846 the students from the missionary institution at Basle wrote that throughout the year there was always one of their number "on a pathless road"—at sea en route to a mission field.

While the Society of Inquiry was writing to colleges and seminaries in the United States and Europe, it also carried on extensive correspondence with missionaries. In its early years, the society corresponded with the London Missionary Society and with Gordon Hall, one of the first missionaries sent out by the American Board of Commissioners for Foreign Missions to India in 1812. In 1821 the students wrote to "the Rev. Dr. Carey, Missionary at Serampore." Addressing him as "Rev. Sir, and tho' unknown Beloved father in Christ Jesus," they expressed their joy in his "truly apostolical" min-istry and asked for correspondence with him, not as equals, but "as youthful disciples—as children, who wish to learn." "Our warfare," they wrote to the Baptist missionary, "is with the common enemy: the enemy not of Baptists or Presbyterians, but of Christianity."

Writing in 1821 to Henry Woodward, the first Princeton student to go overseas as a missionary, the society stated that it was pleasant to correspond with any missionary but especially one "who has occupied the same seats, and listened to the same teachers with ourselves." In 1822 the society began correspondence with the missionaries in the Sandwich Islands; with Pliny Fisk, a missionary in Palestine; and with United States mission stations among the Chickasaw Indians. In 1826 correspondence was opened with "the colony at Liberia." The students steadily extended their corre-spondence with missionaries from different Protestant denominations serving in all parts of the world. For example, in March 1844 they wrote to the Methodist mission in Argentina, the Moravian mission in Jamaica, and the Baptist mission in Burma. The society's letters stressed the interest of the seminarians in the work of all missionaries. Their letter to William Carey stated, "The different names by which we are known in the Christian church, and the different views we take of points not essential, will not be suffered to affect our feelings toward you, or to damp our joy at your success."

The students tried to write interesting and factual letters. The general preface to the register of correspondence of the Committee on Foreign Missions advised writers of letters to missionaries to provide "facts and birds' eye views, not reasonings." A typical letter was sent to a missionary in Bombay on August 1, 1825, from John W. Nevin, the fourth corresponding secretary of the Society of Inquiry. The letter began with news of other seminaries. It reported that Auburn charged only half as much as Princeton and that the General Assembly of the Presbyterian Church was considering a new seminary in Ohio. "Civil and religious intelligences" followed. General Lafayette's visit to America had been "one long triumphant circuit." The canal from Albany to Buffalo was almost complete. Creek Indian difficulties had erupted in Georgia. The letter told of new colleges springing up in the South and West and stated that the new college in Danville, Kentucky, would "stand as a bulwark of truth against the heresy and infidelity of Transylvania University." It reported that there had been frequent revivals recently and that "a new national institution" had been established—a tract society in which "all denominations of true Christians are to cooperate." Some slaveholders had "generously freed their slaves and helped in having them sent away." The letter stated that the Colonization Society had the "promise of mighty moral influence both upon the United States and upon the gloomy desolations of Africa."

A letter sent in 1832 to Lorrin Andrews, former Society of Inquiry member and missionary in the Sandwich Islands, reported increased interest in missions at the seminary, revivals in Princeton, and a growing division in the Presbyterian church. It summarized the recent activities of the various benevolent societies and discussed the Southampton (Virginia) slave insurrection, colonization, and Liberia. It reported the commissioning of two Princeton students as missionaries to Africa with the new Western Foreign Mission Board. The letter concluded with news of general interest—the flood in Ohio, cholera in Europe, wars in Egypt and Mexico, Indian difficulties in the West, and the new constitution of Colombia.

Missionaries valued such letters. Former student John

Freeman wrote from India in 1840 to thank the society for detailed and minute information, welcome because it was news "and not a stereotyped exhortation on pastoral theology" like a letter received from another seminary, "valuable for nothing except the distance it had traveled." Not only did the missionaries appreciate news from America. John Philip, superintendent of the London Missionary Society's work in southern Africa, read his letter from the Princeton students at his mission's stations. He wrote, "It was the occasion of much refreshing to the missionaries and to the people. The poor Hottentots were greatly rejoiced at the accounts you have given us of the success of the Gospel in America."

The students also desired to receive information from the missionaries. Although they hesitated to ask Gordon Hall to write to them since "the moments it will take might possibly have saved a soul," their letters were filled with questions concerning the training and qualifications of missionaries, life and ministry overseas, and missionary strategy and success. In replying to the Princeton students, John Philip stated, "I have had many letters from Europe, inquiring as to the success with which our missionary labours have been attended, but your letter is the first I have seen confessing ignorance as to the manner in which such labours should be conducted, and at the same time praying for information on the subject."

The Society of Inquiry drew up a set of "standing questions" for use by the corresponding secretaries in writing to missionaries. Nine topics were covered. The first set of questions dealt with qualifications and preparation for missionary work. The second topic concerned the question of the missionary call and "duty to the heathen." The third set of questions had to do with preparation for the voyage and outfit—such as what clothes to take and how to pack books so they would not be damaged "by chafing from the motion of the vessel." The fourth topic concerned "missionary employments" and strategy in presenting the gospel to people in other lands. The fifth set of questions dealt with "the state of the heathen"—including religious, social, and civil conditions of foreign peoples. The sixth group of questions concentrated on the missionary's encouragements and trials. The seventh set asked for trustworthy sources of information about the various countries where the missionaries worked. The eighth group of questions asked about climate, population, and government. The ninth set included miscellaneous topics, such as the influence of foreign residents on missionary work.

The Society of Inquiry heard regularly from missionaries, and its records were soon filled with valuable information. Often the missionaries went beyond merely answering the students' questions. Gordon Hall sent to Princeton a report on Hindu worship with beautifully painted pictures of the ten incarnations of Vishnu.

\*    \*    \*

The Princetonians not only read about missions and wrote to missionaries; they also supported missions financially. One of the earliest projects at the seminary was the missionary box in the Oratory where students and faculty put their donations. Special missionary offerings were received at the monthly Concert for Prayer. Money collected by the Society of Inquiry as fines for the absence or lateness of members was used to support missions among the western Indians! In 1821 a garden was being cultivated by students, who gave the proceeds to missions. In the early 1820s most students helped support two little native boys in Ceylon—named "Archibald Alexander" and "Samuel Miller"—who were living with the family of Princeton missionary Henry Woodward. Years later, the Princeton students were supporting another "Samuel Miller."[12] In 1839 he wrote his Princeton benefactors, sending them an exquisitely drawn map of Jaffna and informing them of how he had been challenged by the question of his eternal destiny so that "I lastly ran to Jesus and embraced him as my saviour, master, and leader."

In addition to supporting missions financially, the students became involved in evangelistic and missionary projects of their own. The seminarians did not hesitate to engage Princeton townspeople in serious conversations; one of these recalled a time in her girlhood when she would cross the street if she saw a seminary student approaching "lest he address to her some gentle word concerning her soul"!

The students carried on regular ministries in the vicinity of Princeton. The Society of Inquiry wrote to the Episcopalian students in Virginia on April 9, 1831, "Many of us are engaged in conducting Sabbath schools and social prayer meetings within a circuit of ten or twelve miles around this village." The Princeton Sabbath School Society had been organized in 1815, principally through the efforts of student John S. Newbold. By 1822 there were eighteen schools in Princeton and its vicinity—each with a seminary student as superintendent. The fourth annual meeting of all the Sabbath schools was held on August 31, 1822. Six hundred "scholars" were present to hear an address by Archibald Alexander.

Sunday schools for the African Americans of Princeton and its vicinity were begun by Robert Baird and other students in the early 1820s. Many were taught to read and were instructed in Christianity by the students in these Sunday schools. In the late 1850s Robert Nassau, two other students, and some of the young women of Princeton taught Sunday school in the town's black Presbyterian church—making the school, Nassau wrote, "Cupid's camping ground"!

Some of the student-led Sunday schools and prayer meetings became new churches. Charles J. Jones, converted in 1841 after twenty years as a sailor, studied at Princeton Seminary for three years. During this time he established a prayer meeting in town. Thirty people were converted and formed the nucleus of the Second Presbyterian Church.

Of special concern to the students were the missionary opportunities presented by the men who worked on the nearby Delaware and Raritan Canal. The canal, which connected New York and Philadelphia by inland waterway, was completed in 1834. Ten years later about five thousand men—many of them Roman Catholic immigrants—were working on the busy canal. For a number of years the students brought Bibles and tracts to people living near the canal, who then gave them to the boatmen. Over one hundred Bibles and about fifteen thousand pages of tracts were distributed annually.

In 1845 the students, deciding that the "voice of the living teacher" was also needed, appointed one of their number, William Bannard, as missionary to the boatmen. He was commissioned by the American Bethel Society and supported in part by the Missionary, Bible, and Tract Society of the seminary. Bannard worked for eleven weeks during the summer, visiting over two hundred boats, conversing with four thousand people, and distributing eight thousand pages of tracts. He attempted to obtain a promise from the boatmen that they would stop swearing; he persuaded three hundred of them to sign a petition to close the canal to shipping on Sundays. He sought to awaken churches near the canal to "the importance of cultivating this part of the great field of the world." For a number of years the Missionary, Bible, and Tract Society appointed and supported one of its members as a summer missionary on the canal. One year it also funded the establishment of a reading room with 230 books for the use of the canal workers.

In 1822 the Andover students challenged the Princetonians with a call to "do good" even while in seminary, by adopting some plan for the "long vacation."[13] Both schools, the letter continued, were near large cities which contained multitudes who were "almost as ignorant of Christ as the inhabitants of Hindostan." The Princeton students were already active in mission work during their vacations. Student missionaries were sent out regularly on special missions to neighboring cities and towns and to the "Pines" and other "destitute" parts of New Jersey. They preached and distributed literature; started Sunday schools, Bible classes, and monthly concerts; established religious libraries; and organized churches.

The seminarians joined the college students in 1817 to organize the Nassau Hall Tract Society. Members of the society were frequently seen at the Nassau Street market talking to the farmers and leaving tracts in their baskets. During vacations students gave tracts to travelers and road workers and threw them into passing wagons. By 1822 they had distributed 43,800 tracts—with titles such as "Keeping the Sabbath," "Day of Judgment," and "Swearer's Prayer." The 1846 report of the tract keeper of the Association for Benevolent Purposes stated that almost 20,000 pages of tracts had been distributed or sold by members during the past year.

From the seminary's founding, students were involved in efforts "to circulate among the poor and the destitute the Word of God." Challenged by the example of the English students at Cambridge, the students of the college and seminary formed the Bible Society of Nassau Hall on February 27, 1813. This was the first local, and the first college, Bible society in the United States. It supported the distribution of the Bible among the poor of Newark, the Germans in Pennsylvania, the pioneers of the west, federal soldiers and sailors, and the French in Louisiana. At its ninth annual meeting the Nassau Hall Bible Society was congratulated for "having led the way" among colleges and seminaries.

On July 31, 1827, the Nassau Hall Bible Society resolved to supply a Bible to every "destitute" family in New Jersey within a year. Forty students (thirty from the seminary) agreed to spend their fall vacation in this effort. Over sixty-five hundred Bibles and one hundred thousand tracts were distributed. On January 1, 1828, the Society of Inquiry wrote to students in Edinburgh that now every family in New Jersey had a Bible. The students hoped that the example of the Nassau Hall Bible Society would be followed by the state Bible societies and that "the long prayed for time is near, when there will not be a family in the nation without a Bible." The example of the Princeton students did spread to Bible societies in Pennsylvania, Delaware, Vermont, and Maryland; in May 1828 the American Bible Society decided to supply every family in the United States with a copy of the Bible within two years.

The Bible project revealed an appalling number of people unable to read. A meeting was held in Princeton on December 13, 1827, in which a number of citizens determined to raise forty thousand dollars for "the support of Missionaries and the establishment of schools in destitute parts of the State." The seminary students were involved in this project as well. A year later, the Society of Inquiry reported to the missionaries in the Sandwich Islands that a large part of the money had been collected and that twenty-five schools had been established. The students expected aid from the New

Jersey legislature to establish "one uniform and efficient system of education in the state." The Princeton effort and the newspaper essays of seminary graduate Robert Baird, who was serving as an agent of the New Jersey Missionary Society, resulted in the passing of the school law of 1829, which created the public school system in New Jersey.

Beginning in the 1820s, most of the major benevolent societies employed "agents"—frequently seminary students— to go from town to town promoting their particular cause, distributing tracts, and organizing local auxiliaries. Many of the Princeton students used their vacations for this purpose. During the spring vacation of 1832, Joseph Barr worked for the American Tract Society. In six weeks he traveled over four hundred miles—mostly on foot—preached thirty-four times, and collected $825. "My principal object," he wrote to his father, "was to obtain funds for foreign distribution. This gave me an opportunity of pleading the cause of the heathen world."

During the summer of 1847 the Female Seamen's Friend Society sent Charles J. Jones to New London, Connecticut, as a missionary to the thousand men from the large fleet of whaling ships then in port. Jones visited the ships and boarding houses, distributed Bibles and tracts, and preached on board the vessels and in the various churches. Robert Nassau spent the summer vacation of 1857 as a colporteur for the Presbyterian Board of Publication. He asked for the most difficult field and was assigned to Missouri and Kansas. The following summer Nassau served as a missionary with the Philadelphia Sabbath Association, working among the boatmen on the Pennsylvania Canal.

\*　　\*　　\*

From its earliest days, Princeton Seminary was a center of mission study and activity. The faculty were missionary-minded men; but much of the credit must go to the students. They collected information on missions, challenged each other to missionary commitment, and kept in touch with other students at home and abroad. They worked to evangelize Princeton and the nearby towns and villages and, during their vacations, spread out across the country in mission projects. Before many years had passed, students from the little Presbyterian seminary were preaching the gospel and planting churches throughout America and in many foreign lands. The single most vital force producing Princeton's lively missionary vision was the student-run Society of Inquiry. In Archibald Alexander's opinion,

. . . no part of the exercises in the Theological Seminary has been attended with more manifest good effect than those which appertain to the proceedings of this Society; and there can be little doubt, that some of those who are now laboring successfully among the heathen, received their first missionary impulse from the ideas suggested, the intelligence received, and the solemn scenes which they here witnessed; and when the thoughts of those who have been removed for years from the place of their Theological education, revisit these sacred walls, there is probably nothing which is remembered with deeper interest, than the transactions of the first day of the month.

Graduates did remember the first day of the month. From the Ganges River, John Freeman wrote in 1839 about the practical knowledge and happy hours of Christian communion that the Society of Inquiry had given him. Walter Lowrie wrote from Macao on November 20, 1843: " . . . the thoughts of hallowed seasons in the old Oratory where you meet, have been among the most pleasant of the many pleasant recollections I have brought from the land of my birth." Caleb Baldwin, in China in 1850, remembered "that room where love for the Saviour and love for souls have so glowed in my heart."

# 9

# School of the Prophets

*Statue of George Whitefield at the University of Pennsylvania. The influence of Whitefield was immense in creating vision for the kind of men needed in the Christian ministry.*

Dear Brother, pray for us, that, in this school of the prophets, that Holy Spirit of sanctification and of zeal, which we daily pray may be poured upon all churches, may be poured out in his most plenteous effusions.

SAMUEL MILLER
to Asahel Nettleton
May 19, 1824

DURING the first decades of the nineteenth century the young American nation grew rapidly. As transportation and commerce moved people westward, Kentucky and Tennessee each passed the half-million mark. By 1830, Ohio had almost one million people—more than the population of Massachusetts and Connecticut combined. Protestant Christians were optimistically and energetically working to further evangelism and Christian ideals in the new nation, especially on the frontier.

Cooperating through the Plan of Union, Congregationalists and Presbyterians planted churches in the West. New seminaries were started to assist in the great task of national evangelism and world missions. The second Presbyterian seminary was located at Auburn, New York, in 1818. Catering to the Plan of Union churches, Auburn attracted many students from New England and New York.

The seminary at Hampden-Sydney College (since 1812 a department of the college) was reorganized as a distinct school in 1823. The founder of the new seminary, John Holt Rice, wrote to his friend Archibald Alexander at Princeton:

If . . . a Seminary can be established in the South, many will frequent it, who will not go to the North . . . But my plan is, if we can succeed here, to take Princeton as our model, to hold constant correspondence with that great and most valuable institution, to get the most promising of our young men to finish off at Princeton; and, in a word, as far as possible, make this a sort of branch of that,

[163]

so as to have your spirit diffused through us, and do all that can be done to bind the different parts of the Church together.[1]

The Virginia school came under the control of the synods of Virginia and North Carolina and was appropriately named Union Seminary.

At the General Assembly of 1825, Ashbel Green moved that the Presbyterian church begin a new seminary in the West. Two years later, the theological seminary of Allegheny Town was founded in western Pennsylvania. Allegheny's two full-time faculty members, Luther Halsey and John Nevin, had both taught at Princeton—one in the college and the other in the seminary—and they did their best to transplant the Princeton plan, curriculum, and textbooks.

The Synod of South Carolina and Georgia began a theological seminary in 1828, which located in Columbia, South Carolina, two years later.

The reputation of Archibald Alexander, Samuel Miller, and Charles Hodge was strongly established, however, and continued to attract many students to Princeton. John Adger came from South Carolina in 1829. "The professors at Princeton in my day," he later wrote, "were only three in number, but they were as good in every respect as could be found at that time in this country."[2] In 1830, Thomas Smyth, a student at Highbury College in London, planned to come to America and asked his teachers which seminary he should attend. They told him to go, by all means, where Dr. Alexander and Dr. Miller were. John Lowrie came in the fall of 1832— "attracted by the fame of the senior Professors."[3]

In the early years, students traveled to Princeton by horseback or coach. Some came for hundreds of miles—a journey marked by changes from stagecoach to stageboat and back again, by dangerous ferry trips over great rivers, and by nights in uncomfortable wayside taverns. Traveling from Philadelphia to New York in the 1820s, Frances Trollope— distinguished writer, world traveler, and mother of the famed novelist, Anthony Trollope—described her experience with American stagecoaches: "At Trenton, the capital of New Jersey, we left our smoothly-gliding comfortable boat for the most detestable stage-coach that ever a Christian built to dislocate the joints of his fellow men. Ten of those torturing machines were crammed full of passengers who left the boat with us." Stage-coach travel would have seemed luxurious, however, to some who made their way to Princeton. In November 1833, two young men carrying all their clothes in backpacks reached the seminary for the beginning of the term; they had walked from Tennessee! "Such men are worth helping," J. W. Alexander wrote; "such men do the work of the church."[4]

In 1834, the Delaware and Raritan Canal was completed. Skirting the edge of Princeton, the canal joined Philadelphia with New Brunswick by inland waterway but after one year was no longer used for passenger travel. By this time, the Camden and Amboy Railroad connected New York and Philadelphia (a seven-hour train ride). Stage-coaches met the trains at Hightstown and took students and other travelers into Princeton. Several years later the rails of the Trenton and New Brunswick Line were laid on the banks of the canal, and by 1839 the puffing engine and train of wooden cars, brought students for the seminary and college to the station at the foot of Canal Street.

The little village of Princeton, with its fine old trees and college and seminary buildings, resembled an English university town. Nassau Street was lined with shops and inns on its north side and on the south with the college's four buildings—Nassau Hall, the Refectory, Philosophical Hall (containing the library, classrooms, and two literary societies—Whig and Clio) and the president's house. Three thousand people—more than a fifth of whom were African Americans, both slaves and free—lived in the town.

Since 1823, the president of Princeton College had been James Carnahan: an amiable, honest, unassuming man and a successful preacher and teacher. Descended from Scotch-Irish Presbyterians of the Cumberland Valley in Pennsylvania, Carnahan graduated from Princeton College in 1800.

Ashbel Green had lost the support of the majority of the trustees and resigned at the fall commencement in 1822. During his ten years as president, he had strengthened the faculty and doubled the size of the student body. Of the 356 graduates who left Nassau Hall during Green's administration, twenty became college presidents; four, United States senators; and eleven, congressmen. Many others became ministers of the gospel. It was, however, a period troubled with major college riots. The revival of 1815 had been followed by the "Great Rebellion" two years later, much to Ashbel Green's dismay (who years later admitted that he had made the mistake of thinking that "if the College was once reduced to a state of entire order, it would be likely to remain in that state").[5] The students protested their heavy assignments by nailing up all entrances to Nassau Hall, together with the doors of the rooms of the tutors and religious students. Then rushing up to the top floor—yelling "rebellion! rebellion! fire! fire!"—they broke the windows and rang the bell incessantly. Dr. Green called the militia to besiege the barricaded Nassau Hall, but fortunately it failed to appear, and the students finally grew tired and opened the building. Green was mortified that such a rebellion had occurred under his administration but took comfort in the fact that "Washington's administration was not free from it; nay, we know that there was a rebellion in heaven itself."[6]

Some, including Samuel Stanhope Smith, saw Green as an overly strict disciplinarian; and some historians have viewed his administration as the "nadir" of the college's history. Charles Hodge spoke for the seminary, however, when he recalled Dr. Green's practice of observing the first Monday of the month as a day of fasting and prayer and commented, "This was the spirit in which his administration was begun and continued to the end."[7] John Maclean, who knew Dr. Green well, said that "he was a truly great, good, humble and devout man. . . . He was conscientious and upright, free from deceit and even from the appearance of it."[8]

After Ashbel Green's resignation, the board unanimously elected John H. Rice of Richmond, Virginia. Rice declined and not long afterwards accepted a call to the chair of systematic theology at Hampden-Sydney College. Philip Lindsley served as interim president during the 1822-23 session. He declined the presidency of Princeton, accepting instead the presidency of Cumberland College in Tennessee, where he remained for twenty-six years, playing a notable role in the educational life of the South. On May 12, 1823, the trustees elected James Carnahan. He was later described by one of the college students as "a man of huge common sense, kindness of heart and excellent executive ability."[9]

James Carnahan was born November 15, 1775, near Carlisle, Pennsylvania. He graduated with the highest honor from Princeton College in 1800. After a year of private theological study he became a tutor at the college, continuing his study under President Smith. On December 1, 1803, he married Mary Van Dyke of Mapleton, New Jersey. Carnahan was ordained in 1805 and served as pastor of two Presbyterian churches in New York State. In 1814 he moved to Georgetown in the District of Columbia, where he founded a successful classical academy. He taught there until he was called to the presidency of his alma mater in 1823.

Princeton College was still a small school with a president, one or two professors, and several tutors. In the 1830s, however, the faculty grew to include some of the ablest teachers in the country. John Maclean, son of Princeton's first professor of chemistry, taught ancient languages and literature. He was assisted by Joseph Addison Alexander, the son of Archibald Alexander. Addison's brother, J. W. Alexander, was professor of rhetoric, Latin, and English literature. Stephen Alexander, who studied at Union College and Princeton Seminary and knew Latin, Greek, Hebrew and the major European languages, assisted Dod in mathematics and later taught astronomy and natural philosophy. Henry Vethake taught economics, natural philosophy, and chemistry. John Torrey was called to the chair of chemistry and natural history in 1830 and became one of the country's greatest botanists. Joseph Henry was a brilliant and self taught scientist of international reputation.[10] In 1836, decades before Marconi was born, Henry—with black Sam as his assistant—sent wireless transmissions from his old laboratory to his home, and made experiments in telegraphy which antedated the work of Morse. Henry habitually introduced his laboratory work by saying, "Young gentlemen, we are about to ask God a question." A later professor of church history at Princeton Seminary wrote that Joseph Henry's "exceptional greatness as a man of science gave celebrity to the institution," and his "transparent goodness endeared him to both colleagues and students."[11]

Albert B. Dod, a graduate of both the college and seminary, was a winsome and effective professor of mathematics and of almost everything else. With "flashing wit and silvery voice," he taught physics, philosophy, literature, architecture, and theology. Charles Hodge said of Professor Dod, "There was nothing that he could not make plain." When Dod once attended the annual examination of the cadets at West Point, the students and professors were so impressed with his superior intellect and skillful instruction that they urged the United States government to appoint him chaplain and professor of moral philosophy. Hodge often praised Dod's ability. "His mind was always on the alert, and teeming with thoughts and suggestions," Hodge wrote. "It was a common thing for him, when he entered my study, to say,—'I was thinking, as I came along, of such or such a question,' —announcing some problem in mental or moral science." Hodge continued, "Indeed I do not know that I ever was acquainted with a man, who so constantly suggested important topics of conversation, or kept the minds of his friends more on the stretch."[12] A Presbyterian minister, Dod was a frequent contributor to the *Biblical Repertory*.

As the college had been a "school for statesmen" in the days of Witherspoon, it was now a great institution for the study of science. After Greek, Latin, mathematics, and philosophy, the students looked forward eagerly to their senior year when they had the privilege of studying under Princeton's distinguished scientists—the most able in the country.

As the faculty grew, so did the campus. Behind Nassau Hall, East College and West College were built as dormitories; and the quadrangle was completed in 1837 with the erection of two wooden and stucco buildings, Whig Hall and Clio Hall, for the debating and literary societies. Until the 1830s, the college student body numbered less than one hundred. In 1829 there were seventy students; ten years later 270 young men were enrolled at Princeton. With pride, Professor J. W. Alexander described the final examinations at the college:

I wish . . . our Final Examinations . . . were public. Nothing could do so much justice to our methods of teaching. It lasts from 8 to 10 days; hours 8:30 - 12, and 2 - 5. Most of the subjects (about 16) are, on the English-University plan, from papers, embodying the chief points of the whole subject; the same paper to each; not seen before the moment; no book, reference, or communication allowed. Some of the best scholars answer every question in full . . . . There is perfect silence, and it is a fine moral spectacle to see 70 odd young men so intensely employed.[13]

The college students took much interest in the debates in Clio and Whig, learning to form intelligent opinions and to express them clearly with force and wit. They also showed the beginning of "school spirit" when, in the dead of night, they drove a wagon pulled by four horses to Rutgers College and captured the Revolutionary War cannon which had been sent to New Brunswick during the War of 1812.

The faculty worked hard to promote Christian commitment among the college students. J. W. Alexander wrote, "I never knew a more assiduous pastor than Professor Maclean: he daily talks with some of the youth; and is doing more good than any of us."[14] The two Sunday meetings were well attended, as was the half-hour prayer meeting every evening at 6:30. The Philadelphia Society, founded in 1825 by four students "to promote the personal piety of its members," met once a week for an hour in the evening and held a Sunday morning service for prayer and exhortation.

The college and seminary were closely connected. Every other week, a literary club brought together the teachers of the two schools. College personnel often visited the simple, dignified "seminary" building—its three stories flanked by the homes of Dr. Alexander and Dr. Hodge—to attend classes and worship services. In 1834 a chapel, designed by the noted Princeton architect Charles Steadman, was built a little behind the space between the seminary building and Dr. Alexander's home, facing Mercer Street. Its Greek Revival style and impressive classical columns added a new dimension to the little campus. The six thousand dollars needed for the chapel had been collected in Philadelphia and New York by Charles Hodge. An identical building—in the manner of Whig and Clio Halls on the college campus—

to be placed between the seminary building and Dr. Hodge's home was planned but never built. Across the street from the seminary the Episcopal church was being built; and throughout the town, some half-dozen handsome homes. The colonial red brick and stone of Princeton was giving way to white clapboard houses which lined the town's placid streets. It was a delightful place. J. W. Alexander, who moved back to Princeton in late 1833, wrote of "the greenness, the airiness, the fragrance, the healthfulness, the over—over—overflowing of fruits, and the otherwise varied delightfulness of Princeton."[15]

The students appreciated the convenience and comfort of the seminary. Charles C. Jones settled in at Princeton in October 1829 and wrote his fiancée, "I am now located in the Seminary building in a warm, well furnished, and carpeted room, with *separate bed rooms*, with a class-mate, Mr. Jonathan Trumbull Backus."[16] The catalogue for 1837-38 indicated that there was no charge for either tuition or room, but each student was required to pay $10 per year to the "general expense fund." Board in the refectory cost $1.25 to $1.75 a week. Rooms were heated by fireplaces, wood for which cost $6 to $10 a year.

The 1832 seminary year began with an address by Archibald Alexander entitled "Plea for Absolute Devotion to God in the Work of the Ministry." Alexander told the students:

You are coming forward, my young friends, at an eventful period of the world. Read then the signs of the times. Let every man be found at his post and standing in his lot. Let no one now entering the ministry dream of a quiet or easy life, or of literary leisure.[17]

The students took seriously their call to the ministry and tried to be faithful and diligent. First-year students concentrated on Hebrew (Greek already having been learned in college) and biblical studies and began the study of theology. During the second year, students did exegetical study of the Bible in Greek and Hebrew and worked on theology, church history, and missions. Third-year students continued exegesis and theology and added church government, pastoral theology, and preaching.

The seminarians visited people in and around Princeton and preached on Sundays. From time to time, they found other ways to serve. When an epidemic of sickness broke out in the college, one of the seminary students gave himself with such diligence to nursing the sick that Dr. Alexander expressed doubt as to whether he really remained a student in the seminary. In 1832 cholera struck the canal workers on the edge of town. J. W. Alexander wrote that his brother William, a doctor, had "been with a large proportion of those who have died; some he has watched and rubbed all night; some he has picked up and carried in his arms to their dying beds . . . . Some of the theological students have deserved nobly of our neighbourhood, by their devotion in nursing, etc."[18]

The faculty expected the students to work hard. They also were concerned with the importance of their "taking the requisite amount of wholesome exercise" but could not decide on a plan. Dr. Alexander reported to the directors in 1828 that the system called "gymnastick" was in vogue, but "it has been doubted by many judicious persons, whether the use, especially of some parts of that system, is of a sufficiently grave character for theological students." Many students took their exercise by walking—on crisp autumn days or in the spring when the leaves and buds were first appearing in woods and fields. Sometimes they made their way through lanes and meadows to Pretty Brook, to sit beside the stream and read; sometimes they headed for Morgan's Quarry, or walked beside the canal or along the Millstone River.

The great commission of Christ—"the last command," as the Princetonians often called it—compelled an increasing number of the seminary students to become foreign missionaries. On August 17, 1831, the professors and students observed a day of fasting and prayer with six of their colleagues who were ready to depart for mission work overseas. "They are beloved youth—all of them manifesting a primitive zeal and love," J. W. Alexander wrote; "The Lord go with them and bless them."[19] The next year Joseph Barr, who had transferred to Princeton from Andover to satisfy his Presbyterian father, cut short his seminary preparation to go to Africa.[20] He wrote to his father on September 5,

1832, "After seeking Divine guidance, and consulting my professors, who were unanimous in the opinion that I had better go, I have written to the Board that I will . . . go." On October 12, Barr was ordained by the Presbytery of Philadelphia. Dr. Alexander preached on the command of Christ to make disciples of all nations, and Dr. Miller delivered the charge. Before the ship sailed for Africa, however, Barr was stricken with cholera and died on October 28.

The death of Joseph Barr stirred the seminary. The Society of Inquiry asked Dr. Miller to preach a memorial sermon. Miller, who just days before had lost his own nineteen-year-old son, challenged the students to receive Barr's death as a personal call to missions. He said:

O, if we could see 120, or 130 heroic youths here assembled, all of them burning with the same love and zeal that burned in the bosom of the beloved Barr, what impression, under God, might not be expected speedily to be made on this community; and ultimately on the world?

Archibald Alexander was strongly tempted by an invitation from the Synod of Virginia to become the president of Union Seminary after the death of his close friend, John Holt Rice, in 1831. Despite his years in the North, he was always drawn to his native Virginia. Student John Adger from South Carolina wrote that "old Dr. Alexander was not only by birth a Southerner, but in all the characteristic features of our people."[21] Furthermore, Alexander feared that Princeton would become "a bone of contention" in the rising ecclesiastical conflict in the Presbyterian church. Alexander would have left Princeton in "the capable hands of Charles Hodge" and gone to Union if, as he wrote, "I were younger and more capable of answering their expectations."[22]

John Holt Rice's brother Benjamin was married to Archibald Alexander's sister. In 1833 Benjamin, after a successful pastorate in Petersburg, Virginia, and a short ministry at the Pearl Street Presbyterian Church in New York City, was called to the First Presbyterian Church in Princeton. The fifty-year-old Rice was an effective preacher and a greatly beloved pastor. He made the manse on Witherspoon Street a center of southern hospitality, and his daughters were among the belles of the village. On July 6, 1835, the church burned down again—the fire caused by a skyrocket landing on the roof. A year and a half later, a new building designed by Charles Steadman was ready for use. The brick building, with its Corinthian columns, was much admired as a handsome model of simplicity and good taste. Its gallery and pulpit were designed by Professor Albert B. Dod.

\*   \*   \*

Dr. Alexander's abundant brown hair was turning slightly gray, and he suffered from brief attacks of rheumatism made worse by the east wind. He gave up his long walks in the early mornings, his horseback riding, and swimming—which he loved as a boy and young man. His wife, Janetta, was a help and blessing to her husband—"such a gift as God bestows only on the most favored," their son wrote. He shared everything with her, and "when his spirits flagged, she was always prompt and skilful to cheer and comfort."[23] They both loved music and often sang together their favorite psalms and hymns. They entertained often, and Dr. Alexander was "most elated when his table was fullest."[24] Students came and went constantly, the earlier students of the seminary remembering Mrs. Alexander as "a mother or an elder sister."[25] She was active and successful in gathering support for those in need.

Janetta's mind was quick and her memory remarkable. Despite her poor eyesight, she continued to read the old books she had come to love in her childhood home— Wilson's *Sacra Privata*, Bennet's *Divine Oratory*, Traill's *Sermons on the Throne of Grace*, Flavel's *Treatises*, Newton's *Cardiphonia*, Cowper's *Poems and Letters*, and Boston's *Fourfold State*. She was known to her family as a gifted interpreter of Scripture. James wrote of the "admiration and love" which his brother Addison, the author of a number of commentaries on books of the Bible, had for their mother. "I have seen him, numbers of times, leave his writing to go to her and read the verse he was commenting upon, and ask what she supposed it meant; and I once heard him say, her common sense, in certain matters of this kind, was worth more than all the commentaries in the world."[26]

[173]

The Alexanders had six sons and one daughter. The daughter was named Janetta for her mother. The first son was named for his mother's father, James Waddel; Dr. Alexander named another for himself. The others were named for famous men—Samuel Davies, the Virginia pastor and president of Princeton College; Henry Martyn, missionary; William Cowper, poet; and Joseph Addison, scholar. Dr. and Mrs. Alexander loved and enjoyed their children. James Waddel wrote of his father that "except in hours of devotion, his study was always free to his children, even the youngest; noise made no difference; their books and toys were on his floor. . . ."[27]

The Alexander children probably learned more at home than they did at school. Dr. Alexander taught them spelling, arithmetic, geography, algebra, geometry, the classical languages, and especially the Bible. He selected Scripture verses for them to memorize and rewarded them with little gifts of money. As soon as they could understand English words, he began to teach them Latin, listing each day a number of Latin words with their meanings for them to memorize. When Joseph Addison showed unusual interest and ability in languages, his father wrote out the Hebrew alphabet for the six-year-old boy; a little later he prepared a manuscript Hebrew grammar adapted to his age, with the title page:

Hebrew Grammar
with the points
Translated from Leusden's
Compend of Buxtorf,
For Joseph Addison Alexander
Princeton, New Jersey
A.D. 1819

Dr. Alexander lived next door to the seminary building, and this proximity to his classes made him quite sedentary. His son remarked in wonder that "it is certain that in the last thirty years of his life, he used as little bodily motion as any man of his times; confining himself not only to one apartment, but to one chair." From that chair he could see the distant horizon marked by blue hills, which must have reminded him of his Virginia home. He loved to "sit alone, in silence, generally in the twilight, or musing over the fire, in deep and seemingly pleasurable thought." James Waddel attributed his father's originality, clarity, and "extraordinary readiness at almost any time to rise in extemporaneous address" to this daily and lifelong habit of quiet thought.[28]

On the stroke of the bell for class, Dr. Alexander would emerge from his study, wrapped in his cloak, and step quickly to the seminary building. In his classroom, after reading a passage, he would shift his square spectacles back over his forehead and look out piercingly at the class as he gave his extempore comments in a high, clear voice. He was a gifted teacher and had "the art," his son wrote, "of making every learner willing."[29]

Much of Dr. Alexander's time was spent in personal counseling. J. W. Alexander wrote in 1835, "I know not a busier man in the world than my old father. And half of every day is spent in talking with students privately. True, he does not chase them from room to room, or run through the roll, but he never chains up his gate, or pleads any business to exclude any one, at any hour."[30] Dr. Alexander was able to get quickly to a problem and offered kind, helpful advice. One of his students said that of all Dr. Alexander's strengths, nothing impressed him more than his wonderful knowledge of people and their needs; he described him as "the Shakespeare of the Christian heart."[31] After hearing Alexander preach, a noted figure from the town surmised that "Dr. Alexander must have been very wicked in his youth, or he could not know so well how wicked men felt."[32]

A stream of students and others waited on him for counsel. Charles Hodge once said, "If any student went to Dr. Alexander in a state of despondence, the venerable man was sure to tell him, 'Look not too much within. Look to Christ. Dwell on his person, on his work, on his promises, and devote yourself to his service, and you will soon find peace.'"[33] Dr. Alexander gladly talked with all who came, but he did not want to waste time. Occasionally, during a caller's boring monologue, he was not beyond the temptation to "abstract his eye and his attention, and hum a tune to himself"! Once a zealous student attempted to convert Alexander to the position of total abstinence. Alexander talked with him at some length, but finally his patience forsook him and he said, "Mr. B——, I made up my mind on this subject before you were born." As a general rule, Dr. Alexander never drank wine; but when its use came to be considered sinful by many, he would sometimes, in company, take a glass "for conscience sake."[34] Dr. Alexander greatly disliked religious show or pretense. A man once interrogated Alexander concerning the evidences of his personal piety. Provoked by Alexander's silence, the man exclaimed: "Have you *no religion*, Dr. Alexander?" "None to speak of," was the quiet reply.[35]

Archibald Alexander's first book, *A Brief Outline of the Evidences of the Christian Religion* (1825), was published when he was fifty-three.[36] Thereafter he wrote substantial books on theology, Bible history, Christian life, church history, and a history of African colonization, in addition to several volumes of sermons. He contributed many important articles to the *Biblical Repertory* including such varied topics as: "The Catechism of the Council of Trent," "Evidences of a New Heart," "The Present State and Prospects of the Presbyterian Church," and "Mr. H. Everett's Report on Indian Affairs." These few titles indicate Alexander's interest in theology, the Christian life, the health of the church, and the welfare of neglected people. In the introduction to his *Selection of Hymns* (1831), he explained the value of hymns to Christians, noted the various uses that can be made of them in a person's life, and stated that even those "who seem to be wide apart in regard to many speculative points, can often harmonize in their devotional exercises." Alexander added:

Christians frequently differ more from each other in appearance than in reality: for they who can sincerely and cordially unite in the same prayers, and in the same spiritual songs, must be of one heart and one mind in all that constitutes the essence of religion.[37]

\* \* \*

Archibald Alexander's colleague, Samuel Miller, was a cheerful, polished gentleman who dressed immaculately, walked and stood erectly, and conducted himself with great dignity.

While Alexander was not "a man of rules," Miller led a life of careful routine, with regular walks for exercise, great attention to diet and drafts, and a daily recording of the temperature. He was always punctual and hardly wasted a moment. He worked diligently and followed his own advice to the students—to have, as he expressed it, "something always lying on the anvil." A skillful conversationalist, he had the gift of putting others at ease. Dr. Carnahan remembered how Samuel Miller, during the meetings of the seminary and college professors, would skillfully "touch the key note" which would bring his more reticent colleague, Archibald Alexander, into the conversation. Miller had a fund of anecdotes and amusing stories which he was fond of telling and which others repeated as "Dr. Miller's stories." He told a story with great energy of expression and action. His son wrote that

his voice was one day heard in his study, the tones rising in excitement and emphasis, until they attracted the attention of different members of the family throughout the house. A length he was heard fiercely to vociferate, "Keep your hands off of me, Sir! Keep your hands off of me!" With one accord, the whole body of listeners, thoroughly alarmed, and having called Mrs. Miller from her room as they passed, flew to the study door. Here there was a momentary pause, while Mrs. Miller was put forward, to take the responsibility of entering first. She opened the door with some hesitation, as the alarming sounds had died away; but the others all pressed close after her, and the whole excited company was revealed to President Carnahan of the College, who, quietly seated, was listening with great apparent delight to Dr. Miller, who was upon his feet, throwing all his energy into some amusing anecdote, which he had brought up for the occasion.[38]

Samuel Miller greatly admired Archibald Alexander and readily deferred to him as "the safer and more experienced guide in matters of heart religion." According to Miller's son, fellowship with Alexander was the source, at least in part, of his father's "more decided, constant, and vigorous" spiritual growth after his move to Princeton. The cordial and unselfish relationship between the two men was often mentioned by their students and friends.

Dr. Miller was not as effective a teacher as Dr. Alexander. Some students privately complained that his lectures were "tedious" and "prolix," but William Henry Ruffner found them "rich with most valuable and interesting information."[39] Samuel Miller did not possess the force of personality and authority that so easily enabled Archibald Alexander to hold his students' attention. Charles Hodge remembered when he was a student that "the good Doctor wore out his lead-pencil in thumping the desk to make us behave." However, by his scholarship, courtesy, and exemplary Christian life, Miller gained the respect and love of his students. Charles Hodge often told how, in the summer of 1819, Dr. Alexander gave a lecture to the senior class which greatly impressed the students. William Nevins proposed that in appreciation for such teaching, they establish a scholarship of the class of 1819. A committee was appointed to tell the professors of the plan. Hodge said:

When the committee waited on Dr. Miller, Nevins with his charac-teristic naive frankness told him the whole story, and dwelt on the enthusiasm cherished by the students for Dr. Alexander. Dr. Miller having heard him through, expressed his pleasure in view of what the class had done, and then lifted his hand and said, "My young friend, I solemnly believe that Dr. Alexander is the greatest man who walks the earth!" When we left the Doctor's study, Nevins said to his associates on the Committee, "Well, if Dr. Alexander be the greatest, Dr. Miller is surely the holiest that walks the earth!"

Hodge added, "We were boys then; but this incident serves to show how Dr. Miller was regarded by his pupils."[40]

Irenaeus Prime, a student at Princeton in 1832-33, long remembered Samuel Miller's invitation to him after one of their first classes together: "Will you be so good as to come and take tea with me this evening? I wish you to become acquainted with my family." Before the new student left that evening, Dr. Miller took him into his study and said, "This is my library: while you are in the Seminary it is entirely at your service; take books to your room and use them as long as you please."[41] From time to time, to show their appreciation for him, the students would stand when Dr. Miller entered the classroom; he would bow his acknowledgments as though it were a usual courtesy.

Samuel Miller's wife, Sarah, was a woman of natural ability

and force. Her son was of the opinion that even though his mother had far less education than her husband, she was "perhaps, his superior in mental originality, and independence of thought and investigation." "With equal scholastic acquirements," he wrote, "she would have been, doubtless, the more vigorous thinker of the two." Sarah did not hesitate to express her opinions. One day a man came to talk with her husband, but since Samuel was busy in his study Sarah conversed with him. She discerned immediately that he was a Hopkinsian and "full of disinterested benevolence." When she also discovered that "he was likewise ready to advocate the doctrine of God's being the author of sin," she stated that she "felt inclined to contend with him, and insisted that he had crossed the narrow path of orthodoxy."[42]

Sarah suffered from depression and frequent headaches, which she recognized gave "a sombre hue to her religious experience." She took, her son wrote, "much more gloomy views than Dr. Miller of the world and its vanities." Some "accomplishments of a literary and artistic kind" that Samuel Miller desired for his children she doubted and feared "because of what she imagined their worldly, ensnaring tendency."[43] More economical than her husband, Sarah guarded the family spending with care.

Although traditional in his views of the role of women, Samuel Miller supported women's involvement in benevolent and social ministries. His 1808 sermon for the Society for the Relief of Poor Widows with Small Children was a strong declaration of women's responsibilities to society and the propriety of female charitable associations. Acknowledging the duty of both men and women "to feed the hungry and clothe the naked," Miller recognized the superiority of women in these areas. "They have more sympathy, more tenderness, more leisure and more patience than men," he said.[44] In 1816 Sarah Miller helped organize the Female Benevolent Society of Princeton to educate poor children. In 1825 this society opened its own school with Mrs. Miller as "its chief manager." Before the school was opened, Mrs. Miller brought a number of poor children into her home for daily teaching. She supported the Sunday school for the town's black children. She was greatly interested in the establishment of the Mount Lucas Orphan and Guardian Institute near Princeton and secured for it a considerable endowment. When the school was closed, she transferred a large fund to Ashmun Institute, a school founded by Presbyterians for the training of African Americans.[45]

Sarah Sargeant Miller was a leader among Princeton women in encouraging missionary giving. For many years she was in the habit of putting aside in a drawer every silver dollar that came to her, as belonging to God. This money, above and beyond her usual giving, was saved until she was led to give it to some Christian work. In 1832, she gave her silver dollars to Eliza Thomson. Eliza, with her husband, a Princeton Seminary graduate, was going as a missionary to the Holy Land; and the 131 silver dollars would be used in Eliza's school for girls.

Despite their differences in personality and outlook, Sarah and Samuel Miller were fully agreed, their son wrote, in "their fundamental views of gospel truth and gospel duty"; they agreed also "in being alike ardent lovers of Presbyterianism, as to both its distinctive doctrines and polity."[46] Dr. Miller frequently spoke or wrote of his wife's good qualities. On their anniversary—October 24, 1847—he praised her "strong, discriminating, practical mind," her "physical and moral courage," and her "plain and simple living" that enabled her "to consecrate a larger portion of her means to the Redeemer's kingdom." He then added:

Her piety is as solid, profound, fervent, intelligent and scriptural as I have ever known. It is evidently the governing principle in all her ways. She is really better qualified than many ministers to instruct the inquiring, and to counsel the perplexed and anxious. Hundreds of times have I profited by her remarks on my sermons, and other public performances, more than by the remarks of any other human being.[47]

Twice a day, Dr. and Mrs. Miller and their children gathered for family worship; the mother and father also prayed together during the day.

\*       \*       \*

At Princeton, Samuel Miller's interest turned from scholarly intellectual history to careful study of seminary education, church polity, and theological issues. The growing anti-confessional spirit in American Protestantism was brought close to home for Miller. In 1824 the Reverend John Duncan, a Presbyterian pastor from Baltimore, was elected a director of Princeton Seminary. On the day that he took his seat, Duncan preached a sermon before the board, faculty, and students in which he attacked creeds and confessions. Miller responded by giving the introductory lecture at the opening of the summer session on "The Utility and Importance of Creeds and Confessions."[48] Dr. Miller told the students that the faculty saw themselves "placed under a solemn, nay, an awful responsibility" in their work of educating men for the Christian ministry. "Can you wonder that, having advanced a little before you in our experience in relation to this office," he told them, "we cherish the deepest solicitude at every step you take? Can you wonder, that we daily exhort you to 'take heed to yourselves and your doctrine,' and that we cease not to entreat you, and to pray for you that you give all diligence to approve yourselves to God and his Church able and faithful servants?" The students, too, had an awesome responsibility because in what they were and what they did "the temporal and eternal welfare" of thousands might be involved. Whatever their talents and learning, if they did not have "genuine piety," he said, they would probably be "a curse instead of a blessing to the Church." An equal danger, according to Dr. Miller, was neglect of the doctrine of the church.

The subject of his lecture, the importance of creeds and confessions for maintaining the unity and purity of the visible church, he noted, belonged properly to his own responsibility of teaching church government. He began by outlining arguments in favor of creeds. A "maximum" confession, such as the Westminster Confession of Faith, he believed, was indispensable for harmony and purity in the church. He answered a number of objections commonly brought against creeds—including the charges that they supersede the Bible, interfere with the rights of conscience, and are divisive. He then spoke directly to the students before him in the Oratory:

To you, beloved candidates for the sacred office, let me recommend a sacred regard to this duty. Resist, always, to the utmost of your power, the littleness of sectarian bigotry, and strive to banish it from the church. But, at the same time, cherish among her members an enlightened attachment to that particular branch of the family of Christ in which their lot is cast. For this purpose, strive to promote among them a general and intimate acquaintance with our Confession of Faith, and Form of Government and Discipline, as well as our Catechisms. . . . Never advise the people to take the contents of these public formularies on trust; but diligently to compare every part of them with Scripture, and see how far they agree with the unerring standard. Thus will you be likely to become instrumental in forming solid, intelligent Christians. Thus may you hope to become the spiritual fathers of multitudes, "whose faith shall stand, not in the wisdom of men, but in the power of God."[49]

Standing at his high desk to write, Samuel Miller produced important works on infant baptism, fasting, and public prayer, and prepared many articles and sermons. He contributed regularly to the *Biblical Repertory*, writing on such diverse topics as temperance, the religious education of children, world evangelization, and the proper use of the Sabbath.

Those who knew Dr. Miller were amazed at the amount of work he accomplished. In 1833 he noted in his journal six reasons why he was able to write so much:

1. I do not allow myself to be hurried; or to press my health, strength or spirits beyond what they will bear, by writing at late hours, or by overstrained exertion at any one time. I am very much of the mind of the old Quaker, who, when a traveller on the same road overtook him, seemed to be pressing forward in great haste, and asked with much apparent eagerness, how soon he could reach a certain town, thirty or forty miles ahead, significantly replied, "Thou mayest get there by sunset, if thou wilt go slow enough." The inquirer pressed on, leaving the prudent Quaker to jog along at a slow, but regular, rate. Several hours before sunset, the Quaker overtook his impatient fellow-traveller, some miles short of the town to which he was going, greatly fatigued himself, and his horse fairly fagged out. The Quaker passed him, and reached the same town with ease before the sun went down—all because he had travelled slowly but regularly. I am persuaded that, in every sort of

labor, the old Latin maxim, *Festina lente*, is of exceeding great importance.

2. I have been, for many years, in the habit of going to bed early. I wish always to be in bed a little after ten o'clock, certainly before eleven. Sitting up late, and studying much by candle light, are very destructive to health, and, ultimately, retard, rather than promote, literary labor.

3. I make a point of rising very early: in winter, an hour before day, making my own fire, and getting ready for work, before I can be interrupted by company, etc.; and, in summer, soon after sunrise. This is very important to him who would do much.

4. I try to improve every fragment of time; and although my interruptions are incessant, yet I am so happy as to be able, after an interruption, to take up a subject where I left it, without much loss of time in going back to find the clew. This has long been of great use to me, and made my fragments of time more precious.

5. Whenever I have been compelled to make an extra effort, in the way of studying or writing, I have found incalculable advantage in going through it fasting, or, at least, eating very little. In these circumstances my mental operations are always more active and successful; and I, of course, suffer much less from mental application, and from want of exercise, than if I ate as usual.

6. I must do honor to divine aid. I have always found, that the more I acknowledged God, in my studies, the more comfortably and successfully they proceeded.[50]

✳     ✳     ✳

Archibald Alexander and Samuel Miller became known as "the venerable professors" by "the young men" of Princeton Seminary. They were admired for their many abilities, and they were loved for their Christ-like lives. In an address that he gave in 1874, Charles Hodge looked back to the early days of the seminary and its first two professors. What characterized them most, Hodge said, was that "Christ was as prominent in their religious experience, in their preaching, and in their writings, as He is in the Bible." He continued:

When men enter a Roman Catholic Church, they see before them a wooden image of Christ extended upon a cross. To this lifeless image they bow. When students entered this Seminary, when its first professors were alive, they had held up before them the image of Christ, not graven by art or man's device, but as portrayed by the

Spirit on the pages of God's Word; and it is by beholding that image that men are transformed into its likeness from glory to glory.[51]

The small faculty faithfully taught their students and showed "intense interest" in the work of every graduate; they sought eagerly "all news of the alumni." "The early professors," one Princetonian wrote, "always kept their hands on their former students, wherever they might be, the hands of sympathy, of imagination, of Christian love."[52] Dr. Alexander especially was keenly interested in the places his students went. "There was no man living," his son wrote, "whose acquaintance with the geography and topography of America was more extensive or exact." He often drew maps for missionaries leaving Princeton on some assignment in the South or West, with notations concerning distances and places to spend the night. He constantly studied books of voyages and travels to learn about foreign countries. In his correspondence with missionaries, he sought to add to his knowledge. In 1843 he wrote to Walter Lowrie, "I tell my pupils in foreign countries to send me no prosing sermons. We have enough of this ware here. We want information, minute and accurate." He urged Lowrie to write a book about China, because "we greatly want information respecting that wonderful country." One of the seminary students was "often foiled in trying to communicate to his teacher in their familiar interviews something new or uncommon that occurred to him in his reading or observation, and had to content himself with the resolution to be constantly receiving every sort of information from him without imparting any in return." After seminary, he spent ten years as a missionary in India. On his return, he went, as he said, "with some confidence that he could now find something to say that Dr. Alexander did not know beforehand; but, after a long conversation, he came away with the disheartening impression that he knew more, even about India, than himself."[53]

Dr. Alexander's knowledge of the ministers and churches of his own denomination often astonished visitors. William E. Schenck, Princeton Seminary graduate who became pastor of First Presbyterian Church in Princeton in 1848, wrote that Alexander was acquainted not only with the "present condition, characters, and prospects" of Presbyterian churches but he "was familiar also with their histories from the beginning." "This was the case not only with the more important churches in the cities and larger towns," Schenck added, "but with even the obscurest missionary churches. I have heard him discourse at length about the little preaching places in the Pines of New Jersey, and along the sea shore, or back in the mountains of Pennsylvania, until I marvelled how he could possibly either acquire or retain all his information."[54]

Dr. Alexander followed carefully the travels and ministries of the Princeton students, as they spread out across the country to far-flung congregations; settled in more comfortable nearby places; became missionaries in Asia, Africa, the Near East, or the isles of the sea; or went to preach to the Indian tribes in the West or to the slaves in the South.

\*      \*      \*

Next to Archibald Alexander and Samuel Miller, no man was more admired by the Princeton students than Ashbel Green. With Alexander and Miller, Green was one of the "founders" of the seminary, and since its beginning he had served as the president of its board of directors. He was in Princeton often for the board meetings and the examinations of the students by the faculty and directors. He was pleased to observe, during the examination on didactic theology in May 1831, that the professor required the students "to confirm" their statements "of doctrinal truth from the word of God."[55]

Dr. Green often preached to the students, as he did on May 16, 1831.[56] What he had to say on this occasion, Green stated, would touch a number of topics, some of which he hoped would, "under the divine blessing," be useful to his hearers. He began by urging the students to resist the temptation to "seize on everything at once." They should rather concentrate their energies in seminary on that which is fundamental for a Christian minister—"a knowledge of the Bible, in the languages in which the Bible was given by the inspiration of the Holy Ghost; and a just, accurate, and familiar view of the truths of the Bible, as they are arranged, defended, and illustrated, in our approved systems of theology, and in the Confession of Faith and Catechisms of our church." A knowledge of Greek and Hebrew and systematic theology, Green told the students, must be gained in seminary "or you are never likely to get them."

Dr. Green went on to warn the Princeton men against "the error of thinking that close study . . . is unfavourable to a highly devout spirit, great sanctity of heart and life, and great zeal in preaching the gospel, and endeavouring to win souls to the Saviour." He appealed to "the experience of the whole Christian church"—from Justin Martyr through the Reformation and the Puritan period down to "the Mathers, and Sheppard, and Edwards, and Dickinson, and Burr, and Davies"—to illustrate that great learning and love for God and zeal for souls can go hand in hand. Green added:

I am ready to admit, and do freely admit, that it is very possible a man may be frozen to the core in the ice of Biblical criticism, and even of orthodox doctrine. But I deny that the truths and study of the Bible, and the orthodox faith, ever did, by their direct and proper influence, freeze any man. It was something else, or the want of something else, that froze him, if he was frozen: and if he was ever thawed out into spiritual life and vigour, the truths of the Bible and the orthodox faith, in the hand of the Spirit of God, were the instruments of producing this desirable change.

Dr. Green urged the students to preach the Bible. "Nothing appears to me more objectionable, in the method of preaching which prevails in our country in the present time," he said, "than the sparing use which is made of the Scriptures of Truth." "Give your hearers, if you please, argument and illustration from reason, and sometimes from history, and science, and philosophy," he told the students; "but back and confirm everything you utter by a plain 'Thus saith the Lord.'"

Dr. Green next spoke about "cultivating a missionary spirit." He regretted, he said, that, because of his exhaustion after the long meeting of the board of directors, he had been unable to attend the students' missionary meeting on Friday night. He suggested that the Princeton students "spend one year, at least, in missionary labours" before settling as pastors of established churches. This experience would not only do good to others but also benefit the missionary himself, he said, filling his heart with "tender compassion for perishing sinners." Those who are seriously thinking of devoting their whole lives to missionary labors, "and of going to the heathen on our own borders, or in foreign lands," Dr. Green continued, will "go forth to a work, the most honourable and heavenly, however laborious and painful, in which mortals ever were, or can be, employed."

Dr. Green had planned to talk about the importance of a minister's conduct, his use of money, and his study habits; but he found himself in danger "of running into too much length," and so he concluded his rambling address with "a few observations on revivals of religion." "We hope and trust," he said, "there is no student in this seminary, who is not a cordial friend to such a display of divine grace, as is commonly called a *revival of religion*." He urged the students to spend at least part of their coming vacation "in some place or congregation—easily to be found, blessed be God, at the present time—where a revival of religion exists." He warned the seminarians against ideas and practices which would "mar the blessed work which you seek to promote" and praised the sermon of Dr. Leonard Woods, that Green and the Princeton faculty and students had heard the Andover Seminary professor preach in the First Presbyterian Church on Sunday.[57] Dr. Woods, preaching on I Corinthians 3:6, had insisted that no human soul is ever converted "but by the special and almighty energy of the Holy Spirit" and that we must be careful "to do that, and only that" which God has assigned to us. We must "not attempt to take the work out of God's hands," Green said, "nor to use any means which he has not clearly authorized in his holy word."

In his sermon to the Princeton students, Ashbel Green touched on all the major emphases of Princeton Seminary—dedication to the study of the Bible in the original languages, knowledge of Reformed theology and commitment to the Westminster Standards, the two-fold goal of "piety of the heart" and "solid learning," the cultivation of a missionary spirit, and wholehearted support of revivals. These themes the students heard continually in classes and chapel, in formal presentations and informal conversations. These ideals made Princeton Seminary what it was.

# 10

# The Seminary in the 1830s

*John Breckinridge,*
*Professor of Pastoral Theology*
*and Missionary Instruction,*
*1836-1838.*

May the next year be a happy one, intellectually and spiritually! May less time be wasted than in any former year! May my faculties be better employed than ever before! May I be more entirely devoted to my Master's service! May I daily grow in grace and in mastery over sin! May all my studies and employments be blessed to the sanctification of my soul! The Lord in mercy grant it for the Saviour's sake.

Prayer of
JOSEPH ADDISON ALEXANDER
for 1835

CHARLES Hodge took his place beside his senior colleagues as an essential part of the seminary faculty. He enjoyed his campus home and study, where he would walk up and down singing hymns and occasionally playing the flute or violin for his own enjoyment. He took pride in his garden, and, in 1830, purchased six acres of land adjourning the seminary property for his horses. Every day he recorded the temperature and wind direction and made notes concerning the weather. In April 1832, his mother died so unexpectedly that he was unable to see her. He was greatly saddened but took comfort that his brother, Hugh, was there "seeing and receiving the evidences of her confidence in her Redeemer."[1] Long-time family friend Ashbel Green conducted the funeral service in Philadelphia.

In 1820, as soon as he moved to Princeton, Hodge began to suffer pain in his right leg.[2] Constant walking—especially during the spring of 1833, when he was in New York City collecting money from the Presbyterian churches for the new chapel at the seminary—aggravated his condition; for months he was confined to bed until, gradually, he could sit or stand again. For a number of years he spent most of the time in his study, where his windows overlooked the seminary grounds. On the wall hung a landscape in water colors which Hodge, as a school boy in Philadelphia, had painted—his one work of art. Lying on his couch with his leg in a steel splint, he studied and wrote. His books were kept in a revolving case and his family was often called on to keep them within reach.

[191]

From the summer of 1833 until February 1836, Hodge met his classes in his own house—sometimes in the study, sometimes in the back parlor. The students who came and went noticed the brightness of Dr. Hodge's face despite his constant suffering. Hodge's study was also "for many years the meeting place and intellectual exchange" of the college and seminary.[3] There, the seminary faculty meetings were held, and the college and seminary professors gathered for their regular times of fellowship and discussion. Almost every night a colleague or a visiting minister or scholar stopped in. To Charles Hodge's children, who looked on with great interest, "this study became the scene of the most wonderful debates, and discourse on the highest themes of philosophy, science, literature, theology, morals and politics."[4] Perhaps even more exciting were the chess games between their father and Professor Dod.

Charles and Sarah Hodge's children enjoyed living in their large house and playing on the seminary campus. A student of this time described the oldest son, Archibald Alexander Hodge, as he ran "about the Seminary grounds, a flaxen-haired, blue-eyed, rosy-cheeked little boy of seven or eight summers, and one or two of his little brothers with him."[5] A. A. Hodge later remembered his life and that of his younger brothers and sisters in a home "all radiant . . . with love, with unwavering faith, and with unclouded hope."[6] The children were Dr. Hodge's pride and joy. "His study had two doors," wrote A. A. Hodge, "one opening outwards towards the Seminary for the convenience of the students, and a second one opening inward into the main hall of the home"—for the children. His son continued, "He prayed for us at family prayers, and singly, and taught us to pray at his knees with such soul-felt tenderness, that however bad we were our hearts all melted to his touch." At morning worship in the home, they repeated the Apostles' Creed and then a personal consecration to Father, Son, and Holy Spirit, written by Charles Hodge for his family. Secure in their parents' love and prayers, and encouraged by the piety and enthusiasm of the seminary community, the younger Hodges early committed themselves to Christ and his service. Ten-year-old Archibald and his sister Mary Elizabeth gave a letter on June

23, 1833, to Princeton Seminary graduate James R. Eckard, who was soon to sail for Ceylon. Addressed to the "heathen," it read:

Dear Heathen: The Lord Jesus Christ hath promised that the time shall come when all the ends of the earth shall be His kingdom. And God is not a man that He should lie nor the son of man that He should repent. And if this was promised by a Being who cannot lie, why do you not help it to come sooner by reading the Bible, and attending to the words of your teachers, and loving God, and, renouncing your idols, take Christianity into your temples? And soon there will be not a Nation, no, not a space of ground as large as a footstep, that will want a missionary. My sister and myself have, by small self-denials, procured two dollars which are enclosed in this letter to buy tracts and Bibles to teach you. Archibald Alexander Hodge and Mary Eliz. Hodge, Friends of the Heathen.[7]

\*     \*     \*

The *Biblical Repertory* continued to provide translations and reprints of significant European works for American students. Volume four, published in 1828, contained two long articles translated by Charles Hodge—one by Tholuck on "The History of Theology in the Eighteenth Century" and the other by Stapfer on "The Life of Kant." With the completion of volume four, it was decided in the fall of 1828 to expand the journal to cover the whole field of biblical and theological studies. The volume for 1829 carried the title *Biblical Repertory. A Journal of Biblical Literature and Theological Science; conducted by an Association of Gentlemen*. The "association of gentlemen" included Archibald Alexander, Samuel Miller, and Charles Hodge of the seminary and James Carnahan, John Maclean, and Albert Dod of the college. James W. Alexander, pastor in Trenton, and Joseph Addison Alexander, tutor in the college, were also "copious and important contributors to the Review"; and, according to Charles Hodge, "they soon began to take a leading position in its editorial management."[8] The "association," said Hodge, "was not defined within very strict limits; nor was it controlled by any special terms of agreement. It consisted of the more frequent contributors to the pages of the Journal, who were willing to assume the responsibility before the public of

its character and contents."[9]  The new journal was designed
to furnish Christian readers with "facilities for a right
understanding of the divine oracles."  It would also review
philosophy and literature, refute error, discuss theology and
ecclesiastical polity, and support "the various enterprises of
Christian benevolence."  The journal was "not designed to be
controversial in its character but to state temperately and
mildly, yet firmly and fearlessly, Bible truth in its whole
extent."[10]

In 1830 the name was changed to *Biblical Repertory and
Theological Review* and in 1837 to *Biblical Repertory and Princeton
Review*.  The addition of *Princeton* to the journal's title was
suggested by J. A. Alexander, who pointed to the *Edinburgh
Review* as an example of an important journal with a local
name.  The journal dealt with a broad range of theological
and biblical issues—usually by way of extensive responses to
books, sermons, or articles in other periodicals—but also
included many contributions on matters of science, philosophy, literature, and history.  The *Biblical Repertory and
Princeton Review* was widely read; and Lyman Beecher, an
outspoken critic of Princeton, acknowledged that it was "the
most powerful organ in the land."[11]

\*        \*        \*

Charles Hodge was now teaching Hebrew and Greek, Old
and New Testament literature, exegesis courses in several
biblical books (including a course on the Pauline Epistles), as
well as giving lectures on Biblical criticism and introduction,
Bible geography, and hermeneutics.  One of his students,
John Adger, described Hodge as "a very lovable man" but
added, "I do not think he was a good teacher.  He roused in
us no enthusiasm for either of the Bible languages."[12]
Another student, Theodore Woolsey, came from Yale College
in the fall of 1821 to study Hebrew under Hodge.  He disliked
the Princeton way of teaching it without points and
complained of the "meagreness" of the Greek that he got.
Yet fifty years later Woolsey said that it was under Charles
Hodge that he "imbibed that love, particularly for the Greek
Scriptures, which has been so great that I have sometimes

wished that I might take my Greek Testament with me into heaven."[13]

B. B. Warfield, a student in Hodge's later years, wrote that he had "sat under many noted teachers" and that Dr. Hodge was "superior to them all. He was in fact my ideal of a teacher. Best of all men I have ever known, he knew how to make a young man think." Warfield commented in detail concerning his course in exegesis with Charles Hodge:

He taught exegesis only to the juniors, and although five years have elapsed, the impressions made at that time remain as vivid as though it were yesterday. His very mode of entering the room was characteristic. . . . his carriage was erect and graceful, and his step always firm. The mantle that hung from his shoulders during the cooler months heightened the effect of graceful movement. . . . After his always strikingly appropriate opening prayer had been offered, and we had been settled back into our seats, he would open his well thumbed Greek Testament—on which it was plain that there was not a single marginal note—look at the passage for a second, and then throwing his head back, and closing his eyes, begin his exposition. He scarcely again glanced at the Testament during the hour, the text was evidently before his mind, verbally, and the matter of his exposition thoroughly at his command. In an unbroken stream it flowed from subject to subject, simple, clear, cogent, unfailingly reverent. Now and then he would pause a moment to insert an illustrative anecdote—now and then lean forward suddenly with tearful, wide-open eyes, to press home a quick-risen inference of the love of God to lost sinners. But the web of his discourse—for a discourse it really was—was calm, critical and argumentative. We were expected to take notes upon it and recite on them at our next meeting. This recitation was, however, brief, covering not often more than a quarter of an hour; and we consequently felt that lecturing was the main thing.

This, then, was how he taught us exegesis. The material of the lectures resembled very much his printed commentaries. I thought then, and I think now, that Dr. Hodge's sense of the general meaning of a passage was unsurpassed. He had all of Calvin's sense of the flow and connection of thought. Consequently the analysis of passages was superb. Nothing could surpass the clearness with which he set forth the general argument and the main connections of thought. Neither could anything surpass the analytical subtlety with which he extracted the doctrinal contents of passages. I can never forget how bitingly clear his sentences often were, in which he set forth in few words the gist of a chapter. He seemed to look through a passage, catch its main drift and all its theological bearings, and state the result in crisp sentences, which would have been worthy of Bacon; all at a single movement of mind.

He had, however, no taste for the technicalities of exegesis. He did not shrink from them in his lectures, indeed; but on such points he was seldom wholly satisfactory. His discussion of disputed grammatical or lexical points had a flavor of second-handedness about them. He appeared not to care to have a personal opinion upon such matters, but was content to accept another's without having made it really his own. He would state, in such cases, several views from various critical commentators, and then make a choice between them; but I could not always feel that his choice was determined by sound linguistic principles. He sometimes seemed to be quite as apt to choose an indefensible as a plausible one—guided, apparently, sometimes by weight of name, sometimes by dislike to what seemed to him over-subtlety, and sometimes, it seemed, by theological predilection.

He made no claim, again, to critical acumen; and in questions of textual criticism he constantly went astray. Hence it was that often texts were quoted to support doctrines of which they did not treat; and a meaning was sometimes extracted from a passage which it was far from bearing. But this affected details only, the general flow of thought in a passage he never failed to grasp, and few men could equal him in stating it.[14]

From his early years as professor of Oriental and Biblical Literature, Charles Hodge lectured on the Pauline Epistles. His first major publication was a commentary on the book of Romans, which appeared in 1835. Friedrich Tholuck's commentary on Romans had appeared in 1824; and two American commentaries on the book—by Moses Stuart and Albert Barnes—were published in the early 1830s. Hodge reviewed Stuart's book in the *Biblical Repertory,* praising the author as "the great American reformer of biblical study" but opposing his view of imputation.[15] Stuart, according to Hodge, questioned the "forensic unity" of both Adam and humanity and Christ and the Christian. Hodge criticized Barnes's commentary for its lack of maturity ("Mr. B., to borrow a figure, has plucked his pear before it was ripe") and its "violent . . . attack upon some of the most important doctrines of the church."[16]

Writing on his couch during the winter of 1834-35, Hodge exchanged notes with Dr. Alexander concerning his work on Romans. Alexander suggested changes in style, emphasis, and arrangement. He encouraged Hodge to let the text of the commentary be "pure English" rather than to include Greek, since "by this means it will be studied by all intelligent Presbyterians." He wrote to Hodge, "In the main, I am deeply persuaded that you have brought to view the doctrines which the Holy Ghost intended to reveal by the pen of Paul." Alexander thought that Hodge's book would "do more to confirm the orthodox faith of our church than any book which has been published for a century."[17]

Hodge attempted to defend what he believed was the orthodox view by "a faithful appeal to exegesis"; but—in distinction from Tholuck's and Stuart's works—he was especially concerned with the doctrine of the book of Romans. His commentary opposed the ideas of New England theology concerning imputation, original sin, and inability. Hodge insisted that the guilt of Adam's sin was imputed to all humanity, so that all are born sinners and are totally unable in themselves to change their condition. In commenting on Romans 5:12-21, Hodge referred to no less than sixty scholars. He cited a wide spectrum of orthodox writers, from Chrysostom to "President Edwards," to endorse his Calvinistic interpretation of a passage that he admitted to be both difficult and unpopular. "We are not like the separate grains of wheat in a measure," Hodge wrote, "but links in a complicated chain. All influence the destiny of each, and each influences the destiny of all."[18]

Charles Hodge's commentary on Romans was immediately recognized as an important work.[19] An abridged edition for lay Bible students, published in 1836, circulated widely and was reprinted in England in 1838. Early in 1841 Hodge's 1835 edition was published in French, translated by Adolphe Monod. Monod found Hodge's commentary admirable, although a little too much influenced by his systematic theology. He stated in his preface:

Dr. Hodge belongs to the religious opinion known in America by the name of the "Old School." His doctrine is precisely that of our own churches, and it is exhibited in the Commentary with remarkable distinctness and vigor. If we may venture the inquiry, we would ask as to this point whether the matter is not rather more precise and formal in Dr. Hodge's exposition, than in the Bible itself. We have learned from this Holy Book to have some dread of formulas that are too straitened, and of what Felix Neff, with his usual originality calls "squared doctrines."[20]

In his *Commenting and Commentaries* (1876), Charles Spurgeon wrote that "Hodge's method and matter make him doubly useful in commenting. He is singularly clear, and a great promoter of thought."[21] A later Princetonian, Francis L. Patton, characterized Hodge as "a dogmatic exegete." His commentaries were not primarily grammatical or historical but theological. His chief strength was his ability to seize upon the central idea of a passage. Patton wrote that Hodge "knew Greek, it is true, but, better still, he knew Paul."[22] Conservative modern scholars have praised Hodge's commentary on Romans as a reflection of continental scholarship, theological rigor, and warm evangelical spirit.

\*     \*     \*

In May 1834, Joseph Addison Alexander was appointed Charles Hodge's assistant. In 1833 Alexander had visited Europe, carrying with him a letter of introduction from Hodge to his friend Friedrich Tholuck. Hodge wrote of Alexander, "He is more of a scholar, especially in your favorite field of Oriental languages, than any American within my knowledge, who has visited Europe." Tholuck was not disappointed. He told a friend that Alexander was "the only man who could *always*" give him the right English word for one in German "apparently untranslatable."[23]

The twenty-five-year-old Addison Alexander, third son of Dr. and Mrs. Alexander, was already something of a legend in Princeton. As a child he had shown a love for reading and a phenomenal skill in languages. When he was about six years old he would disappear into the kitchen after the evening meal to read *Pilgrim's Progress* to the woman who cooked for the family, stopping every now and then to comment as he went along. By the age of ten he had mastered the rudiments of Latin, Greek, and Hebrew. He found an old copy of an Arabic grammar on the top shelf of his father's library, and soon he was reading the Koran. He examined with fascination two old Persian manuscripts in the college library.

Recognizing his ability and initiative, his parents postponed his formal education, allowing him freedom to study with family members and private tutors or on his own. In 1824 Addison Alexander entered the Junior class at Princeton College and quickly became the prodigy of Nassau Hall. Some of his fellow students believed that he was superior to most of the college's instructors. He graduated in two years at the age of eighteen. His father wrote to a friend that Addison was "very far superior to anyone of his age I ever saw in literary attainments." He was a good public speaker, and his father thought he probably would become a lawyer or politician. "His views and feelings on the subject of religion are known only to himself," Dr. Alexander wrote; "He is so reserved that nobody attempts to draw him out; but his whole deportment is as correct as it easily could be."[24]

Addison declined a position as tutor in the college and spent the next three years in private study. He took special delight in oriental languages and literature (Hebrew, Arabic, Persian, Syriac, and Chaldee) and read French, Italian, Spanish, and German.[25] It was his custom to pursue his studies in six or eight languages every day. In December 1828 he began the study of Chinese. In learning a new language, his procedure was to find a great classic in that language and work his way through it with a grammar and lexicon. His academic journal gives evidence of his diligence and breadth of scholarship. For example, on January 14, 1828, the eighteen-year-old student read Exodus 29 and 30 in Hebrew; two chapters of *Don Quixote* in Spanish; five pages of *Télémaque* in French; studied the *Gulistan* in Persian; read English essays on Asian philosophy and language instruction; and read seven chapters of James Fenimore Cooper's *Red Rover!*[26] When he was not studying he was writing stories such as "The Quaker Settlement" and "The Jewess of Damascus"; articles on "Greece in 1827," "The Persian Poets," and "The Sea"; and political editorials and poems for the *Patriot*, the *Philadelphia Monthly Magazine*, the *Souvenir*, and the

*Emporium;* or translating Justin Martyr's *Exhortation to the Greeks* for the *Biblical Repertory.*

In 1829 Addison taught Latin, ancient and modern history, geography, and composition at Edgehill School, which he founded with Professor Patton in Princeton. It was during this year that he put his trust in Christ. Robert Baird, seminary graduate and one of Addison's early tutors, visited Dr. Alexander about this time and told how, after their business was handled,

he remarked that as I had taken a great interest in his sons, he had a piece of intelligence to communicate which he was sure would give me much delight. He then stated that he was well satisfied, from a conversation which he had had with Addison the evening previous, that he was a converted man! This he said in a tone of voice which manifested the deepest feeling. Indeed, for some moments afterwards he could not speak, but covered his face with his handkerchief, and gave way to his deep emotions of joy and hope.[27]

Addison's journal, which had before contained scholarly notes and records of his study and writing, showed a new interest:

... in addition to ... literary pursuits, I have been deeply engaged in a study new to me, and far more important than all others—the study of the Bible and my own heart. I humbly trust that I am not what I was. I have still my old propensities to evil, but I have also a new will co-existing with the old, and counteracting and controlling it. My views respecting study are now changed. Intellectual enjoyment has been my idol heretofore; now my heart's desire is that I may live no longer to myself, but in Him in whom I have everlasting life. God grant that the acquisitions that I have been allowed to make under the influence of selfish motives may be turned to good account as instruments for the promotion of His glory. May it not be that my strong and unaccountable attachment from a very early age to unusual studies, &c., was intended as a preparation for God's service in some foreign land? Oh! if I were thought worthy of bearing such a message—but I desire to abstain from all attempts to order my own steps. I have indulged my imagination formerly too much. It must be mortified. My God, for such I, even I, may call thee in the name of Christ—my God, into thy hands I commit myself! In life or death, at home or abroad, in peace and joy or in the dark valley, I design to be thine—thine with a devotedness proportioned to my meanness, misery, ingratitude, infirmity and utter unworthiness of favour. Oh! deliver me from my worst enemy—myself.[28]

Addison was now reading Augustine's *Confessions*; Jonathan Edwards's *Treatise on Religious Affections* ("It put me on my guard against some delusions into which I should have been very apt to fall"); John Owen on *The Grace and Duty of Being Spiritually Minded*; Henry Martyn's *Journals* (noting the resemblance of Martyn's conversion to his own—"It was equally gradual, without strong terrors or remorse, and seems to have resulted as immediately from study of the Scriptures"); and the works of John Newton ("He always speaks from his heart and from his own experience"). Despite his great new interest in Christian writers, Addison resisted placing his "dependence on human aids." He wrote on February 11, 1830:

Men are fallible; and their fallibility is everywhere apparent. I value religious books because they bring into a single point of view, truths which are detached in the Scriptures; and because they show the effects the religion of the Bible has, actually, upon the minds of men. In almost every book, however, there is a tincture of some personal infirmity or error—an overstraining of some one point of view in preference to others. Thus Owen, who wrote his book on Spiritual Mindedness in his old age, when waiting for his last change, was too apt to underrate the social relations and man's duties as a member of society; while Newton, who was wonderfully changed from a wicked slave-dealer to a Christian minister, naturally set too little value on learning, education, &c. It is only in the Book—the Book of Books, that all is symmetrical and consistent; Oh may I love it more and more![29]

On April 24, 1830—his birthday—Addison wrote:

I am this day twenty-one years old, and after looking back upon my past life, and forward to eternity, having also sought instruction in God's Word and at the throne of grace, I desire with few words, but with a fixed heart, to consecrate myself, soul and body, now and forever, to the God who made me. With this intent I now most solemnly renounce the service of the devil, my late master;

abandoning not only certain sins, but *sin* itself; with all its pleasures, honours and emoluments; desiring and beseeching God never more to suffer me to taste the least enjoyment of a sinful nature.[30]

On July 29, 1830, Addison Alexander became adjunct professor of Ancient Languages and Literature at Princeton College. For the next two and a half years he taught his courses, continued his study of languages (adding Portuguese, Danish, and Turkish), and began studying theology with his father. His goal was to become a careful student of the Bible. He wrote, "I have set before me the specific ends of my toils, to become thoroughly acquainted with the *Scriptures*; philologically, theologically, practically; and so to qualify myself for interpreting them properly to others."[31] He sought guidance for his biblical study from his father and the professors at the seminary and attended the religious services there. The Sabbath, now eagerly anticipated as "a precious opportunity of waiting upon God," was used solely for reading the Bible and books on practical religion. In his journal for March 11, 1831, he wrote, "At the conference last Lord's Day, my father urged upon the students the duty of storing their memory with Scripture. I resolved, by way of experiment, to get by heart a portion of Scripture every day, both in English and the original."[32] Eventually he memorized the Psalms in Hebrew and English and the books of Romans and Hebrews in Greek and English.

Joseph Addison Alexander came to the seminary in 1834 and the next year was elected by the General Assembly as associate professor of Oriental and Biblical Literature. The seminary students were not a little awed by their new professor. They saw a short, stout young man, with full rosy cheeks and a large head which they often compared to Napoleon's.[33] They knew that he was "a great scholar" whose "communion," one wrote, "was with the mighty dead and in outlandish tongues"![34] He had a reputation for silence as well as for masterful speech and was known for his exacting discipline. The students had heard that he generally avoided the company of others except for his family and a few close friends. One wrote that Dr. Addison Alexander was "one of the most brilliant men, in all his productions, I have ever seen, perhaps the most so; but in private he is a real character. He is as unsociable as a comet, and looks as grim as a *taurus*."[35] If the seminarians were a little afraid of Addison, the children loved him. Little Archibald Alexander Hodge wrestled with him on the floor, teased him for his stories, and "sat amazed while he sang English, French, German, Italian, Turkish, Latin, Greek, Hebrew, and Arabic songs or chants."[36]

Samuel Beach Jones, who studied at Princeton from 1832 to 1836, later wrote that he had in the course of his life met three teachers of "pre-eminent ability" and that Addison Alexander was "the foremost of them all, for pupils of intellect above the average."[37] The students learned Hebrew from him and appreciated his lectures on Isaiah, the Messianic Psalms, and other Bible books and topics. One seminarian commented that he could not be excelled as an exegete— "His analyses, with which he introduced each exegetical lecture, so concise, so clear, so simple, were themselves far better than most commentaries."[38] Another student believed that Dr. Addison Alexander was "the ablest speaker in the faculty."[39] Another was impressed with his prayers. He wrote, "They had that wonderful concentration and variety with an essential sameness, which you notice in Calvin's prayers at the close of his lectures on the Minor Prophets."[40]

Soon Addison Alexander was teaching little groups of students elective classes in Arabic, Syriac, and Aramaic and giving advanced lectures on Leviticus. A number of these students became outstanding missionaries. Under Alexander's tutelage, Joseph Owen, who became president of the Allahabad Missionary College in India, read the entire Old Testament in Hebrew, the Koran in Arabic, and made considerable progress in the classical language of India by the end of his seminary career. With the coming to the seminary of the brilliant son of Archibald Alexander, the practice of occasional elective courses at Princeton became more standard; and the catalogue of 1834 for the first time listed such extracurricular studies.

Addison Alexander had little patience with slow students— especially if he thought there was evidence of laziness or carelessness—and his remarks could be sharp. He was by no means a patient teacher of Hebrew grammar. One day when a student was performing poorly in conjugating the hiphil forms of a verb, the professor threw down his Hebrew grammar and angrily said, "Gentlemen, I can't spend any more time on these elementary matters. Learn them for yourselves. I shall begin lecturing on Genesis tomorrow."[41] When his temper got the better of him in the classroom, the next prayer he offered in the Oratory was sure to show how sincerely he repented. The students would sometimes ask each other, "What has Dr. Addison been doing for which he is so sorry?"[42] Alexander's attitude toward himself is revealed in this prayer which he wrote in his journal in January 1835:

Mercy and help, O Lord, my sovereign Lord! Thou who lovest little children, make me a little child. Make me humble, simple-hearted, tender, guileless, and confiding. Kill my selfish pride. Shiver my hard heart. Break my stubborn spirit. Make me love my kind by making me to love Thee. O soften me, my Saviour, by showing me thy own tender, bleeding, melting heart. Purge envy from my heart by causing me to live and work for thee. O that this foul fiend were wholly dispossessed! I bless thee for trials: may they do me good. Compel me to remember that I am not my own. Save me from being the object of envy or ill-will. Save me from the wickedness of trying to excite it. Lord, I would give the world for true humility. O, make me—make me humble![43]

God answered his prayer. Addison became more gentle and reasonable in his demands upon his students' time and brains; and his sarcasm and scorching review articles in the *Biblical Repertory* gave way to a gentler style. His biographer wrote, "In after years his feelings greatly softened towards human infirmity."[44] The students did not fail to observe the spiritual growth of their young teacher. One seminarian who studied at Princeton from 1836 to 1839 wrote, "It would be strange indeed if, so conversant as he was with God's Word, and reverencing it as he did, he did not manifest it by his holiness and nearness to God. And especially during the latter part of my course in the Seminary were we impressed with this; and the remark was often made that Dr. Addison was a man that walked with God, and was evidently growing in grace."[45]

J. A. Alexander's election to the Princeton faculty in 1835 marked the beginning of a distinct Old Testament department at Princeton. He declined the chair of Oriental and Biblical Literature in Union Theological Seminary, just established in New York City, and was inaugurated professor at Princeton on September 24, 1838. He became a candidate for the gospel ministry in 1838 and was ordained on his thirtieth birthday, April 24, 1839.

\*       \*       \*

J. A. Alexander became the seminary's fourth teacher in 1834; in 1836 a fifth was added. For some time, the seminary faculty desired to expand the teaching of missions. The 1829 General Assembly appointed a committee of five men including Archibald Alexander, Samuel Miller, and Charles Hodge to consider the possibility of establishing "a Missionary Institution, for the instruction and training of missionaries, under the care of the General Assembly, and in connexion with the Theological Seminary at Princeton." The committee reported to the next General Assembly that in the light of the growing importance of the missionary cause, such an institution was needed. The report stated:

The spirit of the religion of Jesus is essentially a spirit of Missions; and, undoubtedly, one of the first and highest duties of the Christian Church, is to nurture and extend this spirit, and to make all her establishments tributary to its advancement. The importance, therefore, of connecting an institution of the kind proposed, with a Seminary in which a large number of candidates for the holy ministry are assembled, is obvious. Its native tendency, if properly conducted, will be to kindle among the rising ministry, a new and more fervent zeal on behalf of missions; to call forth, animate and prepare larger numbers of missionaries, both for the foreign and domestic field; and, eventually, to diffuse, throughout all our churches more of that deep and practical sense of obligation in reference to this subject, of the want of which we have so much reason to complain, and the increase of which is so earnestly to be desired.

The committee argued that a missionary department at Princeton would benefit not only the cause of worldwide missions but the seminary itself and the American church. The seminary would gain a deeper sense of piety and vital religion by having a department with its primary purpose "to cherish fervent love for immortal souls." The committee affirmed that "every effectual step that is taken to extend the missionary cause, tends no less surely, to promote piety and pastoral fidelity at home."

The committee suggested that "a small and humble beginning" be made by adding to the Princeton faculty a "Professor of Pastoral Theology and Missionary Instruction." His duties would be to teach "everything which relates to the Pastoral office" and especially to collect and impart "instruction on the subject of missions." He would "promote among all the students an enlarged spirit of pastoral fidelity, of missionary zeal, and of liberal preparation and active effort for the advancement of the Redeemer's kingdom."[46]

The report was accepted by the General Assembly, but no action was taken until the directors of the seminary recommended in 1835 that the assembly follow through on its decision. A lengthy debate followed, during which the appointment of a professor of Pastoral Theology and Missionary Instruction was opposed by some members of the assembly. They argued that it was unnecessary, because there were already four professors at the seminary to teach the 120 students, and that it was improper to separate the pastoral training of the students from their instruction in other classes.

These arguments were answered by Charles Hodge in his *Biblical Repertory* review of the 1835 General Assembly. He wrote, "We know no work to which a man could be called, requiring more wisdom, reflection, study, prayer and experience, none more solemn and responsible than to teach hundreds of candidates for the ministry how to win souls to Christ and how to train them up for his kingdom." Hodge pointed out that the new professor would also teach missions and would "have to embody the results of missionary experience as to the best method of evangelizing the world; as to the requisites, trials, duties of the messengers of the gospel in foreign lands; as to the character, necessities and facilities, of the different parts of the missionary field, etc. etc." This work could not be done adequately by the current professors, Hodge argued, who had more to do than some thought— with daily lectures, evening "exercises" three times a week, and Sunday preaching. In answer to the second objection, Hodge said that the new professor would have a special call to exercise pastoral supervision over the students, but not to the exclusion of his colleagues.[47]

After the debate, the General Assembly elected John Breckinridge to the seminary faculty as professor of Pastoral Theology and Missionary Instruction—the first professor of missions in any school in the world. Breckinridge's zeal and ability in the missionary cause were well established by his article "The Claims of Foreign Missions," which had appeared in the *Biblical Repertory* in 1830. The thirty-nine-year-old Breckinridge was a tall, handsome, and courtly Kentuckian. His father, who died when John was nine years old, served as a United States senator and attorney general and was a trusted friend of Thomas Jefferson's. John was reared by his mother and his older brother, Joseph Cabell, who married the daughter of Samuel Stanhope Smith.[48] He studied at Princeton College in preparation for a law career. While in college he was converted during the revival of 1815 and joined the Presbyterian church. He then decided to study for the ministry and entered Princeton Seminary, graduating in 1822 with plans to become a foreign missionary.

In 1823 John Breckinridge married Margaret Miller, the twenty-one-year-old daughter of Dr. and Mrs. Samuel Miller. A few years earlier, a revival in Princeton led by Daniel Baker—who as a student had been greatly used in the college revival of 1815—convinced some of Margaret's friends to pray for her conversion. A short time later, in a small gathering, she heard someone read a sermon by Jonathan Edwards—which brought her, she believed, to "a new view of everlasting things."[49] Like her mother earlier, however, Margaret struggled with doubts until after her marriage, when she finally publicly professed Christ and joined the church.

John Breckinridge became chaplain of the United States House of Representatives during the 1822-23 session and then served as pastor of churches in Kentucky and Maryland. In 1831 he became secretary of the Board of Education in Philadelphia, which was reorganized by the General Assembly in the light of the more than one-thousand vacant congregations in the Presbyterian church and "the immeasurable destitution of the heathen world." Under Breckinridge's leadership, the board—which for years had existed in the shadow of the more active American Education Society—emerged as a vigorous ministry within the denomination. On May 5, 1836, John Breckinridge was inaugurated as a professor at the seminary. Philadelphia friends provided a "delightful" house for him and his family. The house, another work of Charles Steadman, soon was known as "The Ridge."

John Breckinridge's time at the seminary was divided between teaching and fund-raising, necessary and difficult because of the large-scale financial panic of 1837 that for several years slowed business in Princeton and around the country to a crawl. He also assisted the new Presbyterian Board of Foreign Missions but declined appointment in order to continue teaching at the seminary. The board, however, renewed its invitation after the 1838 General Assembly, and Breckinridge resigned from the seminary to become its secretary.

On June 16, 1838, Margaret Miller Breckinridge died after an illness of six months. Her father sadly wrote in his journal, "This is a mournful, solemn day. This morning, soon after breakfast, my eldest daughter departed this life. . . . She suffered much from extreme weakness and frequent pain, but was patient and composed, and departed in the calm enjoyment of Christian hope. Blessed be the God of all grace for this inestimable favor." To a large and deeply moved congregation in the Presbyterian church, Dr. Alexander preached the funeral sermon. He told the grieving friends:

She was brought up among you, from her childhood, and enjoyed the affectionate regards of this community in no common degree, as is manifest by the general and tender sympathy felt on this occasion. By her sweet simplicity, engaging vivacity, affectionate temper and affable manners, our beloved friend endeared herself to her acquaintances and neighbors, wherever she resided. And in regard to her Christian character, she adorned her profession by a consistent life and conversation, in all the relations which she sustained.[50]

In 1840 John Breckinridge went to New Orleans to serve as pastor of the Presbyterian church. Serious throat problems reduced his voice to a barely audible whisper. He left New Orleans for Cabell's Dale, the home where he was born near Lexington, Kentucky. There, on August 4, 1841, he died of "bronchial consumption." Just before he died he said, "I am a poor sinner who has worked hard, and had constantly before my mind one great object—the conversion of the world." After a few moments he added, "Nothing is impossible with God." And a little later he said, "God is with me." Princeton mourned for him; and his picture was soon hanging by the side of Dr. Miller's over the mantle in the home of J. W. Alexander, now professor at Princeton College. Alexander "knew him longer, and better, than any man living," he claimed; and he added, "if we ever knew a man of whom we could truly say, his faults were few, and his virtues transcendent, this was one."[51]

John Breckinridge's brief time as Princeton's professor of missions underscored the seminary's commitment to world evangelization. South Carolinian John B. Adger planned to return to the South as a pastor, but at Princeton he saw that, as great as the need was for ministers in the United States, "every heathen nation was incomparably more destitute."[52] Adger spent twelve years working among the Armenians of Turkey.[53] During the mid-1830s a group of missionary-minded students moved through the college and seminary together and then served overseas. John Morrison, Joseph Owen, and John Freeman went to India. Peter Dougherty became a missionary to the Indians of the Grand Traverse Bay, and Oren Canfield and Jonathan Alward went to Africa.

Africa especially was a challenge and a sorrow to the Princeton students. Joseph Barr had died in 1832 before he could sail for the "dark continent." David White and his wife died within days of reaching Cape Palmas in 1837. Still the students could not believe that Africa was to "be given up." Oren Canfield and Jonathan Alward went in 1841. Alward lived only a few days after his arrival and was buried next to the grave of the Whites. Canfield died of malaria a year later. Robert Sawyer arrived at Monrovia in December 1841. He managed to preach and begin Christian schools before he died, after just two years in Africa. A small beginning, however, had been made in fulfilling Philip Milledoler's charge in 1812 that the students from Princeton plant "the standard of the cross on the remotest shores of heathen lands."

# 11

# The Old Doctrines of Calvinism

*Asahel Nettleton (1783-1843)*
*Reproduced by courtesy of*
*The Connecticut Historical Society,*
*Hartford, Connecticut.*

There are few truths of which I have a more unwavering conviction, than that the sheep of Christ, for whom he laid down his life, shall never perish.

ARCHIBALD ALEXANDER

THE decade of the 1830s was a time of controversy in the Presbyterian church. The burning issues of the day were discussed at Princeton Seminary and presented to a wider audience through the pages of the *Biblical Repertory*. As the church divided into "Old School" and "New School" parties, the seminary faculty were seen at first as "moderates." Dr. Alexander wrote in 1834, "We go on here upon our old moderate plan, teaching the old doctrines of Calvinism, but not disposed to consider every man a heretic who differs in some few points from us." Alexander and his colleagues feared that "through the ultraism of the Old and the New School, the sound and moderate part of the church" was being placed in jeopardy.[1]

The Presbyterian New School party was influenced by theological developments in New England after the death of Jonathan Edwards. This confusing and difficult history (which awaits a competent interpreter) stretches from the time of several of the eighteenth-century students of Edwards (mainly, Joseph Bellamy, Samuel Hopkins, Nathaniel Emmons, and Jonathan Edwards, Jr.) to the death of Edwards Amasa Park in 1900. The earliest of these theologians created a school in American Calvinism which has been described as Edwardseanism, Consistent Calvinism, Hopkinsianism, and the New Divinity. Although these theologians sought to be faithful to the experiential Calvinism of the senior Edwards, traditional Calvinists—as early as 1765—complained that their views represented a "new" system of

[213]

divinity. Much of the motivation for their efforts came from their desire to reconcile Calvinistic doctrines such as election and total depravity with evangelism and moral reform—an unnecessary exercise, according to their opponents, since traditional Calvinistic orthodoxy, they argued, had always been a powerful instrument for revivals, missions, and reform.

The New Divinity theologians taught that God permitted sin as the necessary means of achieving the greatest good. They presented the atonement as the outworking of God's love or a demonstration of his moral government rather than as a substitutionary satisfaction for sin. They described sin as self-love and taught that true virtue consisted in "disinterested benevolence"—even to the point of being willing to be damned for the greater glory of God. While some opponents saw the New Divinity as a serious deviation from Reformed orthodoxy, others tolerated it as an unusual—and not particularly helpful—expression of Calvinism.

A more radical break with Jonathan Edwards and the old Calvinism came with the New Haven Theology, defined primarily by Yale Divinity School professor Nathaniel W. Taylor (and therefore sometimes called Taylorism). Taylor attempted to "improve" Edwards's famous analysis of the freedom of the will and to counter Hopkins's view of the sinner's powerlessness before regeneration. The direction of his thinking was seen in the title of his 1818 treatise, *Man, A Free Agent Without the Aids of Divine Grace.* On September 10, 1828, Taylor took the bold step of presenting his views directly to the Connecticut Congregational clergy, gathered at Yale chapel, in his famous hour-and-a-half sermon, *Concio ad Clerum* (Advice to the Clergy). Taylor rejected the traditional doctrines of original sin and regeneration and taught that people are not born sinful but become sinners at their first moral act. Though people sin inevitably, Taylor believed that their self-determining will has "power to the contrary," so that they remain morally responsible. Similarly, people have the power to effect their own regeneration but lack the will to do so until the Holy Spirit makes a forceful appeal to their understandings. The Holy Spirit helps to influence the person to change—like the solicitations of a friend—but does not act to change the heart of the sinner. Preachers, therefore, must confront sinners and urge them to accept salvation. This was a reasonable and, to some, an attractive revival theology; but, as Sydney Ahlstrom has commented, it meant that "revivals came to be understood less as the 'mighty acts of God' than as the achievement of preachers who won the consent of sinners."[2] By accentuating human agency, Taylor and his followers hoped to provide a way in which Calvinism could be reconstructed to appeal to a democratic American culture; but, by adopting presuppositions of their deistic and liberal opponents, they actually hastened the downfall of Calvinism in New England.[3]

The Princetonians distinguished the "somewhat modified Calvinism" of the New Divinity from the more radical recasting of Edwards's thought in the New Haven School. Dr. Alexander and his colleagues saw themselves as traditional Calvinists but also as true followers of Jonathan Edwards. Although they rejected Edwards's metaphysical idealism and distrusted some of his theological speculations, they stood with him on the major doctrines of the trinity, the imputation of Adam's sin, the bondage of the will, and the atonement.[4] They held that Adam's sin was imputed to all his descendants (although they did not agree with Edwards as to exactly how this happened) and that, in the atonement, Christ—by suffering the punishment of sin for his people— satisfied the justice inherent in God's inviolable law. Alexander and the Princetonians labored to teach and defend these doctrines while they admitted that, like all divine mysteries, these truths transcended human reason. They believed that the New Divinity innovations were unnecessary and the New Haven views downright heretical. Charles Hodge described the New Haven theology as "the pressing out of one corner of the system of President Edwards, to results from which that good and great man would have revolted."[5]

\*     \*     \*

The New England theology, in its various forms, had become a source of apprehension and controversy in the Presbyterian church. In 1810 Samuel Miller had defended the moderate Hopkinsian Gardiner Spring before New York Presbytery when the Brick Presbyterian Church of New York City had called Spring, a graduate of Yale, as its pastor. Spring's sermon before presbytery—on "Human Ability"—revealed a strong strain of New Divinity thinking and created a heated debate. Only when Samuel Miller interceded for Spring, on the grounds that he was a "very pliable man," did the presbytery relent and install him at the Brick Church. Miller's friend and associate, Philip Milledoler, opposed Spring's acceptance by the presbytery. Years later, Milledoler described what he called "the whole amount" of his difference with Samuel Miller—"he considered me as acting conscientiously in this case, yet as carried away by the ardour of my feelings; and I considered him as carried away, by his natural amiability and Christian charity, beyond the bounds marked out for those who are set for the defence of the Gospel."[6]

Ezra Stiles Ely, who had zealously opposed Gardiner Spring, moved to a Philadelphia church and argued against Hopkinsianism so incessantly that the congregation split. The undaunted Ely prevailed on the Synod of Philadelphia, in the fall of 1816, to adopt a "pastoral letter" advising presbyteries to resist "the introduction of Arian, Socinian, Arminian and Hopkinsian heresies." The General Assembly's committee, under Samuel Miller's leadership, commended "the zeal of the Synod in endeavoring to promote a strict conformity to our public standards" but regretted that "zeal on this subject should be manifested in such a manner as to be offensive to other denominations, and especially to introduce a spirit of jealousy and suspicion against ministers in good standing, which is calculated to disturb the peace and harmony of our ecclesiastical judicatories."[7] Miller's pacific temper on these occasions characterized the stance of his Princeton colleagues as well.

Although the Princeton professors were all "Old Calvinists," the seminary had not escaped the influence of the New Divinity. Student C. C. Jones wrote to his fiancée in December 1829 that the Princeton students were divided into two parties: the majority holding to Dr. Alexander's views and the minority advocating the New England theology. The Princetonians, however, refused to condemn those who in their opinion did not deny teachings central to the system of doctrine of the Westminster Standards. "It is not enough that a doctrine be erroneous, or that it be dangerous in its tendency," wrote Charles Hodge; "if it be not subversive of one or more of the constituent elements of the Reformed faith, it is not incompatible with the honest adopting of our Confession. It cannot be denied that ever since the Reformation, more or less diversity in the statement and explanation of the doctrines of Calvinism has prevailed in the Reformed Churches."[8] Hodge argued that "none of the sober-minded among the Old School had ever deliberately regarded" the views of the Hopkinsians "as putting a man beyond the pale."[9]

In the Princeton view, however, the New Haven teaching did subvert the foundations of the Reformed faith.[10] The important difference between Samuel Hopkins and Nathaniel Taylor, they believed, was that for Hopkins regeneration was solely the work of the Holy Spirit, but Taylor told the sinner that he had the ability to act to escape his damnable condition. Charles Hodge and the Princetonians saw in Taylor's views a radically different expression of Christianity from traditional Calvinism. Since its inception, Hodge wrote, Christianity has been plagued by the conflict between two competing doctrinal systems. The one, he said, "has for its object the vindication of the Divine supremacy and sovereignty in the salvation of men; the other has for its characteristic aim the assertion of the rights of human nature. It is specially solicitous that nothing should be held to be true, which cannot be philosophically reconciled with the liberty and ability of man."[11] These competing outlooks, Hodge believed, were again at war in the nineteenth century, each claiming to be the true representation of biblical faith and asking for the allegiance of the church.

One major area of battle between Princeton and its New England opponents was the doctrine of original sin. Archibald Alexander was convinced that "the old doctrine of the ancient church, which traces all sins and evils in the world to the *imputation* of the first sin of Adam," was scriptural teaching. "If the doctrine of imputation be given up, the whole doctrine of original sin must be abandoned," Alexander wrote. "And if this doctrine be relinquished, then the whole doctrine of redemption must fall, and what may then be left of Christianity they may contend for that will; but for ourselves, we shall be of the opinion that what remains will not be worth a serious struggle." Alexander's views "set the general tone and specific boundaries for [Charles] Hodge's work and inspired him to a most vigorous historical and exegetical investigation of the doctrine of the imputation of Adam's sin."[12]    Charles Hodge treated the subject in two articles in the *Biblical Repertory* in 1830 and 1831 and in his *Commentary on the Epistle to the Romans,* first published in 1835.[13]

From the vantage point of 1871, Charles Hodge summarized the long history of the doctrinal conflict between Princeton and the New England views that influenced New School Presbyterians:

For more than sixty years certain differences of opinion had prevailed in our body on the nature of the relation between Adam and his posterity, the nature of original sin, of the sinner's inability, of the influence of the Holy Spirit in regeneration and sanctification. But so long as all parties held that men are born into the world, since the fall, in a state of sin and condemnation; that this fact was due to the sin of Adam; that men are dependent on the Holy Spirit for their regeneration; and that it is due to the sovereign and supernatural interposition of the Spirit that one man is converted and not another, the authority of the Church in the exercise of discipline was not invoked. But when it was taught that all sin consists in the voluntary violation of known law; that men since the fall, are not born in a state of sin; that they are not chargeable with guilt or moral pollution until, having arrived at years of discretion, they deliberately violate the divine law; that all men have plenary ability to avoid all sin; and, having sinned, to return unto God and do all that he requires at their hands; that God cannot prevent sin, or the present amount of sin, in a moral system; that he cannot effectually control the acts of free agents without destroying their liberty; that in conversion it is man, and not God, who determines who do, and who do not, turn unto God; that election is founded on the foresight of this self-determined repentance on the part of the sinner;—when these doctrines came to be taught in our church, it was seen that the vital principles, not of the Reformed faith only, but even of Catholic Christianity, were involved.[14]

\*     \*     \*

Old School Presbyterians, troubled by New England theology, also worried about the type of revivalistic preaching which was being introduced into their churches. A hundred years earlier, during the 1730s, a "surprising work of God" renewed Dutch Reformed, Presbyterian, and Congregational churches in the Middle Colonies and New England. A decade later it became a "Great Awakening," when George Whitefield tirelessly preached to immense gatherings and small congregations from Savannah to Boston. The revival, which converted thousands and left its mark on American life, divided Presbyterians into Old Side and New Side churches.

The First Great Awakening had become a distant memory, but scattered revivals continued here and there. Around the turn of the century, a new wave spread through the land, converting sinners and renewing churches in the East and on the southern frontier. This movement, known later as the Second Great Awakening, gathered momentum in the early decades of the nineteenth century. Presbyterians, many of whom had been aggressive in their evangelism since the days of Whitefield, at first welcomed the revival as a deterrent to "infidelity" and as a check on the spiritual declension threatening the nation. Princeton Seminary reflected the power of this Second Great Awakening. Archibald Alexander was converted during its early Virginia phase and preached in the midst of revivals during his youthful ministry. He saw the revival's power and sometimes its frenzy—in meeting houses, in wilderness clearings, in school yards, and pioneer villages—among young and old. The majority of the students in Princeton's early years—including a number of converts from the notable awakening which occurred in 1815 at Princeton College—were products of revivals. By the 1820s, however, the revival had become a matter of controversy. The popularity of untrained preachers, the acceptance of doctrinal outlooks more in line with the democratic mentality of the nation, emotional excesses, and new approaches to evangelism all created considerable disturbance among Presbyterians. Some broke away completely from the doctrinal and educational requirements of Presbyterianism (such as those forming the Cumberland Presbyterian Church and the Disciples movement of Barton Stone and Thomas Campbell); others remained Presbyterian but modified their message and practice; while still others (including Princeton) tried to distinguish between true revival and its false expressions.

*　　*　　*

The Princetonians greatly appreciated the ministry of Asahel Nettleton.[15] Samuel Miller met Nettleton in New England in 1820 and was drawn at once to the renowned evangelist. Nettleton was born on April 21, 1783, in North Killingworth, Connecticut. He grew up without Christian influences and was thinking of opening a dancing school when he was converted in 1801. Poor health prevented his becoming a foreign missionary. Nettleton graduated from Yale in 1809 and remained there for postgraduate studies. When he was asked to take a preaching assignment in eastern Connecticut, his ability as an evangelist was immediately evident and he was ordained in 1811. "So fruitful was his preaching, so self-effacing and cooperative was he, and so decorous and unsensational were his methods, that he was soon in great demand not only in Connecticut but in New York and elsewhere in New England."[16] Conservative in practice and retiring in manner, he was scrupulous in his attempt to avoid unnecessary attention to himself and to involve the local pastors fully in his ministry. He was known to leave in the middle of a series of meetings if he felt that people were looking too much to him to produce a revival. He stressed total dependence on God's sovereign grace and rejected any techniques that could be interpreted as "getting up a revival." Powerful but sober sermons and a reverent, orderly atmosphere became trademarks of his revival meetings. Early supporter Lyman Beecher described Nettleton's preaching as "discriminatingly doctrinal, giving a clear and strong exhibition of doctrines denominated Calvinistic." In some of his sermons, Beecher added, there was "unsurpassed power of description, which made the subject a matter of present reality." James W. Alexander, who heard Nettleton preach on three occasions, wrote that although he was "one of the most solid, textual, and methodical speakers, he usually laid no paper before him. His speaking in the pulpit was exactly like his speaking by the fireside."[17] In addition to preaching, Nettleton systematically visited homes, conducted personal conferences, and provided careful follow-up instruction. His greatest effectiveness, in Beecher's opinion, was in "the ubiquity and power of his personal attention where exigencies called for it, and the little circles which he met daily, when many were interested, to instruct and guide."[18]

Charles Hodge probably had Asahel Nettleton in mind when he wrote in 1835:

We have often admired the wisdom of those men whose ministrations have been so pre-eminently blessed, in purposely avoiding to excite any such expectation [of results due to their presence]. It was almost an invariable rule for them not to go where they had been specially invited and great expectations aroused of the results of their visit. They appeared among the people without any flourish of trumpets, or note of preparation, and without allowing the word revival to be mentioned, laboured to awaken the church and to bring the careless under the power of the truth.[19]

However much Nettleton pleased Princeton, his preaching fell out of favor with many of the New England ministers because of his tenacious insistence on preaching the old Calvinistic doctrines of original sin and divine election. His later work was publicly eclipsed by the more sensational career of Charles Finney—a revivalist Lyman Beecher compared unfavorably to Nettleton in 1827, when he wrote that Finney was "as far removed from the talent, wisdom and judgment and experience of Nettleton, as any corporal in the French army was removed from the talent and generalship of Bonaparte."[20]

\*  \*  \*

Named after the hero of a popular novel by Samuel Richardson, Charles Grandison Finney was born in Connecticut on August 29, 1792. He grew up in the frontier wilderness of Oneida and Jefferson Counties in central New York—often called the "burned-over district" because of the numerous movements, experiments, and religious revivals which for years swept through that area. Finney, a striking-looking, dynamic young lawyer, with a worldly spirit and large ambition, was converted in 1821. After a time of soul-searching, he had knelt and prayed in the woods near his home in Adams, New York, until he was "most wonderfully quiet and peaceful." The next morning, a man came into the law office of Wright and Wardwell where Finney was employed and said, "Mr. Finney, do you recollect that my cause is to be tried at ten o'clock this morning? I suppose you are ready?" Charles Finney replied, "Deacon Barney, I have a retainer from the Lord Jesus Christ to plead his cause, and I cannot plead yours."[21]

Charles Finney attended the Presbyterian church in Adams and soon found himself at odds with the Calvinistic sermons of the energetic young pastor, Princeton graduate George Gale. Gale stressed the sovereignty of God, election, original sin, and limited atonement. Finney's reading of Blackstone's legal commentaries taught him that only those violations of the law that were committed voluntarily with a will that was free could be justifiably punished. He was enraged to discover that Calvin and the Westminster standards of the Presbyterian church taught that the human will was in bondage, encumbered with inherited guilt and not free to obey God. Gale preached on the necessity for repentance and saving faith, but he made it clear that one could not repent and believe in his own strength. To teach that people were mired in sin and unable to exert moral choice, Finney thought irrational and utterly unfair. He soon came to believe that people were not sinners from birth but from choice; they were endowed by nature with all the power of moral agency. Because it was in their power to do so, it was, therefore, their duty to repent, believe, and obey the gospel. It was, after all, what Finney himself had done. "Gospel salvation," he later wrote, "seemed to me to be an affair of something to be accepted; and that it was full and complete; and that all that was necessary on my part, was to get my own consent to give up my sins, and accept Christ."[22] Entirely ignorant of the long history of Pelagianism, Finney was convinced from his reading of the Bible (influenced, certainly, by his legal training) that the broken relationship with God could be healed if mankind would simply turn to him in repentance.

Despite their differences, Finney and Gale became friends.[23] The pastor guided the zealous new convert through the steps of coming under care of the Saint Lawrence Presbytery and supervised his study for the ministry (after Finney's application for a scholarship had been turned down by Andover, Princeton, and Auburn seminaries).[24] Finney's study with Gale was "little else than controversy." He wrote that his minister

used to insist that if I would reason on the subject, I should probably land in infidelity. And then he would remind me that some of the students had gone away infidels, because they would reason on the subject, and would not accept the Confession of Faith, and the teaching of the doctors at that school. He furthermore warned me repeatedly, and very feelingly, that as a minister I should never be useful unless I embrace the truth, meaning the truth as he believed and taught it.[25]

Finney, however, preferred to go directly to the Bible and "to the philosophy or workings" of his own mind for his theology.

Finney's studies were gradually eclipsed by his evangelistic efforts. At his licensure exam on December 30, 1823—after only six months of study—one presbyter asked Finney if he subscribed to the Westminster Confession of Faith. Incredibly, Finney claimed that he had not even read it! More incredibly, the presbytery licensed him anyway and sent him as a missionary to Jefferson County, where he preached "in school-houses, and barns, and groves."[26] He was ordained on July 1, 1824, and moved his operations south to Oneida County.

After sensational revival campaigns in the towns of western New York, Charles Finney turned to the major cities of the eastern seaboard. Lyman Beecher, observing Finney's power and recognizing that he and Finney were in theological agreement, made an uneasy peace with him at the General Assembly of May 1828 in Philadelphia.[27] During 1828, Finney preached in "Anti-Revival" Philadelphia, with numerous conversions but no widespread awakening. He next turned to New York City—"Satan's last outpost," he called it—where he was supported by wealthy laymen of New England background and Congregationalist conviction. With their financial resources and the enthusiasm that Finney's preaching generated, these prominent New Yorkers founded several new "Free" Presbyterian churches (with free seats for all in contrast to the normal pew-rent system of most churches of the day).

In 1830 Finney went to Rochester, New York—a boom town on the newly completed Erie Canal—where he conducted the first city-wide evangelistic effort in American history. With support of all the Protestant churches, he followed a broad, undenominational approach in presenting the gospel. The Rochester revival, the most successful of Finney's career, wedded temperance meetings with evangelistic appeals (and the use of "anxious seats" on a large scale). The revival, which reached out to over one hundred miles around Rochester, affected the moral atmosphere of the entire area and added hundreds to the churches. Finney next preached in Boston; he then returned to New York City in 1832 to become pastor of the Second Free Presbyterian Church (also called the Chatham Street Chapel), which met in a renovated auditorium holding 2,500 people.

In 1835 Finney became the professor of theology in the new Oberlin College in Ohio, while continuing to serve as pastor in New York. On March 13, 1836, he resigned from the Chatham Street Chapel and announced his intention to demit the ministry of the Presbyterian church and transfer his ordination to the Congregationalists. The magnificent new Broadway Tabernacle, built to Finney's specifications, was constituted a Congregational church and Finney became its pastor. A year later he sadly tendered his resignation at the tabernacle to concentrate on his teaching at Oberlin. Finney, however, continued to spend large blocks of time in evangelistic preaching in the eastern states and in England.

Charles Finney's powerful, colloquial, direct, and denunciatory style of preaching and his "new measures" appealed to some and shocked others. The "new measures" (many of which had been used by the Methodists for years) included "protracted" (night-after-night) meetings; lay exhortation; the practice of praying publicly for the conversion of people by name; public praying by women in mixed audiences; the invitation to come forward; and hasty admission of converts to church membership. The "new measures" appeared to some to be necessary parts of a revival. For true Calvinists, however, this was to confuse human contrivances with outpourings of divine grace.

Finney had vehemently rejected what he termed the "strait jacket" theology of Princeton Seminary and despised its "Old School" doctrines. He advocated a doctrine of the atonement which demonstrated the love of God and made it possible for people to repent. He rejected the doctrine of total depravity, insisting that the prevailing "cannot-ism" must be replaced by telling sinners that they had the power to experience immediate conversion. He urged sinners "to make themselves a new heart and a new spirit" and pressed "the duty of instant surrender to God." The function of the Holy Spirit, Finney said, was to persuade people to make the right choice. Ultimately the decision rested with the sinner. He criticized ministers who "preached repentance and at the same time told people that they could not repent." He summed up his disgust in the words of the popular anti-Calvinistic jingle, "You can, but you can't; you will, but you won't; you're damned if you do, and damned if you don't"!

Asahel Nettleton undoubtedly had Finney in mind when he said in a sermon:

There are many who think they see a great inconsistency in the preaching of ministers. "Ministers," they say, "contradict themselves—they say and unsay—they tell us to do, and then tell us we cannot do—they call upon sinners to believe and repent, and then tell them that faith and repentance are the gift of God—they call on them to come to Christ, and then tell them that they cannot come."

That some do preach in this manner, cannot be denied. I well recollect an instance. A celebrated preacher, in one of his discourses used this language: "*Come unto me,* all ye that labour and are heavy laden, and I will give you rest." In another discourse, this same preacher said: "No man *can come unto me* except the Father which hath sent me draw him." Now, what think you, my hearers, of such preaching, and of such a preacher? What would you have said had you been present and heard Him? Would you have charged Him with contradicting himself? This preacher, you will remember, was *none other than the Lord Jesus Christ!* And, I have no doubt, that many ministers have followed His example, and been guilty of the same self-contradiction, if you call it such.[28]

At Park Street Church in Boston, in the autumn of 1831, Finney preached a sermon from Ezekiel 18:31 entitled "Sinners Bound to Change Their Own Hearts." God's part in conversion, Finney said, was to influence the sinner to change; but "the sinner actually changes, and is therefore himself, in the most proper sense, the author of the change."[29] Asa Rand published a lead article entitled "The New Divinity Tried" in his paper, the *Volunteer,* in which he exposed the errors of Finney's sermon. In a dignified and respectful but relentless manner, he accused the New Divinity of ignoring not only the doctrine of the Westminster Confession of Faith, but also the many scriptures that teach the imputation of Adam's sin to his descendants with the result that all are born in sin, defiled in the faculties of soul and body, possessed of a nature that is the opposite of good, and utterly unable to change their condition. According to Rand, Charles Finney reduced the work of the Holy Spirit in salvation to "a small and weak thing," trivializing his essential role in making people "willing and able to believe."[30] Rand's article, reprinted in a sixteen-page booklet, created a furor. Benjamin B. Wisner of the Boston Old South Church, who had been the key figure in Charles Finney's coming to Boston, defended Finney's orthodoxy, although he admitted that Finney was deficient in his view of the work of the Holy Spirit in regeneration.

\*      \*      \*

Princeton had watched these developments in the Presbyterian church with great concern. The faculty were unhappy with the theological innovations of the New England Calvinists and the revival practices of Finney and his followers, but they had followed a course of caution and patience. Charles Finney's "New Heart" sermon and Wisner's review of Rand's criticisms, however, could not go unchallenged. In April 1832, the *Biblical Repertory* published Charles Hodge's twenty-six-page "Review of 'The New Divinity Tried.'"[31] Hodge saw nothing new in the New Divinity except that these old teachings were now "being held by men professing to be Calvinists." Hodge upheld Asa Rand at every point and at one point went beyond Rand. He agreed with Rand that the tendency of Finney's mode of evangelism rested largely in the sinner's own determination and so minimized the role of the Holy Spirit. But Hodge added the serious charge that Finney's approach gave insufficient attention to Christ's work. "Christ and his cross are practically made of none effect," Hodge wrote; "the constant exhortation is, to make choice of God as the portion of the soul; to change the governing purpose of the life; to submit to the moral Governor of the universe." Where in all of this, Hodge wondered, was the mediator? "The sinner is led to God directly . . . he is not urged, under the pressure of the sense of guilt, to go to Christ for pardon."[32]

The Princetonians saw a connection between the theology and methodology of Charles Finney and his followers. "That the new measures and the new divinity should have formed an intimate alliance," Charles Hodge wrote in 1835, "can surprise no one aware of their natural affinity."[33] Just as the New Divinity placed an emphasis on the sinner's ability to choose either good or evil, so the new measures were designed to increase the pressure on the person to make a self-conscious and immediate choice to accept Christ. In his preface to the Princeton edition of Halyburton's *Memoirs*, written in 1833, Dr. Alexander compared the conversion of Thomas Halyburton with those of the present day:

While, in our day, conversions are multiplied beyond all former precedent, there is much reason to fear, that many of them will not bear to be brought to the touch-stone of God's word. With many, conversion has become a slight and easy thing, the mere hasty purpose of an hour; and unaccompanied by those deep views of depravity, and those soul-comforting views of Jesus Christ, which are here described. The consequence is, that multitudes who profess conversion, do not exhibit, in any satisfactory degree, the spirit of Jesus Christ, in meekness, humility, benevolence, and self-denial of their character.[34]

Samuel Miller offered an even more negative assessment of the new measures when he wrote in 1833:

When this exciting system of calling to "anxious seats,"—calling out into the aisles to be "prayed for," etc., is connected, as to my certain knowledge, it often has been, with erroneous doctrines;—for example, with the declaration that nothing is *easier* than conversion;—that the power of the Holy Spirit is not necessary to enable impenitent sinners to repent and believe;—that if they only resolve to be for God—resolve to be Christians—*that* itself is regeneration—the work is already done:—I say, where the system of "anxious seats," etc., is connected with such doctrinal statements as these, it appears to be adapted to destroy souls wholesale! I will not say that *such* revivals are never connected with sound conversions; but I will be bold to repeat, that the religion which they are *fitted to cherish*, is altogether a different one from that of the Gospel.[35]

During the winter and spring of 1834-35, Charles Finney gave a series of twenty-two lectures in the Chatham Street Chapel on the subject of revivals. First published in *The New York Evangelist*, the series was quickly put into book form, with the title *Lectures on Revivals of Religion*. In the first lecture, Finney set forth his definition of a revival. It "is not a miracle, or dependent on a miracle in any sense," he said. "It is a purely philosophical [i. e., scientific] result of the right use of the constituted means—as much so as any other effect produced by the application of means."[36] Here Finney directly contradicted the older view of Edwards, Whitefield, the Princetonians—and practically everyone else until then— that revivals came only in God's good time. Throughout his lectures, Finney praised the Methodists for their warm preaching and soul-winning successes and heaped criticism upon the Presbyterians. Presbyterian ministers, he said, did not "pour out fire" upon their hearers and, despite their great learning, had been outstripped by the Methodists in the size of their churches. "We must have exciting, powerful preaching, or the devil will have the people, except what the Methodists can save," Finney warned. Much of the blame rested, Finney said, upon "the traditions of the elders," as he scornfully called the doctrines of Calvinism. He denounced the system of doctrine of the Westminster Confession of Faith (which he referred to elsewhere as "this wonderful theological fiction").[37] Particularly the doctrine of election had stifled Presbyterian preaching, he claimed, as it inhibited immediate response by telling sinners that although they must repent they could not. He saved his most withering blast for the General Assembly. "These things in the Presbyterian Church," he exclaimed, "their contentions and janglings are so ridiculous, so wicked, so outrageous, that no doubt there is a jubilee in hell every year, about the time of the meeting of the General Assembly."[38]

The Old School counterattack was not slow to come. Its chief answer was a ninety-seven-page article by Princeton College professor Albert B. Dod, contained in two issues (July and October 1835) of the *Biblical Repertory*.[39] With biting sarcasm, Dod faulted Finney's literary style and knowledge of history and pointed out his errors in biblical and theological matters. In July, Dod dealt basically with Finney's book of sermons and concluded that his teachings were "neither more nor less than the old Pelagian notions." In the October issue, Dod turned to Finney's *Lectures* and found two major problems. First, he pointed to the extremism promoted by Finney's approach. Second, and more serious, was the unsound doctrine that accompanied the revival practices of Finney and his friends. There was, he wrote, "a close and logical connexion between Mr. Finney's theology and his measures." The abstractions of the New Haven theology had come to life in "the coarse, bustling fanaticism of the New Measures." Dod called upon Finney to perform "his plain duty" and leave the Presbyterian church for another "within which he can preach and publish his opinions without making war upon the standards in which he has solemnly professed his faith." Dod concluded his second article with the harsh words—"Nor will we withdraw our charges against him, until he goes out from among us, for he is not of us."[40]

\*       \*       \*

While the Princetonians firmly opposed the New England theology and Finney's revivalism, they were not opposed to different methods and new ideas. On March 27, 1832, J. W. Alexander wrote:

One man has anxious meetings, another anxious seats, a third calls them out in the aisle, a fourth invites them to his study, a fifth visits them at home. Here are diversities of methods, but no ground, I think, for violent controversy. Various methods have been blessed, to my knowledge, in various revivals, and new ones are yet to be invented. On this subject, I think our old men are too tenacious. Nothing is worse in my estimation, *because* it is new, unless indeed it be doctrine. It is hard to determine in all cases what measures are the best, but almost any are better than total listlessness.[41]

Although the Princetonians disapproved of many of the new measures, they did not reject "protracted meetings." Such meetings, John Breckinridge wrote, "combine the labours and prayers of many ministers, and of a whole church at once; they protract and deepen the impression of the truth upon the principle and after the manner of the Sabbath." This practice, he declared, is "as old as the Kirk of Scotland, yea, as the Church of Christ; and are virtually recommended in our directory for worship." Breckinridge admitted that some do oppose revivals on principle and therefore "do well nigh as much harm as all our errorists and innovators." Having to choose between the opponents of revival and the innovators, Breckinridge wrote, would be a "real calamity"— "like selecting between stupor and intoxication; between madness and death."[42]

The Princetonians attempted to avoid these extremes. There was no one in the Presbyterian church who had studied more closely the whole subject of revivals than Archibald Alexander. His lifelong positive attitude toward revivals was partly due to his early experiences in Virginia. His warnings concerning the dangers of emotional excesses, unbiblical methods, and doctrinal deviations were not the observations of a detached critic. It was Dr. Alexander's custom to lecture to the seminary students "fully and frankly" on revivals. He urged them to seek God's blessing in reviving their churches. He prepared them for the criticism that Calvinistic preaching would produce the complacent attitude that since people were "dead in trespasses and sins," they were excusable and need make no effort "until it should please a sovereign God to work." Alexander answered that "the true system is, to exhort sinners to be found in the use of God's appointed means; that is, to be diligent in attendance on the word, and at the throne of grace. . . . While they are reading, or hearing, or meditating, or praying, God may, by his Holy Spirit, work faith in their hearts."[43] He argued that the opposite doctrine that people "can repent, at any moment, by a proper use of their own powers" was much more likely to produce overconfidence, postponement of action, and a failure to make a Christian commitment than his own Calvinistic emphasis on God's ultimate sovereignty. The sober opinions which Dr. Alexander calmly maintained became the settled judgment of a large part of the Presbyterian church, through the preaching and writing of his students.

In 1832, William B. Sprague, pastor of the Second Presbyterian Church in Albany, New York, issued a book with the same title that Finney later used, *Lectures on Revivals of Religion*.[44] Sprague had observed the revivals for years; and now, in his book, he tried to distinguish between false excitements and true awakenings. Twenty leading ministers of six denominations gave their views in letters written for the appendix of Sprague's book. Archibald Alexander discussed the problems of modern revivalism and then briefly set forth the Princeton view of "genuine revivals, where the gospel is preached in its purity, and where the people have been well instructed in the doctrines of Christianity."

In some cases revivals are so remarkably pure, that nothing occurs with which any pious man can find fault. There is not only no wildness and extravagance, but very little strong commotion of the animal feelings. The word of God distils upon the mind like the gentle rain, and the Holy Spirit comes down like the dew, diffusing a blessed influence on all around. Such a revival affords the most beautiful sight ever seen upon earth. Its aspect gives us a lively idea of what will be the general state of things IN THE LATTER-DAY GLORY, and some faint image of the heavenly state. The impressions on the minds of the people in such a work are the exact counterpart of the truth; just as the impression on the wax corresponds to the seal. In such revivals there is great solemnity and silence. The convictions of sin are deep and humbling: the justice of God in the condemnation of the sinner is felt and acknowledged; every other refuge but Christ is abandoned; the heart at first is made to feel its own impenetrable hardness; but when least expected, it dissolves under a grateful sense of God's goodness, and Christ's love; light breaks in upon the soul either by a gradual dawning, or by a sudden flash; Christ is revealed through the gospel, and a firm and often a joyful confidence of salvation through Him is produced: a benevolent, forgiving, meek, humble and contrite spirit predominates—the love of God is shed abroad—and with some, joy unspeakable and full of glory, fills the soul. A spirit of devotion is enkindled. The word of God become exceedingly precious. Prayer is the exercise in which the soul seems to be in its proper element, because by it, God is approached, and his presence felt, and beauty seen: and the new-born soul lives by breathing after the knowledge of God, after communion with God, and after conformity to his will. Now also springs up in the soul an inextinguishable desire to promote the glory of God, and to bring all men to the knowledge of the truth, and by that means to the possession of eternal life. The sincere language of the heart is, "Lord what wouldst thou have me to do?" That God may send upon his church many such revivals, is my daily prayer; and many such have been experienced in our country, and I trust are still going forward in our churches.

Alexander believed that the ideal would be that of continuous genuine revival, in which sinners were constantly being converted and the church renewed. He acknowledged, however, that it seemed to be God's will to send "seasons of refreshing." If God, he wrote, "chooses to water his church by occasional showers, rather than the perpetual dew of his grace . . . we should rejoice and be grateful for the rich effusions of his Spirit in any form and manner."[45]

Dr. Alexander did look for and rejoice in genuine revivals. He circulated his writings on revivals and religious experience in a number of papers before collecting them into a book in 1841. In his *Thoughts on Religious Experience* he studied specific examples, with observations concerning the nature of conviction, the experience of conversion, sanctification and its accompanying spiritual conflicts, and death and dying.

[232]

Charles Hodge's views on revivals were expressed in a number of writings for many years. In 1835, he stated that "as in every individual Christian there are seasons of more or less devotional feeling, fidelity, and activity, so it is in every church." Revivals, though not the only mode of spiritual progress, are precious manifestations of divine power. In most cases, Hodge stated, "the work commences silently in the hearts of a few praying people; the sacred fire gradually spreads through the church; the word is preached with more point and fervour; prayer is offered with greater importunity and faith; the Spirit descends with power upon the people, and they are in the midst of revival before the word has been pronounced."[46]

The Princetonians participated enthusiastically in these times of revival. According to J. W. Alexander, "there was no preacher whose services were sought with greater avidity during . . . seasons of religious warmth" than his father.[47] The Society of Inquiry reported on April 8, 1831, that increasing attention was being given to religion in Princeton. Prayer meetings were held in the Presbyterian church every morning at six o'clock. By September, there had been two hundred conversions in "the little societies under the care of the seminary students." In 1837, professors Alexander, Miller, and Breckinridge preached in a revival which reached nearby New Brunswick and produced five hundred "hopeful conversions." The annual report of the Committee on Revivals for the year 1841 described a revival then taking place in the vicinity of Princeton: it "commenced at Penn's-Neck" through the work of student Thomas Malcom—or actually, the report stated, "in his increased prayers and faith." "Hopeful conversions" had reached nearly one hundred. In 1844 Dr. Alexander wrote to a young relative, "We had a precious shower of grace here, without any new measures or any undue excitement."[48] Most of the seminary students agreed with their teacher in opposing "extraordinary measures" while supporting revivals. The Committee on Domestic Missions and Revivals of the Society of Inquiry said of a revival in the Third Presbyterian Church in Philadelphia, "One of the most remarkable things attending this revival was the fact that there was nothing remarkable about it!"

During times of revival, students often left the seminary temporarily to assist in the work. In March 1848, the pastor of the old Tennent Church in Monmouth County, New Jersey, came to Princeton to ask for help with the revival in his area. Dr. Alexander sent three students, who, after a week of hard work, returned to their studies reporting that "the blessing that rested upon the people seemed to fall on us."

Princeton's understanding of revival in the traditional Calvinistic and Edwardsean sense carried great weight with many American Christians, but Finney's message and method were in greater harmony with the thought and activism of the period. As Andrew Jackson, who was elected president in 1828, brought into politics a powerful democratizing force, so Charles Finney was a leader in the democratization of American Christianity.[49] Preaching the complete freedom of the human will in moral issues, and rejecting traditional methods and authoritative creeds, he fit perfectly the optimistic mood of the rapidly expanding country.

Princeton, however, was firm in its commitment to the older views. "The mournful truth is, that spurious and fanatical excitements have so commonly been dignified by the name of revivals," wrote Charles Hodge, "that that term, so dear to the American churches, has in a measure lost its sacred import, and no longer stands as the certain symbol of the manifestation of the divine power."[50] The Princetonians persisted in viewing religious awakenings as the "surprising" work of God—powerful, unpredictable, and diverse. In the context of the Revival of 1858, James W. Alexander wrote:

The principle should never be forgotten, that while the great laws of the divine government and the dispensation of grace remain the same, the Supreme Giver varies his modes of bounty, with reference to differences of country and period. Apostolic awakenings were in some things unlike those of the Reformation day. The quiet, spring-like renewal of vital godliness, under Spener, Francke, and the Pietists, bore little external resemblance to the prodigious revolution under the Wesleys, Whitefield, Edwards, the Tennents and the Blairs. The very remarkable awakenings in which Dr. Nettleton and his friends were instrumental differ again from the times of refreshing in which we live. Let us not limit the Holy One of Israel.[51]

During this time of change and rising tensions in the Presbyterian church, Princeton Seminary attempted to hold, as Dr. Alexander had said, "the old doctrines of Calvinism." For the Princetonians, this meant tolerance of theological ideas which did not violate the system of doctrine taught in the Westminster Confession of Faith but determined rejection of those that did. It meant holding to a positive and lively view of revivals without embracing compromising theology or questionable methodology. Charles Finney—who stood for much of what Princeton opposed—left the Presbyterian church for Congregationalism in 1836; but the problems facing the church and the seminary were far from over.

# 12

# Our Beloved Zion

*Samuel Miller,*
*Princeton's second Professor,*
*at age 72.*

Our religion is not, as someone has said, like the moon, giving light without heat, nor like the stove, giving heat without light, but like the sun, giving perennial light, and warmth, and life.

JAMES WADDEL ALEXANDER

THE Plan of Union of 1801 formally sanctioned Congregational-Presbyterian cooperation in church planting. It made it possible for Presbyterians and Congregationalists in any community to form one congregation, call a pastor from either denomination, and join either the local presbytery or the congregational association. This "presbygational" arrangement—as it came to be called—worked in favor of the Presbyterians, because many of the churches formed were received into local presbyteries. But in doctrinal matters, a tide of New England Theology began to flow into the Presbyterian church. Old School Presbyterians were distressed to realize that, through the Plan of Union, the doctrine which they so heartily disapproved was becoming part of their beloved church.

Another problem facing Presbyterians was the expanding activity of the extra-ecclesiastical voluntary associations. Sensing that the divided denominations were by themselves inadequate to accomplish the task of Christianizing the new nation and the world, American Protestants formed a number of voluntary societies to promote missions, education, and a variety of benevolent reforms. The American Board of Commissioners for Foreign Missions (1810), the American Bible Society (1816), the American Education Society (1816), the American Colonization Society (1816), the American Sunday School Union (1817), the American Tract Society (1826), the American Home Missionary Society (1826), and the American Temperance Society (1826) were the "great eight." Numerous lesser societies promoted prison reform, Sabbath observance, recovery of prostitutes, and many other causes. The multiple good works of "the Evangelical United Front," as it was called, were promoted by revival preaching and by thousands of local chapters. With headquarters in Boston, New York, and Philadelphia, these organizations had interlocking directorates of a few wealthy eastern business men, mostly New School Presbyterians and New Divinity Congregationalists. Huge amounts of money were collected. By the 1830s, the combined budgets of the fourteen largest societies easily rivaled the major expenditures of the federal government. Hundreds of delegates came to New York each May for the "anniversary meetings"— a major event in the American Christian calendar. At first almost all Presbyterians supported these organizations; but by 1830 participation in certain of the societies had become a matter of dispute.

Controversy erupted first concerning the American Education Society—the most powerful of the organizations which provided financial aid for men studying for the ministry. As a result of its financial involvement with students, the society functioned as a kind of informal accrediting agency of theological seminaries. In 1829 the General Assembly of the Presbyterian Church had reorganized its Board of Education—to provide financial support for ministerial candidates—and called upon the churches to support it. Dr. Carnahan, president of Princeton College, published an article in the July 1829 issue of the *Biblical Repertory*, in which he set forth his objections to the American Education Society. Professor Stuart of Andover replied in the October issue; there was a rejoinder from the "conductors" of the Princeton journal. When a separate edition of Stuart's article, with a sixteen-page postscript, was published, it was reviewed in the January 1830 issue of the *Biblical Repertory*. Archibald Alexander explained the issue to a South Carolina pastor in 1831: "The question which now presses itself on the attention of every Presbyterian, is, whether we had best give up this whole concern into the hands of the A. E. S.; or whether we should endeavor, *as a church*, and by our constitutional judicatories to retain some control over the education of the candidates for the ministry, within our limits." Princeton believed, Alexander stated, "that this is a concern, which above others, should be managed by the church in her distinctive capacity"; but he greatly regretted "that the spirit of party has become so dominant."[1]

In 1832 Samuel Miller insisted, in a letter to the American Home Missionary Society, that he had no prejudice against voluntary associations and saw great need for these organizations that, in his opinion, could "gain access to many places, and accomplish many things, which an ecclesiastical board could not do." At the same time, he was firmly committed to the continuation of the Presbyterian Board of Missions, independent and separate from the American Home Missionary Society. In his *Letters to Presbyterians on the Present Crisis in the Presbyterian Church in the United States,* Miller continued to view both voluntary societies and ecclesiastical boards as useful and necessary but insisted that the Presbyterian church, as a church, must guard its doctrine and government and prepare its ministers. Miller wrote that although he was still supportive of certain voluntary societies, he now was convinced that "voluntary associations for conducting domestic missions and for educating young men for the holy ministry, ought never to be encouraged by those who prize the purity and peace of the church."[2]

Archibald Alexander approved and recommended the Bible Society, the Tract Society, and the Colonization Society, but stated that the work of training its ministers and establishing churches must come under the direct jurisdiction of the Presbyterian church.[3] Charles Hodge agreed that for certain activities, such as those sponsored by the Bible and tract societies and the American Sunday School Union, interdenominational cooperation was quite proper; but other ministries, such as the education of ministerial candidates and the supervision of their work, only the church itself could properly conduct. "The men who decide where and how the rising ministry are to be educated, and who determine where they are to go when their education is completed," Hodge wrote, "have the destiny of the Church in their hands." "People may cry out against all this as high churchism," he added, but "it is Presbyterianism"![4]

While Princeton was carefully discriminating between Hopkinsianism and Taylorism, and between legitimate and unacceptable interdenominational cooperation, other Presbyterian leaders had become convinced that the situation in the Presbyterian church was critical; they pressed for the prosecution of heresy or the division of the church. Ashbel Green took the lead in marshaling the conservative forces with three articles in the *Christian Advocate* in 1831. He defined the parties in the church as "Old School" and "New School" and stated that the major difference was that the "New School" allowed "a far greater latitude of construction" in its view of subscription to the Westminster Confession of Faith. J. W. Alexander appreciated the concerns of Dr. Green but wrote on March 10, 1831, "It is devoutly to be wished, that in 'contending for the faith,' which is enjoined, they may not 'strive,' which is forbidden."[5]

The 1831 General Assembly saw the first great clash between the two parties. Albert Barnes, a graduate of Princeton Seminary and pastor of the Presbyterian church at Morristown, New Jersey, had published a sermon in 1829 on "The Way of Salvation." He advocated doctrines that sounded more like New England—and Charles Finney—than Princeton. When Barnes was called the next year to the distinguished First Church of Philadelphia, the presbytery seized the opportunity and charged him with doctrinal error. The case went to the General Assembly in 1831, which acquitted him with an admonition against unguarded statements. New School adherents were heartened by their victory, but Dr. Green and his supporters were not about to give up. They were greatly thwarted, however, when the General Assembly allowed the creation of a second presbytery in Philadelphia, based on the "elective affinity"—a procedure which had already been used in New York City to allow a New School presbytery to function without Old School interference. From now on, the Old School Presbyterians in Philadelphia would have to challenge the New School men at the level of synod or general assembly, where the outcome was in much more doubt than in the smaller, more easily controlled presbytery.

Old School Presbyterians put forth their case in a series of ten lectures delivered in Philadelphia during 1831-32. In his introduction to the publication of the lectures, Ashbel Green stated that "in the Presbyterian Church, at the present time, doctrines not in accordance with our public standards, are freely promulgated, both from the pulpit and the press." He praised the Westminster Confession of Faith as the most accurate statement of the truths of the Bible; and so its teachings, he urged, "must be more favourable than any other to the advancement of genuine Christianity."[6] Among those giving "the Spruce Street Lectures" were Charles Hodge ("On the Nature of the Atonement"), Samuel Miller ("On Ecclesiastical Polity"), and John Breckinridge ("On Christian Missions").

Doctrinally, the sympathy of Princeton was clearly on the side of the Old School. But Charles Hodge and his colleagues disagreed with many, perhaps most, of their Old School brethren "as to the wisdom adopted for securing a common object."[7] After the General Assembly of 1831, Samuel Miller acknowledged that "the apprehensions of danger, felt by our friends of the Old School, are well founded"; but he urged restraint. He wrote:

Do you ask, What can and ought to be done? My reply is—(1) Let the friends of the Confession of Faith and of Presbyterianism be aware of the danger, and fully awake to its reality and character. (2) Let them calmly, humbly, and prayerfully preach the truth, and maintain it, not in a pugnacious and irritating manner, but mildly and firmly, in all their public and private acts, especially in all of their admissions of young men to license and ordination. (3) Let them show, by their indefatigable labor and zeal, that they are real friends of revivals of religion, which many of the New School brethren seem to wish to insinuate is not the case. (4) Let them treat their New School brethren mildly and affectionately, differing from them as little as possible in other matters, and guarding, as much as possible, against all exciting and dividing measures, and having as little warfare as possible consistently with regard to the truth.[8]

The stance of the Princetonians, described by Robert Baird as "men of the mildest spirit and most moderate sentiments," did not please some of the Old School leaders. J. W. Alexander wrote to John Hall on June 14, 1831, "Our Princeton men are considered by certain *soi-disant* standards as 'sneaking,' 'on the fence,' etc. There certainly is such a thing as right-eous moderation, and those who have practiced it have, as far as I know, in every age stood between two fires, incurring the wrath of both sides."[9] On October 11, he returned to the same topic:

You are aware that the Princeton men are in very ill odour with the *extrême droite* of the Philadelphia Presbytery. The Repertory is considered a craven publication, because it did not take sides at once on the Barnes controversy. Now all this is exceeding impolitic in the Philadelphia gentlemen. By excluding as "fence-men" all who have not fully participated in their panic, they run the risk of reducing their party to a mere handful. The truth is, the Princetonians are as thoroughly old-school in their theology as Dr. Green himself, but they are unable to see that it is the path of duty to denounce every dissentient individual.[10]

In 1833, Samuel Miller contributed to the *Presbyterian* a series of letters on the crisis in the Presbyterian church.[11] He expressed the fear that the Presbyterian church might split, recalling vividly the pain his father felt when the church had divided earlier into Old Side and New Side parties. Dr. Miller's first letter dealt with "Adherence to our Doctrinal Standards." Miller rejected both "absolute uniformity in the mode of explaining every minute detail of truth," which some advocated, and the acceptance of "all sorts of unscriptural opinion, except the extreme of heresy," which others appar-ently held. "If we cannot adopt some course between these ruinous extremes, and with a spirit of mutual affection and accommodation walk in it," Miller added, "there is an end of our long cherished union." The Westminster divines, stated Miller, had minor differences among themselves, but they were "all substantial and sincere *Calvinists*, and framed the Confession in such a manner as that those who differed, in respect to these minor shades of opinion, might all honestly adopt it." Miller put the issue clearly before the church:

And now, at the close, I ask, "What will you do?" The question is not, whether, in opposing erroneous opinions, you will patronize a system of "ultra" rigor, of inquisitorial strictness. This I have never approved, and have no wish to see applied. But the question is, whether you will honestly and with good faith maintain the system of doctrine which every minister elder of the Presbyterian Church has solemnly engaged to sustain?[12]

J. W. Alexander wrote concerning Miller's articles: "It is a sincere attempt at pacification; and, like all such attempts, will displease the extremes."[13]

The New School controlled the general assemblies from 1831 through 1834. By 1832 many were expecting a split in the Presbyterian church. J. W. Alexander wrote on January 17, 1832, "Let us pray for something better. I mean, that the pious, humble, moderate, and (moderately) orthodox should come out from the ultras of both sides, and cohere as the Presbyterian church."[14]   Archibald Alexander preached a sermon on "The Pastoral Office" to the Princeton alumni during the 1834 General Assembly in Philadelphia.[15]   He said:

Much, very much, depends upon the decisions of this body, at the present sessions. It does not behoove me to dictate, or even suggest to you, what in particular should be done; but it is right that I should exhort you to lay aside all prejudice, passion, and party spirit, and with sincere and honest hearts, in the fear of God, to consult and act for the real welfare and the best interests of our beloved Zion, as you will answer for it at the tribunal of Jesus Christ, before which we must all soon appear. If now, while the ark of God is in your keeping, you should give it a wrong touch: if your measures should tend to destroy the purity, disturb the peace, or break the unity of this extended section of the Christian church, how awful your accountability. If through any want of wisdom or fidelity on your part, this well-organized society, should fall into dissension or disunion, what a triumph will you afford to the enemies of our common Christianity, and to those religious sects, which cherish feelings of envy and jealousy towards the Presbyterian Church.[16]

After the 1834 General Assembly, desperate Old School leaders called a special party convention and adopted "The Act and Testimony" (written by Robert J. Breckinridge) as a statement of their principles. About 375 ministers eventually signed the document; but many others, equally orthodox and equally concerned for the purity of the church, did not.

Charles Hodge wrote to his brother on November 21, 1834, "The Philadelphia men, Dr. Green, etc., etc., are driving matters to an extremity, and if they succeed we shall be ruined for the next ten or twenty years."[17] Hodge feared that "The Act and Testimony" would split the Old School portion of the church and that the stricter party would withdraw from the church, leaving the seminary completely under the control of the New School.

The *Biblical Repertory* published articles in October 1834 and January 1835 concerning "The Act and Testimony." The professors of the seminary sympathized with the general concerns of the leaders of the Old School and stated that "the fear of God, reverence for his truth, and love for his church, seem clearly to have presided over the composition of this important document." But Hodge and his colleagues could not accept "The Act and Testimony" for three main reasons. First, it constituted a new and unauthorized test of orthodoxy, rather than simply setting forth a testimony "against errors and disorder." Second, "The Act and Testimony" presented an untrue view of the state of the church by claiming that "alarming errors" were rampant. Third, the real effect of the document was division and not reform, because only the strictest Old School men could possibly agree with every statement. Charles Hodge wrote, "It is an act of gross injustice to multitudes of our soundest and best men; it is the effectual means of splitting the church into fragments, and of alienating from each other men, who agree in doctrine, in views of order and discipline, and who differ in nothing, perhaps, but in opinion as to the wisdom of introducing this new League and Covenant." Hodge urged that reform take place in a calm, orderly, constitutional manner, without the play on emotions that had been used by "The Act and Testimony" group. He defended the position of the Princetonians in the *Biblical Repertory* in January 1837. Hodge wrote:

We adhere to our principles, and disclaim all co-operation in any extra-constitutional measures, until the crisis shall arrive, when we shall have to decide between a good conscience and disunion. We are well aware that many of our brethren, with whom we agree on most points, differ from us on this. Nor can we shut our eyes to the indications, which are increasing in number and significance every week, which render the disruption of our beloved church a very probable event. Its probability, however, does not render it, in our apprehension, less to be deprecated. We believe the principle to be erroneous, and fear the consequences will be disastrous.[18]

Hodge added, however, that the chief blame for the crisis did not rest "on those who feel constrained, by their regard for truth, to effect a separation, even by disruption of the church, from the advocates of error" but "principally upon those who have driven them to this extremity."

"The Act and Testimony" men were greatly offended by Princeton's position. The Synod of Philadelphia passed a vote which amounted to a formal declaration of lack of confidence in the seminary. There was talk of shifting its support to Western Theological Seminary or starting a new seminary. The Princeton party was characterized as "trembling brethren" and "compromisers." They were suspected of lack of courage or excused as "secluded professors" and so less informed of the situation than active pastors would be. In late 1836 a delegation of Old School leaders came to Princeton to argue their case. They met with the three senior professors of the seminary and J. W. Alexander in Dr. Hodge's study. The meeting was friendly but did not alter the convictions of the two sides. The Princetonians continued to find themselves under attack from both parties. This resulted in financial pressures on the seminary; and for several years the faculty was frequently without salary. Dr. Alexander was hard-pressed, and Charles Hodge managed by borrowing from his well-to-do brother, Hugh, who generously rescued Charles by loans and gifts when his professor's salary was delayed or fell short.[19]

The Old School achieved a large majority in the 1835 General Assembly; but the New School was victorious in 1836. In 1835, Lyman Beecher, pastor of Second Presbyterian Church in Cincinnati, and well known for his New England views, had been charged with heresy, slander, and hypocrisy by Dr. Joshua L. Wilson, pastor of Cincinnati's First Presbyterian Church. Wilson claimed that Beecher denied original sin, imputed guilt, and people's inability to save themselves. Beecher was acquitted by the presbytery, the Synod of

Cincinnati, and by the 1836 General Assembly, where he delivered a statement of strict orthodoxy. The *Biblical Repertory* was satisfied with his statement but questioned his sincerity; and, in its 1837 review of his *Views in Theology*, it highlighted discrepancies between his earlier published works and orthodox Calvinism.

Meanwhile, Albert Barnes, having reiterated his views in a new commentary on Romans, was charged again with heresy before the Presbytery of Philadelphia.[20] Appeals were made to the synod and to the 1835 General Assembly. Here the Old School had a sufficient majority to condemn his writings and to depose him from the ministry. The next year, however, the General Assembly—with the New School in control—reversed the action of 1835 and restored Barnes to his pulpit. Samuel Miller voted to sustain the appeal of Barnes; but Miller's subsequent motion to instruct him "to be more careful" to conform his writings to the Confession of Faith failed by a vote of 109 to 122.

The 1836 General Assembly also made several significant decisions related to the controversy over the Presbyterian church's support of certain benevolent societies. For some time, the Old School had been threatening to dissociate the church from the American Board of Commissioners for Foreign Missions and the American Home Missionary Society. The New School majority defeated a proposal to replace the ABCFM with the Western Foreign Missionary Society—a mission agency of the Pittsburgh Synod—and almost succeeded in merging the denomination's home mission board with the AHMS. As a final blow to the conservatives—and especially the Princetonians—the assembly expressed its support of the founding of Union Theological Seminary in New York City, a New School–oriented seminary that would operate outside the control of the denomination.

Many Old School leaders were now ready to withdraw if they could not gain a majority and force the New School from the church. Samuel Miller opposed secession. He believed that only a minority of Old School men would withdraw and that this would leave all the funds and institutions of the church in New School hands. Archibald Alexander dreaded schism, but he "slowly and reluctantly arrived at the conclusion that the two parties could not much longer remain together."[21]

A pre-assembly Old School Convention in 1837 adopted a "Testimony and Memorial" that claimed that the New School party was riddled with heresy. The Princetonians had long attacked the "Pelagianism" of New Haven but refused to identify all New England theology as heresy; they believed that relatively few Presbyterians held the New Haven views. Samuel Miller claimed in 1833 that "nineteen-twentieths of our ministry and eldership are not liable, in any considerable degree to the charge in question." In 1836 Charles Hodge concurred, stating that the New Haven party was "very inconsiderable as to numbers."[22] A year later he wrote that "the majority of the church is sound, and sound as Presbyterians."[23] Hodge believed that matters were included in the charges of the "Testimony and Memorial" that "even the friends of sound doctrine could not regard as proper grounds of discipline."[24] Hodge saw his position and that of his Princeton colleagues as "difficult and delicate." He wrote in January 1837:

On the one hand we respect and love the great mass of our old school brethren; we believe them to constitute the bone and sinews of the Presbyterian church; we agree with them in doctrine; we sympathise with them in their disapprobation and distrust of the spirit and conduct of the leaders of the opposite party, and we harmonize with them in all the great leading principles of ecclesiastical policy, though we differ from a portion of them, how large or how small that portion may be we cannot tell, as to the propriety and wisdom of some particular measures.[25]

Ashbel Green and many others went to the General Assembly of 1837 determined to leave the church if the New School party gained control. When the Old School discovered that it had a majority, it moved quickly and decisively to "abrogate" the Plan of Union of 1801—an "unnatural and unconstitutional" arrangement, according to the Old School, which had produced "much confusion and irregularity." The Old School majority then made this abrogation retroactive in order to effect a separation from the "Congregationalism" resulting from the Plan of Union. By a series of "abscinding acts," they expelled the Synod of Western Reserve and three Synods of New York—Utica, Geneva, and Genessee—from the Presbyterian church. By this bold action, the General Assembly removed from its membership over five hundred ministers and churches and approximately sixty thousand church members and thus reduced the voting strength of the New School by half. The Old School majority went on to make the Western Foreign Missionary Society the sole mission board of the denomination and warned the ABCFM and the AHMS not to consider themselves part of Presbyterian work at home or abroad.

Princeton was represented at the General Assembly by Archibald Alexander. He voted for the abrogation of the Plan of Union and the excision of the Synod of Western Reserve but against the excision of the three synods in western New York. The Synod of Western Reserve was largely Congregational; but, in Dr. Alexander's opinion, the New York synods contained a majority of properly organized Presbyterian churches. He believed that the move to expel these synods was unnecessary to secure the reform of the church.

The Princeton men agreed with Alexander at every point except for the matter of the "excision" of the three synods of western New York. Samuel Miller and John Breckinridge approved of the General Assembly's action; Archibald Alexander and Charles Hodge, along with Professors Maclean, Dod, and J. W. Alexander of the college, preferred a plan which required Congregational churches in those synods to become presbyterially organized or to withdraw from the Presbyterian church. The *Biblical Repertory*, in reporting the action of the General Assembly, implied approval of the expulsion of the three synods of New York despite the disagreement of the Princeton men on this point. A note was added before publication stating that some of the "conductors" (meaning Dod, J. W. Alexander, and Hodge) felt that there was not sufficient evidence to justify the move. Several others, particularly Breckinridge, resisted the addition of the note, believing it likely to do harm. It was a struggle for Hodge to go against the strong opinion of his friends, but he would not yield. Hodge wrote to his brother on July 26, 1837, "Dr. Alexander did just what he ought to have done. He said he could not see the grounds of my scruples, and thought the thing inexpedient, but gave his cheerful assent to my saying in the note just what I pleased." Hodge was thankful that the matter was handled "without producing a breach" and that he had "still a good conscience." He told his brother that he would wonder when he saw the note "how little a matter has kindled such a flame."

The New School declared the "disowning acts" of 1837 "null and void" and sent commissioners to the next General Assembly, meeting at the Seventh Presbyterian Church in Philadelphia. No sooner had the opening prayer been offered than a New School spokesman arose with certain resolutions. The moderator pronounced him out of order, since, until the roll was called, there was no house to deliberate. The commissioner appealed from the chair to the house. The moderator replied that there was no house to appeal to. Chaos ensued, as the New School commissioners gathered in the aisles of the church. Amid shouts and tumult, they declared themselves the "Constitutional Assembly" and voted to adjourn to the First Presbyterian Church, where they organised a separate Presbyterian denomination. Nearly equal in size to the Old School, the New School's greatest strength was in New York State and in the upper Midwest. Most Presbyterians in the Middle States and in the South remained with the Old School.

Princeton was by now firmly in support of the assessment of the situation which others of the Old School had reached earlier. On June 11, 1837, Charles Hodge wrote to his brother:

I think substantial justice has been done, though there may, in some cases, have been some informality in the mode of doing it. . . . The simple truth is, that the church has tolerated the Congregationalized portion of the body until its very existence was in danger.[26]

Samuel Miller wrote to William Sprague on August 7, 1837:

I feel persuaded, that, however, repulsive or indefensible those acts may now appear, the more they are reflected on, and the more their bearings and consequences may disclose themselves, the more will sound and judicious men be reconciled to them. I do believe, that, long before the meeting of the next Assembly, the friends of truth and order will be convinced that the last Assembly had no other method of effectually putting an end to controversy, and restoring harmony to our beloved church, than by taking the course which they did.[27]

J. W. Alexander, who had deplored the controversy—and wrote in 1831, "O for a corner where Theological warfare is unknown"—now saw some good in the conflict. On August 10, 1837, he wrote:

I hope I shall never so far undervalue charity as not to lament the false fire kindled in church controversies; but I comfort myself with the thoughts, that what we love we always contend for; that the most flourishing seasons for piety have been those of the most active debates: witness the days of Augustine, of Luther, of the English Nonconformists; that the conservative principle of Protestantism is discussion of all points; and that the friction of debate is temporary, while the gain on the side of truth is permanent.[28]

Later in his life, Charles Hodge looked back over the division of the church in 1837 and stated that the Princeton men were in entire sympathy with the main principles of the Old School party.

They sided with them as to the right, and, under existing circumstances, the duty, of the church, to conduct the work of education and foreign and domestic missions by ecclesiastical boards, instead of voluntary, independent societies. They agreed with that party on all doctrinal questions in dispute; and as to the obligation to enforce conformity to our Confession of Faith on the part of ministers and teachers under our jurisdiction.[29]

The New School, to test its claim to the true succession and its entitlement to the funds and institutions of the Presbyterian church, brought suit in early March 1839. The trial drew together some of the most distinguished men of both churches and excited great interest across the United States. The court room was crowded with eager spectators trying to follow the complexities of church doctrine and polity.[30] When the New School won a favorable court decision in its suit, a dismayed Charles Hodge wrote to his brother, "We are, in the eye of the law, a secession from our own church; the New England men have succeeded in getting that church to themselves. . . . It is very painful to think of Princeton Seminary going to ruin; for it must go to ruin in the hands of New School men. They have a Seminary in New York, and cannot possibly supply both with students." Hodge hoped that the Old School could hang together, but he was fearful that if it lost its name and property it would "break into little fragments and cease to have much power to do good."[31] The case was appealed to the Supreme Court of Pennsylvania, which finally declared the Old School to be the legitimate successor of the General Assembly of 1837. Three years later, the New School quietly discontinued the suit.

\*     \*     \*

Meanwhile, Charles Hodge, urged by Old School leaders, was working hard on his *Constitutional History of the Presbyterian Church in the United States*.[32] He hoped that it would "tend to increase the respect and affection of Presbyterians for the church of their fathers." He also wanted, in the light of the current controversies, to demonstrate Old School principles in the history of the Presbyterian church from its founding to 1789. A. A. Hodge wrote:

It is believed that in the execution of this work Dr. Hodge fully proved that the founders of our Church in the United States intended to plant a true Presbyterian Church, a genuine daughter of the Church of Scotland, and that the terms of ministerial communion among us have been from the beginning, and by the constitution of the Church continue to be, the real belief and honest profession that "the System of Doctrine taught in the Holy Scriptures," is the one contained in the Westminster Confession of Faith and Catechisms. [33]

A. A. Hodge admitted, however, that the book was "the least natural, and most laborious work" that his father ever undertook.[34]

As Charles Hodge attempted to give his interpretation of the First Great Awakening and the Presbyterian Old Side-New Side controversy of the 1740s, he found himself, perhaps for the first time, in serious disagreement with Dr. Alexander. The Old Side Presbyterians had opposed George Whitefield and attempted to block the entrance of Log College graduates into the ministry of the church; they criticized the New Side's "disorderly way, contrary to all Presbyterian rules." The New Side attacked the "unconverted ministry" of their opponents and vigorously supported the revival. In his history, Hodge rejected the validity of the emotional outbursts of the eighteenth-century revivals and, in lengthy detail, identified these experiences with mental disorders. They are "nothing but one form of an *infectious* nervous disease," he wrote, "generated by strong impressions on the imagination and lively emotions."[35] He sharply criticized Jonathan Edwards for allowing the emotional phenomena to continue under his ministry and rebuked George Whitefield and William Tennent for their harsh judgment of the religious condition of ministers.[36] In analyzing the Old Side–New Side controversy, Hodge stated that "some of the best and some of the worst men in the church were found on either side," but placed himself more in sympathy with the Old Side by his strong opposition to the irregularities and breaches of Presbyterian church order that marked New Side pronouncements and actions.

Dr. Alexander was deeply pained. He wrote Charles Hodge a long letter expressing his strong conviction that "the Old Side were a great deal worse and the New Side a great deal better" than Hodge had presented them. Alexander's letter gave Hodge "a great deal of uneasiness," but he felt he had to stand by his interpretation.[37] Hodge realized that his history, especially his treatment of "the Whitefieldian revival," would "give more or less offence" to a great many of his friends. Accordingly, he chose to publish his book with William S. Martien rather than to risk bringing controversy to the Presbyterian Board of Publication.[38]

Archibald Alexander's own history of the First Great Awakening and the Presbyterian schism appeared in 1845, entitled *Biographical Sketches of the Founder, and Principal Alumni of the Log College, together with an account of the Revivals of Religion under their ministry*.[39] Alexander agreed that there were faults on both sides but clearly considered Old Side errors far more serious. Tennent and the New Side men transgressed the rules of order and spoke uncharitably of their brethren, but the Old Side opposed the revival. Alexander wrote, "Men may continue to maintain in theory an orthodox creed, and yet manifest such deadly hostility to vital piety, that they must be considered the enemies of the cause of God, and the work of the Spirit."[40] The zeal and spirit of the New Side men also greatly appealed to James Waddel Alexander. In 1847, he observed: "So far as my researches go, Presbyterianism has never and nowhere made striking advances, except when the body of preachers and people has been animated with a zeal for truth and saving souls, such as at the very time has been a little too strong, methodistical, pietistical, enthusiastical, in the eyes even of many sound, good sort of brethren."[41]

In time, Charles Hodge came to a more positive view of the value of the First Great Awakening. He wrote in 1847:

We avow our full belief that the Spirit of God does at times accompany the means of grace with extraordinary power, so that many unrenewed men are brought to the saving knowledge of the truth, and a high degree of spiritual life is induced among the people of God. We believe also that such seasons have been among the most signal blessings of God to his church, from the day of Pentecost to our own times. We believe, moreover, that we are largely indebted for the religious life which we now enjoy to the great revivals which attended the preaching of Edwards, Whitefield, and the Tennents; and at a later period, of Davies, Smith, and others, in Virginia.[42]

The division of the Presbyterian church in 1837 left the Old School "in a state of almost unprecedented doctrinal homogeneity." One might well doubt, the history of the Old School in the *Presbyterian Re-union Memorial Volume* stated, "whether any other Christian communion of equal size has ever excelled it, as to unity in the reception of an evangelical creed of such extent as the Westminster Confession and Catechisms."[43] Beginning with the establishment of the Board of Foreign Missions in New York City in 1837, the Old School quickly organized a complete range of assembly-controlled agencies for its missions and benevolences. And Princeton Seminary was the Old School Presbyterian Church's intellectual, theological, and spiritual center.

# Old School Princeton

*Lenox Library, 1843, with the new Lenox Library,
1879, in the background.*

[Princeton] has become inexpressibly dear to me as a magnificent stronghold of Christian culture and orthodox faith, on the walls of whose institutions the smile of God gleams like the light of the morning.

THEODORE L. CUYLER

PRINCETON Seminary emerged from the turbulent 1830s with an international reputation for thoughtful, vigorous defense of Presbyterianism. One of several major Calvinistic voices in the country, the seminary carried on lively debates with New School Presbyterians, New England Congregationalists, and the Mercersburg theologians. Princeton was no longer the only American Presbyterian seminary. Auburn was the seminary of the New School churches of New York. In the South, there were Union Seminary of Virginia and Columbia Seminary in South Carolina, and Western, Lane, and New Albany (Indiana) served the church in the western states. In August 1833 over one hundred students gathered at Cincinnati's Lane Seminary—the largest single class of theological students ever assembled in an American school. Converted to the antislavery position by the abolitionist Theodore Weld, and disgusted with the board's opposition and President Beecher's vacillation, almost all of these Lane seminarians withdrew the following year—many of them going to Oberlin to study with Charles Finney. Union Theological Seminary was founded in New York City in 1836 by a group of New School laymen and four ministers—all graduates of Princeton Seminary—as a school "around which all men, of moderate views and feelings, who desire to live free from party strife, and to stand aloof from all the extremes of doctrinal speculation, practical radicalism, and ecclesiastical domination may cordially and affectionately rally."[1] Auburn, Lane, and Union (New York)

were New School institutions. Of the five Old School seminaries, three—Union (Virginia), Columbia, and New Albany—were under synodical supervision; and two—Princeton and Western—were under the control of the General Assembly.

For a short time after the Old School-New School division Princeton Seminary's enrollment declined, but by the mid-1840s it was higher than ever. Andover, with 153 students in 1844, was still the largest American seminary; but Princeton had 110 students and Union of New York enrolled 90. The General Theological Seminary of the Episcopal Church in New York had 74 students, the "theological department" at Yale had 72, while only 27 students were studying in the "theological department" at Harvard.

The decade of the 1840s was "the golden age" of Princeton. Funds continued to be a challenge; but the seminary was greatly encouraged by the efforts of alumnus Cortlandt Van Rensselaer. Between 1843 and 1845 he raised approximately $100,000, for which he accepted no remuneration. The influence of the Princeton professors was now at its height. Archibald Alexander and Samuel Miller were renowned and beloved; Charles Hodge was just reaching his prime; and Joseph Addison Alexander showed great promise as one of America's most competent Bible scholars. Study with these four men was intellectually demanding and spiritually challenging. Theodore L. Cuyler, who studied at Princeton from September 1843 to May 1846, described the atmosphere of the seminary as "deeply and sweetly Evangelical." The faculty—"those wise men"—he said "taught us not only to think, but to believe."[2] William Miller Paxton, a student at the seminary from 1845 to 1848 and later a member of its faculty, wrote, "I well remember that when I was a student, no young man could pass through his first year without being constrained to re-examine his personal hope and motives for seeking the sacred office."

\*      \*      \*

In 1840 the General Assembly elected Charles Hodge to the aging Archibald Alexander's chair as professor of Exegetical and Didactic Theology. Dr. Alexander favored the move and promoted it, although Hodge was very reluctant. He did not relish this change in direction and the enormous work involved in moving from the exegetical to the theological department of the seminary. He had hoped the plan would not be approved but refused to oppose Dr. Alexander's wishes, and so accepted the new position. Archibald Alexander's title now became professor of Pastoral and Polemic Theology—a description which well suited this genial man, who was able, to an unusual degree, to be both pastoral and polemic.

Charles Hodge moved into theology, although he continued to teach his class in the Pauline Epistles to the juniors. A. A. Hodge saw the change as providential; he believed that his father had greater potential for excellence in theology. Furthermore, Charles Hodge had been prepared for systematic theology by twenty years of work in the original languages of Scripture and by teaching exegesis. This enabled him to make his theology "a simple induction from the teachings of Scripture"—and so to develop a system in which "all its elements and proportions" were "inspired and controlled by the Word of God."[3]

For several years after Charles Hodge became professor of theology, Dr. Alexander continued to give the lectures while Hodge catechized the class on different topics, adding his own explanations and remarks. Then the two men shared the lecturing until Hodge finally assumed responsibility for the department on his own. William Miller Paxton's class "heard" Dr. Alexander's "lectures upon Didactic Theology as well as those of Dr. Hodge." Paxton wrote:

Dr. Hodge gave us a subject with massive learning, in its logical development, in its beautiful balance and connection with the whole system. Dr. Alexander would take the same subject and smite it with a javelin, and let the light through it. His aim was to make one point and nail it fast. I always came from a lecture with these words ringing through my mind, "A nail driven in a sure place."[4]

Like his mentor, Charles Hodge greatly appreciated the older theologians. In 1844 he closed a review of a new book from Germany with these remarks:

After all the alleged improvements in theological research, we never feel so much disposed to take down one of the old Latin dogmatic writers of the seventeenth century, as immediately on closing a fresh work from Germany. These antiquated writers have a thousand faults, it may be; they are stiff, they are prolix, they are technical, they are intolerant and austere, they are scholastic in their distinctions, but they have one great merit—they always let us know what they mean. Their atmosphere, if wintry and biting, is clear.[5]

Charles Hodge agreed with Dr. Alexander that Turretin's *Institutio Theologiae Elencthicae* was "incomparably the best book as a whole on systematic theology" and continued its use as the principal text.[6]   In addition to Turretin, Hodge's students read Hill, Dick, and Knapp.   George Hill (1750-1819), principal of St. Mary's College in St. Andrews, was a leader of the moderate party of the Church of Scotland and author of *Lectures on Divinity.*  John Dick (1764-1833) was a theologian of the Scottish Secession church who had received an honorary doctorate from the College of New Jersey in 1815.  His *Lectures on Theology* (1834) was frequently reprinted and became the standard system of theology among the Seceders.  Georg Christian Knapp (1753-1825), professor of theology at Halle, published his *Lectures on Christian Theology* in 1827.  Moderately orthodox, he attempted to reconcile revelation with reason.

Hodge assigned his classes a topic in Turretin—usually twenty to forty Latin pages.  In class he led a discussion in the form of questions and answers, forcing the students to think through the topic for themselves.  He then assigned a list of about twenty-five questions to be prepared for the following week's class.  Hodge maintained that the best method of teaching theology involved "the use of the text-book, the living teacher, practice in writing, and an active drill in verbal questions and debates."[7]  Later, Hodge added his own lectures to the other class exercises.  Students appreciated Hodge's clear and consecutive lectures.  "His thoughts move in rows," they often said.[8]  William Henry Ruffner, who transferred from Union Seminary in Virginia for the 1846-47 session, found that Hodge's weekly lecture on theology presented "a subject in a stronger manner than we can find it treated in any textbook."[9]

The students loved Charles Hodge. Dr. Hodge "is one of the most excellent of men," wrote James P. Boyce; "so modest and yet so wise, so kind and fatherly in his manner, and yet of so giant an intellect, he is a man who deserves a world of praise."[10] C. A. Salmond recalled his theology classes with Hodge in the 1870s:

Always earnest in the class-room, he was never morose. His powerful face wore a habitual expression of refined geniality, which at times would relax into a smile, as a student recalled unwittingly some incident of the past. The writer, for instance, who happens to be a Scotchman, was being examined one day on the Sacraments. He was asked to give the Shorter Catechism definition of baptism, and had proceeded a little way, when, under the impression that he had begun the wrong answer, he stopped short. Doctor Hodge, with a naive smile, remarked—"You are the first Scotchman I ever caught!" But by this time the student had got on the rails again, and glided swiftly to the end, without further let or hindrance, to the amusement of the class. "That reminds me," said the Doctor quietly, "of a Scotch lady I once knew, who, when asked to repeat the sixth commandment, replied: 'I'll soon do that, if you'll only start me.'"[11]

\*       \*       \*

With Charles Hodge's move to theology, Joseph Addison Alexander became the professor of Oriental and Biblical Literature. He organized the Old Testament department at Princeton and gained for it an international reputation. In the first half of the nineteenth century, American Protestants were introduced to the critical methods of biblical study emanating mainly from German universities. The new approach rejected the miracles, questioned traditional ascriptions of authorship and date of Old and New Testament books, and raised grave questions about the authority of the Bible. The Bible was seen as the product of a growing religious awareness gradually evolving from primitive superstition rather than a revelation from God. The young Alexander quickly emerged as Princeton's response to the technical arguments raised by the radical critics. He appreciated the linguistic research and learning of the European critics; and although disagreeing profoundly with their presuppositions and conclusions, he urged the necessity of learning from them: "The true course with respect to German labours and researches is not to look away from them or cover them with dust, but to seize upon their valuable products and convert them to our own use. . . ."[12] Both Charles Hodge and J. A. Alexander did just this. John W. Stewart has stated that "it is doubtful if any other American theologians were better informed of the German scholarship about the Bible."[13]

The critics (or, as Alexander called them, the "neologists") erred, not because they were too critical or scholarly but because they were neither critical nor scientific. They were not impartial scholars but held that "the general presumption is against the truth and authenticity of everything traditional or ancient and in favor of whatever can by any means be substituted for it."[14] Although he believed that criticism should not adhere slavishly to tradition, the younger Alexander insisted that correct method grants the tentative validity of received opinion until compelling contrary evidence be uncovered. The essential difference between his critical principle and that of the Germans was, he wrote, the "same as that between the principle of English jurisprudence, that a person accused is to be reckoned innocent until he is proved guilty, and the rule adopted in the criminal proceedings of some other nations, that he ought to be held guilty till he proves his innocence."

J. A. Alexander became the American disciple of Ernst Hengstenberg, the conservative German scholar who, Alexander wrote, "maintain[ed] that religious truth is clearly revealed in a positive form, and must be definitely held on the authority of Scripture."[15] But as great as his respect was for Hengstenberg, Calvin was his delight. While reading Calvin's commentary on Isaiah in 1843, he wrote, "Such sense! such piety! such style!"[16]

Alexander's Old Testament study focused on biblical prophecy, which he saw as an artistically unified painting in which the foreground—the history of Israel—is depicted specifically and the background—the Messianic era—is presented in general contours. He rejected the dual-sense theory because it suggested "harsh transitions" between the

[264]

two testaments. The prophets did not view the two covenants as separate entities but rather as different aspects of the story of the one "people of God." Alexander stressed the "general prophetic intimations" of the Old Testament and opposed those who tried to establish the fulfillment of Messianic prophecy by reference to "minute and disputable points." In his New Testament research, Alexander emphasized the literary unit of each of the gospels, rejecting both critical efforts to uncover a single primary source and orthodox fascination with gospel harmony.

Charles Hodge wrote that although J. A. Alexander was "perfectly familiar with the writings of German rationalists and sceptics from Ernesti to Baur and Strauss, they affected him no more than the eagle is affected by the dew on his plumage as he soars nearer the sun."[17] Neither did he unduly involve his students in critical studies. Theodore Cuyler remembered that Dr. Alexander "no more disturbed us with the much-vaunted conjectural Biblical criticisms than he disturbed us with Joe Smith's 'golden plates' at Nauvoo."[18]

As always, Addison Alexander charmed the faculty children. Caspar Wistar Hodge never forgot visits, as a child, to Dr. Alexander's rooms in the "Tombs"—the basement of the seminary chapel; and he never forgot "Wistar's Magazine." This was a handwritten production which appeared every other week for two or three years, much to the shared delight of the scholar who produced it and the little boy who eagerly awaited the next issue.[19] One of these contained, among other things, a ludicrous account of a "terrible fire that broke out to-day in the Kisterbock stove" and an advertisement for a "Seminary for Chickens" in the backyard, where "Professor Chanticleer" taught "crowing" and "Peter Pullet" was the "Clerk of Faculty."[20] Another issue tells the story of "Yes and No"—two boys, James and John, one of whom could not say yes and the other who could not say no. James L. Beffo (the editor), Gaspard de la Foix, Sophonisba Saltmarsh Pepperwell, Dr. Bald, Mrs. Bald, Old Black, Peter Arun, The Man, Mr. Flag Ship, Don Barbarossa, Oliver Oaf, Ossifrage, Captain Cumberland, and M. W. Mott appeared in the successive numbers of the magazine. When not entertaining children, Addison Alexander amused himself by playing the flute, reading the *Thousand and One Nights* in Arabic, or studying Ethiopic, Polish, or Malay.

\*     \*     \*

In 1841, Charles Hodge's *Way of Life* was published by the American Sunday School Union to present, "for the use of educated youth," the great doctrines of the Bible.[21]  As Hodge wrote the book, he submitted it, chapter by chapter, to Archibald Alexander for his advice.  Dr. Alexander suggested shorter chapters, because he found that he was "often turning to see how many pages remain before the termination of the chapter."[22]  Alexander wondered whether the American Sunday School Union would accept Hodge's strongly doctrinal emphasis, but the book was published with the title *The Way of Life* substituted for Hodge's "The Narrow Way."  With three questions in the preface, Hodge set forth his purpose: "Are the Scriptures really a revelation from God?  If they are, what doctrines do they teach?  And what influence should those doctrines exert on our heart and life?"  The book was immediately popular.  The *Boston Recorder* commented, "We doubt whether any book of our day can be named which promises a greater amount of immediate or even enduring good to Zion than this . . . .  It is heart-searching, enlightening, stimulating and strengthening to faith and every other Christian virtue."[23]  *The Way of Life* was quickly reprinted in England by the London Religious Tract Society.[24]  Years later Dr. James McCosh, president of Princeton College, said at Hodge's semicentennial, "Nor is it only among the theologians that the name of Dr. Hodge is known and appreciated; it is esteemed by the thinking portion of the common people.  I remember that when Dr. Hodge's 'Way of Life' was added to the library of the [Scottish] congregation with which I was connected, there was a keen competition between a servant girl and a hand-loom weaver, as to which should get the first reading."[25]

Also in 1841, Archibald Alexander's *Thoughts on Religious Experience* was published.  Many of these chapters had already appeared in the Presbyterian *Watchman of the South* and had been reprinted in other papers of different denominations.

These were collected and published in a single volume by the Presbyterian Board of Publication, along with some new material by Dr. Alexander—"Letters to the Aged," "Counsels of the Aged to the Young," "Counsels to Christian Mothers," "Letter to a Mourning Afflicted Widow," and "Letter to a Bereaved Widower."

\*      \*      \*

New student Darwin Cook arrived at Princeton Seminary in 1842. He described the school and the town in a letter to his mother:

There is a gate and a gravel walk through the middle of the yard to the front door of Alexander Hall; on the right is Dr. Hodge's house, and on the left there is a brick house among the trees. Dr. A. Alexander lives there. . . . That other little building with white pillars is the chapel where I live—that is, I have a room under it. You can't see where I get through the hatch-way into the underground room of the chapel. . . . Dr. Hodge is a little red-faced man, round and snug. . . . Dr. Alexander is a little old man whose chin sticks out sharp as you can think. His voice is fine and soft like a woman's though it is round and pleasant. . . . There are some of the handsomest gardens in this neighborhood that you ever saw. You have no conception how some live and spend money here. They keep a gardener, perhaps for a thousand dollars a year, who cultivates three quarters or an acre and doesn't raise anything at all really useful but those little flowers just calculated to please the eye. Ah, some people's "eyes stand out with fatness" while others are starving with hunger.[26]

The strongly opinionated Cook was a Presbyterian from nearby Pennsylvania, but Princeton Seminary attracted students from many places and backgrounds. In 1837-38, Lutheran student Frederick Augustus Muhlenberg studied at Princeton. The next year Der Minasian Senakerim, an Armenian from Turkey, entered the seminary. Among the students who entered Princeton in 1838 was John Miller, one of Dr. and Mrs. Miller's five sons, all of whom attended Princeton College.[27] One became a physician and three became lawyers. When John decided to study for the ministry, his father was delighted and wrote:

My dear son has just taken his place in our Seminary as student of theology. I have been ever anxious that all my sons should be ministers of the Gospel; and as each one, in succession, made choice of a profession for life, my heart almost sank within me to find that they all, with one accord, turned away from the ministry of reconciliation to some secular calling. I began to fear that no one of them would choose the best of all employments. At length, however, I am gratified to find [John] turning his mind toward this noble, heavenly profession. . . . I would unspeakably rather, if I know my own heart, see him an able, faithful, successful minister of the gospel, than President of the United States, or the occupant of an imperial throne.[28]

In December 1843, J. W. Alexander sent a seminary catalogue with the names of the students to his friend John Hall. He added by way of explanation, "Mr. Webber has been a Texan major. Thomas Thomas is a Welshman. Mr. Byers is a Nova-Scotian licentiate. W. Scudder is a Ceylonese."[29] Another student in 1843 was Archibald Alexander Hodge. His fellow students had compassion for him "as likely to be smothered under the combination of his two great names"![30] He had graduated from Princeton College, where he showed great aptitude for mathematics and science. He was Professor Joseph Henry's "favorite pupil" and worked with his teacher on original experiments with the telegraph.[31] He taught for a year in the Lawrenceville Academy and was, for another year, tutor at the college and assistant to Henry. At the seminary he was one of a group of students—Hodge, Lacy, McPheeters, Phillips, and Scott—who were especially interested in the study of systematic theology. These men distributed among themselves the task of taking down a verbatim record of Dr. Hodge's lectures, which they put together in a connected form. One day Archie surprised his father by an especially competent essay on a difficult question; and Dr. Hodge, with "an expression of pleased astonishment on his face," insisted that he read it to the class.[32] In 1844 Samuel Davies Alexander, Dr. Alexander's fifth son, joined Archibald Alexander Hodge and the other students at the seminary. He had graduated from Princeton

College in 1838 and studied civil engineering before deciding for the ministry.

During the summer of 1843 Archibald Alexander spent two months in his native Virginia. On June 29 he addressed the alumni association of his old school, now named Washington College. He stressed the importance of a regular, lengthy, liberal education, with general knowledge as well as special knowledge in one area. He asserted that religion is "infinitely the most important and necessary part of education." "Leave this out," said Alexander, "and it will be doubtful whether our schools will not do more harm than good, for sound morality rests on religion as its basis." The excitement of the day and the heat of the building were too much for the seventy-one-year-old preacher. He faltered, turned pale, and slowly sank back into the chair behind him. He was carried out into the open air but, to the amazement of the concerned audience, Dr. Alexander returned. Speaking from his chair, he continued his address, refusing to listen to those who urged him to rest. In hushed silence, the people listened intently as Alexander paid tribute to his old teacher of Liberty Hall Academy, William Graham. He described Graham's service to the Christian church and to the cause of education in Virginia. Archibald Alexander, who was the sole survivor among the teachers and students of the early days of the school, exhorted his hearers to "seek salvation through the infinite merits of the Redeemer." The deeply moved assembly was not without tears as he closed with the words: "Having now finished what I wished to communicate, at this time, I must, my beloved friends, take a solemn and lasting farewell of you all; never again expecting to see the faces of most of you in the flesh. May Heaven's richest blessings attend you."[33] Dr. Alexander's address at Washington College was just one of many that he gave during his visit to Virginia. In August, J. W. Alexander wrote, "My father has returned. He was gone sixty-four days, and in that time delivered thirty-two public discourses." The son expressed his gratitude for the preservation of his "honoured parents to an old age of cheerfulness, health and activity."[34]

\* \* \*

In 1843 the first seminary library building was completed. One of the arguments that had been made for one school rather than several, when the Presbyterian church was debating the best approach to theological education, was the possibility of a really great library in a single seminary. At the beginning, the professors and students had used the college library. But they soon began collecting books for the seminary library, first placed in the home of Dr. Alexander. The directors voted to spend one hundred dollars in 1812 to purchase "books immediately wanted." The seminary paid $77.49 for two copies of Parkhurst's work on the Hebrew language, six copies of Wilson's introduction to Hebrew, and two Hebrew Bibles. In 1817, the books were moved into a second-floor room in the new seminary building. The collection, which in 1825 was named the Green Library in honor of Ashbel Green, slowly grew through purchases and gifts. A collection of books and pamphlets came from Dublin in 1818; and in 1834 a splendidly published and bound set of Charles Simeon's *Horae Homileticae* was sent to the library as a gift from the author. Charles Hodge served as book agent for the seminary during his time in Europe and continued to maintain contact with European book sellers. In 1838 came the first of a remarkable collection of twenty thousand pamphlets, assembled by William B. Sprague, on topics related to early American preaching and religious history. The library of Charles Nisbet was obtained in 1838 and that of John Breckinridge in 1842.

The new library building was given by New York philanthropist James Lenox. He was the son of Robert Lenox, a Scottish immigrant who became one of the five wealthiest men in New York City. Both father and son served as trustees of both Princeton College and Princeton Seminary. Mr. Lenox purchased five acres between Mercer and Stockton streets, across from the seminary building, for the library site. When completed in 1843, the new building of brown sandstone and Italian marble—an outstanding example of early American Gothic architecture—boasted handsome woodwork and furnishings of black walnut, windows of amber glass to protect the books from sunlight, and ten thousand volumes.[35] James Lenox, a devoted bibliophile who owned the first Gutenberg Bible in the United States, regularly presented volumes to the library, including writings by his favorite Scottish authors.[36]

The deed of May 5, 1843—when James Lenox transferred title of the new library to the seminary—summarized the theological convictions of the faculty, directors, and supporters of Princeton.

PROVIDED ALWAYS AND NEVERTHELESS and upon this condition that if at any time or times hereafter the said parties of the second part [Princeton Seminary] shall pass from under the supervision and control of the General Assembly of the Presbyterian Church in the United States of America now commonly known and distinguished as the Old School General Assembly and its successors, or if at any time or times hereafter the leading doctrines declared as the confession of faith, and catechisms of the Presbyterian Church, such as the doctrines of universal and total depravity, the doctrine of election, the doctrine of the atonement, the doctrines of the imputation of Adam's sin to all his posterity and of the imputation of Christ's righteousness to all his people for their justification, the doctrine of human inability and the doctrine of the necessity of the influence of the Holy Spirit in the regeneration, conversion, and sanctification of sinners, as these doctrines are now understood and explained by the aforesaid Old School General Assembly, shall cease to be taught and inculcated in the said Seminary, then and in either case the Grant and Conveyance, hereby made, shall cease and BECOME NULL AND VOID.[37]

\*      \*      \*

Justin Perkins, missionary to Persia, and Nestorian bishop Mar Yahannan visited Princeton in 1842. Perkins later wrote that he found more students at Princeton interested in missions than in any other seminary that he visited in the United States. The bishop, who had welcomed the first American missionaries to Tabriz in 1833, was the object of intense interest to the young seminarians. In 1843 the students were visited by a member of the Episcopal mission to China; three Christian sailors, including a Seminole Indian; an agent from the Jews' Benevolent Society; and John Morrison, Princeton graduate and Presbyterian missionary to India. About this time Levi Spaulding, a member of the first contingent of

American missionaries who went to India, spoke at Princeton. "He was as nearly like my conception of the Apostle Paul as anyone I ever beheld," Theodore Cuyler wrote. "The tears flowed down our cheeks as we listened to Spaulding's recital, and the result of his visit was that more than one of our students volunteered for the work of foreign missions."[38]

Foreign missions continued to attract some of the best of the seminary students. In November 1843, J. W. Alexander wrote, "Five young men of the Seminary are assigned to China. One of these and another during the long vacation, paid two thousand family-visits in the Pines; everywhere giving advice, books, etc. One of the four, Culbertson, was an army-officer, and highly honoured at West Point."[39] Another was A. W. Loomis. When he left Princeton, Dr. Miller prayed with him and gave him a book. "It was the Life of Brainerd," Loomis wrote, "a large and ancient copy, which he took from its shelf, wrote in it his name and mine, and presented it with his benediction."[40] The faculty sent their missionary students out with their blessing and kept in touch with them. In 1837 John Adger, now in Turkey, received two very long letters from Archibald Alexander, "each letter consisting of eight pages about a foot long, and fully as wide." Dr. Alexander wrote to Walter Lowrie in China in 1843 concerning the fall enrollment at the seminary, Dr. Hodge's improving health, the new library ("one of the handsomest libraries in the world"), the visit of Lowrie's father to address the students, the conferring of an honorary doctorate on J. W. Alexander ("so that I must now consent to be called the old Doctor"), and discussions in the Presbyterian church concerning the eldership and millenarianism.

\*     \*     \*

In December 1843 William Cunningham visited the United States as the head of a delegation from the Free Church of Scotland, to present the cause of that new denomination and receive financial assistance. Meetings were held in the country's largest cities, with Dr. Cunningham giving the major address at forty of these. The thirty-eight-year-old theologian came to Princeton three times during his American trip.

J. W. Alexander described the distinguished visitor:

Height about 6 ft., and large in proportion; a stout but finely
formed man; very handsomely dressed, and in an eminent degree
the gentleman, in every thing but excess of snuff. Age, I reckon,
about 41; spectacles. A shock of thick curly hair. He has no airs of
patronage. Powerful reasoning and sound judgment seem to be his
characteristics; and he is a walking treasury of facts, dates, and
ecclesiastical law. I heard him for an hour, on Friday, in a speech
to the students. Indescribable Scotch intonation (but little idiom)
and convulsion of body, but flowing, elegant language, and amazing power in presenting argument. Though his manner is rugged
and uncouth, and he has no sign of imagination, yet when he gets
on tender topics of religion, he is so scriptural, and so sound, that
one is affected by what he says. I have seldom listened to a man
with more instruction.[41]

William Cunningham was impressed with Princeton Seminary. He wrote to his wife of his "great pleasure in the society
of the theological professors here, who are all men eminent
for their talents and learning, and are known in Britain by
their writings." A. A. Hodge well remembered "those . . .
days, the pleased excitement of our father, as he lay back
upon his easy chair listening to Dr. Cunningham as he strode
gesticulating through the study with his long arms laying
down the principles and narrating the story of the great Free-
Church Exodus, or when our father walked with him in
the larger parlour, or once or twice, when the February sun
shone clear in the paths around the house."[42] The two men
became friends at once. Charles Hodge remarked, "I do not
recollect of ever having met any one to whom I was so much
drawn . . . on such short acquaintance."[43] Cunningham
always maintained that he had greater confidence in the
theological opinions of Charles Hodge than in those of any
other living theologian.[44]

William Cunningham was back in Princeton in March
1844. Sunday morning, March 16, he preached in the
seminary chapel on II Corinthians 5:14,15—"a most able
sermon," according to J. W. Alexander, "uniting the
highest degrees of plainness, argument, and unction." In the
evening, Cunningham preached on Hebrews 7:26—"a noble

sermon, as plain and unillustrated as before, but mighty in argument, and robustly eloquent."[45]

The April 1844 issue of the *Biblical Repertory* contained an article by Charles Hodge in support of the "Claims of the Free Church of Scotland," excerpts of which Cunningham read to the Free Church General Assembly. Hodge stated that "our Scottish brethren" are suffering for the "right to regulate [their] faith and practice by the Word of God," free from state control. Their struggle, Hodge asserted, is for "a truth essential to the purity and prosperity of religion, and consequently their cause is the cause of Christ." Hodge continued:

We doubt not that the clear exhibition of [the] truth [of the Headship of Christ], by the Scottish delegates, will be a means of spiritual good, for which all our contributions will be a most inadequate compensation. Nay, were we to increase them a hundredfold we should still be their debtors, if only we are made to feel, more than we have hitherto done, that Jesus Christ is indeed our Lord. It is this more than anything else that has interested us in their mission. We have felt under some of their addresses as we never have felt before. We have had clearer views of the intimate connection between the practical recognition of Christ's kingly office and the life of God in the soul, and we think we see one of the principal sources of that strength of character, elevation of mind, and constancy in trials which Scottish Christians have so often exhibited. Let any man, with this principle before his mind, read the history of Scotland, and he will have the solution of the mystery of servant girls and labourers dying on the gibbet or at the stake for a question of Church government. Let him contrast the bearing of Knox, Melville, or Henderson when they stood before kings—we will not say with the slavish adulation of the unworthy bishops of King James, but—with the spirit of such good men as Cranmer, and they will see the difference between believing that Christ is King and believing that the king is Head of the Church.[46]

\*       \*       \*

On October 3, 1844, Dr. Alexander preached the sermon at the installation of his son James Waddel as pastor of the Duane Street Church in New York City. He took his text from II Timothy 2:15—"Rightly Dividing the Word of Truth"—and presented many of the themes of his own long ministry. He noted that the preacher is a workman. "Two sorts of men," he said, "should . . . be excluded from the gospel ministry: first, those who will not work; secondly, those who know not how to perform their work aright." The preacher, Archibald Alexander continued, must know how to rightly divide "the word of truth." That means that he must carefully distinguish God's truth from error and from "philosophy, and mere human opinions and speculations." "Many who do not reject the truth," Alexander said, "yet so cover her with robes of their own weaving, that she cannot be seen in her lovely simplicity." Furthermore, "the skillful workman must be able to distinguish between fundamental truths, and such as are not fundamental." "All Bible truth is important," Dr. Alexander said, "but some truths must be known and believed, or the person cannot be saved." "All truth is essential to the perfection" of the Christian system; "fundamental truths, to its existence." Rightly dividing the word of truth also requires that the preacher arrange it in such order and present it in such a manner "that it may be most easily and effectually understood." He will "declare the whole counsel of God," but "in due order, at proper times, and with a wise reference to the strength and spiritual attainments of our hearers."

Most importantly, Dr. Alexander asserted, "a good workman will so divide the word of truth, as clearly to distinguish between the law and the gospel; between the covenant of works and the covenant of grace." By insisting on this point, the Princeton professor said, Luther began the Reformation; he called it "the article of the standing or falling of the Church." If the preacher misses the mark here, "you will find him bewildered, and bewildering his hearers everywhere else." He will preach "another gospel" which "brings no good news to lost sinners; but sets men at work to get into paradise at the old gate, which was long ago shut up, and has for thousands of years been guarded by the fiery-flaming sword of Divine justice." While preaching grace, Dr. Alexander said, the good workman will not neglect to set forth "the holy law of God in its spirituality, extent, and binding obligation . . . for where there are none sick, there will be no need of a physician; and where no law is preached, there will be no conviction of sin, and none crying out, 'what must we do to be saved?'" "Let the law be faithfully proclaimed, as binding on every creature, and as cursing every impenitent sinner," stated the preacher, "and let the utter inability of man to satisfy its demands be clearly set forth, not as an excuse, but as a fault; and then let the riches of grace in Christ Jesus be fully exhibited and freely offered, and let all—however great their guilt—be urged to accept of unmerited pardon, and complete salvation." Dr. Alexander concluded his sermon by remarking that his own ministry was "fast coming to a close." "One of my greatest consolations," he said, "is to see younger ministers raised up by the Great Head of the Church, to fill the places of us who must soon leave the stage." The need is for "ministers of the highest qualifications," he added; "and of all qualifications none is so indispensable as deep, unfeigned, spiritual piety—a heart imbued habitually with the Spirit of Christ, and disposed to count all things but loss for his sake."[47]

\*       \*       \*

The Princeton community was saddened by the death of Princeton College professor Albert B. Dod on November 20, 1845. During his week-long illness, he was cheerful and calm. Charles Hodge, who counted the forty-one-year-old Dod among his closest friends, was especially grieved. He wrote to William Cunningham in Scotland, "His death is the greatest loss I have ever sustained in the death of friends." Hodge added, "I had often known of men's dying in peace or in triumph, but to see a man dying cheerfully in the full possession of his intellect, in calm, unexcited confidence in Christ as his God and Saviour, was to me a perfectly novel sight." As friends repeated Scripture promises to him, Dod replied with feeling, "I thank you for that. God bless you for that." When Hodge quoted the words "Whosoever believeth that Jesus is the Son of God, is born of God," Dod replied, "Thank you for that," and attempted to raise his friend's hand to his lips.[48]

J. W. Alexander, now a pastor in New York, paid tribute to Dod, his former colleague at Princeton College. "It is my deliberate opinion," he wrote, "that I never saw his superior in extent of knowledge, in exactness in certain branches, in capacity to teach, in power of colloquial argument, in generous enthusiasm. . . . There is something very pleasing to me, in the almost universal expression of sorrow among all classes in New Jersey, and especially among his pupils. His dying exercises strike me as truly gracious."[49] Charles Hodge gave the funeral address for his friend. Professor Dod had left him with a message for the college students. Lifting his eyes from his manuscript, Hodge pointed to the students sitting in the gallery and, with tears pouring down his face, gave them Dod's last message "with a gust of emotion that went through that audience like the sweep of a storm through the forest."[50] With the death of Professor Dod, Charles Hodge lost a friend, and Princeton, a wide-ranging scholar. When a volume of essays from the *Princeton Review* came out in 1847, it included seven articles by "the late distinguished Professor Dod"—on capital punishment, phrenology, "the vestiges of creation," analytical geometry, Oxford architecture, revivals of religion, and Dr. Beecher's theology.[51]

\*     \*     \*

Charles Hodge continued to suffer with his leg. Various remedies were attempted. Sixty leeches were placed on his groin; a thin piece of tree bark was burned on the leg, which "of course," commented Hodge, "burns to a crisp the skin under it." Professor Joseph Henry brought his battery and "applied galvanism" to Hodge's leg but, according to A. A. Hodge, "without any known effect." His condition slowly improved, however, and on June 19, 1843, he attached a note to his daily record of the weather—"walked to town for the first time in ten years." The year before, he had been able to attend his first General Assembly. In 1846 he was again a commissioner and was elected moderator. The following year, at the assembly in Richmond, Hodge, as retiring moderator, gave the opening sermon: an appeal based on the principles of Thomas Chalmers for a "sustentation fund," with which the entire church would provide for every minister an adequate salary.

By now, Charles Hodge's influence in the Old School Presbyterian church was immense. He was serving on the Board of Domestic Missions and on the Board of Foreign Missions and would later become a trustee of Princeton College and a member of the Presbyterian Board of Education. From 1835, Hodge reported on each General Assembly for the *Biblical Repertory*. His yearly account was so popular that a friend commented that "there is no inducement to prepare a good article for the July number, because every one turns at once to that on the General Assembly which absorbs all interest."[52]

In 1846, Archibald Alexander's *Brief Compend of Bible Truth* was published. Originally written for the blind, it was enlarged and reprinted for "plain, common readers" who desired a brief and simple presentation of Christian doctrine.[53] That same year, Joseph Addison Alexander's first volume on Isaiah was published. Ten years earlier, on June 21, 1836, he had written in his journal, "I began my notes in Isaiah and wrote on the first ten verses of chapter xlix."[54] In 1842, overwhelmed with the immensity of his task, he laid the work aside, planning to publish first on the minor prophets. He prepared a commentary on Obadiah but soon took up Isaiah again. His journal noted the progress of his work. For example, on November 2, 1843, he wrote:

Read Jarchi, Kimchi, Aben-Ezra, the Michlal Jophi, Luther, Calvin, Grotius, Junius, Cocceius, the Dutch Annotations, Pool's Synopsis, Vitringa, Clericus, Gill, J. H. Michaelis, J. D. Michaelis, Lowth, Rosenmüller, Augusti, Gesenius, Maurer, Hitzig, Hendewerk, Barnes, Henderson, De Wette, Ewald, and Umbreit, on Isaiah x. 33, 34. Wrote the first draft of a commentary on these verses.[55]

Addison Alexander wanted to write a popular commentary but decided to write for ministers—in order to afford them "a partial succedaneum for the many costly books" and to enable them "to profit by the latest philological improvements and discoveries." He explained his purpose: "Let the professional interpreter content himself with furnishing the raw material in a sound and merchantable state, without attempting to prescribe the texture, colour, shape, or quantity of the indefinitely varied fabrics into which it is the business of the preacher to transform it." Alexander treated

Isaiah "as the work both of God and man, a divine revelation and a human composition, the contents of which are never to be dealt with in a manner inconsistent either with the supposition of its inspiration or with that of its real human origin." Against the stream of a growing number of critics, Alexander held to the unity of Isaiah. The entire book, he insisted, was characterized by the common "origin, mission, sins and sufferings, former experience and final destiny of Israel," which he called the "Church of the Old Testament."[56] Alexander sent copies of his new book to Joseph Owen, John Freeman, and Walter Lowrie—former pupils, now missionaries—and returned to work on the last thirty-one chapters of Isaiah.

With several dozen large volumes open on the high desks placed from one end of his study to the other, Addison Alexander stood to study and write. His youngest brother, Henry Martyn Alexander, watched him work and said, "He was much troubled with toothache and the hot weather affected him a good deal, and I have often heard him say that the best relief from both of these annoyances was some difficult passage to explain."[57] In 1847 the second volume, *The Later Prophecies of Isaiah,* was completed.[58]

The year 1847 brought changes to the Charles Hodge household. Until then, both parents and all eight children had lived together in Princeton without interruption. The children's education through college had all taken place at home or in the town's college. In 1847 Hodge's oldest daughter, Mary Elizabeth, married William M. Scott, an 1846 Princeton Seminary graduate. Mary Elizabeth and William moved to Danville, Kentucky, where he took up his work as professor of ancient languages at Centre College. That same year, Archibald Alexander Hodge and his wife departed as missionaries to India. For the first time the Hodge family circle was broken, and Hodge was deeply moved. It was painful "to marry a daughter," he admitted; and joy and sorrow mingled as he said good-by to Archie. "Our family was never completely regathered on earth again," A. A. Hodge later wrote, "for before the son returned from India, the Mother was making the beginnings of the home in heaven."[59]

\*  \*  \*

Ashbel Green was busy writing an account of his own life.[60] On September 3, 1844, J. W. Alexander wrote, "Dr. Green goes on with his autobiography. I prize his company: he is living on the verge of heaven. I always envied his most comfortable fixedness of opinion on all subjects."[61] For several years, he was unable to walk or to speak clearly and spent almost all his time in prayer and Bible reading. Near the end he said, with great effort, to a friend, "Once a man, and twice a child!" On May 19, 1848, while the General Assembly was meeting, he died. Dr. Green was almost eighty-eight years old.

After his pastorate and the presidency of Princeton College, Green had returned to Philadelphia, where, at sixty-one, he became editor of *The Presbyterian*, "on condition that the title should be changed from a sectarian to a catholic form." The paper was renamed *The Christian Advocate*, and Green was its editor for twelve years. Despite poor health and recurring dizziness, he continued to preach regularly, serving the African-American church in Philadelphia for two and a half years. His last sermon was preached in this church on July 16, 1843, when Green was eighty-two years old.

Dr. Green was a lifelong student of the Bible. In his seventy-fifth year, his diary still included such notes as "Studied Hebrew closely all day." In 1837 he began to write a biography of John Witherspoon, his loved and admired teacher and model. First chosen as a commissioner to the General Assembly of 1790, Ashbel Green was seldom absent after that. For twelve years he served as its stated clerk. When the General Assembly met in Philadelphia in 1846, Green, eighty-six years old and ill, wanted once again to be present. As soon as he entered the door, supported by two friends, the entire assembly stood and remained standing until he was helped to a seat.

Ashbel Green has been called "the indispensable man for many of the projects of the Presbyterians in the early republic."[62] He was a leader in the formation of Princeton Seminary. He promoted its cause in presbytery and General Assembly, wrote its "Plan," donated land for its campus, and contributed generously to its library. It was often said that Dr. Green more than anyone else could be considered "the father of the institution."[63]   From June 30, 1812, until the end of his life, Green was president of the board of directors of the seminary, although his relationship with his Princeton friends was severely strained during the Old School-New School controversy in the 1830s. He was also a leader in promoting revivals and missions. He worked tirelessly to convince the church to establish its own Presbyterian boards and wrote the history of early Presbyterian missions.

Dr. Green's determined mind and eloquent speech made him a man of influence and power. William S. Plumer considered Green the best lecturer he ever heard and praised the "extraordinary powers of natural arrangement of his thoughts." His critics, however, called him "the pope of the Presbyterian Church." It was said that his influence was such that he could make a motion in the General Assembly and without giving a single argument take his seat and his motion would be carried. Dr. Green was, of course, aware of his reputation. Reflecting on his own history, and perhaps on lessons that he had learned in his long ministry, he said to a young minister who visited him in his Philadelphia study in 1838:

No doubt, you have heard of me as the old Pope of the Presbyterian Church, very bigoted and strait-laced in my opinions, and a great heresy hunter; so you will not suspect me of being timid and time serving in what I am about to say to you on the subject of theological controversy; but my advice is, that you let it alone. Have your own opinions on all important subjects matured, and be prepared to maintain them; but do not preach polemically, by bringing into the pulpit the controversies of the Church.[64]

Some criticized Ashbel Green as stern, dictatorial, and aloof; but James Waddel Alexander spoke for many at Princeton and elsewhere when he described him as "one whom in our childhood we wondered at, in our youth dreaded, and in our riper years revered and loved."[65]

On May 22, 1848, Dr. Green's friend and colleague for thirteen years at Second Presbyterian Church in Philadelphia, J. J. Janeway, preached Green's funeral sermon at the First Presbyterian Church in Princeton. His text was Philippians 1: 21—"For to me to live is Christ."[66] Dr. Miller and President Carnahan offered prayers, and Ashbel Green was buried in the Princeton Cemetery beside the graves of the other presidents of Princeton College.

\* \* \*

During the summer of 1849, Sarah Hodge had visited her daughter and son-in-law in Kentucky and had returned in September, as her husband reported to his brother, "wonderfully well, fatter and stronger than before her journey, and in excellent spirits."[67] She became ill, however, later in the same month. Her doctors were optimistic that she would recover, but she steadily grew worse. Hugh Hodge visited as frequently as possible, but all he could do was comfort and encourage. As the end drew near, Charles watched by Sarah's bed, praying with her and comforting her with the words of "How sweet the name of Jesus sounds," "Jesus, lover of my soul," and other favorite hymns. On December 18, in the afternoon, she sank so low that the family feared that she could not live until sundown. Her husband asked her, "Do you love the Lord Jesus?" She replied, "I hope so." He asked, "Do you trust in him?" "Entirely," said Sarah. "Is he precious to you?" Charles asked. "Very," she responded, and then added, "inexpressibly. He is my all in all." Early Christmas morning, after talking about her children—all of whom were there except her oldest son (still a missionary in India)—and "giving them to God," she "softly and sweetly fell asleep in Jesus." The family knelt around her bed "in consecrating prayer to God."[68]

Sarah Hodge was buried in the Princeton Cemetery, and her husband had this inscription engraved on her tomb:

> Sarah Bache,
> wife of
> Rev. Charles Hodge
> departed this life,
> December 25th, 1849,
> aged 51 years.
> An Humble Worshipper of Christ,
> She Lived in Love and
> Died in Faith.

Truthful Woman, Delightful Companion,
Ardent Friend, Devoted Wife.
Self-sacrificing Mother,
We Lay You Gently Here, Our Best Beloved,
To Gather Strength and Beauty
For the Coming of the Lord.
A Grain of Wheat is not Quickened except it Die.

Charles greatly missed his beloved Sarah, wife of over twenty-seven years and mother of his eight children. A year and a half later he wrote to his brother, "No day has intervened that I have not often and literally shed tears to her memory; no week has passed that I have not been twice or oftener to her grave." On November 12, 1850—the twenty-second anniversary of Hugh Hodge's marriage—Charles wrote to his brother that he could still recall distinctly the appearance of his Sarah on Hugh's and Margaret's wedding day:

The night before we were in New Brunswick. In the morning we went to New York in the steamboat. We put up at Bunker's. I know the room we occupied. I know where Sarah sat at dinner, and what she ate. In the afternoon Miss Boyd came to her aid in dressing. I can see her as she sat by Margaret on the sofa in the evening, and how she smiled when I called her "old Mrs. Hodge." It is thus I can recall her by associating her with particular times and places. The general recollection is painfully vague; these definite associations are poignantly vivid. And yet I assiduously cultivate them as part of the homage due her memory. No human being can tell, prior to experience, what it is to lose out of a family its head and heart, the source at once of its light and love.[69]

\*     \*     \*

Addison Alexander had moved from the chapel basement to the John Breckinridge house, and then to the first floor of the seminary building, on the side next to Charles Hodge's house. Restless and easily bored, he often moved his residence and continually rearranged his furniture. Sometimes, young Caspar Wistar Hodge would help him reorganize his library, "and when all was done, he would feel quite refreshed, and say that it was 'the next best thing to moving.'"[70]

He changed the structure of his courses from year to year (and sometimes in the middle of the course). He never called the roll two days in the same order. He loved to vary his vacation trips—traveling to Canada, New England, Virginia, and occasionally to the West. His colleague Alexander T. McGill commented, "Nothing but old doctrines and old friends could he adhere to with immutable interest and fondness."[71]

Addison carried a heavy teaching load. In 1845 he taught Hebrew grammar, Old Testament, Messianic Prophecies, the Acts of the Apostles, and lectured on Bible interpretation, criticism, and archaeology. When the second volume of his Isaiah commentary was completed, he began piling up sheets for his book on the Psalms. His brother wrote, "Addison has saddled himself with a tremendous job . . . but his working power exceeds anything I ever dreamt of."[72] In another place, James compared Addison's ability to take on major projects to John Breckinridge's "immense journeys" to collect money for Christian causes. When asked how he could undertake such long trips, Breckinridge had replied that he never looked upon them "as things which must end." "Addison tells me," James wrote, "he finds the same thing good in his commentary." He added, "Our Lord's maxim about taking thought for the morrow, seems to have very wide applications. We might accomplish more if we were not foolishly asking ourselves so often, how long such and such a great work would take us."[73]

For six months during 1847, Addison Alexander was the regular preacher at Tenth Presbyterian Church in Philadelphia, during pastor Henry A. Boardman's trip to Europe. The church was packed every Sunday, clear to the outer door, and many were unable to find room even in the aisles. During that winter Addison preached his most famous sermons—"The Faithful Saying," "The City with Foundations," "Awake, Thou that Sleepest," and "The Broken and Contrite Heart." The following November he began another six-month preaching engagement, this time at Second Presbyterian Church in Philadelphia. His sermons, "very unequal" according to his brother, were often elegant and sometimes forceful and moving.[74] Charles Hodge wrote that

Addison's sermons "were always instructive and often magnificent. He would draw from a passage of Scripture more than you ever imagined it contained."[75] In his *Recollections of a Long Life,* Theodore Cuyler recalled some famous American preachers he had heard, including his Princeton professor—J. A. Alexander. He wrote:

Oh, how his grandest sermons linger still in my memory after three-score years—like the far-off music of an Alpine horn floating from the mountain tops! . . . His voice was peculiarly melodious, especially in the pathetic passages; his imagination was vivid in fine imagery, and he had an unique habit of ending a long sentence in the words of his text, which chained the text fast to our memories. The announcement of his name always crowded the church in Princeton, and he was flooded with invitations to preach in the most prominent churches of New York, Philadelphia, and other cities. One of his most powerful sermons was on the text, "Remember Lot's Wife"; and he received so many requests to repeat that sermon that he said to his brother James in a wearied tone, "I am afraid that woman will be the death of me."

Cuyler added, "I enjoy the perusal of the rich, unique, and spiritual sermons of my beloved professor and friend; but no one who reads them can realize what it was to listen to Joseph Addison Alexander in his highest and holiest inspirations."[76]

\*　　\*　　\*

The centennial of Princeton College was celebrated on June 29, 1847. James Sproat Green, son of Ashbel Green, presided. The younger Green was a local lawyer of distinction, a United States district attorney, a trustee of the college, and, from 1818 to his death in 1862, treasurer of the seminary. J. W. Alexander delivered the centenary address and Samuel Miller led in prayer. Dinner followed—an occasion of high academic festivity with many toasts and speeches.

On November 3, 1847, Samuel Miller wrote to the seminary directors submitting his resignation. To Dr. Miller's surprise, they refused to accept it and asked him to remain at the seminary. Though feeble, he taught his classes and continued to write. His last publication, *Thoughts on Public*

*Prayer*, was dedicated "to the younger ministers, and candidates for the ministry, in the Presbyterian Church in the United States" on October 31, 1848—his seventy-ninth birthday.[77] On March 20, 1849, Dr. Miller again resigned. This time the directors accepted his request, voting to continue his salary and giving him the title Emeritus Professor of Ecclesiastical History and Church Government.

With Dr. Miller's retirement, there was a growing sentiment in the Presbyterian church to move Joseph Addison Alexander into the church history department. Addison's father did not favor the idea. On April 13, 1849, he wrote to his son James Waddel that Addison, to be sure, had spent enough time teaching Hebrew, but that he was now in a good position to teach anything related to the Bible. Dr. Alexander stated that Addison, however, was willing to accept whatever decision the General Assembly made. "We cannot tell beforehand," added the elder Alexander, "who would be a pleasant colleague."[78]

It was not Addison but his brother, James Waddel Alexander, who was elected by the 1849 General Assembly to Samuel Miller's chair of Ecclesiastical History and Church Government. J. W. Alexander was a scholarly man of fine literary talents. His father once said to Henry Boardman, "My son James has always been a sort of walking Cyclopaedia." He studied at Princeton College and Seminary and taught mathematics and classics at the college. He then served his father's old congregation at Charlotte Court House in Virginia, living in the same house where his father had lived thirty years earlier. He became pastor of the Presbyterian church in Trenton, New Jersey, in 1829. On June 18, 1830, he married Elizabeth Cabell, daughter of a Virginia physician. The wedding took place at Ingleside in Charlotte County, Virginia, with the Reverend William Plumer—a Princeton graduate and now a pastor in Petersburg—conducting the service. It was a happy marriage. James Waddel wrote in 1833 of "the unspeakable and increasing joys of Christian wedlock; joys which become purer and more exquisite as they lose the adventitious glare of early romance; joys which are increased by affliction, and raised by religion to the very summit of terrestrial blessings."[79]

In 1833 J. W. Alexander was appointed professor of Rhetoric and Belles-Lettres at Princeton College. During his eleven years at the college he preached over sixty times a year; for seven years he was the pastor of the African American Presbyterian church on Witherspoon Street. An avid writer, he produced a large number of books, including *The American Mechanic and Working Man, Good, Better, Best; or, the Three Ways of Making a Happy World* (reprinted in London, with an introduction by Robert Smith Candlish); and many articles for the *Biblical Repertory* and other journals and magazines.[80] Charles Hodge commented that he heard J. W. Alexander say that "the only trouble he found in writing was turning the leaves."[81] His great love, however, was preaching; and in 1844 he accepted a call to the Duane Street Presbyterian Church in New York City. There he developed a deep concern for the needs of the great city and attempted to lead the church into a bold and fresh approach to the poor and the lost. Although he preferred to remain a pastor, the forty-five-year-old J. W. Alexander—like his father thirty-seven years earlier—bowed to the decision of the General Assembly. With his wife and family, he returned to Princeton, and to the delightful company of his mother and father and brother. On November 20, 1849, he gave his inaugural address on "The Value of Church History to the Theologian of our Day." He greatly enjoyed studying and teaching church history. He did extensive reading in Augustine and the Pelagian controversy. On March 5, 1850, he wrote, "Renewed studies of Luther have made me admire and love him more than ever."[82]

The students were exceedingly pleased with their new professor. He was a handsome man with impressive dark eyes and the bearing of a Christian gentleman. During 1850 he lectured on homiletics—the only year he taught this course—and James P. Boyce, who entered Princeton in 1849, said that in the area of "sacred rhetoric" Dr. J. W. Alexander was "the most delightful lecturer" he had ever heard.[83]

The seminary faculty was a close-knit family: Archibald Alexander; his two sons; his old friend, Samuel Miller; and his spiritual son, Charles Hodge. They were bound together by kinship and friendship and by theological conviction.

Samuel Miller wrote to Henry Boardman in 1849, "The union in our faculty has been complete.  And the solid basis of the whole, has been a perfect agreement, on the part of all of us, in an honest subscription to our doctrinal formularies."[84]

# 14

# The Duty of Controversy

*Charles Hodge's study, where he met his classes
from 1833 to 1836 when he suffered from lameness.*

He that declines controversy "on principle," or from motives of convenience or prudence, has thereby renounced his confidence in the truth—that truth of which it has been truly said, that it is "like a torch, the more it's shook, it shines."

BENJAMIN BRECKINRIDGE WARFIELD

**P**RINCETON was a quiet little village loved by its scholars and townspeople. The college, with its impressive architecture, ample lawns, and spreading trees, dominated the town. Several blocks away the seminary clustered around its main building. On sunny days and during quiet evenings the great debates of the time could appear distant and unreal. But Princeton—both college and seminary—was very much involved in the issues agitating the church and the nation, and its voice was heard.

The Princetonians did not relish controversy but neither did they shun it. They were committed to defending the faith, but they attempted to do so with Christian charity. As always, Archibald Alexander established a high standard for Princeton. In a sermon preached in 1844 he asked the question, ". . . must the servant of God yield the truth to any one who chooses to impugn it, or is he at liberty to make a compromise with error for the sake of peace?" Alexander answered, "by no means," and then set forth in a few words the principles that should guide the Christian in controversy:

He is bound to contend for the faith once delivered to the saints, and to hold fast the form of sound words which he has received. Controversy will be necessary so long as error exists, but two things are strictly forbidden: first, unprofitable contention, the tendency of which is "to subvert the hearers;" and, secondly, angry contention, for "the servant of the Lord must not strive, but be gentle to all men." No man has a right to compromise a single truth, for this is the sacred deposit which he, in common with other ministers, holds for the edification of the Church; and which they are bound to commit to other faithful men, to be transmitted to those who may come after them.

It is not our duty to enter into controversy with all those who may differ from us in matters not fundamental. "Him that is weak in the faith receive ye, but not to doubtful disputations." "For one believeth that he may eat all things; another, who is weak, eateth herbs. Let not him that eateth despise him that eateth not; and let not him that eateth not judge him that eateth, for God hath received him. Let every man be fully persuaded in his own mind." In all such cases, if God's glory be the end, the person will be accepted, although he may be in trivial error. To seek the honor and glory of God, is the grand characteristic of all true Christians. "For none of us liveth to himself, and no man dieth to himself. For whether we live, we live unto the Lord; and whether we die, we die unto the Lord; whether we live, therefore, or die, we are the Lord's."[1]

Samuel Miller defended religious controversy as necessary, though painful, by pointing to the polemical character of Jesus' preaching and that of the apostles. He illustrated his point:

The church, in this conflict, may be compared to persons striving to ascend an agitated and rapid river, when the wind and the tide are both strong against them. They can advance only by hard rowing; and the moment they intermit their efforts they fall down the stream. The church has to fight for every inch of ground; and whenever she ceases to contend for the truth, she ceases to advance. She may contend with an improper spirit. If she does this, it is her mistake and her sin. But to contend no more, is to disregard the command of her Master in heaven, and betray his cause to the enemy.[2]

Charles Hodge told his classes that the motive of polemics "should be love of truth." One must treat one's opponent with respect and fairness, he said. The views of one's opponent and "the state of the controversy should be clearly understood" and must not be misrepresented in the debate. Although it is justifiable to show the error of a position by tracing its consequences, Hodge said, "we ought not to charge the person embracing it with holding these consequences."³ The Princetonians recognized the importance of "holding the truth"—and of holding it "in love."

The first issue of the reorganized Princeton journal in 1829 maintained that it was "not designed to be controversial in its character, but to state temperately and mildly yet firmly and fearlessly, Bible truth in its whole extent." Later, however, Charles Hodge stated that a journal "consecrated to the support of truth" should be controversial as "a matter of course." Those who question the necessity of such controversy, he added, need only recall that "the Bible is the most controversial of books. It is a protest against sin and error from beginning to end."⁴

One of the earliest controversies to engage the Princetonians was with the Unitarians. From the middle of the eighteenth century, liberal ideas had been proclaimed by an increasing number of Boston clergymen. In 1787, King's Chapel in Boston—the first Episcopal church in New England—became the first Unitarian church in America. In 1805 Henry Ware was appointed Hollis Professor of Divinity at Harvard, and soon America's oldest college was firmly in liberal hands. The Harvard Divinity School, which gradually took shape between 1811 and 1819, professed to be simply Christian, but its faculty and students were Unitarian. In 1819 William Ellery Channing, the quiet and dignified young minister of the Federal Street Church in Boston, took the occasion of Jared Spark's ordination at an explicitly Unitarian church in Baltimore to set forth the major themes of "Unitarian Christianity."⁵

Channing's sermon drew many replies. Professors Moses Stuart and Leonard Woods of Andover presented the trinitarian rebuttal. So did Lyman Beecher and his friend Nathaniel W. Taylor, professor of theology at Yale. In answering the Unitarian arguments, they attempted to make orthodox doctrine more palatable, and more reasonable, than the teachings of Unitarianism. The New Divinity position on freedom of the will and other doctrines, however, appeared to the Unitarians to be "decidedly anti-Calvinistic." The Unitarian *Christian Examiner* reviewed Beecher's famous sermon, "The Faith Once Delivered to the Saints," preached in October 1823, and gleefully declared:

It begins with asserting, in as strong and unqualified language as was ever used by an Arminian or Unitarian, the doctrine of man's actual *ability* and *free agency* . . . . On the subject of *original sin*, and *native depravity*, our author is hardly less unsound in his orthodoxy, for his statement of the Atonement might also be adopted by all Unitarians of whom we have any knowledge.[6]

Princeton's response to Channing's sermon came when Samuel Miller was invited to preach at the installation of Princeton Seminary graduate William Nevins as pastor of the First Presbyterian Church in Baltimore. Miller argued that a "fatal decline of orthodoxy" occurred as creeds were called into question and charged the Unitarians with "soul-destroying errors." Jared Sparks, the minister of the Baltimore Unitarian church, was present to hear Miller's sermon and addressed a series of letters to Miller in the recently founded *Unitarian Miscellany*. Miller, after months of sustained "peltings," responded in December 1821 with *Letters on Unitarianism; Addressed to the Members of the First Presbyterian Church, in the City of Baltimore.*[7] "The system of the Unitarians," he wrote, "is nothing less than a total denial and subversion of the Christian religion." Unitarianism was, therefore, "the most delusive and dangerous" error that had "ever assumed the Christian name." Orthodox supporters expressed gratitude, but liberals such as Sparks were incensed and considered Miller "the arch-bigot of his day."[8]

Dr. Miller was uncomfortable when his *Letters* provoked Moses Stuart of Andover to write his *Letters on the Eternal Generation of the Son of God* (1822). Stuart was concerned to answer Channing; but at the same time he frankly diverged from the main tradition of trinitarian thought—questioning the use of the word "person" and rejecting the doctrine of the eternal generation of the Son. "The fathers in general," Stuart said, "nurtured in the bosom of heathenism and emanation philosophy . . . do not appear to have apprehended anything repulsive in the doctrine of generation as to the divine nature. I am unable to agree with them here."

In his rejoinder to Stuart, *Letters on the Eternal Sonship of Christ, Addressed to the Rev. Prof. Stuart, of Andover*, Samuel Miller expressed fear that the Unitarians might claim "premature triumph on seeing two professed friends of Orthodoxy differing in opinion"; but he made it clear that Princeton regarded the doctrine of the eternal generation of the Son as "highly important."[9] Stuart's denial of it, he stated, was a major concession to "the enemies of truth." Miller argued that the "threefold mode of existence" presupposes an inner-trinitarian society of persons existing from eternity, so that from the beginning the Father has never existed without the Son and Spirit. "The Father is Father *as such*, and the Son is Son *as such*, not by incarnation, adoption, or office, but by nature," Miller stated. The immanent trinity consists not merely of attributes which become manifestations in time through the economic trinity of persons, but trinity consists truly and really of three persons. Since the Godhead exists eternally and essentially as persons, the second person is eternally begotten. Miller's favorite analogy, borrowed from Jonathan Edwards, was that of the sun, which has never existed without sending out beams of light.

Moses Stuart had objected that he could not understand such a "palpable contradiction" as that contained in "eternal sonship." Samuel Miller asked in reply how this doctrine was any more mysterious than the doctrine of the trinity, the omnipresence of God, or, for that matter, any doctrine of Scripture. Miller stated that we are bound to use language which conveys to our minds very inadequate ideas of the things we are trying to express, especially when speaking of the trinity. Stuart had objected to the language of the Nicene Creed as implying the subordination of the second person; but to Miller the sonship of the second person is unique, and neither inferiority nor subordination is intended by the creed.

Samuel Miller's historical skill was evident in his examination of the history of the doctrine of the trinity. He showed that eternal generation was a part of the orthodox teaching of the church from the Council of Nicaea to the present—although he admitted that possibly the language chosen to express this eternal unity of substance and distinction of persons in the Godhead was not always the most fortunate. Miller, however, made his point: both the persons of the Godhead and their relationship are eternal. The Son is the Son not merely by office but by nature—and eternally.

\*     \*     \*

As the Princeton teacher responsible for church government, Dr. Miller enlarged his already considerable knowledge in this area. As we have seen, Miller, in 1809 when he was pastor in New York City, had preached a sermon on "The Divine Appointment, the Duties, and the Qualifications of Ruling Elders." The sermon was published and was widely read. In 1816, the General Assembly of the Presbyterian Church placed Miller, with two others, on a committee to revise the Form of Government. He became, perhaps more than any other man, the recognized Presbyterian authority in matters relating to polity and order. Presbyteries and sessions frequently sought his counsel on the fine points of ecclesiastical law.

In 1821 Samuel Miller greatly enlarged his 1809 sermon and published it as *An Essay, on the Warrant, Nature and Duties of the Office of the Ruling Elder, in the Presbyterian Church*, dedicated to "the ministers and elders of the Presbyterian Church in the United States."[10] "That we make so little of this office [of ruling elder], compared with what we might do, and ought to do," Miller wrote in the introduction to his book, "does really appear to me one of the deepest deficiencies of our beloved Church." Miller was convinced that a recovery of the full significance of the office would "be, at once, one of the surest precursors, and one of the most efficient means, of the introduction of brighter days in the Church of God."[11] Miller's *Essay* began with the declaration that "our once crucified, but now exalted Redeemer, has erected in this world a kingdom which is his Church." It is important to organize the church, Miller believed, according to the divine pattern. He then presented the biblical warrant for Presbyterian church government, focusing especially on the scriptural basis for the office of elder. Miller believed that the eldership was one order of ministry divided into two functions—ruling and teaching. He wrote:

It is plain that, according to early and general usage, Ruling Elders ought not to be styled *laymen*, or *lay-Elders*. They are as really *in office*; they as really bear an office of *divine appointment*; an office of a *high and spiritual nature. . .* as any other officer of the Christian Church. They are as really a portion of *God's lot*; as really set over the *laity*, or body of the people as the most distinguished and venerated minister of Jesus can be. Whether, therefore, we refer to early usage, or to strict philological import, Ruling Elders are as truly entitled to the name of *Clergy*, in the only legitimate sense of that term, that is, they are as truly *ecclesiastical officers* as those who "labor in the word and doctrine."[12]

Miller then traced the history of the office of elder from the church fathers through the Reformation up to contemporary times. The book ended with a practical section on the qualifications and duties of elders. "We have no reason to expect," wrote Miller, "that the piety of the mass of members in any church will rise much higher than that of their Rulers and Guides. Where the latter are either lifeless formalists, or, at best, but 'babes in Christ' we shall rarely find many under their care of more vitality or of superior stature." While Miller stressed the Presbyterian understanding of the office of ruling elder, he was concerned not "to depreciate the ecclesiastical order of other denominations." He wrote that wherever he found those "who evidently bear the image of Christ" and "who appear to be engaged in advancing his kingdom," he could "hail them with unqualified affection"— whatever form of church order they held. Miller concluded his *Essay* with the statement that his daily prayer was "that all the Evangelical Churches in our land may be more and more united in principle and effort, for extending that 'kingdom which is not meat and drink, but righteousness and peace and joy in the Holy Ghost.'"[13]

Miller's *Essay* became an important landmark in the history of Presbyterian polity. Thomas Chalmers called it "the very best work that has been given to the church on that subject."[14] When John Lorimer set about researching his own study of *The Eldership in the Church of Scotland* (1841), he found that surprisingly little had been written on the subject, even in the country where the office of elder had achieved its highest respect. He wrote, "The most complete treatise which I have seen on the subject, and to which I gladly acknowledge my obligations in the following pages, is a work

'On the Office of the Ruling Elder, by Dr. Samuel Miller, Professor of Ecclesiastical History in . . . Princeton, New Jersey.'"[15] A Scottish visitor to the United States in 1844 indicated in his journal his pleasure at meeting the author of the important work on elders and added that "the old gentleman seemed much gratified to be told that his treatise on the eldership had done excellent service in reviving the order in Scotland; by instructing us anew in our own principles."

As a pastor in New York City, Samuel Miller had emphasized the importance of the office of ruling elder as a check on clerical power—having the Episcopalians especially in mind. In his 1809 sermon on "The Divine Appointment, the Duties, and the Qualifications of Ruling Elders," he had stated that elders might "render more signal and important services to the cause of Christ, than many laborers in Word and doctrine." Miller had signified the importance he attached to the office by ordaining ruling elders with the laying on of hands. During his Princeton years, Miller's attention turned—at least temporarily—from the challenge of Episcopacy against Presbyterian ordination to a Presbyterianism threatened by Congregational laxity and confused by lay-controlled voluntary societies. James P. Wilson, Presbyterian pastor in Philadelphia and Miller's boyhood friend, openly espoused Congregational church polity in a long series of articles in the *Quarterly Christian Spectator* between 1823 and 1828.[16] Lay preachers flourished on the frontier, and prominent laymen assumed leadership of the powerful voluntary societies. Having resurrected the dead order of the ruling elder, Miller now turned to restore the minister's office to its proper position. He labored to erect a fence around several areas of the ministry into which he saw the laity inappropriately intruding. In 1823, in an article for *The Christian Advocate* entitled "Thoughts on Lay-Preaching," Miller, while appreciating the increased efforts of the laity since the beginning of his ministry, expressed his concern over the rise of lay preaching. In his *Letters to Presbyterians* (1833), he acknowledged the "large and most important sphere of duty in the Church of God" that belongs to laymen but warned that when "they venture beyond the limits" of their office and "encroach upon the appropriate functions of ecclesiastical office, their agency becomes a source of mischief, and not of benefit."[17]

Miller now stressed the fact that the ruling eldership provided a scheme of checks and balances: restraining, on the one hand, a churchly aristocracy lording it over the laity and, on the other hand, an intrusion of laymen into the functions of the clergy. This balance of power, achieved by means of the biblical and historic office of ruling elder, he described as "Presbyterian republicanism." Miller saw the office of ruling elder as a major source of help and support for pastors and an honorable and legitimate sphere of service for laymen. He wanted to take the work of benevolence out of the hands of the voluntary societies and place it within the church under the direction of ruling elders. He urged each church, under superintendence of its elders, to form its own "auxiliary Bible association; a society for aiding in Foreign Missions, and another for aiding in Domestic Missions; a Tract society; a Temperance Society; and an Education Society."[18]

Samuel Miller admitted that he had modified some of his earlier opinions in a "few minor points" but claimed that "in reference to the Divine warrant and the great importance of the office," his convictions had become "stronger than ever."[19] He still tried to set forth the importance and dignity of the office of ruling elder and to explain its appropriate role. The minister, Miller held, is to preach and administer the sacraments, whereas the ruling elder is to represent the people in the governing of the church. The minister and ruling elders share in the work of pastoring and discipling the flock. Miller struggled to articulate the tensions that Presbyterians have always felt—that the ruling elder is an ordained officer with equal ruling authority to that of the teaching elder, but the teaching elder is a leader among equals (*primer inter pares*).

After the 1837 division, controversy continued among Old School Presbyterians on "the church question." Some, led by James Henley Thornwell of South Carolina and Robert Jefferson Breckinridge of Baltimore, Maryland, and Lexington, Kentucky, advocated further reforms in matters of polity and order. They held a view of Presbyterianism which claimed that church polity was set forth in scripture as clearly as doctrine. The question of the legitimacy of "church boards" agitated Old School Presbyterians during 1841 and 1842, and in 1843 there was a debate in General Assembly on "the elder question." Thornwell took the lead on the board issue and Breckinridge became the spokesman on the role of ruling elders. Proud of the fact that he had served as both a ruling and a teaching elder, Breckinridge defended the participation of ruling elders by the imposition of hands in the ordination of ministers, and argued for the necessity of the presence of ruling elders in forming a quorum of presbytery.

From November 26 to December 24, 1842, in the pages of the *The Presbyterian,* Samuel Miller (writing under the pseudonym "Calvin") published a series of five articles entitled "The Rights of Ruling Elders." Miller stated that the Breckinridge view of the eldership was an innovation in Presbyterian history, although Miller admitted that in 1808 he had ordained ruling elders by the imposition of hands. As late as 1831 Miller had supported the idea of ruling elders participating in the ordination of ministers. In a letter to a ruling elder in Baltimore, he had written, "I fully concur with you in your opinion that Ruling Elders ought *upon principle* to lay hands, with Teaching Elders in all ordinations." But he urged patience, stating that "we are not yet . . ., I suppose, prepared for such a step."[20] By the 1840s, however, Miller had abandoned his earlier views and now opposed ruling elders participating in the laying on of hands in the ordination of ministers.

From January 14 to February 18, 1843, Breckinridge (under the name "Presbyter") argued in *The Presbyterian* for one order of elder, or presbyter, with diversity of office. The sharply divergent views of Miller and Breckinridge were reviewed by Charles Hodge in a lengthy article in the *Biblical Repertory* of April 1843. Hodge argued that Breckinridge's strict views on polity were supported by neither the Bible nor the church's constitution; the church was free, therefore, to govern itself according to the general principles revealed in the scripture. Further, Hodge agreed with Miller that there are three distinct officers in the church—bishops or ministers, elders, and deacons. Breckinridge replied that in rejecting the *jus divinum* view, Hodge had laid the axe to the "root of our whole doctrine of Church order, which might well enough have been expected from an Erastian, a Prelatist or a New Schoolman—but surely not from Princeton."[21]

Following Samuel Miller's sermon on the eldership, the 1843 General Assembly voted down an overture from West Lexington Presbytery requiring that ruling elders be included in the ordination of ministers and also ruled that any three ministers in a presbytery could form a quorum to transact business. Miller voted with the majority in these decisions, while Breckinridge and Thornwell argued that ruling elders should be ordained in the same way as ministers, by the laying on of hands, and asserted the right of equal participation by ruling elders in the ordination of ministers. They also held that no church court could be properly constituted without one or more ruling elders present. In the 1843 fall meeting of the Synod of Philadelphia, Breckinridge carefully laid out his views of the fundamentals of Presbyterian polity in a two-hour address printed as "Presbyterian Government Not a Hierarchy, But a Commonwealth." Professor Albert Dod answered in the April 1844 issue of the *Biblical Repertory* that Breckinridge's views were supported neither by scripture nor history. Breckinridge was incensed that the Princeton review had been written by a minister without charge—a man he described as "an Evangelist who teaches Mathematics and lectures on Architecture in Nassau Hall." The debate continued with Thomas Smyth, Presbyterian minister in Charleston, South Carolina, supporting the Miller-Hodge position, and Robert Lewis Dabney of Virginia upholding the Thornwell-Breckinridge view. The Presbyterian church followed Princeton's lead on church polity and the eldership, but the views of Breckinridge, Thornwell and Dabney eventually became the position of the Southern Presbyterian Church.[22]

\*     \*     \*

The Episcopal controversy revived with the appearance of John Cooke's *Essay on the Invalidity of Presbyterian*

*Ordination.* Samuel Miller responded by reissuing in 1830 his *Letters Concerning the Constitution and Order of the Christian Ministry.*[23] In 1835 he wrote a little booklet entitled *Presbyterianism the Truly Primitive and Apostolical Constitution of the Church of Christ.* It was reprinted in Scotland in 1842 as part of a volume on Presbyterian church government, edited by John Lorimer, minister of Free St. David's Church of Glasgow. While stressing that the visible church "is made up of all those throughout the world, who profess the true religion, together with their children," and deploring the separation of Christians in competing denominations, Miller nonetheless was convinced that the Presbyterian church was "more truly primitive and apostolical in its whole constitution, of *doctrine, worship, and order,* than any other Church, now on earth."[24]

In 1840, the Presbyterian Board of Publication issued an abridgment of Miller's *Letters on the Christian Ministry* under the title: *The Primitive and Apostolical Order of the Church of Christ Vindicated.* The Anglo-Catholic *Tracts for the Times,* recently reprinted and extensively circulated in the United States, occasioned this new edition of Miller's defence of Presbyterianism against prelacy. Miller did not view the issue as an inconsequential debate on church polity but as involving "matters of infinite moment." The *Tracts for the Times,* he asserted, "turn away the attention of their readers from the Saviour, as the only ground of confidence, and direct them to the fables, the genealogies, and the miserable revived superstitions of Romanism."[25] Samuel Miller insisted that he was not attacking Episcopacy but merely showing that Episcopalians had been "utterly wrong and unjust" in attacking Presbyterianism. Miller, ably supported by J. A. Alexander, continued to defend Presbyterian principles in many reviews and articles in the *Biblical Repertory.* "It was no bitterness against his Episcopal neighbours," Miller wrote, "no love of controversy, no restless ambition, no desire to intrude into another denomination for the purpose of making proselytes, that dictated an attempt to defend his beloved church." Reviewing this long controversy with Episcopacy, a later Princeton Seminary professor wrote that Samuel Miller "marshalled the proofs for Presbyterianism with great ability and popular effect, and kept his temper better than any of his opponents."[26]

Samuel Miller—who said that he loved "to have a nail in every building intended for the glory of God or the good of man"—gladly contributed to a fund for constructing an Episcopal church across the street from the seminary. When an old acquaintance wrote in 1847 that because of his location he had joined the Episcopal Church, Miller replied that although he had no personal acquaintance with the minister, he understood that he was a decidedly evangelical man. He added:

From all that I have ever learned, I feel persuaded, that he preaches the Gospel substantially and faithfully. Of course, assured that he is engaged in leading souls to Christ, and, through his atoning sacrifice and life-giving Spirit, to heaven, I can cordially resign you, if you allow me to say so, to his evangelical care. In my opinion, you judge correctly, in thinking that you cannot go essentially wrong, in joining yourself to any Protestant denomination, by the ministry of which inquiring souls are directed, as the ground of hope, not to rites and ceremonies, but to the atoning blood and perfect righteousness of the Saviour of sinners.[27]

\*     \*     \*

Although Samuel Miller was "the recognized authority of the Presbyterian church in all matters relating to her polity and order," Charles Hodge had become an even greater force in American Presbyterianism.[28] The power of Hodge's opinion was demonstrated in his response to the decision of the 1845 General Assembly, which declared that Roman Catholic baptism was not Christian baptism.[29] As early as 1831 the question of "popish" baptisms had come before the assembly. Both Samuel Miller and Archibald Alexander served on various committees appointed to study the question. No report came to the assembly from this effort, but both Alexander and Miller expressed their personal views. Dr. Alexander believed that an "ecclesiastical decision" would be a mistake and held that the "only wise and peaceable course" would be to "permit every minister . . . to act agreeably to his own honest convictions."[30] Dr. Miller was persuaded that "the

precedents of the early Church, the decision of the Reform-
ers, and sound principle" all favored acknowledging Roman
Catholic baptism as valid Christian baptism.[31] In 1835 the
General Assembly had declared that the Roman Catholic
Church had "essentially apostatized from the religion of our
Lord and Savior Jesus Christ" and therefore could not be
recognized as "a Christian Church." In 1840 the General
Assembly voted that a sermon on "the evils of popery" would
be delivered annually to the assembly, with Robert J.
Breckinridge appointed to give the inaugural sermon.[32]

It was not surprising then that the question of the validity
of Roman Catholic baptism was decided in the negative by
the 1845 General Assembly. What was surprising was the
margin of the vote, 173 to 8! Hodge lamented the assembly's
decision as a great blunder and said so in his annual review of
the General Assembly in the *Biblical Repertory*.[33] Hodge
argued that the position of the assembly had been taken "in
opposition to all previous practice and to the principles of
every other protestant church." He stated that like the
Presbyterians, the Roman Catholic Church used water and
baptized in the name of the trinity. In fact, added Hodge,
"there is not a Church on earth which teaches the doctrine
of the Trinity more accurately, thoroughly, or minutely,
according to the orthodoxy of the Reformed and Lutheran
churches, than the church of Rome." Hodge acknowledged
that many serious errors abound in the Catholic Church, but
maintained that it was part of the visible church. Here he
followed the Reformers, especially Francis Turretin, who
declared that in its papal hierarchy and attendant corruption
Rome is "antichristian and apostate," but that it is yet
Christian in that there are "people of God" still remaining
in it. Despite its errors, Hodge insisted that the Roman
Catholic Church retained truth "enough to save the soul."
Catholics, he stated, hold the doctrines of the incarnation
and the trinity; "they teach the doctrine of atonement far
more fully and accurately than multitudes of professedly
orthodox Protestants." They believe in the forgiveness of
sins, the resurrection of the body, and in eternal life
and judgment. Hodge chastised the assembly for its ill-
considered decision. It is sin "to reject as reprobates any real

followers of Christ," he stated; "the cause of Protestantism suffers materially from undiscriminating denunciations heaped upon the church of Rome."[34] Hodge's position provoked considerable response—mostly negative. With typical understatement, Hodge said that his view did not meet with "the approbation of a large portion of our brethren."[35]

In April 1846, Hodge answered his critics with an article entitled "Is the Church of Rome Part of the Visible Church?"[36] He argued that "the order and teaching of the Romish Church is in many respects corrupted and overlaid by false and soul-destroying abuses" but that "the great body of people constituting the Roman Catholic Church do profess the essentials of the true Christian religion, whereby many of them bear the image of Christ, and are participants of His salvation." The Catholic Church, however corrupt, accepts the general truths of the ecumenical creeds and so is, he asserted, "a part of the visible church on earth."[37] Charles Hodge's views on the Roman Catholic Church were not only more moderate than those of many in the Presbyterian church but also those of more "liberal" ministers such as Lyman Beecher and Horace Bushnell. Hodge courageously resisted the nativistic spirit of the time and led the Presbyterian church to safer and saner ground. The General Assembly rescinded its 1845 position and left the decision concerning Roman Catholic baptism to each local church session.[38]

*       *       *

When Charles Finney's *Lectures on Systematic Theology* was published in two volumes in 1846, Charles Hodge subjected it to close scrutiny in the *Biblical Repertory*.[39] Hodge began:

This is in more senses than one a remarkable book. It is to a degree very unusual an original work; it is the product of the author's own mind. . . . The work is therefore in a high degree logical. It is as hard to read as Euclid. Nothing can be omitted; nothing passed over slightly. . . . There is not one resting place; not one lapse into amplification, or declamation, from beginning to close. . . . The author begins with certain postulates, or what he calls first truths of reason, and these he traces out with singular clearness and strength to their legitimate conclusions. We do not see that there is a break or a defective link in the whole chain. If you grant his principles, you have already granted his conclusions. Such a work must of course be reckless. Having committed himself to the guidance of the discursive understanding, which he sometimes calls the intelligence, and sometimes the reason, and to which he alone acknowledges any real allegiance, he pursues his remorseless course, regardless of any protest from other sources. The scriptures are throughout recognized as a mere subordinate authority. They are allowed to come in and bear confirmatory testimony, but their place is altogether secondary.[40]

"The true and Christian method is to begin with the doctrines," Hodge countered, "and let them determine our philosophy, and not to begin with philosophy and allow it to give law to the doctrines."

Hodge objected to Finney's assumption that liberty and ability are identical. He wrote, "It is a dictum of philosophers, not of common people, 'I ought, therefore, I can.' To which every unsophisticated human heart, and especially every heart burdened with a sense of sin, replies, 'I ought to be able, but I am not.'" Hodge continued, "As the doctrine, the very opposite of Mr. Finney's assumed axiom, is thus deeply and indelibly impressed on the heart of man, so it is constantly asserted or assumed in Scripture." Hodge still felt (as he had in 1832) that in Finney's doctrine of salvation "Christ and his cross are practically made of none effect." He wrote that "it shocks the moral sense of men to say that a pirate, with all his darkness of mind as to God, and divine things, with all his callousness, with all the moral habits of a life of crime, becomes perfectly holy, by a change of will, by forming a new intention, by mere honesty of purpose."[41] Finney's theology had far too much emphasis on human reason and human ability, and far too little on the Scriptures, the atonement, and the Holy Spirit, for Charles Hodge.

By the time of the publication of his *Lectures on Systematic Theology*, Charles Finney had embraced a perfectionist doctrine of sanctification. By 1839 he had drifted somewhat from his earlier Wesleyan ideas to the view that "entire and permanent sanctification is attainable in this life on the ground of natural ability."[42] Then he began to teach that "the baptism of the Holy Spirit" was normative for all Christians, although he did not himself experience this second work of grace until 1843. He described what happened—"My confidence in God was perfect, my acceptance of his will was perfect, and my mind was as calm as heaven."[43] No one is perfect, responded Hodge, who is not perfectly like Christ. Hodge quoted many biblical passages where the writers, in spite of their greatest attempts to live consistently holy lives, were forced to confess their failures. "Need any reader of the Bible," he asked, "be reminded that the consciousness of sin, of present corruption and unworthiness, is one of the most uniform features of the experience of God's people as there recorded?" Yet Finney expected people "to believe that 'honest intention' is the whole duty of religion," and if they have that they are perfect. Finney's religion "is something exceedingly different from what good people in all ages have commonly regarded it," Hodge concluded.[44]

Charles Finney offered a lengthy rebuttal to Hodge in the next issue of *The Oberlin Quarterly Review*. He did little more, however, than attack Old School theology and concluded with a statement with which Hodge would have agreed fully: "I freely admit that this writer and myself have exceedingly diverse views of the nature of true religion."[45] Hodge apparently did not see the need to respond further.[46]

\*     \*     \*

While Charles Hodge was refuting Finney's theology, he was also following carefully the views of John Nevin and Philip Schaff, the two outstanding teachers in the little seminary of the German Reformed church at Mercersburg, Pennsylvania. As noted earlier, Nevin studied at Princeton Seminary and taught Charles Hodge's classes while Hodge was in Europe. He was professor of biblical literature at Western Seminary for a decade, before moving to Mercersburg in 1840. Hodge always regarded Nevin "as the greatest of his pupils" and maintained respect for him, although their friendship was greatly strained by their heated debates.

John Nevin was joined in 1844 by Philip Schaff, a brilliant young Swiss theologian who had studied with Hodge's friends Tholuck and Hengstenberg, but who also drew much inspiration from Schleiermacher and Neander. Schaff abandoned prospects for a distinguished career at a European university to teach church history and biblical literature at Mercersburg. He delighted in saying of himself, "I am a Swiss by birth, a German by education, and American by choice." [47]

Through their books and articles in the *Mercersburg Review*, Nevin and Schaff emphasized the objective, sacramental, and liturgical factors in theology and began an important movement which Sydney Ahlstrom has called "the most creative manifestation of the Catholic tendency in American Protestantism."[48]   They stressed the incarnation —rather than the atonement—as the central Christian doctrine.  Christ, they said, was a spiritual force active in the world through his ongoing incarnation in the Christian church. They criticized modern American "Puritanism," new-measures revivalism, and denominationalism, and called for a return to sixteenth-century Protestantism with its high view of the church.  The "sect system," which flourished under the American separation of church and state, drew its spiritual capital from Puritanism, they argued.  It is unhistorical and unchurchly, zealous for the sovereignty of God but not for the body of Christ.  They gave much more credit to the medieval and Catholic heritage than was common in American Protestantism.  They believed that "the Lord still has great things in store" for the Roman Catholic Church.  The historical development of the church, they declared, reveals by its richness and diversity how the Christian faith fulfills and culminates every human or historic tendency.

In the pages of the *Mercersburg Review*, commented Sydney Ahlstrom, the scholarship of Nevin and Schaff "roved over the whole history of the Church, to greatest effect probably when they drew lessons from the early centuries and patristic writings, stressing subjects that Protestants had ignored, giving vitality to the doctrine of the Church as the body of Christ, and emphasizing its objective and visible character."[49] Despite important differences, Princeton had much in common with the Mercersburg theologians, which may explain Hodge's sharpness of tone—largely absent in his other polemical writings.

Philip Schaff's inaugural address at Mercersburg, in which he opposed "Romanism" but argued for a movement toward an "evangelical Catholicism," was published as *The Principle of Protestantism, as Related to the Present State of the Church* in 1845. It was aggressively introduced by Nevin. The work attracted Hodge's attention; and he quickly produced an extensive review in the *Biblical Repertory* entitled "Schaff's Protestantism."[50] Hodge agreed with Schaff that the church must maintain the faith of the Reformation; but he utterly rejected the Mercersburg argument that American Protestantism, including conservative Presbyterianism, had deviated from Reformation norms by acceptance of sectarianism, rationalization of the Lord's Supper, and minimization of the visible church. Hodge praised Schaff's exposition of the great doctrine of justification by faith, the first distinguishing principle of Protestantism, as "thoroughly evangelical"—and good reading for "our new school brethren." He was disturbed, however, by Schaff's ambiguity on the question of how we become Christians. Is it by faith or is it through the church? "German writers have many characteristic excellencies," he wrote, "but they have also some characteristic faults. They are seldom very intelligible."[51] Hodge concurred with Schaff's treatment of the supremacy of Scripture as the rule of faith, the second distinguishing principle of Protestantism. He feared, however, that Schaff attributed much more weight to the traditions of the visible church than is consistent with the Protestant principle. Against Schaff's accusation of sectarianism, Hodge argued that "more real brotherhood" exists "between the evangelical denominations of America than is to be found in the church of Rome, the Church of England, or in the Reformed or Lutheran church of Germany." He added, "The true unity of the church is therefore, in a measure, independent of external ecclesiastical union." Schaff blamed the Puritans for separating from the established Church of England and condemned the recent secession of the Free Church of Scotland. Although Hodge admitted that "sectarianism" is "a very serious evil," he insisted that some "separations are a duty which we owe to God and to the real unity of the church whenever unscriptural terms of communion are enjoined."[52] Hodge considered Romanism "immeasurably more dangerous than infidelity"—not a greater evil—but more dangerous to Protestantism because "a false religion is more likely to spread than mere irreligion." But he maintained that the fear of some that Nevin and Schaff were tending toward prelacy and Rome was altogether unfounded.

Hodge was soon to change his mind about Nevin. In *The Mystical Presence, A Vindication of the Reformed or Calvinistic Doctrine of the Holy Eucharist* (1846), Nevin argued for a return to what he held was Calvin's view of the "real spiritual presence" in the Lord's Supper. Nevin leveled serious criticism at the American Calvinistic tradition—including Jonathan Edwards and Charles Hodge and the Presbyterians—for what he considered their spiritualistic, subjective, and memorialistic views of the Lord's Supper. Hodge's review of Nevin's book ("Doctrine of the Reformed Church on the Lord's Supper") sharply charged Nevin—who "should know better"—with having abandoned what Hodge considered true Reformed orthodoxy.[53] Nevin vigorously set forth Calvin's teaching on the "mystical" presence of Christ in the Lord's Supper, while avoiding the doctrine of election. Hodge, less inclined to a full-orbed sacramental theology, championed the eternal decrees. Hodge believed that the *Consensus Tigurinus,* drawn up by Bullinger and Calvin, represented the best Reformed statement on the Lord's Supper.[54]

Hodge argued that Nevin and the Mercersburg Theology—too much influenced by Schleiermacher—united "God and man through the incarnation of the first and deification of the second." He judged that Nevin's Christology exaggerated the unity of the two natures of Christ in a manner reminiscent of the ancient Eutychian heresy. He believed that Nevin's soteriology—participation in the life and grace of Christ made available through the church—substituted a theory of inherent righteousness for the doctrine that God graciously "imputed" Christ's righteousness to the elect believer. He felt that Nevin's theology diminished the role of the Holy Spirit. Even though Hodge may have erred in minimizing the historical learning and significance of Nevin's work on the Lord's Supper, he was right in detecting in him a move toward Roman Catholicism. According to James H. Nichols, Nevin's later views displayed "strong sympathies for Roman Catholicism and an emotional alienation from Protestantism."[55] In 1854, Hodge wrote that his former student and old friend had "forfeited entirely the confidence of the Protestant community."[56]

Philip Schaff, however, remained a popular and respected spokesman for Protestantism and became a highly regarded church historian. His important work of 1846, *What is Church History? A Vindication of the Idea of Historical Development*, was "a milestone in the history of American historical theory."[57] Building on the views of his teacher Ferdinand Christian Baur, Schaff set forth the first American exposition of the "idea of 'organic' development" in the successive ages of the church. The church's own doctrine, life, worship, and government are progressively transformed, Schaff argued, by the "uninterrupted presence of Christ . . . in and among his people." The church's development is dialectical as well as organic, Schaff believed. It proceeded by way of the opposition and reconciliation of logical principles, as well as by the gradual unfolding of a new life principle. Although far from accepting all his ideas, some Princetonians took a positive view of Schaff's work. J. W. Alexander wrote to a friend on June 29, 1846:

I wish you would read *Schaff's* famous book [*What is Church History?*]. Cry out as we may, he tells us some plain truths, and reveals things which none but a transatlantic eye could discern. It is a most exciting and suggestive volume, with a figment for the hypothesis, but great genius, learning, and truth in many of the details. I have always felt the force of what he says about the Puritans having cut to the quick, in regard to externals; about the charity we should have for Papists; and about the evils of innumerable sects. But he goes fearfully far, about visible unity.[58]

J. A. Alexander was "a warm admirer of the talents, attainments, and piety of Professor Schaff, and thought him better fitted than any man in America to write the great popular work on Church History."[59] In 1857, Alexander wrote to encourage Schaff in his writing, praising him for the "intellectual and literary merit" of his books and for "the good old Protestant principles" found in them.[60] Charles Hodge was not as enthusiastic about Schaff, however. He was afraid that Schaff's "organicism" predisposed him to see in the evolution of Christian consciousness the growth of orthodox dogma, never a possible devolution from the Christian gospel. When Schaff's *History of the Apostolic Church* appeared, Hodge criticized it for containing a strong "anti-Protestant leaven."[61]

In 1870, Philip Schaff joined the Presbyterian church and became a professor at Union Theological Seminary in New York. He taught Hebrew and Bible until 1877, when he was appointed professor of church history. His three-volume *Creeds of Christendom* appeared in 1877 and became a valuable and standard reference work. He founded the American Society of Church History in his home in 1888. *A History of the Christian Church*, in seven volumes, was completed in 1892. An ecumenical churchman, Schaff played a significant role in the World Conference of the Evangelical Alliance in 1873 and, two years later, participated in the founding of the Alliance of the Reformed Churches in the Jerusalem Chamber at Westminster Abbey.[62]

\*     \*     \*

The Romantic mood—flowing from Jean-Jacques Rousseau, Immanuel Kant, and Samuel Taylor Coleridge—transformed European intellectual life during the early nineteenth century, with its stress on intuition, aesthetics, poetry, and feeling in reaction to the logical and rational features of the Enlightenment. It influenced Mercersburg, left Princeton unaffected, and flourished in New England transcendentalism. In his 1838 address to the graduating class of the Harvard Divinity School, Ralph Waldo Emerson put forth the transcendentalist agenda. He demanded a complete recasting of religious life and thought, saying that ministers should replace their "faith in Christ" with a "faith in man like Christ's." In "masterly studies" for the January 1839 *Biblical Repertory*, J. W. Alexander and Albert Dod reviewed the rise of "transcendentalism" and examined in detail Cousin's system.[63] Alexander's exasperation with Emerson's address came out when he confessed that he lacked "words with which to express our sense of the nonsense and impiety which permeate it. . . . There is not a single truth or sentiment in the whole Address that is borrowed from the Scriptures. And why should there be? Mr. Emerson, and all men, are as truly inspired as the penmen of the sacred volume."[64] The article by Alexander and Dod attracted much attention and was reprinted in the United States and Europe.

In 1840, Hodge in an article entitled "The Latest Form of Infidelity," presented one of his earliest comprehensive judgements of romantic idealism. He wrote:

It knows no intelligent or conscious God but man; it admits no incarnation, but the eternal incarnation of the universal spirit in the human race; the personality of men ceases with their present existence, they are but momentary manifestations of the infinite and unending; there is neither sin nor holiness; neither heaven nor hell.[65]

\* \* \*

Horace Bushnell attended Yale Divinity School and began a long ministry at Hartford's North (Congregational) Church in 1833. In 1847 he wrote *Christian Nurture*, in which he set forth the thesis that "the true idea of Christian education is: that the child is to grow up a Christian, and never know himself as being otherwise." Rejecting the American emphasis on revivalism, Bushnell believed that conversion was ideally a gradual lifelong process of growth and deepening awareness. Charles Hodge reviewed the book, carefully summarizing Bushnell's argument. Like Bushnell, Hodge lamented the undue reliance on periodic religious excitements to the neglect of "family training" and "pastoral instruction." Hodge concurred that in American religion there was "disproportionate reliance placed on the proclamation of the gospel from the pulpit as almost the only means of conversion; and in the disposition to look upon revivals as the only hope of the church." He agreed that there is "a connection between faithful parental training and the salvation of children."[66] These were not new ideas to Charles Hodge. Years earlier, on the occasion of the baptism of his first daughter,

Hodge had written to his mother:

I have great confidence in the effect of religious truth upon the infant mind. Children are so susceptible, their associations are so strong and lasting, that it does not seem strange that the effect of early education should so frequently be felt through life. And if we add to this God's peculiar promises to those who endeavor to bring up a child in the way in which he should go, we shall see that there is abundant reason to hope that exertions properly directed will be crowned with success.[67]

Only after twenty-two pages of largely affirmative comment did Hodge come to the point that Bushnell had made the regeneration and sanctification of the soul too much a "natural" process. Bushnell rejected the doctrine of human depravity and taught that the influence and training of children by parents were fully adequate to correct natural corruption and effect regeneration. Bushnell assumed, according to Hodge, "that men are not by nature the children of wrath, that they are not involved in spiritual death, and, consequently, that they do not need to be quickened by that mighty power which wrought in Christ when it raised him from the dead." He wrote, "The whole tenor of this book is in favour of the idea that all true religion is gradual, habitual, acquired as habits are formed. Everything must be like a natural process, nothing out of the regular sequence of cause and effect." While Hodge appreciated Bushnell's insistence on the importance of "Christian nurture," he could not accept his downplaying of human sinfulness. "He has not advanced an inch beyond Pelagius," Hodge wrote.[68]

Soon there was another quarrel with Horace Bushnell. Influenced by the romanticism of Coleridge and by the American tradition of transcendentalism, Bushnell saw Christianity not so much as a matter of doctrine but as "spirit and life" flowing from "Christ dwelling in us." In the course of history, Bushnell believed, the "living words that Jesus spoke to the world's heart" hardened into dogmas which then brought conflict and schism. To cure this deplorable situation, Bushnell proposed a theological program of "Christian comprehensiveness," in which the insights of all Christians would be combined "in a grand comprehensive unity." This was possible, Bushnell argued, because all religious language is necessarily figurative and poetic; therefore absolute doctrinal statements are impossible.

In his 1848 lecture at Andover Seminary, "Dogma and Spirit," Horace Bushnell spelled out his views, emphasizing the ambiguity and imprecision of religious language and the mysterious quality of religious knowledge. He argued that knowledge received intuitively was superior to knowledge gained by observation and reflection. Bushnell's insistence that verbal communication is "essentially evocative, symbolic, and social in nature" made a literal appeal to scriptural and creedal statements impossible.[69] Theology, he believed, was a barrier to religious truth; and the low state of New England Christianity, he stated, was due to its concern for dogma at the expense of spirituality. Bushnell set forth these views again in his "Preliminary Discourse on Language" that appeared in his 1849 work, *God in Christ.* "Creeds are poems and theologies fabrics of images," he wrote, "directing us to truths of the spirit in the only way they can: by indirection." For the church to achieve a true reviving of religion, it had to move beyond a conception of the gospel as a system of propositions and formulas to a vision of Christianity as a spiritual and life-giving power. True knowledge of God, Bushnell said, came through "faith, right feeling, spirit, and life."[70]

Bushnell's ideas created a flurry of responses. Henry B. Smith, professor at Amherst College, answered Bushnell in an address on the "Relations of Faith and Philosophy," given at Andover Seminary. Smith claimed that evangelical faith and human philosophy are complementary, since both deal with the facts of reality from different perspectives. Philosophy, said Smith, must understand that the Christian faith is based on a revelation historically attested and presents as "another series of facts" the experience of believers across the centuries. Philosophic unbelief is unsound, Smith argued, because it is unphilosophical "for philosophy to be dogmatic in the face of a recognized reality." Insisting that "in Jesus Christ is to be found the real centre of the Christian economy," and commending Schleiermacher and German evangelical theology, Smith concluded that Christianity gives "what man most needs, and, unaided, never could attain."

Smith's answer to Bushnell, despite its debt to German philosophy, was sufficiently orthodox to pass Charles Hodge's scrutiny.

Edwards A. Park, Andover's leading theologian, also got into the debate when he delivered an address ("The Theology of the Intellect and That of the Feelings") to a convention of Congregational ministers in Brattle Street Meeting House in Boston on May 30, 1850. Park tried to appropriate and soften the ideas of Bushnell and still defend the theologian's traditional function by distinguishing between doctrinal statements suited to rational analysis and religious expressions that satisfied the cravings of the pious heart. He argued that the theology of the intellect and the theology of the feelings express the same truths—one in a rational form and the other in aesthetic terms. The two theologies are related and intertwined, Park stated. "The theology of the intellect enlarges and improves that of the feelings, and is enlarged and improved by it."[71] Even though Park gave primacy to the theology of the intellect (since only a theology that persuaded the head could reach the heart), his views caused great concern at Princeton. Charles Hodge believed that Park's critique conceded far too much to Bushnell.

Hodge replied to Park, and a lengthy exchange of over 265 pages took place in Park's *Bibliotheca Sacra* and Hodge's *Biblical Repertory* during 1850 and 1851. Hodge believed that Park was too much influenced by Schleiermacher's efforts to ground Christianity in religious feelings and set out to state the proper understanding of the objective and the subjective in the Christian faith.[72] He readily admitted that there are cognitive and emotive sides to truth, but he objected to the idea that there are two kinds of truth or two theologies. Park's proposal, Hodge stated, meant that "if an assertion of Scripture commends itself to our reason, we refer it to the theology of the intellect, and admit its truth. If it clashes with any of our preconceived opinions, we can refer it to the theology of the feelings, and deny its truth for the intellect." Hodge insisted that figurative language properly used and understood did not make a concept any less precise or intelligible. Figurative language in the Bible and in the creeds, he said, was addressed to the intellect as well as to the feelings and, consequently, was just as intelligible and descriptive as the most literal language. Neither can one separate the faculties of intellect and emotion in the individual. Hodge insisted that "both Scripture and consciousness teach that the soul is a unit." There is perfect consistency between the intellectual apprehension of truth when viewed in order to be understood and when contemplated in order to be felt. However different the language employed when expressing thoughts and feelings, there cannot be "two conflicting theologies." "The theology of the feeling is the theology of the intellect in all its accuracy of thought and expression," Hodge maintained.[73]

For Charles Hodge, Christianity was a unified experience. It was both an intuition, or a feeling of trust, and a rational assent to the objective truths taught in Scripture. Hodge attempted to explain the true relation between the two. They are not independent, he argued, nor does the intellect merely interpret the feelings, as Schleiermacher taught. Hodge set forth three biblical principles which he used in addressing the issue. First, "the Bible never recognizes that broad distinction between the intellect and the feelings which is so often made by metaphysicians." The understanding is darkened and the heart depraved. Secondly, "the Scriptures as clearly teach that holiness is necessary to the perception of truth. In other words, that the things of the Spirit must be spiritually discerned." Thirdly, "the Bible further teaches that no mere change of the feelings is adequate to secure this spiritual discernment. . . . The eyes must be opened in order to see wondrous things out of the law of God." "The glory of God, as it shines in the face of Jesus Christ," wrote Hodge, "must be revealed, before the corresponding affections of admiration, love, and confidence rise in the heart." God acts upon the whole soul, producing "the intuition of the truth and glory of the things of God." Therefore there must be perfect harmony between the feelings and the intellect—"they cannot see with different eyes, or utter discordant language." Distinguishing between knowledge and comprehension, Hodge argued that even though Scripture and the creeds contained mysteries that could not be understood by finite minds, they nonetheless provided knowledge about those mysteries in rational terms. Hodge believed that Bushnell's ideas and Park's use of them threatened the scientific nature of theology and the rational foundations of the faith. Park, almost immediately, recanted the liberal implications of his concessions and remained a conservative Calvinist in the increasingly liberal New England scene.

In 1849 Horace Bushnell had published his *God in Christ.* Hodge admired Bushnell's "vigorous imagination and adventurous style" but stated that he failed to put forth "a consistent and comprehensive theory on the great themes of God, the Incarnation, and Redemption." Bushnell, Hodge charged, "is Rationalist, Mystic, Pantheist, Christian, by turns, just as the emergency demands."[74] Bushnell responded to criticism from Hodge and others by moderating his position and attempting to set forth a more comprehensive exposition of Christianity in *Christ in Theology* (1851). Bushnell's *Vicarious Sacrifice* was published in 1866. The cross, for Bushnell, was a declaration not of the satisfaction of our sins but of their cancellation within the being of God; so that, having expressed his displeasure over sin and painfully accepted the consequences, God affirmed his moral government of the world and influenced sinners by the example of his love. Hodge saw in this not a biblical exposition of the doctrine of the atonement but a rational explanation.[75] Bushnell later moved toward the Athanasian doctrine of the Trinity and the Anselmic insistence that God was "satisfied" by Christ's atoning death.

\*     \*     \*

For years now the Princetonians had been setting forth the old truths, as they understood them, from the Bible and the teachings of the Reformed faith. In the pages of the *Biblical Repertory* they had defended the "evangelical scheme" against "Infidels, Papists, Socinians, Pelagians, Arminians, and Enthusiasts." In 1846 a collection of *Theological Essays,* taken from the *Biblical Repertory,* appeared in book form. When these were reprinted in Scotland ten years later, Patrick Fairbairn, who was professor of divinity in the Free Church College, Aberdeen, wrote in a prefatory note:

For an exact and discriminating knowledge of the peculiar doctrines of Calvinism, of the fundamental grounds on which they rest, of the false admixtures on the one side, and the dangerous concessions on the other, with which at successive periods they have been associated, and of the relations in which they stand to a true and a false philosophy, the Essays under consideration could not easily be surpassed. And it adds materially to their value, that they are not dry vindications of a theoretical and systematic orthodoxy, but the profound and earnest reasonings of men, who felt that, in contending for Calvinism, they were contending for the great interests of truth and righteousness—of men, of whom it is scarcely too much to say, that on them, the mantle, not merely of Edwards, but of Calvin himself, seems peculiarly to have fallen.[76]

Not only was Princeton praised by scholars and churchmen for its stalwart defense of Reformed orthodoxy, but simple Christians faithfully prayed for and supported its work. Robert and Marian Hall gave $2,500 to endow a scholarship at Princeton.[77] The Halls, brother and sister, had been brought up under the ministry of John Brown of Haddington in Scotland. They emigrated to America in 1785, settling in Orange County, New York, where they taught school. Living frugally, they saved enough money to give modest sums to several Christian organizations. When it was suggested that the scholarship be called the Hall Scholarship, Marian Hall replied, "I dinna wish my worthless name to be remembered after I am dead and gone, but I do wish to do something for the cause of true religion, which shall maintain the truth, as long as the Kirk shall lead, and, therefore, I wish the Scholarship to be named *Ed.*" When asked for the meaning of the name, she said, "And dinna ye ken, young mon? E'en go and read your Bible." She directed the questioner to Joshua 22:34, which records that the children of Reuben and the children of Gad called the altar at the Jordan *Ed*, "for it shall be a witness between us that the Lord is God." "I believe in the doctrines of the Bible, as expressed in the Confession of Faith, the Larger and Shorter Catechisms of the Presbyterian Church," said the old lady, "and I wish that the Scholarship be called *Ed*, as a witness between us and the Theological Seminary, that the Lord is God."[78]

# 15

# The Church and the Country

*Charles Colcock Jones,
Princeton student in 1829
and 1830, and Presbyterian
"apostle to the slaves."*

The only practicable efficacious remedy for social evils . . . is and must be a religious one, that is, one founded not in mere prudential changes of man's mutual relations, but in their common relation to their common God, whether considered as their master and preserver, as their sovereign and their judge, or as their Saviour and Redeemer.

JOSEPH ADDISON ALEXANDER

A S churchmen and theologians debated ecclesiastical
and theological topics, the entire nation wrestled with
political and social issues. During his ministry in New
York City, Samuel Miller was avidly involved in politics as a
Jeffersonian Democrat. After he came to Princeton, he
regretted his "talking and acting and rendering" himself so
conspicuous "as a politician" during his earlier period; and
he wrote that for a clergyman "to talk of the Saviour will have,
usually, a better political effect, than to talk of party men or
measures."[1]   Archibald Alexander had little interest in politics, seldom voted, and never preached a "political" sermon.
But Charles Hodge wrote to his brother on September 17,
1841, that politics was "a subject second only to religion in
importance."[2]

There were some political issues which stirred all the
Princetonians. In 1830, President Andrew Jackson signed the
Indian Removal Act, which relocated the Native Americans to
lands west of the Mississippi River. During debates and tensions which followed, the Princeton students were highly
critical of "the cruel and oppressive measures" against the
Indians; they warned that "national sins" would be visited
with "national judgements."[3] The students were outraged
when two missionaries were imprisoned by the state of
Georgia for refusing to leave the Cherokee Territory. They
wrote that the missionaries had been subject to "the most
inhuman treatment ever experienced by free citizens in our
country."[4]   Charles Hodge too was deeply distressed. He

[323]

wrote his brother, "Verily, I think I could in such a case join a rebellion, with a clear conscience, as I am sure I could with a full heart."[5]

In 1847 the United States declared war on Mexico. The students considered it a "calamity"; and, without commenting on the justice of the war, Archibald Alexander wrote that Mexico and the United States ought to be "united in the bonds of amity" and not exerting all their power to destroy one another. He called on American Christians to humble themselves in penitence before God to pray for peace and to pray that great good might come out of the evil, especially the opening of Mexico for the preaching of the gospel.[6] J. W. Alexander shared his father's dismay. He wrote:

How can I pray for a blessing on our fight with Mexico! Poor creatures, they have done as little against us as we could have expected. As a Christian nation, we should have sent them the Gospel; but now, unless God interpose wonderfully, we shall rob and invade them. Who knows but that we may find ourselves engaged with a stronger than they?[7]

When there was a celebration in New York on May 8, 1847, for the American victories in Mexico, J. W. Alexander wrote, "I feel like preaching on 'charity . . . rejoiceth not in iniquity—vaunteth not itself.'"[8]

\*     \*     \*

The great issue of the day, however, was slavery. For the first fifty years of its existence, Princeton Seminary—students and professors—wrestled with the problem. Almost all agreed that it was a great evil and ought to be abolished. A Society of Inquiry report charged that because of slavery, "the glory of this far famed republic is sullied, religion is dishonoured, and humanity mocked."

Samuel Miller, though he was a slaveholder's son, had attacked slavery sharply during his New York days. In 1793, the twenty-four-year-old Miller preached:

It is a truth denied by few, at the present day, that political and domestic slavery are inconsistent with *justice*, and that these must

[324]

The Church and the Country

necessarily wage eternal war. . . . Humanity, indeed, is still left to deplore the continuance of domestic slavery, in countries blest with Christian knowledge, and political freedom. The American patriot must heave an involuntary sigh, at the recollection that, even in these happy and singularly favored republics, this offspring of infernal malice, and parent of human debasement, is yet suffered to reside.[9]

Four years later, in a speech before the New York Society for the Manumission of Slaves, Miller anticipated the Princeton position when he called for the abolition of slavery in a "gradual manner; which will, at the same time, provide for the intellectual and moral cultivation of slaves, that they may be prepared to exercise the rights and discharge the duties of citizens."[10]

The General Assembly of 1818 passed unanimously a "Declaration of Slavery" (written by Ashbel Green), stating that slavery was "a gross violation of the most precious and sacred rights of nature . . . utterly inconsistent with the law of God . . . totally irreconcilable with the spirit and principles of the Gospel of Christ." The assembly's statement urged that it was "manifestly the duty of all Christians . . . as speedily as possible to efface this blot on our holy religion, and to obtain the complete abolition of slavery throughout Christendom, and if possible throughout the world."[11] After 1818, the Presbyterian church, however, found that further statements on the subject produced great dissension; and they adopted a much more cautious approach. A committee on the issue of slavery, chaired by Samuel Miller, reported to the 1836 General Assembly

that the great Founder of our Religion, and his inspired Apostles, in proclaiming the Gospel of his grace to Jews and Gentiles, among whom domestic slavery was established by law, did not denounce it as one of those evils which He required to be immediately abolished; but chose rather to enjoin upon masters and slaves those duties which are required of them respectively by their Master in heaven; and to inculcate those benevolent and holy principles, which have a direct tendency to mitigate the evils of slavery, while it lasts, and to bring it to a termination in the most speedy, safe and happy manner for both parties.[12]

The statement was too weak for some and too strong for others—or, as one member of the committee put it, it was "for some, too likely to make trouble, and for others, too unlikely to make it." After debate, the assembly adopted a short resolution postponing the subject indefinitely.

Charles Hodge set forth his views—and those of Princeton—on slavery in three significant articles in the *Biblical Repertory*—"Slavery" (1836), "Abolitionism" (1844), and "Emancipation" (1849).[13] Hodge's position remained constant, as he wrote in his article on the 1864 General Assembly: "We have not changed our ground on the subject of slavery. We hold now precisely what we held in 1836, when the subject was first argued in these pages."[14] He always asserted that the Bible opposed both the pro-slavery position and that of the abolitionists. The "fanatical pro-slavery doctrine," he thought, was not held by "one educated man in a hundred, or even in a thousand." Abolitionism, which insisted that slaveholding is a sin, ran counter to the Old Testament, which permitted slavery, and to the New Testament, which nowhere condemned slaveholding. Indeed, as Hodge pointed out, Jesus and the apostles received slaveholders into the fellowship of the church. The scriptural view, Hodge wrote, neither forbids nor commands slavery, but regulates it according to biblical requirements for both slaves and masters. In reference to the growing sectional tensions on this issue he asserted, "Let the North remember that they are bound to follow the example of Christ in their manner of treating *slavery*, and the South, that they are bound to follow the precepts of Christ in their manner of treating their *slaves*." Hodge and the Princetonians abhorred the evils of slavery, deplored the agitation of the abolitionists, avoided condemnation of slaveowners, and aimed at peaceful emancipation—meanwhile arguing that slavery must be made to conform to the biblical mandate of honest service and fair treatment. Acting on biblical principles, they argued, would result in "the speedy and peaceful abrogation of slavery" and "the gradual elevation of the slaves to all the rights of free citizens."[15]

Until the 1830s, most people opposed to slavery were committed to the "gradualist" position regarding emancipation.

In 1836, Samuel Miller explained his position to an English correspondent by writing, "I am a warm friend to abolition as speedily as is consistent with the best interests of the slaves themselves."[16] Some Americans, however, began to fear that "gradualism" was merely an excuse for indefinite postponement and took a more aggressive approach. The 1837 murder of Princeton Seminary graduate and abolitionist editor, Elijah Lovejoy, in Alton, Illinois, sent "a shock as of any earthquake" across the land, according to John Quincy Adams.[17] Many switched over to "immediatism," but others—including the Princetonians—were repelled by what appeared to them an unworkable and irresponsible demand. Like many other nineteenth-century Americans, they were committed to a stable and hierarchical society and alarmed by the terrors of the French Revolution and the disorders of Jacksonian democracy. They therefore resisted abrupt change and radical measures, supporting social change through orderly processes and believing that God was already at work in the system of things.

J. W. Alexander wrote, "I am more and more convinced that our endeavours to do at a blow, what Providence does by degrees, is disastrous to those whom we would benefit."[18] Charles Hodge held that slavery "should be left to the operation of those general principles of the gospel which have peacefully ameliorated political institutions, and destroyed domestic slavery throughout the greater part of Christendom."[19] Christianity worked by changing the hearts of people who then, in their normal lives as citizens and leaders, would gradually and carefully nudge society in a more just direction. True reform, Hodge believed, resembled the work not of a western farmer hacking down great forests to make room for corn, but that of a humble mason working on a great cathedral, "placing a single brick or stone into the glorious edifice." Hodge's view of "providential progress"[20] and his "constructive conservatism"[21] recognized progress and welcomed it when it appeared but was unlikely to provide much impetus for change. The Princetonians were, as they often claimed, "friends of the slaves," but they failed to align themselves clearly and positively with the oppressed in the face of real injustice and tyranny. In so many areas,

Princeton Seminary was a challenge and inspiration to thousands of people. In the matter of slavery, however, its message was timid, conventional, and unremarkable.[22]

The Princetonians believed, as Charles Hodge wrote in 1849, that in time slavery would be "peacefully and healthfully abolished."[23] In the meantime, they supported African colonization and missions to the slaves as proper steps to emancipation, while insisting on the principle that the organized church should not legislate on moral issues where the Bible had not spoken explicitly. "It is plain that the church has no responsibility and no right to interfere with respect to the slave laws in the South," Hodge wrote in 1844; "We have other and higher duties."[24]

\*     \*     \*

African colonization was a plan with a long history. Several years before the Revolutionary War, Samuel Hopkins had proposed that some blacks should be educated and sent back to Africa as teachers and pastors. In 1800, the Virginia legislature asked Governor James Monroe to correspond with President Thomas Jefferson regarding the purchase of land in Africa to colonize free blacks. The first public meeting of the American Colonization Society was held in Princeton in 1816, and the professors and most of the students were present. The colonization plan did not attack slavery as such but attempted to influence it indirectly by providing a solution to the problem of the free blacks, thus encouraging owners to free their slaves.

Archibald Alexander, according to his son, had the Colonization Society "more at heart than anything in the world."[25] Alexander argued that the enemies of colonization should "either propose some method by which these degraded and down-trodden people may be rendered more comfortable and respectable here" or "cease to throw obstacles in the way of their emigration to a country where they may have the opportunity of enjoying the real blessings of freedom." He deplored the contempt for the blacks which "exists, and which is perhaps stronger in the free than in the slaveholding States."[26] Alexander also saw the colonization of Christian blacks in Africa as the means of evangelizing that great continent.

In spite of mounting opposition to the idea of black colonization, the American Colonization Society was for years the only truly national organization that even professed to deal with the issue of slavery. Archibald Alexander, writing in 1846, asserted that it had accomplished more "to promote emancipation than all the abolition societies in the country."[27] The Colonization Society served "as an awakening force and as a transitional organization," but it brought about the freedom of only a few blacks and diverted the attention of many—including the Princetonians—from more creative and productive efforts to deal with the problems of slavery and racial prejudice.[28]

\* \* \*

Princeton saw great value in missions to the slaves. J. W. Alexander wrote, "Slavery must and will end; I hope peaceably; but, anyhow, we ought to save the souls of this generation."[29] Archibald Alexander, who had given special attention to the slaves in his ministries both in Virginia and in Philadelphia, told the seminary students that taking the gospel to the slaves was "one of the most interesting and inviting fields of missionary labour in the world."[30] According to Alexander, the best means of abolishing slavery was to preach the gospel. Although he did not deny that it may have been the duty of some to try to bring about the abolition of slavery more directly, he said that it was not the work of ministers as such, especially in the southern states.

A number of Princeton students responded to Archibald Alexander's advice, including a young Georgian, Charles Colcock Jones. In 1832, Jones organized the "Liberty County (Georgia) Association for the Religious Instruction of the Negroes" and became a full-time missionary to the slaves. Dr. Alexander wrote that Jones, while a student at the seminary, "formed his purpose, and the outlines of his plan, and zealously endeavoured to enlist others in the cause of the neglected slaves."[31] C. C. Jones became the leading missionary to the slaves in the antebellum South, and his Princeton professors and the students followed his missionary career with great interest. In 1843 Archibald Alexander wrote that C. C. Jones had "as good a claim to the name of a philanthropist as anyone."[32] The importance of the work of evangelizing the slaves—primarily to prepare them for heaven, but also to prepare them for freedom—the Princetonians believed, could not be overestimated. The students and professors were not exhibiting a lack of compassion for the slaves but were being true to their deepest convictions when they sought to give them something they themselves greatly valued—the best possible gift for this life and the next.[33]

*       *       *

Princeton, it was often said, had a larger proportion of African Americans than any town in the free states. Until 1846 black Presbyterians worshiped together with white members at First Presbyterian Church. When the new church was being built in 1836 and 1837, the eighty black communicants met separately. A majority of the white pew-holders favored organizing them as a separate church. In a letter written on November 17, 1837, J. W. Alexander declared, "I am clear that in a church of Jesus Christ, there is neither black nor white; and that we have no right to consider the accident of colour in any degree." Alexander believed, however, that the blacks were unwise in insisting on returning, because the abolitionist movement had contributed to the "exorbitant and inhuman" prejudice of "the lower classes of whites against blacks."[34] The separation was gradual. In 1840 a special building was constructed for the use of the black members, and finally in 1846, the session reported that ninety people were dismissed "to form a church under the name of the First Presbyterian Church of Colour of Princeton." In 1848 the name was changed to the Witherspoon Street Presbyterian Church.

In 1843 a runaway slave from Maryland was tried in Princeton under the fugitive slave law, and tension in the town was high. The jury ruled in favor of the owner. The slave was held in close custody in an upstairs room in the

Nassau Inn during a night and a day while an effort was made to purchase him. A woman from the South, a descendant of John Witherspoon, paid $550 and set the man free. The former slave worked and repaid her, often showing with pride "the book opened for him, in which his ransom was charged on one side, and his work credited on the other side of the account, until in the course of three or four years, he cancelled the debt."[35]

\* \* \*

Historians have frequently noted the shift in the viewpoint of American Christians during the nineteenth century, from a friendly but watchful stance toward the nation to an increasingly pronounced dedication to America as God's chosen people. A recurring theme in mid-century sermons was the parallel between ancient Israel and the United States. The Princeton professors and students shared in this enthusiasm and agreed that God not only had caused the light of the gospel to shine in America but also had created a unique Christian nation. One Princetonian, however, was not comfortable with the belief that America was God's chosen nation. Joseph Addison Alexander objected to the way American Christians frequently described the nation as God's new Israel. He said:

Such is the force of words, to influence as well as to express thought, that by dint of constant repetition, men may actually come at last to think themselves a chosen and peculiar people, not only in the spiritual Christian sense, but in the national external sense.[36]

Alexander argued that there was a decided contrast between ancient Israel and modern America. Israel as a nation was in fact "the chosen and peculiar people of Jehovah. We, in this respect, have not, and never had, the shadow of a claim to take precedence of our fellow Gentiles." As the Jews thought that the Messiah was to be a national deliverer, so "there is great danger of our thinking, or at least of our acting, as if we thought that he came to save *us*, and to secure us in the undisturbed enjoyment of our temporal and spiritual comforts, and that the rest of the world must be

[331]

consigned to his uncovenanted mercy." Alexander reminded American Christians that they had not been entrusted with the oracles of God as an exclusive possession but as a responsibility. God had placed before them a great, effectual door into the world.

Princeton Seminary took the task of world evangelization seriously. During its early history, virtually every student was a member of the Society of Inquiry on Missions. In 1844 the number of members was one hundred, with almost twelve hundred seminary students on its rolls since its beginning in 1814. Some of these students were now missionaries, preaching the gospel message they had learned at Princeton and establishing churches throughout the world.

# 16

# Two Great Lights

*Page from the Diary of Lewis Miller, York, Pennsylvania.*

Thank God, that Princeton Seminary has a history!  The past is safe. The memory of the two eminent men who were its first professors and who gave it character rests over it as a halo, and men will tread its halls for their sake with something of the feeling with which they visit the tombs of the good and great.

CHARLES HODGE

IN the summer of 1812 three students began their work at Princeton Seminary. During the year 1850 almost two hundred young men were enrolled. They rose early, usually about 4:30 in the morning, and in cold weather built fires in their stoves. Some took short walks before the 6:45 a.m. prayer meeting. Breakfast was in the refectory—a separate building constructed in 1842. The fare was plain but abundant. Many of the students formed themselves into "little clubs" and studied the Shorter Catechism during mealtimes. There were classes to attend in the morning and afternoon and daily chapel. Most students took a walk before supper. There were meetings nearly every night in the week, then there was study until bedtime.

John Byers, a graduate of the University of Glasgow, entered Princeton soon after arriving in America in 1848. He found himself, as he said, in a different atmosphere from any he had ever experienced and believed that he was really converted in his first year at the seminary. David Wilson came in 1849. After three weeks at Princeton he wrote to a cousin that a feeling of brotherhood existed among the students, as well as an earnest, practical spirituality. "One must be pious," he wrote, "to enjoy himself among saints, and diligent to respect himself among students."

In 1850, John Nevius decided to study for the ministry and wrote his mother, a New School Presbyterian, that he was going to Princeton because it had "by far the most celebrated and efficient faculty."[1] David Tully of the class of 1850 described the famous faculty:

Dr. Archibald Alexander had the keenness of a Kentucky rifle-man in his insight into spiritual experience; Dr. Addison Alexander was a whirlwind as a teacher and a preacher; Dr. Samuel Miller was a prince in church history and the Chesterfield of the Presbyterian Church; and Dr. Charles Hodge was the greatest analytic mind that this country has produced, certainly since the days of Jonathan Edwards.[2]

After 1845 a number of Baptist students from the South entered Princeton, the division between Northern and Southern Baptists having made many reluctant to attend Newton or Hamilton seminaries. Janetta Alexander and her daughter-in-law, Elizabeth Cabell Alexander (James Waddel's wife) took a special interest in the southern students. The senior Mrs. Alexander said that she knew the Baptist students better than the Presbyterians because they were "more inclined to be sociable."[3] On September 19, 1849, J. W. Alexander described some of the new seminary students: "Of Scots and Hibernians we have about a dozen, several being Glasgow graduates; also a Baptist preacher, and wife, from Charleston. Last year there were five or six Baptists, all most promising men."[4]

*     *     *

On Sunday, August 19, 1849, Samuel Miller drove five miles to the church at Dutch Neck, where he had often preached. He told the pastor that he very much wished to "preach Jesus" to the congregation that he and Archibald Alexander had served for over ten years until the church was finally able to call its own pastor. His text that day was Hebrews 6:19— "Which hope we have as an anchor of the soul, both sure and stedfast; and which entereth into that within the veil." The pastor, George Ely, described the sermon:

He first spoke of the *differences* between the anchor of a ship and *"hope"* as the anchor of the soul. Several of these differences were noticed, but the one upon which he dwelt with the greatest feeling and fervency was, that whilst the anchor of the ship takes hold *on things below*, "hope," the anchor of the believer's soul, takes hold *on things above.* Here he had to leave his notes; his feelings became intense, and his soul was too full of deep emotion to be restricted by anything previously written. His "hope," for the moment, seemed to be changed into full fruition; the "soul" and its "anchor" to be both together *"within the veil."*

Dr. Miller told the little congregation, "Whether or not this may be the last time that I shall address you, is a matter of small importance. But you may inquire how does this 'hope' appear to an old man standing just upon the verge of the grave?" Lifting up both his hands, with which he was supporting himself upon the pulpit, he exclaimed, in a voice faltering with emotion, "Oh! Inexpressibly delightful." It was the eighty-year-old Samuel Miller's last sermon.

For several years Dr. Miller had been in failing health, but by carefully guarding his strength he had been able to continue his work. As the new school term began in August 1849, he was determined to carry on with his teaching. He met his class with the seniors twice a week—sometimes walking the quarter of a mile to the seminary, sometimes being driven in his carriage. After a few weeks it was clear that he could not continue. His family gathered for a last reunion, and friends and former students came to bid him farewell.

Nicholas Murray, an Irishman, who studied under Dr. Miller at Princeton from 1826 to 1829 and who had served the First Presbyterian Church in Elizabethtown, New Jersey, since 1833, visited his beloved teacher. When Murray entered the library, he saw the feeble and haggard Miller— one half of his face shaved, and soap on the other half, with the barber standing behind the chair. After a few moments of conversation, Dr. Miller said that since this would be their last visit on earth "it [would] be well to close it with prayer." "As I am too feeble to kneel," the old man said, "you will excuse me if I keep my chair." Murray knelt at his feet, and the barber laid aside his razor and brush and knelt by his side. As the former student tried to prepare himself to pray, Dr. Miller began—thanking God for his great mercy in calling them "into the fellowship of the saints" and then "into the ministry of his Son." He thanked God for their friendship as student and teacher and then as ministers of the gospel, and concluded:

And now, Lord, seeing that thine aged, imperfect servant is about to be gathered to his fathers . . . let the years of thy young servant be as the years of his dying teacher; let his ministry be more devoted, more holy, more useful; and when he comes to die, may he have fewer regrets to feel in reference to his past ministrations. We are to meet no more on earth; but when thy servant shall follow his aged father to the grave, may we meet in Heaven, there to sit, and shine, and sing, with those who have turned many to righteousness, who have washed their robes and made them white in the blood of the Lamb. Amen.[5]

After visiting Samuel Miller on November 14, J. W. Alexander wrote that he had never seen "a gentler decline, or a more serene, collected looking into eternity." Later Alexander commented that heaven seemed "just as much ajar, as his next-door bedroom."[6] Dr. Miller was too ill to be present at the inauguration of J. W. Alexander, his successor in the faculty. "I should meet you with less of sadness," Alexander told his Princeton audience

were it not for the absence of that venerable man, whose induction to this chair I distinctly remember six-and-thirty years ago, whose paternal guidance many of us have since enjoyed, and whose useful and eminent discharge of this function might well cause trembling in his successor. Let us therefore, hasten to look away from men, even the best, to the Great Head of the Church, who will bless both his aged servant and this school to which his life has been devoted.[7]

Later in December, Dr. Miller greeted Samuel Alexander with the words "Almost home."[8] J. W. Alexander came to see him on a cold December 31. The younger man greeted Dr. Miller and apologized for his cold hand. Miller replied, "Christ's hand is never cold! He has propped me up and led me and comforted me, more than I am able to express, and I wish you affectionately to thank Him for it in my name." Alexander knelt down and prayed with him.[9] Dr. Miller's physician son, Dickinson, was with him; and his granddaughter, Margaret Breckinridge, read the Bible to him. When she read from Paul's epistles, Miller expressed a strong desire to see Paul. When she closed the Bible, or paused in her reading, he often whispered, "Blessed Gospel! Blessed Gospel!"

On Sunday, January 6, he was very near death. His wife asked him to pray that his mantle might fall on one of his sons who was standing by the bed. He replied, deeply moved, "Oh, not *my* mantle, not *my* mantle! Let him look at such men as Dickinson, and Edwards, and Davies—men who were faithful laborers in their Master's vineyard. Pray that their mantle may fall upon him."[10]

Archibald Alexander, nearly seventy-eight years old, preached that morning in the seminary chapel and came in the evening to visit his old friend. He remained with him for awhile, then prayed and said to Miller, "You are now in the dark valley! . . . I shall soon be after you!"[11] A few hours later, Samuel Miller died. His son wrote, "He had often prayed for himself and others, that, in the dying hour, they 'might have nothing to do but to die'; and the prayer was perceptibly and most mercifully answered in his own experience."[12]

The funeral was a solemn occasion. The thirty-six-year-old seminary had not until now buried a professor. At two o'clock in the afternoon, the procession formed at the home of Samuel Miller; the seminary students were led by the Presbyterian, Episcopal, and Methodist pastors of the town. At the First Presbyterian Church, the seminary choir chanted, "with solemn and appropriate emphasis," the words "Blessed are the dead who die in the Lord. . . ." Dr. Alexander gave the sermon from the book of Hebrews—"These all died in faith." He included his friend and colleague in that list of Abel, Enoch, Noah, and Abraham. He spoke of Samuel Miller's love for teaching and preaching and his reputation as a writer, which, he said, was "as wide spread and honoured on both sides of the Atlantic, as that of any other American divine." He said of his old friend, "I have never known a man more entirely free from vain glory, envy, and jealousy" and reminded the sorrowing company of seminarians and friends that "the crowning glory of his life was his piety."[13] Dr. Carnahan led in prayer, and the procession formed again and moved slowly to the old cemetery already called "the Westminster Abbey of America." Dr. Miller was buried near the graves of the college presidents Burr, Edwards, Davies, Witherspoon, Smith, and Green. The epitaph, prepared by

Charles Hodge, stated that Dr. Miller had served for twenty-one years as pastor of the First Presbyterian Church of New York City and for thirty-six years as professor of Ecclesiastical History and Church Government at Princeton Seminary—"In both callings, faithful and edifying; an acceptable and evangelical preacher; a learned and assiduous teacher; a voluminous and celebrated author. . . . He lived esteemed by thousands, and died amidst light and joy from the Lord Jesus Christ, in whom was all his hope."[14]

\* \* \*

The Reverend William Edward Schenck was now pastor of First Presbyterian Church in Princeton, Dr. Rice having resigned in 1847. Born and educated in Princeton, the new pastor was soon filling an important place in the religious life of the town. There were three Presbyterian and two Methodist churches (including a Presbyterian and a Methodist church for African Americans) and an Episcopal church in town. To these were added the Roman Catholic church in 1850 and the Baptist church in 1852. Through the generosity of its members and especially Paul Tulane, First Presbyterian was for the first time in eighty-nine years free from debt. An iron fence was erected in front of the church, and arrangements were made for illuminating the church by gas—replacing the dim light of oil lamps and the candles of earlier years.

Early in 1850, revival came again to Princeton. On the communion Sunday a few weeks before the revival began, not a single new member was added to First Presbyterian Church. Dr. Alexander spoke to the congregation that day. The pastor later wrote, "I have always believed that those remarks were instrumental, under God, of bringing believers to the throne of grace to supplicate more earnestly for a revival of religion."[15] A time of student disturbances at the college late in 1849 gave way to much "seriousness" before the Day of Prayer for Colleges on January 28. Dr. Hodge and Dr. Hope spoke in the new college chapel, and many were stirred. Christians went from room to room urging the gospel message upon their fellow students. Prayer meetings were held throughout the campus and at First Presbyterian Church. Students met in their rooms for intercessory prayer. People could remember no such time in Princeton since 1815. J. W. Alexander wrote on March 9 that the whole college was "seeking God."[16] Dr. Archibald Alexander, whose preaching had been a major factor in the earlier awakening, was a vital part of this revival. For six or seven weeks, services were conducted every evening except Saturday; and Dr. Alexander, although he was nearly eighty years old, preached repeatedly. One of the college students remembered his sermons "addressed almost exclusively to the conscience" and his reading of the Scriptures interspersed with timely comments "as barbed arrows into the heart."[17] After the meetings had gone on for several weeks, Dr. Alexander was consulted about whether to continue them longer. He advised that they should be held as long as people demonstrated hunger for the Word of God. "Divine truth," he said, "never yet surfeited a hungry soul. Only be careful to let it have nothing but truth."[18]

Charles Colcock Jones, Jr., transferred from South Carolina to Princeton College in the summer of 1850. Even though he found the food "only tolerable" and the students rather rowdy, he was impressed with the Christian atmosphere of Princeton. He wrote to his parents on August 13, 1850:

This college beyond a doubt affords the finest religious and moral training, if one will but improve it, of any I have ever known or heard. On last Sabbath (as an example of what was just stated) we had prayers at half-past six, prayer meeting at nine, church at eleven, Bible class at three, church in town at four, prayer meeting again at five, and church in the Presbyterian church at half-past seven P. M. Thus is the day almost totally occupied with the public and private exercises of devotion, prayer, and praise. Beside these ordinary hours of worship on Sabbath, we have during the week a prayer meeting attended by some one of the professors—usually Dr. Maclean.[19]

This schedule was undoubtedly too much for many students, but young Jones assured his parents that he wanted "to be present at these meetings as often as practicable, and to endeavor to make a proper use of these means which the God of Heaven hath placed in our power."

A few days later, Jones wrote about a sermon he had heard from Dr. Alexander at the Presbyterian church:

[I] was struck with the force and pointedness of his discourse. He appears very aged, though apparently enjoying a green old age. His voice is very fine, and his neck is quite bent. . . . I was so much pleased with his sermon that upon my return to my room I wrote a skeleton of it while fresh in the memory, his style striking me as a very lucid and clear one. This was the first of a course of lectures which he intends preaching to the young men of college, and others in general, delivering one every Sabbath night.[20]

Jones then gave Alexander's text—Proverbs 1:10 ("My son, if sinners entice thee, consent thou not")—and, from memory, his three main points and eighteen subpoints!

\*  \*  \*

Dr. Alexander continued to preach and teach and to promote the interests of the seminary that was so dear to his heart. In May 1850 he sent out a letter explaining the financial needs of Princeton and asking for help. "My connexion with the Seminary, with which I have been identified from its origin, cannot be long," he wrote; "it is among the wishes nearest my heart to see the institution established on a firm foundation and in a flourishing condition before I leave it."

In 1850 he completed and published a volume of *Practical Sermons.* He wrote in the preface:

As this is probably the author's last literary work, it is his earnest desire and prayer, that it may be useful in promoting evangelical and experimental religion. . . . There is nothing in these sermons which will be found offensive to the lovers of evangelical truth in other denominations. The author, in a long life, has found that real Christians agree much more perfectly in experimental religion, than they do in speculative points; and it is his belief, that a more intimate acquaintance among Christians of different denominations would have a happy tendency to unite them more closely in the bonds of brotherly love. May the time soon come when all the disciples of Christ shall form one great brotherhood under the name of CHRISTIANS![21]

Until almost the very close of his life Dr. Alexander continued to teach his classes. His son wrote:

At the stroke of the bell, he might be seen without fail, issuing from his study door, and going across the small space which divided the Seminary from his grounds; much bent, and with eyes turned to the ground as he paced slowly on, wrapped in his cloak and with his profuse silver locks waving in the wind; but often, as if at some sudden dash of thought, he would quicken his steps almost to running and ascend the threshold with alacrity.[22]

He preached his last sermon to the students in the seminary chapel on September 7, 1851. His text was Isaiah 54:13—"All thy children shall be taught of the Lord." The next Sunday, at Princeton's First Presbyterian Church, he took his place at the communion table by the side of the pastor and spoke to the congregation, urging them as pilgrims to a faithful and hopeful life. It was his last public service.

That summer and fall Dr. Alexander had been busy preparing new lectures in order to teach Samuel Miller's class in church government. He wrote sixty-three pages on "Church Polity and Discipline" before an unfinished sentence signaled his final illness. On October 15, J. W. Alexander arrived home from six months in Europe. The next day he took the train to Princeton, where he found his father very weak. His son wrote:

The affairs of the Church employ far more of my father's words than any family concerns. He talked an hour with me on the prospects of the truth in Scotland. The whole tone of his discourse is free from . . . "shows," being precisely what it always was—passing with childlike ease from the settling of a bill to the grace and glory of the gospel. He said, "I have this morning been reviewing the plan of salvation, and assuring myself of my acceptance of it. I am in peace. The transition from this world to another, so utterly unknown, is certainly awful, and would be destructive, were it not guarded by Christ; I know he will do all well."[23]

A few days before he died, Alexander told William Schenck that "if such be the Lord's will" he was ready and even preferred "to go now." "My affairs have all been attended to, my arrangements are all completed, and I can think of nothing more to be done." He added:

I have greatly desired to see my son James before my departure, and sometimes feared I should not have that privilege; but the Lord has graciously brought him back in time to see me, having led him safely through much peril on the ocean. My children are all with me. The Church of which you are Pastor is prosperous and flourishing. The Seminary Faculty is again full, and the institution is in an excellent condition. . . . The Lord has very graciously and tenderly led me all the days of my life. . . . Yes, all the days of my life. *And He is now with me still. In Him I enjoy perfect peace!*

Dr. Alexander then bade farewell to his former student and friend, adding the words, "Continue as you have begun, and have done thus far, to preach Christ and Him crucified, scripturally, plainly, earnestly, and God will continue richly to bless your ministry, even as here He has so lately done." Schenck attempted to thank Dr. Alexander for his kindness to him, but the old man said quickly, "You must thank God for that; all kindness and all friends are his gifts. Give my love to your wife and children." Once more, very slowly, he said, "Give my love and a very affectionate farewell to your wife and children."[24]

There were last visits with Charles Hodge, who later said that "he never saw and never imagined a deathbed where there was so little of death."[25] He told how Dr. Alexander, with a smile, handed him "a white bone walking-stick, carved and presented to him by one of the chiefs of the Sandwich Islands, and said, 'You must leave this to your successor in office, that it may be handed down as a kind of symbol of orthodoxy.'"[26] A. A. Hodge saw his father standing in his study weeping, exclaiming, "It is all past, the glory of our Seminary has departed."[27]

When relieved from pain, Dr. Alexander said that it was due to the ministration of angels and added, "They are always around the dying beds of God's people." He acknowledged that his theological views were "what they have always been," and, on another occasion, stated, "All my theology is reduced to this narrow compass, Jesus Christ came into the world to save sinners."[28] Recalling the desire of a certain pastor for good books, he asked his family to find the man's address and order for him a set of twenty-four volumes from the American Tract Society. When his family returned from church and spoke of Charles Hodge's sermon, he said warmly, "He is a noble man." On October 22, Archibald Alexander died peacefully.

Two days later, in the First Presbyterian Church, the funeral sermon was preached by John McDowell, the oldest director of the seminary. The text was Revelation 14:13—"And I heard a voice from heaven saying unto me, write, Blessed are the dead that die in the Lord from henceforth; yea, saith the Spirit, that they may rest from their labours: and their works do follow them." The choir sang "Why do we mourn departed friends?" Seminary graduate and pastor of the Franklin Street Presbyterian Church in Baltimore, William S. Plumer, concluded the service in the church with a psalm and prayer. In the bright autumn sun the funeral procession extended from the church almost to the old graveyard on Witherspoon Street: first the 250 students and professors from the college; then more than a hundred members of the Synod of New Jersey, with clergymen from neighboring cities and towns; next the coffin, borne by elders of the Presbytery of New Brunswick and accompanied by Dr. Alexander's six sons (and Charles Hodge, who claimed to be a true son also); and finally the 140 students and directors of the seminary. At the grave site, the seminarians stood to the west, the college students on the east, the synod on the north, and townspeople to the south—a balanced tribute to the work and interests of Princeton's first professor.

College student Robert Hamill Nassau—with dreams of becoming a famous soldier or a great orator—was at Dr. Alexander's funeral. It created in him a deep longing for spiritual peace and purpose in his own life and, a few weeks later in a field near Princeton, he gave himself to God. Alexander's students, almost two thousand now scattered around the world, mourned the death of their beloved teacher. J. B. Adger remembered him as "a simple-hearted, straightforward man." When David Wilson—who had just opened the Archibald Alexander High School in Liberia—heard of Dr. Alexander's death, he wrote from Africa to the Society of

[345]

Inquiry at Princeton, "Other good men there are, but there is no other Archibald Alexander"!

Archibald Alexander, Mark Noll has written, was "a forceful and engaging personality of nearly heroic proportions."[29] About five feet, seven inches tall, Alexander was a small, slender man. He was never arrogant or domineering, but he was an outstanding leader. Contemporaries, such as Henry Boardman, often placed the "secret of his power" in the "*combination* of excellencies which his character presented —in his blended piety and wisdom; his simplicity and consistency; his sound sense and spirituality; and his heart sympathy with everything good, and kind, and useful."[30] He was a firm Calvinist, a scholar of note, a preacher of real power, an effective counselor, and a quiet leader. In his own life he combined strong convictions with such mildness and fairness that contemporaries often designated him a "moderate man", and a modern writer calls him a "winsome conservative."[31] His secret of leadership was that he knew where he stood— and he stood there. A. A. Hodge wrote that Archibald Alexander, "more than any man of his generation, appeared to those who heard him to be endued with the knowledge, and clothed with the authority of a prophet."[32] The *Schaff-Herzog Encyclopaedia of Religious Knowledge* (1891) stated that "it is not too much to say that [Archibald Alexander] gave tone to the Presbyterian Church in America, and the high water mark to her piety."

Dr. Alexander created and shaped Princeton Seminary. He impressed his viewpoint and personality upon it as few men have ever stamped an institution. He modeled both "piety" and "solid learning"—and he would not let the seminary lose sight of either. From him came all the motifs of the Princeton theology, but Dr. Alexander was not content to teach Bible and doctrine. "He aimed to send out warriors of the cross."[33] The students sometimes playfully called him "the pope." They had "unbounded confidence," as one of them wrote, "in his sanctified common sense."[34] Another commented on "his wonderful sagacity and acquaintance with the human heart." "His powers of managing and trimming into shape all sorts of characters, such as come here, are remarkable," he added.[35] Another, Elijah Lovejoy, spoke for many when he wrote his father soon after he began his studies at Princeton, "Come here, and I will introduce you to one of the best men in the world—Dr. Alexander."[36]

\*　　\*　　\*

Princeton would always remember Archibald Alexander's colleague, Samuel Miller, as a godly, diligent, humble man —a sound Presbyterian and the "most perfect model of a Christian gentleman."[37]   Naturally of quick temper, Miller learned to control it as his Christian duty.  Once in public a remark of Miller's was criticized roughly and cynically by another minister.  Samuel Miller sat so perfectly still that one of his sons afterwards asked him whether he had really heard the ill-tempered words.  Dr. Miller believed that "a professor's example as a devoted, laborious, faithful minister, was, above all things else, a requisite for the successful training of ministers."  He gave himself unstintingly to that task for the last thirty-six years of his life.  On coming to Princeton, Samuel Miller had resolved not to merge his "office as a minister of the Gospel, in that of professor."  He preached until the end.  Dr. Alexander said of him after his death, "I think I may say, that I never knew a minister, who delighted more in preaching the Gospel."[38]   Miller worked hard to make up for the scholarly deficiencies he felt when he came to the seminary in 1813.  He became a competent teacher in his areas of church history and church government.  A historian has recently written, "Seldom has the history of doctrine had a more enthusiastic and capable defender.  Miller breathed the history of Christian doctrine with a naturalness that comes only after long hours pouring over patristic, medieval, Reformation and modern works."[39]  Dr. Miller was resolute in his determination to maintain the order and purity of the church, but he did so with large charity, love of peace, and so much dread of giving pain that he was criticized by some as being overly tolerant.

The most profound comment on the significance of Archibald Alexander and Samuel Miller for Princeton Seminary came from the man who knew them best.  At the re-opening of the seminary chapel on September 27, 1874,

## Charles Hodge said:

The first signal manifestation of the divine favor to this Institution was the selection of Dr. Archibald Alexander and Dr. Samuel Miller as its professors, and their being spared for nearly forty years to devote themselves to its service. . . . The favor of God to this infant Seminary, was manifested in its being intrusted to the hands of men pre-eminently qualified for sacred trust.

They were in the first place eminently holy men. They exerted that indescribable but powerful influence which always emanates from those who live near to God. Their piety was uniform and serene; without any taint of enthusiasm or fanaticism. It was also Biblical. Christ was as prominent in their religious experience, in their preaching, and in their writings, as he is in the Bible. Christ's person, his glory, his righteousness, his love, his presence, his power, filled the whole sphere of their religious life. . . . When students entered this Seminary, when its first professors were alive, they had held up before them the image of Christ, not graven by art or man's device, but as portrayed by the Spirit on the pages of God's word; and it is by beholding that image that men are transformed into its likeness from glory to glory. It is, in large measure, to this constant holding up of Christ, in the glory of his person and the all-sufficiency of his work, that the hallowed influence of the fathers of this Seminary is to be attributed.

It often happens, however, that men are very pious without being very good. Their religion expends itself in devotional feelings and services, while the evil passions of their nature remain unsubdued. It was not so with our fathers. They were as good as they were pious. I was intimately associated with them, as pupil and colleague, between thirty and forty years. In all that time I never saw in either of them any indication of vanity, of pride, of envy, of jealousy, of insincerity, of uncharitableness, or of disingenuousness. I know that what I say is incredible. Nevertheless it is true. And it is my right and duty to scatter these withered flowers upon their graves. Most men have reason to rejoice that their bosoms are opaque, but these holy men, as it always seemed to me, might let the sun shine through them.

Another characteristic of the men of whom I speak was their firm and simple faith in the Scriptures, and in the system of doctrine contained in the standards of our Church. Their faith was founded on the demonstration of the Spirit, and therefore could not be shaken. No Sunday-School scholar, no mother in Israel, could be more entirely submissive to the teachings of the Scriptures than were these venerable men. There was something sublime and beautiful in the humility of old Dr. Alexander, when he found himself at the feet of Jesus. There was no questioning of the reason, no opposition of the heart. The words of Scripture were received as the revelation of what is true and right from the highest source of truth and goodness. No one can estimate the influence of this trait of the character of our first professors operating through forty years on successive generations of their pupils.

There are theologians who exhort men to think for themselves, and to receive nothing on authority. And others who crave after novelty and aspire after originality. And others who have a philosophical disposition. It pleased God that the first professors in this Seminary should belong to neither of these classes. They exhorted their students to be humble rather than high-minded. They had no fondness for new doctrines, or for new ways of presenting old ones; and they dreaded the thought of transferring the ground of faith from the rock of God's word to metaphysical quicksands. For this reason Princeton Theological Seminary was regarded by the illuminati in every part of the land as very umbrageous, impenetrable to any ray of new light. This did not move the men of whom we speak. They had heard Christ say of certain men that the light that is in them is darkness. And knowing that man is blind as to the things of God, they thought it safer to submit to be guided by a divine hand, rather than, with darkness within and darkness without, to stumble on they knew not whither.[40]

Princeton's first two professors had done their work well. For forty years they worked hard to raise up biblically competent and spiritually strong preachers for the Presbyterian church and for other denominations, for ministry in the United States and throughout the world. They also were concerned to leave the seminary in good hands so its work might continue unhampered. In this, too, they succeeded.

# 17

# Our Elisha

*Charles Hodge, age 49.*

[Charles Hodge] realized pre-eminently his own ideal of a teacher, which he once set forth to me in one of those sentences so characteristic of him, having the power of aphorisms that in an instant let in a flood of light upon a subject, and contain the seeds of thought: "The requisites of a good teacher are Knowledge, Ability, Fidelity and Tact," adding, that "many who have the first three, fall for want of the last."

LYMAN H. ATWATER

WHEN Archibald Alexander and Samuel Miller died, many—including Charles Hodge—believed that "the glory had departed" from Princeton. Hodge, however, was well prepared to assume leadership. Respected as a skilled exegete of Scripture and a careful and perceptive theologian, admired as a knowledgeable and loyal church-man, and loved for his piety and humility—Hodge was an ideal successor to Archibald Alexander and Samuel Miller. At Hodge's semicentennial celebration in 1872, a speaker reviewed the first great transition in Princeton Seminary's history and commented, "The mantle of our Elijahs has certainly fallen upon our Elisha."[1]

Charles Hodge was widely recognized as the leading spokesman for confessional Calvinism in America and as a figure of international reputation. The story is told of one of the theological students of the Free Church of Scotland who had thoughts of taking a session at Princeton with Charles Hodge. A canny Scot—who wanted to make sure beforehand that study taken overseas would count as part of his divinity course—he consulted Professor William Cunningham. "Count!" said Cunningham, taking a pinch of snuff and speaking in a curious falsetto voice which he sometimes used when he wanted to be emphatic, "of course it would. My only difficulty is this: whether a session there under Hodge should not count [as] *two*."[2]

Charles Hodge was the senior professor of the little faculty made up of the two Alexander brothers and young William

Henry Green. J. W. Alexander soon returned to the pastorate, however, accepting a call to the Fifth Avenue Presbyterian Church in New York City. He loved Princeton but believed that he had no special aptitude for teaching, and he missed pastoral work. He had written on October 15, 1849, "I miss my old women; and especially my weekly catechumens, my sick rooms, my rapid walks, and my nights of right-down fatigue."[3] He felt keenly "the evils of the academic manner" and the tendency of the clergy "to be much with the rich and the lettered, instead of being lights to the world."[4] He returned to New York; and soon he was busy serving his large congregation, writing the life of his father—a seven-hundred-page biography which was published in 1854—and preaching in city missions to the poor.[5] On December 2, 1851, he wrote:

My mind works incessantly on such themes as these:—the abounding misery; the unreached masses; the waste of church energy on the rich; its small operation on the poor; emigrant wretchedness; our boy-population; our hopeless prostitutes; our 4,000 grog-shops; the absence of poor from Presbyterian churches; the farce of our church-alms; confinement of our church-efforts to pew-holders; the do-nothing life of our Christian professors, in regard to the masses; our copying the Priest and Levite in the parable.[6]

\*    \*    \*

With the resignation of his brother from the seminary, J. A. Alexander was transferred to the chair of ecclesiastical history. Two years earlier, when the move was contemplated, Addison had complained that he felt little desire to "undertake a new work which, in order to be well done, should have been begun much earlier" and that would require him "to leave the terra firma of inspired truth for the mud and sand of patristical learning."[7] Despite his great reluctance to move from Bible to history, Addison Alexander was soon absorbed in the study of church history and tried, with some success, to teach with his old fire and enthusiasm. One of his students, Ezra F. Mundy, recalled his studies with J. A. Alexander. He told the Alumni Association in 1921:

The flower of the faculty in those days was Dr. [Addison] Alexander. I wish that the present generation of students could have the privilege of hearing him lecture. . . . When our class entered, he had the subject of Ecclesiastical History. Before that time he had been teaching languages for ten or fifteen years. But he seemed to have Ecclesiastical History with all the names and dates and facts in his memory. He used no manuscript. He simply talked to us about Ecclesiastical History, and he could give dates and names and figures with wonderful agility.[8]

A later Princeton Seminary professor of church history said that J. A. Alexander's "extraordinary powers of acquisition, interpretation, and expression, combined with his scholarly methods, his breadth of view, his Catholic temper, and his sound judgment, made him in nearly every respect an ideal professor of ecclesiastical history."[9] Despite his ability, however, Addison Alexander found teaching history frustrating. His restlessness manifested itself especially in his history course, and the students complained that he was "so fickle." He tried to teach the whole subject in one year, at the same time disapproving of the common tendency of separating church history from secular history. He soon came to the conclusion that a seminary course in church history can only give the method of study and prepare students for their own future investigation of the subject.[10]

Addison now lived in his father's campus house, with his mother, two brothers, William and Archibald, and their sister, Janetta. He was fond of watching the people who passed by his gate. He knew all the school children—their names, ages, and special interests. He loved to look at the lazy carts, the men on horseback, and the fancy pleasure carriages as they moved along the street. In the winter he was a delighted spectator of the sleighs, enjoying the merry jingle of their bells. During July 1852 he took his mother on a trip through New England; and the next summer he went to Europe accompanied by his student and friend, Caspar Wistar Hodge—the twenty-two-year-old son of Charles Hodge.

The gifted and versatile Addison Alexander continued his work in Bible while adding lectures in church history. Charles Hodge told Henry Boardman that "our rule here is to urge Addison to do whatever we can find he is *willing* to do." His journal records his teaching plan for 1853-54:

First class. Lectures on Church History, twice a week with recitations. Second class. 1. Thorough exegetical study of the Acts of the Apostles. 2. First part of lectures on Church History as above. Third class. 1. Lectures and lessons on Old Testament History. 2. Lectures and lessons on Connection of the Old and New Testament. 3. Thorough exegetical study of the Gospels.[11]

From time to time, Addison also taught courses in the Harmony of the Gospels; studies in Joshua, Revelation, and other Bible books; and Syriac and other languages. One student, Andrew Hepburn, said that Old Testament History was "the most popular" and, he thought, Dr. Alexander's "favourite course."[12] These lectures to the (third) entering class, according to student James P. Boyce, "consisted really of lectures on the English Bible, and awakened great enthusiasm, so that Presbyterian pastors in Philadelphia would run out to Princeton to hear them."[13] According to Charles Hodge, J. A. Alexander's students often said that "he made the Bible glorious to them."[14]

While carrying on his heavy load of teaching at the seminary, Addison Alexander was writing steadily on his commentaries. He completed his three-volume commentary on the Psalms in 1850 and planned to produce, with Charles Hodge and J. W. Alexander, a commentary on the whole New Testament.[15] Addison was to take the Gospels and Acts, his brother James the Pastoral Epistles, and Hodge the remaining books. Although they did not accomplish their original plan, Hodge wrote commentaries on Ephesians (1856), I Corinthians (1857), and II Corinthians (1859); and Addison Alexander completed Acts (1857), Mark (1858), and began work on Matthew.[16] Samuel Davies Alexander, a pastor in New York, described his brother's work on his commentaries:

The greater part of the commentaries on the Psalms, the Acts, and Mark, were written in New York. During the winter, amidst the pressure of professional labour, he found time to read and digest all known commentaries on the book in hand; and then, when his vacation began, he would proceed to New York, leaving his books behind him, and in his room in a hotel or in my study, would write from eight o'clock in the morning until five in the afternoon. Of course, human nature could not endure this long stretch of intense mental action. So at intervals he would throw down his pen and take up some book of light literature, which he would read for twenty or thirty minutes, and then resume his pen. Dickens, especially his Sketches, was his favourite in these moments. In my library, I have a collection of the early history of the different States of the Union and early travels in America, and in looking over these books, which amount to a hundred or a hundred and fifty volumes, I find his marks in nearly all of them; showing that in the intervals of labour he had beguiled himself in this way.

Sometimes, on some hot day in August, I would find him at his table with his coat off, toiling away at his work. One day in particular, I remember, he had been for several hours considering a most difficult passage, and as I entered he threw down his pen saying, with a glow upon his face that I shall never forget, "Well, this is the most delightful and exciting occupation that I can conceive of, it is better than any novel that I ever read."

It was just this exalted delight that stimulated him in all his work. At times this spirit would flag; and I have known him to cease from writing for two or three days, spending the time in walking the streets, or looking over the volumes in some of the libraries; and then the work would suddenly begin again with new ardour.

The table at which he wrote was generally placed at a window in my study looking out upon one of the noisiest streets in the city, but he often told me, that when engaged in writing, he was absolutely deaf to the noise of cars and omnibuses that were continually passing. In Princeton, while preparing his subject, I have seen thirty commentaries open before him at once. But in New York he would have nothing but his Hebrew Bible and Greek Testament: and I have never seen him use a Lexicon at these times. I once asked him, "How can you get along without your commentaries on these difficult points?" He answered, "I know what they all have said."

On one occasion he was talking to me about some obscure point in a passage, mentioning the different explanations that had been given of it, and stating the reasons why he considered them all unsound, when suddenly he said, "I have it!" and seizing his pen, wrote down a clear and natural explanation of the doubtful passage.

He never put pen to paper on the Lord's Day; never even read on subjects connected with the work in hand: but employed his time in reading hymns and devotional works, and while in New York attended church three times a day. He heard all the ministers then settled here, prominent and obscure, but I never heard him once make an unfavourable criticism. One Sunday, coming in from church, he said, "I heard Mr.——, preach on the First Psalm: he used my exposition very fully; that is what I like; that is what I write my commentaries for."[17]

\*     \*     \*

Three weeks before Archibald Alexander died, William Henry Green was inaugurated professor of Biblical and Oriental Literature. The twenty-six-year-old Green—tall, energetic and dignified—was born within thirteen miles of Princeton. He came from a prominent and famous family. Descended from Presbyterian ministers on both sides of his family, he was a direct descendant of Jonathan Dickinson, Princeton College's first president. His uncle Henry Wood-hull Green was chief justice of New Jersey and chancellor of the state's equity courts; because of his health, he had declined an appointment by Abraham Lincoln as chief justice of the United States. Another uncle, John Cleve Green, amassed a fortune in the China trade, banking, and railroads and became a generous benefactor of the College of New Jersey and Princeton Seminary.[18] Henry Woodhull Green, John Cleve Green, and another uncle, Caleb Smith Green, Jr., all served as members of the Princeton Seminary Board of Trustees, as did three of William Henry Green's cousins—for a combined period of service of almost a hundred years.

Despite his family's many Princeton connections, William Henry Green went to Easton, Pennsylvania, where he lived with his grandparents and attended Lafayette College, graduating before he was sixteen. He was known as "a sunny-faced, bright-eyed boy," who was not only the outstanding student in the school but one who "never missed college prayers in the chapel at five o'clock in the morning, winter and summer!"[19] For relaxation, Green played chess or read French translations of the sixteenth-century Italian poet Tasso. After graduating in 1840, he served as a tutor in mathematics at Lafayette for two years. He joined the First Presbyterian Church in Easton and, along with many Lafayette students and teachers, faithfully made his way down College Hill to listen to the sermons of the pastor, John Gray—a Scotch-Irish immigrant who had attended the University of Glasgow.

William Henry Green spent a year at Princeton Seminary, where he became at once the foremost scholar. A fellow student said that Green "took to Greek as if he had been born at Athens; he took to Hebrew as if he had been the son of a rabbi in Jerusalem." He spent another year at Lafayette as professor of mathematics and then returned to Princeton. Green completed his seminary work in 1846 and was appointed instructor in Hebrew when J. A. Alexander was assigned Old Testament History to permit Dr. Miller to reduce his teaching load. For two years, Green taught Hebrew at the seminary and served as stated supply in the churches of Princeton.

In 1849, at twenty-four years of age, William Henry Green accepted a call to one of the most influential churches of Philadelphia, Central Presbyterian Church. His installation sermon was given by J. A. Alexander. Speaking on I Peter 5:1-4, Alexander presented an "irrefutable argument for ministerial parity" and a "sublime picture of 'the appearing of the Chief Shepherd,' and of 'the crown of glory' reserved for faithful ministers."[20] On May 20, Green preached his first Sunday morning sermon at Central Church; his text was Genesis 1:1. Green's congregation found him to be "one of the ablest and most acceptable preachers in Philadelphia" and "a laborious, faithful and sympathetic pastor."[21] Here he began a life-long interest and ministry as an effective speaker to children. One of his former seminary students met him in Philadelphia and, impressed with the difference between their present relationship and that of their daily encounters in the classroom at Princeton, greeted him with the remark, "Dr. Green, I am delighted to meet you, so to say, on English ground."[22] Before long, however, Dr. Green would be drawn back to teaching Hebrew and Old Testament at Princeton.

In 1851, William Henry Green was elected by the General Assembly meeting in St. Louis to the chair of Biblical and Oriental Literature. At Green's inauguration in September, Samuel Beach Jones, pastor of the First Presbyterian Church in Bridgeton, New Jersey, charged the new professor to give himself to the defense of the Bible against modern critics. Green assured the seminary and its friends that he intended to do just that. "The winds may roar and the floods may dash tumultuously," he said, "but when the tempest clears away and the waves recede, it will be seen that [the Bible] still stands."[23] Dr. Green and his family took up residence on Stockton Street, just off Nassau Street, within easy walking distance of his classroom; and he settled in to his disciplined routine of study, teaching, and writing—seldom broken, except for summer trips to the shore, entertaining seminary guests, or preaching on Sundays in Princeton or in a nearby town.

William Henry Green faced a challenge. He had to follow the brilliant Addison Alexander and teach along with the beloved Charles Hodge. His first class contained some outstanding students—Robert Watts, James P. Boyce, Caspar Wistar Hodge, and Isidore Loewenthal. Although Green was not as brilliant as Addison Alexander, he better understood the needs of the average students. As a teacher he stood somewhere between the exacting Addison Alexander and the mild-mannered Hodge. He knew how to encourage the students to persistence in the study of Hebrew but held to high standards of work, soon impressing everyone with the fact that a good knowledge of the Old Testament language was a *sine qua non*. Green's students felt the pressure of his expectations and often commented that in his classroom they were not "under grace" but "under law." One student noted ominously in his diary, "Examination in Hebrew—Dr. Green!" The students, however, respected and admired their young professor. One described him as

tall, straight, strongly knit, energetic; with brown hair, firm mouth, piercing blue eyes that looked out from under heavy brows; dignified in manner, reserved, modest, at times almost to diffidence, earnest, reverent, and without self-seeking; thorough in his own work and rigorous in the recitation room, meeting his classes with unfailing regularity, going straight from the lecture-room to the study, evidently swayed by the sense of duty.[24]

Dr. Green was one of America's foremost linguists. He taught Hebrew, Aramaic, and Arabic; and he added Sanskrit after a delegation of students requested classes in that language in 1860. His *Grammar of the Hebrew Language* was published in 1861 and was reputed to be the finest such work produced by an American scholar. It went through five editions, and remained a standard text for decades. Green's students in the exegesis of the Psalms and Isaiah read Addison Alexander's commentaries and worked with the Septuagint and Vulgate as well as the Hebrew text. In his classes in hermeneutics and Bible introduction, he sought to bring the students into "a living, working knowledge of the Word of God." Because of his great knowledge of the Old Testament, William Henry Green's students called him "Rabbi" and "Mount Sinai." They were impressed with his earnestness and fairness, and often heard his favorite expression, "Turn on all the light." They also found him to be a man of sympathy and great gentleness in dealing with those in trouble. One of them, John D. Davis, remarked that many a student went to Dr. Green's study for permission to be absent from seminary due to a serious illness or death in his family. He went, said Davis, "perhaps, regarding Dr. Green as a stern and distant professor. He went revering Dr. Green. In that study he had a revelation. He came away *loving* Dr. Green."[25] The modest, hardworking professor served as seminary librarian after Archibald Alexander's death and supplied the newly organized Second Presbyterian Church for a time.

\* \* \*

In 1853 Henry A. Boardman, pastor of the Tenth Presbyterian Church in Philadelphia since his ordination, was elected by the General Assembly to be professor of Pastoral Theology at Princeton Seminary. Born at Troy, New York, on January 9, 1808, Boardman graduated from Yale in 1829 and from Princeton Seminary in 1833. He had decided not to go "to a large city" to serve; but, when the call came from the new church in Philadelphia, Boardman, after consulting with his Princeton professors, was "satisfied that the pillar of cloud had moved in this direction and that there was neither peace nor safety except in following it." When Boardman was elected to the Princeton faculty, his congregation, on June 7, 1853, adopted seven resolutions strongly opposing his move. The next day he received a letter from 115 business and civic leaders urging him to remain in the city. "We feel that your departure from Philadelphia," they wrote, "would be a loss not easily repaired to the public Christianity of a great commercial metropolis."[26] Boardman declined the appointment to Princeton.

The following year, the assembly elected Alexander Taggart McGill as professor of Ecclesiastical, Homiletic, and Pastoral Theology. Of Scotch-Irish descent, McGill was born in Pennsylvania in 1807 and trained in the Scottish Seceder tradition. He graduated from Jefferson College at the age of nineteen and remained there as tutor of Latin for two years. Seeking a milder climate for his health, he went to Milledgeville, Georgia, where he was principal at the Baldwin Academy. He studied law and received several important appointments from the Georgia legislature, including the dangerous work of surveying the lands of the Cherokee Indians prior to their removal to the West. Visiting Missionary Ridge, Tennessee, McGill was so impressed by the good work of the missionaries that he decided to enter the ministry.

Alexander McGill studied at the seminary of the Associate [Presbyterian] Church in Canonsburg, Pennsylvania, and was ordained in 1835. After several years of ministry in the churches of that denomination, he accepted a call from the Second Presbyterian Church (Old School) of Carlisle, Pennsylvania. The Seceders then suspended McGill from the ministry, but the Presbytery of Carlisle refused to recognize the validity of the action. In 1842, McGill became a professor at Western Seminary—teaching church history and church government and, later, oriental and biblical literature. He spent the school year of 1852-53 at Columbia Theological Seminary in South Carolina, and then returned to Western. He was elected to the faculty of Princeton Seminary in 1854 by a unanimous vote of the directors. Charles Hodge, pleased by this solid agreement, said to William Henry Green, "The hand of God is in this."

The McGills moved to Princeton and into the house in which the John Breckinridges and the J. W. Alexanders had lived. Faculty and students welcomed them, and Dr. Addison Alexander made friends with the children of the family, writing a little biography of one of the girls composed from her conversation about the place and playmates she had left behind.

*       *       *

Princeton Seminary now had four teachers—Charles Hodge, J. A. Alexander, William Henry Green, and Alexander McGill. Robert Hamill Nassau, whose conversion resulted from what he saw and heard at the funeral of Archibald Alexander, graduated in 1859 and went on to a distinguished career as a missionary doctor in Africa. He wrote of "the four wonderful men" who had been his instructors:

For Dr. Addison Alexander, I had such extreme reverence that it amounted almost to dread. His colossal memory amazed me. Dates were his playthings. Though I knew the facts and incidents of Church History, *dates* I never attempted. Had he examined me on them, I would have failed. I think that I never ventured to speak to him outside of the Lecture-room (except in Oct. 1857, when I was on the committee for the catalogue). Though, I felt sure, from his prayers in the Oratory, that he had a heart more tender than his sometimes sharp remarks might have indicated.

Dr. McGill was our "Pastor." It was to him that I went when I needed some advice. He was the first person who caused me to see the beauty and consistency of Presbyterianism. I wondered why church sessions did not faithfully carry it out.

With all my profound respect for Dr. Hodge, I was not "afraid" of him. In our recitations on his Lectures (of which, of course, I took full notes) I observed that he seemed pleased at my replies, when I used, instead of his words of my notes, the wording of the Westminster Catechism. *That* was easy for me to do. (I thus had a reply for any one who objected to children being taught Catechism, on the ground that they could not understand it. Of course, they did not. Neither had I, in my childhood. But memorising is easy in childhood. With that Catechism in my memory it was an advantage to have its splendid "form of words" when I reached an age at which I *could* understand them.)

Dr. Green I loved. He impressed different members of the Class very differently. Some, failing to understand, did not like him. They thought him stern and severe. He was not. His words seemed so; but, coming to him in a trustful manner, I found him kind and helpful. When he offered instruction in Arabic, as an extra course, I was one of five who gladly accepted it.[27]

\*     \*     \*

When the students returned to Princeton in 1852, they found new gas lights in the town stores and at the seminary—although the college buildings were still lit by candles and lamps. The next year James H. Brookes, the son of poor Tennessee farmers, came to the seminary. With only ninety-six cents in his pocket, he secured a room provided free for needy students in the basement of the chapel—fittingly dubbed "the Tombs." He refused help from the Presbyterian Board of Education, preferring to go through on his own or not at all. He borrowed fifty dollars from a relative in Baltimore, using five dollars of it to buy some secondhand furniture. Brookes was put off by the relative affluence of the Princeton students and professors. He "stormed inwardly against the cut of the average theologue's coat" and "his white necktie" and, as a silent protest, he frequently "stuck his trousers into his boots and paraded Princeton's streets." Brookes believed that his education at Princeton was "imperfect." The average seminary graduate, he said, "knew too much about the Bible, but not enough of the Bible." A strong premillennialist, Brookes objected to Princeton's postmillennial eschatology. Not surprisingly, the strong-minded young man left Princeton after one year to become pastor of the First Presbyterian Church in Dayton, Ohio.[28]

In 1853, John Maclean, the son of Princeton's first professor of chemistry and a true Princetonian by birth and experience, succeeded James Carnahan as president of the college.[29] Maclean graduated as the youngest member of the class of 1816. He became tutor, professor, and then vice president at the college—teaching, at various times, mathematics, Latin, Greek, natural philosophy, and Christian evidences. When James Carnahan resigned, some board members pushed for a new president who was an acknowledged leader in the Presbyterian church or for a layman distinguished in the world of science. Some favored J. W. Alexander, but he was "as firm as a rock" for Maclean, and on

December 20 John Maclean was elected.

James Carnahan had served thirty-one years—longer than any other president.[30] After a time of serious decline, when the enrollment dropped to sixty-six, the college—with a strengthened faculty, including Albert B. Dod, John Torrey, and Joseph Henry—began to prosper again. Much of the credit for the recovery goes to the skill and wisdom of the young vice president, John Maclean. Carnahan paid high tribute to his colleague when he said that Maclean "was always at his post without shrinking."[31] A later Princetonian characterized Maclean as "a man of quick intelligence, able to turn himself to almost any teaching work, always ready to change his work or to add to it, and always willing to accept a reduction of income."[32] It is not surprising that the president praised such a faculty member! The bachelor professor gave much time and energy to the students. They often recalled seeing "Johnny" in his long cloak, carrying tea kettle and food, on his way to visit a sick boy or, in case of serious illness, bringing the patient into his own house. C. C. Jones wrote his parents on March 1, 1852:

Never have I seen a more perfect model of a kind, benevolent, and tender-hearted professor. Is anyone sick or in distress? Is anyone depressed in spirits or under serious impressions? Anyone poor or deserving of sympathy? Dr. Maclean is ever ready to relieve his every necessity and administer that healing balm of consolation which only the troubled can best appreciate, which none save the kindhearted know how to bestow or are willing to impart. Long will I cherish his numerous good deeds, and ever hold his character in lively remembrance. It is truly astonishing what an influence a professor may deservedly obtain over the minds of students placed under his care. . . .[33]

A later Princeton president said that Maclean "watched over young men so carefully and never rebuked a student without making him a friend."[34] Maclean also took a keen interest in matters outside the college. He played a major role in the founding of New Jersey's public school system. As a member of the New Jersey Prison Association, he sometimes walked ten miles to Trenton on Sundays to conduct services in the state prison.

\*     \*     \*

The 1850s were good years for Charles Hodge. On July 8, 1852, he married Mary Hunter Stockton, widow of Lieutenant Samuel Witham Stockton of the United States Navy. Mary's father, Andrew Hunter, was a Presbyterian clergyman, chaplain in the army and the navy, and for four years professor of mathematics and astronomy at Princeton College. Her brothers followed military careers—Major General David Hunter was a Union officer in the Civil War and Dr. Lewis B. Hunter was a surgeon in both the United States Army and Navy. Charles had known Mary since she was fifteen. She had been like a sister to Sarah, Hodge's first wife, and was loved by the Hodge children. Charles Hodge wrote to John Johns, "She has come into my family as an old friend, every heart already her own, and we all feel her presence as a token and assurance of God's favor."[35] Hodge took pride in his garden and horses. He loved a game of chess or backgammon, played croquet in the summer, and enjoyed reading an occasional novel (which the younger Hodges placed about). He maintained his interest in politics and read several newspapers daily. His study was still "the family thoroughfare," alive with the play of children and, before long, grandchildren. He bought a beautiful farm on the Millstone River three miles from his house, where he could keep his horses.

On New Year's day, 1854, J. A. Alexander wrote in his journal that he heard Dr. Hodge preach in the chapel on Romans 1:16. During the day, Alexander followed his pattern of Bible reading in various languages—Ecclesiastes in Hebrew and Greek, I Kings in Hebrew and Latin, Deuteronomy in Hebrew and Aramaic, and Mark in Greek and Syriac. In the afternoon, he "made a few remarks at Conference, and heard a powerful discourse from Dr. Hodge on time considered as a talent."[36]

That spring Alexander Duff, the first overseas missionary of the Church of Scotland, visited Princeton during his American trip. The seminary eagerly looked forward to hearing the famous missionary. "Dr. Duff has again disappointed us,"

Charles Hodge wrote to his brother on March 15, 1854; "he is not to come for a month. This makes it doubtful whether we shall see him at all."[37] Duff did come, however, and years later Daniel McGilvary, a first-year student, recalled his scathing criticism of the church for "playing at missions" and his impassioned appeal for missionaries.[38] Duff's great two-hour missionary sermon in the Broadway Tabernacle of New York City electrified the immense crowd of two hundred clergymen and many of the leading men and women of the city. Princeton Seminary graduate Theodore Cuyler heard him there and wrote, "I leaned over toward the reporter's table; many of the reporters had flung down their pens—they might as well have attempted to report a thunder storm." When the sermon was over, James W. Alexander said, "Shut up now this tabernacle. Let no man dare speak here after that."[39]

On a stormy March night in 1855 when most of the students were hard at work in their rooms, the silence was broken by the cry of "fire!" Fifty-three years to the day after the fire of 1802, Nassau Hall burned again. But the old walls stood. When the rebuilding began, the Georgian architecture was this time altered by heavy Florentine arches and four-story square towers added to each end of the building.

Ashbel Green Simonton was one of the students who entered the seminary in the fall of 1855. He noted in his journal that the class was an unusually large one and that it numbered one "colored" man as shading to the picture. Simonton made a number of resolutions that he carefully wrote in his journal—"regular attendance on the devotional exercises of the Seminary," "daily and fervent secret prayer," "study of the devotional parts of the Bible and the reading of works on experimental religion and memoirs of Christians distinguished for sincere and heartfelt piety," and "constant and close communion with God." In October he had a life-changing experience. He wrote in his journal:

I have listened to-day to a very interesting sermon from Dr. Hodge on the duty of the church as a teacher. He spoke of the absolute necessity of instructing the heathen before success in the spread of the Gospel could be expected, and showed that any hopes of their conversion based upon the extraordinary agency of the Holy Spirit directly communicating truth were unscriptural. This sermon has had the effect of leading me to think seriously of the foreign mission field. The little success apparently attending missionary operations had tended to dissuade me from thinking of going. But I see I have been wrong. That the heathen are to be converted to God is clearly revealed in the Scriptures and I am convinced that day is coming rapidly. Those who are now laboring are preparing the way and God will not suffer their labor to be in vain. He who lays the foundation will receive an equal reward with those who perfect the building. I had never before seriously considered the question as to my duty to go abroad, always taking for granted that my sphere of labor would be somewhere in our great and rapidly growing country. It is however, I feel convinced, a matter to be taken into deep consideration whether since most prefer to remain it is not my duty to go.[40]

Early in 1856 there were clear indications of the presence of God's Spirit at Princeton, both in the college and seminary. Increased interest in prayer meetings and evidence of seriousness "even in the external deportment" of the students were noted by Ashbel Green Simonton. On Sunday, May 11, 1856, J. A. Alexander was in New York City for the installation of his brother Samuel as pastor of the Fifteenth Street Presbyterian Church.[41] J. W. Alexander gave the sermon. Already, commissioners were arriving for the Old School Presbyterian General Assembly. J. W. Alexander was pleased with the assembly and wrote that "the general impression is that there has never been a more harmonious, judicious, and respectable body."[42] J. A. Alexander listened with admiration to Dr. James Henley Thornwell's sermon on foreign missions. He also attended some of the sessions of the New School Presbyterian General Assembly, which was meeting at the same time in the city. He heard with great interest the debate on slavery. Robert Lewis Dabney of Virginia accompanied J. A. Alexander back to Princeton and spent a day with him there. Dabney wrote:

He received me with quiet, but genuine kindness. I ascertained that he was suffering with an aching tooth, and was much struck with the self-sacrificing spirit in which he declined to retire (as I urged him), and knowing that I had but the one day which I could possibly spend, devoted himself to my entertainment, without betraying his annoying pain in any manner. Our talk was chiefly of matters pertaining to our own profession and the Church. I ascertained that he was a man who thought for himself, and had original views, many of them far from harmonious with prevalent and fashionable ecclesiasticism.

I was much struck with the fact that one who was so much a man of the closet as he, should have so much practical knowledge of society and human nature. During the day I remarked, that there seemed to be a great difficulty in combining practical knowledge of men and affairs with thorough scholarship, in our young men; because the study which secured the latter necessarily shut them out of the publicity which taught the former. He very quietly replied, that there was a way by which the recluse in his study might acquire a correct knowledge of human nature; by the study of his Bible and his own heart. I have no doubt that this remark gave the key to his own character, as concerned this trait of it. There was a remarkable absence of egotism and dogmatism, for one who must have been conscious of powers and acquirements, and who had been so much complimented and applauded.[43]

\* \* \*

The "greatest commercial alarm" ever experienced in the United States shook Americans during the summer and fall of 1857. J. W. Alexander, pastor of New York's Fifth Avenue Presbyterian Church, returned from Europe to find that God had made "distresses touching worldly estate to awaken desire for durable riches and righteousness." Jeremiah Calvin Lanphier, for eight or nine years a member of Dr. Alexander's church, had begun work as a lay missionary of the North Dutch Church in July 1857. As he distributed Bibles and tracts house to house, he prayed for the people of lower Manhattan. On September 23, he began a midday prayer meeting in the third-story lecture room of the church on Fulton Street. Only six people attended that first prayer meeting, but by mid-January the entire church building was crowded and many were turned away. Daily noon meetings—attended largely by businessmen—in churches, theaters, and warehouses spread throughout New York City. Christians "of different names"—Old and New School Presbyterians, Methodists, Baptists, Episcopalians, and others—joined together under the leadership of lay-men "to read the Word, to sing, and to cry unto God for the outpouring of his Holy Spirit."[44] An observer reported:

The prayer-meeting became one of the institutions of the city. Christians in distant parts of the country heard of them. They prayed for the prayer-meetings. When they visited the city, the prayer-meeting was the place to which they resorted. The museum or theatre had no such attractions. Returning, they set up similar meetings at home. The Spirit followed, and the same displays of grace were seen in other cities.[45]

There was "a revival of prayer"—not only in New York City but all over the land. Hundreds of Old School Presbyterian ministers met on December 1, 1857, for a convention on revival in Pittsburgh and later for one in Cincinnati. Meanwhile, in New York City the revival continued. On March 17, Burton's Theater near City Hall was opened for the noonday prayer meeting; it was packed to every corner half an hour before Dr. Theodore Cuyler, pastor of Market Street Presbyterian Church, began the service. This "work of grace," commented J. W. Alexander, was marked by "decorous stillness, reverent waiting upon God, and a tender sense of the heavenly presence."[46] Secular newspapers covered the revival, which the *New York Times* called "one of the most remarkable movements since the Reformation."[47] Reporters were amazed at the moving and orderly impulse to pray that they observed. Very little preaching was done. The New York revival spread, and soon awakenings were common throughout the nation. To further the revival and "to give individual souls in the various stages of awakening or quickening under Divine influence, the needed instruction, counsel, and guidance," J. W. Alexander wrote sixteen tracts for distribution at police and fire stations and throughout the city.[48] Samuel Irenaeus Prime, a student at Princeton Seminary during 1832-33 and now editor of the influential *New York Observer*, described the revival in a book published in 1859, entitled *The Power of Prayer: Illustrated in the Revival of 1857-58.* "The pen of an angel," he wrote, "might well be employed to record the wonderful works of God in the city of New York, during the years 1857-58."[49] *The Power of Prayer* attained a circulation of over 175,000 copies, with reprints in Europe, Africa, and Asia.

On January 17, 1859, Addison preached for his brother James at Fifth Avenue Presbyterian Church in the morning, and James preached for another brother, Samuel Davies Alexander, at Fifteenth Street Presbyterian Church in the afternoon. James recorded that he felt "the solemnity" of sitting in the pulpit with one brother in the morning and the other in the afternoon. He longed, he wrote, to preach "with more simplicity—less of the conventional, less regard for rule, less care for criticism, less notice of the literary element, less regard for custom, more as Calvin, as Luther, as Paul preached." "As life runs on," he continued, "I feel the seriousness of my situation as a minister, but, oh, how little improvement! Oh, my ascended Lord and Master! be pleased to anoint me afresh for my ministry, send me some new and special grace, and cast me not aside as a useless instrument: for Christ's sake. Amen."[50]

\*　　\*　　\*

Following the great revival, ninety-five students matriculated at Princeton Seminary in 1858—the largest number ever to enter the seminary during the nineteenth century. And from Princeton went out a steady and growing stream of graduates to the church at home and to missions abroad. In 1856, the students at Auburn Theological Seminary wrote to the Princeton Society of Inquiry, "What good Princeton Seminary has already done we cannot estimate. The bones of her sons are buried in almost every land." During the summer of 1857, the news of the Sepoy Mutiny in India startled England and America. Among the victims were eight American missionaries, including Princeton graduates Robert McMullin and John Freeman and their wives. Freeman, who came to Christ while reading Richard Baxter's *Call to the Unconverted*, finished his work at Princeton in 1838 and went to India that same year. With his wife, he operated a home for orphan children at the mission center in Allahabad and then served in the Christian village of Fatehgarh. Robert McMullin's missionary call was confirmed by a conversation with three or four senior students one Sunday afternoon at the seminary. He and his wife arrived in Calcutta in January 1857, just a few months before the mutiny occurred. On September 12, 1857, the saddened college and seminary students joined with townspeople at the First Presbyterian Church for a day of fasting and prayer for missions in India.

The Society of Inquiry on Missions had enjoyed strong support through the years. Between 1844 and 1859, about eighty percent of all the Princeton Seminary students became members. In 1859, however, the Society of Inquiry was replaced by a new organization with a more general purpose—the Alexander Missionary, Theological, and Literary Society of Princeton Theological Seminary. Named for Archibald Alexander, the new society stated its purpose as "the promotion of a spirit of inquiry after truth, of skill in presenting and maintaining it, and the information of the members upon matters of religious and general intelligence." The Alexander Society sponsored the monthly Concert of Prayer for Missions and conducted a weekly literary meeting, which featured discussion of a topic in theology, philosophy, ethics, church polity, or literature. The first discussion took place on October 28, 1859, on the topic "Ought slavery to be abolished?" The recording secretary reported the first meeting: "Commencing with that most important of all questions, 'slavery,'—we settled it as 'forever' as the Congressional actions on the same subject have done repeatedly and were then prepared to turn our attention to every variety of topics whether practical or visionary, religious, literary, sectarian, political, metaphysical, theological, moral, ecclesiastical, educational, controversial or ethical." The Alexander Society, however, failed to attract strong student support. A committee appointed in 1861 to investigate reasons for this problem reported that the lack of interest was due to "a want of appreciation of the importance of fluency and earnestness in extempore speech." Princeton men, the report continued, were ahead of students in other seminaries "in scholarship and ability to grapple with a subject" but were "far less acceptable and impressive to the public as preachers."

The committee's note that Princeton was not producing great preachers may have been due to the change in the seminary faculty. Archibald Alexander had been an impressive preacher, and Samuel Miller was, in his own more formal style, effective. Francis Wayland, Baptist minister and president of Brown University, wrote to J. W. Alexander in November 1854 to congratulate him on his biography of his father. "I now see why Princeton has made good preachers," he added. In a later letter, Wayland expressed the doubt that Princeton would ever again make "as good ministers" as when Dr. Alexander and Dr. Miller "were the sole teachers."[51]

The present faculty did not possess a great preacher to inspire and challenge the students in this important area. Charles Hodge could move audiences, but contemporaries did not see him as a preacher. J. A. Alexander's sermons were solid, valuable, and sometimes great; but he had not served as a pastor and concentrated more on writing and teaching than on preaching. Young William Henry Green had a short ministry in Philadelphia, where his preaching was compared favorably with that of Albert Barnes, Henry A. Boardman, and the other Presbyterian ministers of the city. Dr. Green preached hundreds of sermons during his career as a professor at Princeton—delivering them, it was said, with "stately dignity, rapid utterance, [and] intense sincerity of mood and manner."[52] Green's major contribution, however, was in Old Testament studies to answer the higher critics. J. W. Alexander was a fine preacher who effectively modeled the preacher-professor role of Princeton's first two teachers, but he taught at the seminary for only two years.[53] "Preaching Christ," he once said, "is the best, hardest, sweetest work, on this side of beholding him." "There is a wonderful vitality and permanency in experience which is built on the preaching of Christ," he wrote. This is accomplished, he believed, not by "polish or literature in sermons," but by "something earnest, real, and affectionate," which requires nothing less than "a direct and specific influence from on High."[54]

Francis Wayland, in one of his letters to J. W. Alexander, deplored the tendency of seminaries to become "schools for theological and philosophical learning, and elegant literature, rather than schools to make preachers of the gospel." Alexander replied on November 15, 1854, "Most heartily do I assent to your remarks about the literary tendencies of our theological seminaries. I feel it in my heart. Having left the desk for the pulpit, I feel it more."[55]

For some time, respected Christian leaders had been expressing doubts about the effectiveness of theological seminaries in producing preachers and pastors. In 1845, Robert J. Breckinridge criticized the seminaries in his book *The Christian Pastor.*[56] Three years later, Gardiner Spring of New York City's Brick Presbyterian Church complained that the seminaries were investing "mere scholars, those who know more about books than men, and more of the theological halls than the pulpit" with the task of educating ministerial candidates. He called for a return to the older practice of training in the parish setting.[57] Stung by these criticisms, Charles Hodge and J. A. Alexander replied in the July 1848 issue of the *Biblical Repertory.* They wrote:

Dr. Spring avows his preference for the private method of theological education, by pastors, to the public or academical method now almost universally adopted in this country. His argument is reducible to these three propositions; that the ministry has sensibly deteriorated; that this deterioration has in part arisen from theological seminaries; and that this deteriorating influence of seminaries is owing, in great measure, to the practice of making men professors who have no pastoral experience.[58]

Hodge and Alexander produced some telling arguments to counter Dr. Spring's three propositions, but they did not fully appreciate the danger that Breckinridge, Spring, and others feared. Seminary professors must be not only competent teachers in their areas of responsibility, but they also should be men of pastoral experience who have the ability to preach clearly and powerfully the Word of God. The Princeton faculty tried to teach their students to be sound students and strong preachers, but they clearly missed the skill and example of their first two professors, who drew on years of pastoral ministry and preaching experience to teach and inspire the students to be great preachers.

# 18

# Transitions

*The brilliant Joseph Addison Alexander
joined the Princeton Faculty in 1833
and held three different chairs before his
death in 1860.*

I never go to Princeton without visiting [the graves of the Alexanders—father and sons], and I never think of them without having my poor staggering faith in God and in regenerated humanity strengthened. Let us uncover our heads and thank God for them!

ARCHIBALD ALEXANDER HODGE

**D**URING William Henry Green's journey to Europe in the autumn of 1858, Joseph Addison Alexander again taught Hebrew at the seminary. His colleague Alexander McGill wrote, "The whole term of this employment was one of exhilaration to him; like that of a child recovering possession of a toy which he had been tired of once, and now recognized in all its original attractions."[1] For several years Addison Alexander had had a strong and growing conviction that he was not in the right department. His ability and desire led him "to the scientific exposition of the Bible, to its literature and archaeology and philology, and to the training of interpreters of a new school."[2] Early in 1859 he proposed that church history be reunited with church government in Dr. McGill's department and that he move to New Testament. Alexander was hesitant to press for the change, however, because of the large amount of work this would give to McGill; McGill was hesitant because, he said, "the students and the Church at large would regret to see any department on which [J. A. Alexander] had entered with his strength, relinquished to any other man."[3] The trustees and the General Assembly agreed, however, and Dr. Alexander moved from church history to Hellenistic and New Testament Literature, the third chair he had held at Princeton.[4] He reported the change and reviewed his life of scholarship in a letter to his brother James:

Though I never should have made the recent move without your strong concurrence and advice, and though I have consulted you at

[377]

every step, I feel that I have not yet put you in complete possession of my views and feelings. . . . This I cannot do without being a little autobiographical; to which I am the less averse because this is a critical juncture in my history, not only on account of the proposed change in my position, but because I have just finished my half century. I need not remind you of my early and almost unnatural proclivity to Oriental studies. . . [which] were continued after my college course, at which time I read the whole of the Koran in Arabic and the Old Testament in Hebrew. It is nevertheless true that I had begun already to be weaned from Anatolic to Hellenic studies. . . . Thus I began my [teaching at the seminary] with a divided heart, and though I never disliked teaching Hebrew, but preferred it much to all my other seminary duties, I still spent much time upon Greek in private. . . . My interest in the language soon extended to the literature of the Hellenistic Jews, inspired and uninspired, as a distinct and well-defined department of ancient learning. It is this that I have always had before my mind, as my proposed field of study and instruction in my many schemes and efforts to attain my true position. It is not merely the New Testament literature, strictly so called, that I wish to cultivate—though that does lie at the foundation, and gives character to all the rest; but I covet the privilege of making excursions, without any violation of official duty, into the adjacent fields of Hellenistic learning, having still in view as my supreme end, the defence and illustration of the Bible, but at the same time opening a new field for literary culture in this country, and thus gaining for myself a more original position than that of simply sharing Green's professorship. I wish it to be fully understood, if the proposed change should be carried out, that while the New Testament department will have greater justice done it than was possible at any former period, it will have something new connected with it; which can only be suggested by a new name, the novelty of which is therefore an advantage, if it be not otherwise objectionable, which I cannot see to be the case. The more I reflect upon it, therefore, the more clearly I perceive that no description could more perfectly express what I have carried out for myself, than that of "Hellenistic and New Testament Literature."[5]

Less than three months after he received this letter from his brother, James was dead. He had gone to Virginia in June 1859 to try to recover from a serious illness. He and his wife visited her brother, Dr. James L. Cabell, professor of comparative anatomy and physiology at the University of Virginia in Charlottesville. They moved on to Warm Springs, where, on June 17, James wrote:

A Sabbath quiet in this lovely spot. Though my health is less encouraging, I thank God that I have so lively a sensibility to the beauties and glories of his creation. The sights, sounds, and odours are all rural, all mountainous. Every bird and flower and tree, and the variety is great, seems placed aright in a beautiful harmony with the whole. Gentle ascents of mountains on several sides, enclosing this happy valley; grassy up to a certain point of their smooth sides, then merging into thick forests, the line of junction being marked with beautiful shades; herds and flocks ever and anon emerging into the light. It is a country of springs, and the sound of water is much in our ears. Oh, that men would praise the Lord for his goodness.[6]

The Alexanders went next to Red Sweet Springs and—in the same state in which he had been born fifty-five years earlier—James Waddel Alexander died on July 31, 1859. Before his death he sent messages of farewell and comfort to his congregation and family members, and he assured his wife and friends around his bed that his hope was in Christ. They suggested that he not try to talk further, but he added:

Let me add one word more . . . If the curtain should drop at this moment and I were ushered into the presence of my Maker, what would be my feelings? They would be these. First, I would prostrate myself in the dust in an unutterable sense of my nothingness and guilt. Secondly, I would look up to my Redeemer with an inexpress- ible assurance of faith and love. There is a passage of Scripture which best expresses my present feeling: I know whom I have believed—some persons put in a preposition and say, I know *in* whom I have believed. This is not correct, Christ himself is the object of the Apostle's faith. I know *whom* I have believed, and am persuaded that he is able to keep that which I have committed unto him against that day. That is all I have to say.[7]

The body of J. W. Alexander was brought back to Princeton, and he was buried in the old cemetery beside the graves of his parents.[8] On October 9, there was a memorial service at his church in New York. Charles Hodge gave the sermon from Acts 9:20—"He preached Christ." He praised

Alexander as an "accomplished" scholar, skillful writer, "erudite" theologian who "embraced the faith of the Reformed Churches in all its integrity," and a beloved pastor who "preached Christ." Albert Barnes, New School Presbyterian pastor in Philadelphia, stated that J. W. Alexander had combined "as many qualities to constitute a useful minister of the gospel as any man now living." Barnes added:

> Though enrolled with the Old School branch of the Presbyterian Church, he had no bitterness of spirit towards his brethren of the other branch, or towards any Christians of any denomination. He was not indifferent to truth, or to those views of truth by which the Presbyterian body is separated from other denominations of Christians; but my apprehension is, that he regarded those distinctions as of much less importance than the great doctrines of Christianity, in which all are united. I regard him as a man who was eminently qualified to commend religion, pure, simple, spiritual, kind, charitable, heavenly, as we find it in the New Testament, to his fellow men. . . .

Irenaeus Prime, editor of the *New York Observer*, praised Dr. Alexander as a "model preacher" and a faithful pastor. "How fond he was of the daily prayer-meetings," Prime wrote, "how his soul longed for a revival of religion and the conversion of sinners!"[9]

Addison Alexander simply stated the fact of James's death in his journal and drew a heavy black line under the words. He himself was not well—suffering from diabetes. He did not take good care of himself. In fact, as Charles Hodge said, "it would be hard to find an educated man more profoundly ignorant of the structure of the human body or of the functions of its organs. Hence he was constantly violating the laws of health."[10] His condition was worsened by depression following the death of his beloved brother. It was his practice at this time to pace slowly up and down in his yard along the bark path lined with lilac bushes—usually with a book in his hands. Because of his health he gave up lecturing in November 1859 but continued to study. He returned to his commentary on Matthew on January 3, 1860, after five weeks of "confinement and inaction." The commentary ends with chapter sixteen, but, anticipating his death, Alexander completed an analysis of the closing chapters on January 18. His journal, kept faithfully for so many years, ended fittingly with the entry for January 25, 1860—"Reading as usual." He was reading Coverdale's Bible and the Targum of Jonathan. One of the last books he read was Adolphe Monod's *Les Adieux.* The marked "pages of his Flavel" showed that he was now "drawing water out of the wells of salvation."[11] He read with great joy the passage on the resurrection in Charles Hodge's commentary on Romans. Just before his life ended, he went about his room repeating softly the words of Isaac Watts's hymn—"Show pity, Lord, O Lord, forgive; Let a repenting rebel live." He died on January 28, 1860, and was buried beside his father, mother, and brother.

Thus Princeton lost, at age fifty, the brilliant scholar who had filled almost every chair in the seminary. It was, according to A. A. Hodge, "the most disastrous blow the institutions of Princeton ever experienced"—perhaps not forgetting the death of Jonathan Edwards in 1758. With the exception of the death of his wife Sarah, it was for Charles Hodge the greatest sorrow of his life. He wrote, "We have lost the greatest and one of the best men I ever knew."[12] Hodge believed that there was not "a man in the [Presbyterian] Church who had a more simple childlike faith in the entire Scriptures from Genesis to Revelation" than Princeton's great linguist and scholar.[13] The next Sunday Afternoon Conference, wrote William Henry Green, was "the most solemn one I have ever attended. The subject which had been assigned on the previous Sunday, without a thought of the loss which we were to experience in the interval, was 'The Lord reigneth.'"[14] Dr. Hodge broke down while attempting to read the words "Let not your heart be troubled" and passed the Bible to Dr. Green.

Addison Alexander was missed, not just at Princeton but throughout the church. The next month Charles Hodge received a beautiful letter from James Henley Thornwell, the great Southern Presbyterian theologian. Thornwell wrote:

I cannot describe to you the interest with which I have read your letter, nor the thoroughness of the sympathy with which I have entered into your case. My heart bled for you from the very beginning, for I knew precisely how you felt under the severe bereavement. My own mind was so greatly shocked that for successive days and nights I could think of nothing but the irreparable loss which the church had sustained. It was not my good fortune to be personally known to the deceased; but I admired his genius, his learning, his piety and eloquence. I was proud of him as a product of the Presbyterian Church in America, and he had not a friend on earth who felt a heartier satisfaction in the growing brilliancy of his name. His commentaries on Acts and Mark I regarded as models, as nearly perfection in their kind as human skill could make them, and I have been in the habit, not only of recommending them, but of insisting on my classes procuring and studying them. Then his modesty was equal to his worth. So free from vanity, from ostentation, from parade and pretensions.

But my dear brother, God reigns. Let us rejoice that we have this bright and beautiful light so long among us. It was given in grace, and it was removed not without wisdom and mercy.[15]

In May, Charles Hodge told the General Assembly of the Presbyterian Church:

In the death of Joseph Addison Alexander we have lost our great glory and defense. Permit me, Mr. Moderator, to express my own individual convictions. I regard Dr. Joseph Addison Alexander as incomparably the greatest man I ever knew—as incomparably the greatest man our church has ever produced. His intellect was majestic not only in its greatness but in its harmonious proportions. No faculty was in excess, and none was in defect. His understanding, imagination and memory were alike wonderful. Everything was equally easy to him. Nothing he ever did seemed to reveal half his power. His attainments in classical, oriental and modern languages and literature were almost unexampled. His stores of biblical, historical and antiquarian knowledge seemed inexhaustible. To all these talents and attainments were added great force of character, power over the minds of men, and a peculiar facility in imparting knowledge. His thorough orthodoxy, his fervent piety, humility, faithfulness in the discharge of his duties, and reverence for the Word of God, consecrated all his other gifts. His complete mastery of every form of modern infidelity enabled him to vindicate the Scriptures as with authority. He glorified the Word of God in the sight of his pupils beyond what any man I ever saw had the power of doing. Princeton is not what it was, and can never expect to be what it has been. You cannot fill his place. The only compensation for such a loss is the presence of the Spirit of God.[16]

Dr. Joseph Addison Alexander was dead, but through his students and his commentaries he continued to serve the church he loved. Charles Hodge said that "Dr. Addison's life was in a great measure hidden. He never appeared in church-courts or in religious conventions. But although he lived very much *by* himself, he did not live *for* himself. All his powers were devoted to the service of Christ, as writer, teacher, and minister of the gospel."[17] And one of his students, Theodore Cuyler, later wrote, "A thousand pulpits are the richer for the accumulations of that one busy and beautiful life,—that career of labour and love."[18] Another student inspired and challenged by Dr. Alexander was Thomas V. Moore, who became a pastor and wrote commentaries on Scripture which set "a standard of popular exposition . . . which has not been surpassed and rarely equalled." In the preface to his book on *Zechariah, Haggai and Malachi*, Moore paid tribute to J. A. Alexander and "his honored father."[19]

\*     \*     \*

In 1845 Charles Hodge had begun to give the lectures on church government as Samuel Miller's health declined. Hodge's address "What is Presbyterianism?" was published by the Presbyterian Board of Publication in 1855 and reprinted with a commendation by "the strictest Presbyterians of Scotland." Some, however, especially in the southern part of the Old School Presbyterian church, sharply disagreed with Hodge's presentation of Presbyterianism. There were two areas of debate. The first concerned the nature of the office of ruling elder. Agreeing with Samuel Miller's later position, Hodge opposed the one-office view (which made ministers and elders one order) as "subversive of Presbyterianism," because it provided for no lay representation in the government of the church. The second issue had to do with the extent of directions for church government in the Bible. Hodge held that the New Testament establishes Presbyterian polity in its major points but does not prescribe in detail the precise organizational form of the church. Within the limits of biblical principles, Christ left his church free to do its work under the guidance of God's providence and the Holy Spirit, in the manner found to be most effective under the changing conditions of time and place.

This issue was met head-on in the 1860 General Assembly—the last before South Carolina seceded and the nation was divided. The May weather in Rochester, New York, was delightful and the fellowship pleasant. Southerners were pleased with their hospitable reception, and even the antislavery commissioners praised the Christ-centered and powerful preaching of the ministers from the South. Soon Charles Hodge and James Henley Thornwell, the greatest theologians in the Old School Presbyterian church, met in "titanic conflict" on the specific question of whether the boards of the church were consistent with the principles of biblical Presbyterianism.[20] Thornwell—eagle-eyed and small in stature—spoke powerfully in favor of a change. He argued in clear, earnest, impassioned language that "the form of government for the church, and its modes of action, are prescribed in the Word of God, not merely as to its general principles, but in all its details." Then, for forty minutes, Hodge held forth the position that "the church is to be governed by principles laid down in the Word of God" and that beyond those prescribed directions "the church has a wide discretion in the choice of methods, organs and agencies." The assembly voted—234 to 56—in favor of Hodge's view, but the issue continued to be debated with great feeling and learning in the pages of the *Biblical Repertory and Princeton Review,* the *Southern Presbyterian Review,* and other publications.[21]

In 1860 Dr. McGill was teaching pastoral theology, homiletics, church government, and ecclesiastical history and also was busy in the "external affairs" of the seminary—a necessary task which took much more than half his time. Dr. Green was fully occupied with Old Testament, and Dr. Hodge was busy with systematic theology. The seminary needed two more teachers—one for the New Testament chair left vacant by the death of J. A. Alexander and another to take ecclesiastical history and ecclesiology.

Caspar Wistar Hodge, Charles Hodge's thirty-year-old son, was proposed for the New Testament position. Caspar had grown up at Princeton Seminary and was the companion, pupil, and friend of Addison Alexander. Caspar Hodge later wrote:

It was when I was a school-boy, about ten or eleven years old, that he took a fancy to attach me to him more permanently. Going on some errand to his study in his father's house, he entertained me in a long conversation, and engaged me to come again with the promise of writing something for me. . . . While visiting him in this way, he began to teach me. The first lessons I recollect from him, entirely apart from my school tasks, were in the Latin verb.[22]

When Caspar was about twelve, Addison Alexander proposed—much to the boy's joy—to take him from school and personally to prepare him for college. For the next two years, Caspar was with Dr. Alexander almost constantly, studying in his room and often going back at night to read with him. He entered Princeton College and graduated in 1848 at the head of his class. He was interested in science, served as secretary to Professor Henry, and gave some thought to the medical profession. He was Greek tutor at Princeton College during 1850-51. J. W. Alexander wrote, "He is the best Grecian I ever saw of his age."[23]

Caspar Hodge then decided to enter the seminary and study for the ministry. He graduated in 1853 and served the Ainslie Street Presbyterian Church in Brooklyn for three years before accepting a call to the Presbyterian church in Oxford, Pennsylvania. Now, in 1860, there was thought of bringing the young pastor from his small-town parish to the chair left vacant by J. A. Alexander. His father believed that Caspar would greatly object—"first because he regards himself as unfit, and secondly because he would prefer to get along without being called upon to make so much exertion"—but he also believed that his son had the talents and learning which the post demanded. In April 1860, Charles Hodge wrote to his brother, "Wistar is dreadfully mad about it, and hates the whole thing."[24]

For ecclesiastical history and ecclesiology, "the eyes of all the friends of Princeton were now eagerly turned to Robert Lewis Dabney of Prince Edward, Virginia, who had already acquired the well-deserved reputation of being one of the very ablest teachers of theology which the American church had ever produced."[25] Dr. Dabney was teaching theology and homiletics at the little Virginia seminary at Hampden-Sydney and serving as pastor of the college church. Dabney, who had just refused a call to New York City's Fifth Avenue Presbyterian Church, greatly appreciated the Princetonians. He once sent a short list of books to a young man who had asked his advice—including "Alexander's Moral Science," "as many of Calvin's and Addison Alexander's Commentaries as you can [get]," and "Hodge on Romans."[26]

Prior to the 1860 General Assembly that would make the decision concerning the Princeton faculty Charles Hodge wrote to Dabney, explaining Princeton's need and urging him to accept the position. "Now, my dear sir," Hodge wrote on March 24, 1860, "would that I could sit down by your side, or even at your feet, stranger as I am, and beg you, with many prayers and supplications, to consent, should God see fit to call you to come and help us in our great sorrow and need." Two more letters from Charles Hodge and a letter from Alexander McGill failed to persuade Dabney to leave Union Seminary. Dabney replied that he was reluctant to move north for personal reasons—"I must finally rupture the ties of affection and dependence which bind me to my servants, must see my black household scattered abroad, to be reassembled no more, and must subject my wife to domestic arrangements untried by her"—but that he was attempting to determine his duty "in the fear of God alone." In asking himself the question "In which position shall I be likely to effect most for Christ and his church?" Dabney decided that "by going away I shall inflict an almost fatal injury on a minor interest of the church in order to confer a very non-essential assistance on a major interest of the same church." Unstated in his correspondence with Hodge and McGill was Dabney's reading of the political situation. He believed that the country would be forced into war before he could "get a fair start in Princeton" and he would have to return to "his own state and people."[27]

Upon Dabney's refusal, the General Assembly of 1860 assigned Dr. McGill to the chair of Ecclesiastical History, elected Benjamin Morgan Palmer of New Orleans to the chair of Pastoral Theology and Sacred Rhetoric, and elected Caspar Wistar Hodge to the chair of New Testament Literature and Exegesis. Palmer, whose mind was long made up that his place was in the pastorate, declined; but Hodge accepted the appointment. At Princeton he joined his father and his youngest brother, Francis Blanchard Hodge, who had just begun his seminary study. The shy Caspar Hodge read his lectures and never seemed entirely comfortable in the classroom. Students, however, more and more appreciated his carefully prepared and up-to-date courses and loved him for his sensitive and warm spirit. A member of one of Caspar Wistar Hodge's first classes later wrote:

I think we all appreciated Dr. Hodge's position. We had all been students of Dr. Addison Alexander; we felt the burden that was on Dr. Hodge as his successor, and accorded him a deferential sympathy. I never heard a remark made that I can recollect that expressed the contrary. His course with us that year was inevitably an imperfect one. He took Dr. Alexander's Mark for one subject, and went through part of it with us exegetically. He has since repeatedly said to me with emphasis, "Your class treated me very kindly." Then he began to put his very life into the construction of that course of lectures which afterwards made so strong and brilliant an impression. I don't believe that any professor, especially with his retiring, reserved, and undemonstrative temper, ever made so strong an impression upon his students.[28]

The General Assembly of 1861 moved Dr. McGill to the chair of Church Government and the Composition and Delivery of Sermons and elected James C. Moffat professor of Church History. Moffat was born at Glencree in the south of Scotland on May 31, 1811. As a boy he listened with bright interest to the stories his mother told him from the Bible and *Pilgrim's Progress.* While caring for sheep he read all the books he could find. He became a printer's apprentice and, using the hours saved from sleep in the early morning before work, he read the great works of English literature and taught himself Latin, Greek, Hebrew, French, and German. He came to America in 1833 and was introduced by a friend of his father's to Dr. Maclean of Princeton College. James was admitted, by examination, to the junior class and graduated in 1835.

After a short time as a private tutor and graduate student at Yale College, James Moffat returned to Princeton as tutor in Greek. In March 1838, Professor J. W. Alexander wrote, "We have a most promising young man now a tutor here, for whom I wish I could find a good place. His name is Moffat; once a shepherd's boy in Glencree. His linguistic attainments are extraordinary, in languages both ancient and modern."[29] In 1839 Moffat went to Lafayette College as professor of Greek and Latin, and in 1841 he became professor of Latin and Modern History at Miami College in Oxford, Ohio. He prepared himself for the ministry by his own study and was ordained by the Presbyterian church. He became professor of Biblical Languages and Literature at the new Presbyterian seminary in Cincinnati before returning in 1853 to Princeton College as professor of Latin and history and, later, Greek language and literature. In 1861 he moved to the seminary, where he followed Samuel Miller, the Alexander brothers, and Alexander McGill as Princeton's professor of Church History.

# 19

# War and Peace

*Thomas V. Moore, who trained at
Princeton Seminary, 1839-42,
and became one of the leaders of the
Presbyterian church in the South.*

We ourselves have nearly finished our course, and should strive to have our hearts filled with gratitude for the good in the past, and with joyful anticipation of blessedness in the future. Life for us is substantially over, and we have little to expect beyond the present, so far as this world is concerned. Our last days, however, may be our best, if we are only filled with the assurance of God's love, and with devotion to his service and submission to his will.

CHARLES HODGE
to his brother
December 20, 1867

WHILE the seminary was reorganizing after the death of J. A. Alexander, the nation was moving rapidly toward secession and war. Warm friendships between southern and northern students at the college were strained as the Dred Scott decision was followed by John Brown's raid, the raid by the election of Lincoln, and Lincoln's election by secession. On December 20, 1860, South Carolina became the first of eleven states to constitute the Southern Confederacy. In April 1861, northern students at Princeton College showed their loyalty to the Union by raising the national flag over Nassau Hall. The faculty removed it, but, with great indignation, the students put it back in place and there it remained. When the news came in June that war had actually begun, over a third of the three hundred students left for their southern homes. There were many sad scenes at the railroad station by the canal as groups of students told each other good-by, pathetically conscious that they might soon be facing one another as enemies in the great clash of armies.

The war brought deep sorrow to the college faculty. Loyal to the Union, they could not forget their former pupils from the South, so many of whom were now fighting under Robert E. Lee and the Presbyterian "Stonewall" Jackson. When President Maclean received a letter from south of the Potomac, wishing Old Nassau "a long prosperous life in spite of the troubles which agitate the outer world," or when word came that a young man who recently had sat before him in chapel had been killed in battle, he was deeply saddened. Maclean's album of photographs, preserved in the Princeton library, reveals the breadth of his sympathies; for side by side with portraits of Grant and Farragut is one of Robert E. Lee.[1] Over four hundred Princeton College students and alumni served in the war; a large number were officers on both sides. Sixty-seven men from the college were killed or died, the loss borne equally by the Federals and the Confederates—and borne doubly by Maclean because he knew and loved each one.

Across the street at the seminary there was also great sadness. The beloved Archibald Alexander had been a Southerner, and his love for his native Virginia was well remembered. Charles Hodge, now Princeton's spokesman, was loyal to the northern cause, but his patriotism was tempered by his Christianity and his Presbyterianism. William B. Sprague, Hodge's fellow student at Princeton Seminary and since 1829 pastor of the Second Presbyterian Church in Albany, New York, agonized over Princeton's southern students' and graduates' hearty support of the Confederacy. "How is it that so large a number who have been educated here," he asked, "with whom many of us have taken sweet counsel, and some of whom we have all delighted to honor, have identified themselves with an enterprise, designed to lay waste this goodly inheritance which our fathers bequeathed to us?" Sprague added, "I know many of them so well, and they have had a place in my heart so long, that I could not, if I would, answer this question in any other spirit than that of the most enlarged charity." Still, Sprague confessed, there was not "a fact in the whole history of the Church" that confounded him more "than that our Southern brethren should, with such apparent cordiality and unanimity" have supported the "Rebellion." [2]

Many Presbyterians, especially those in the South, held that the Bible and the Westminster Confession asserted the doctrine of the spirituality of the church—the church is purely a spiritual body and must not meddle with any secular or political matter. In the Old School Assemblies of 1859 and 1860, James Henley Thornwell—"a man of lovely character but inexorable in debate"—argued brilliantly for the church's involvement only in those things which the Bible absolutely commands or permits. Charles Hodge, however, believed that it was sometimes necessary for the church to speak in areas of political concern. In the July 1860 issue of the *Biblical Repertory*, he wrote in protest of the view that "the action of the state, however inconsistent with the Word of God, could not be testified against." This "new doctrine" of the spirituality of the church, asserted Hodge, put "a muzzle" over the lips of the church and prevented "her exercising one of the highest and most important prerogatives." A compromise statement on this issue was adopted by the 1860 General Assembly, which on the one hand "disclaim[ed] all right to interfere in secular matters" and on the other "assert[ed] the right and duty of the Church, as God's witness on earth, to bear her testimony in favor of truth and holiness and against all false doctrines and sins." Hodge was pleased. Although he never denied that the church was essentially spiritual, he could never agree that the church should be denied the right of speaking on social and political matters. He later wrote:

There is indeed a sense of the words in which the church has nothing to do with politics. She has no right to pronounce judgment on purely secular matters, or upon such questions which ordinarily divide men into political parties. But politics, in the wide sense of the word, includes the science of government, the policy of states, and the duties of citizens. The plain principle which determines the legitimate sphere of the action of the church, is, that it is limited to teaching and enforcing moral and religious truths as revealed and determined by the sacred Scriptures.[3]

Hodge's article in the January 1861 issue of the *Biblical Repertory*—"The State of the Country"—was a calm attempt at conciliation.[4] While praised as "moderate, fair, and reasonable," it was denounced by some Southerners and by many abolitionists in the North. Stirred by Benjamin Morgan Palmer's ringing Thanksgiving sermon—preached in New Orleans on November 29, 1860—Hodge had come out more strongly than ever before against slavery, angering many of Princeton's southern friends.

\*      \*      \*

As the nation moved toward war, the Princeton community met on February 6 to remember one of its own. Mrs. Samuel Miller, eighty-three years old, died on February 2. Both the seminary and the college cancelled classes and a large congregation gathered at First Presbyterian Church for the funeral service. The text of the sermon was Psalm 92:14— "They shall still bring forth fruit in old age." Charles Hodge led in prayer. Sarah Miller's body was then taken to the town graveyard, where she was buried beside her husband.

\*      \*      \*

The election of Abraham Lincoln in 1860 was soon followed by the secession of South Carolina, and on February 4, 1861, delegates from six states of the Deep South met in Montgomery, Alabama, to organize the Confederate States of America. In April 1861, with the firing on Fort Sumter in Charleston harbor, the War Between the States began. That same month another article by Charles Hodge on "The Church and the Country" appeared in the *Biblical Repertory*. It was a plea for the unity of the church, despite the breakup of the country. "We are historically one church," Hodge wrote; "with the blessing of God, our church may survive this conflict, and present to the world the edifying spectacle of Christian brotherhood unbroken by political convulsions."[5] The Old School Presbyterian church was the largest Protestant denomination in which the North and South were still united. When the General Assembly met at the Seventh Presbyterian Church in Philadelphia in May 1861, only 264 commissioners were present because many Southerners did not attend. Charles Hodge later described the scene: "The eyes of the whole country were converged on the house in which the Assembly sat. The secular press was clamorous for an open avowal of allegiance. Threatening murmurs against clerical traitors were heard on every hand."

On the Friday after the assembly opened, Dr. Gardiner Spring of New York City introduced a resolution which called for the appointment of a special committee "to inquire into the expediency of this Assembly making some expression of their devotion to the Union of these States, and loyalty to the Government." After days of stormy debate and parliamentary maneuvers, "the Gardiner Spring Resolutions" that affirmed that Presbyterians must do all in their power "to strengthen, uphold, and encourage" the federal government of the United States carried by a vote of 156 to 66. Hodge submitted a protest, in which he was joined by fifty-seven others, which stated: "We deny the right of the Assembly to decide the political question, to what government the allegiance of Presbyterians as citizens is due, and its right to make that decision a condition of membership in our church." The assembly accused the protesters of wanting to "recognize, as good Presbyterians, men whom our own government, with the approval of Christendom, may soon execute as traitors." Hodge later explained his position:

Those who resisted the action of the Assembly were themselves. . . loyal to the Constitution and the Federal Government. . . . Why then did they refuse to avow [the Spring Resolutions] in and through the General Assembly? For the same reason that they would refuse, at the command of an excited multitude, to sing the "Star Spangled Banner" at the Lord's Table. They refused because in their judgment it was wrong and out of place. . . . The General Assembly had no right to decide the political question, as to what government the allegiance of Presbyterian citizens is due.[6]

Stung by the "Gardiner Spring Resolutions" and motivated by their own regional loyalty, forty-seven southern presbyteries, during the summer and fall of 1861, severed their relationship with the Old School General Assembly. On December 4, at the First Presbyterian Church in Augusta, Georgia, they organized the General Assembly of the Presbyterian Church in the Confederate States.

When the war came, Hodge praised the United States as the great Protestant power and defender of civil and religious freedom. He deplored secession as a rebellion of the South to perpetuate and extend slavery and to overthrow "this glorious union." Even though Hodge rejected the doctrine of the "spirituality of the church," as some formulated it, he nevertheless believed—as he wrote in 1862—that "zeal for a good cause, or the fervour of patriotic feeling, has led, and may again lead, the church to forget the limits set to her authority as a teacher or a judge."[7]  Charles Hodge and the *Biblical Repertory* continued to support the North throughout the war but attempted to take what Hodge called a "national" rather than a "radical" position. However—like most Christians North and South—Hodge believed that his side was right. He wrote to his brother on July 15, 1862, "I still have full confidence that God is on our side, and that He will bring us safe, and I trust purified, out of all our troubles."[8]

\*     \*     \*

Isabella McLanahan Brown of Baltimore—widow of George Brown, wealthy civic leader and owner of the Baltimore and Ohio Railroad—had indicated to her pastor, Princeton graduate John C. Backus, her intention to provide the necessary funds for another dormitory at the seminary. The outbreak of the war in 1860 caused Mrs. Brown, who like many in Baltimore sympathized with the Southern cause, to abandon her plan—until Dr. McGill wrote to her that a student from Virginia in the grey uniform of a Confederate soldier was attending classes and mingling on friendly terms with the other students.[9]  The news of his reception at a northern school during hostilities persuaded Isabella Brown to contribute $30,000 for the construction of the dormitory. Completed in 1865, Brown Hall housed eighty students and within a few years was equipped with gas heat, for which the students each paid $10 a session.

\*     \*     \*

The news of the capture of Richmond by Union troops on April 3, 1865, was received with great rejoicing at Princeton. The bells of the seminary and college rang and the national flag flew over schools and town.  A huge bonfire was built on the college campus, and Dr. McGill and other professors of the college and seminary gave patriotic speeches from the steps of Nassau Hall.  On April 9, Palm Sunday, the guns were silent at Appomattox.  General Lee surrendered the Army of Northern Virginia, and Jefferson Davis and his cabinet fled southward.  President Abraham Lincoln was shot on Good

Friday. He died on Saturday. At the seminary, the junior class had just assembled for New Testament Literature with Professor Caspar Hodge when the news came. Hodge, after a short prayer, dismissed the class. Charles Hodge stepped out on the porch at the side door of his study and called to one of the students, "My little grandson tells me that something has happened to President Lincoln." The student reported the news. With quivering lips, Hodge said, "O, it cannot be, it cannot be!" He turned, weeping, into his house. An hour later the bell rang and the seminary community gathered for prayer.

\*     \*     \*

Princeton again was saddened that year when Betsey Stockton, the former slave, missionary, and educator, died. The president of the college, John Maclean, and the senior professor in the seminary, Charles Hodge, conducted her funeral service. The students of the two schools were there, as well as mourners from New York and Philadelphia. Betsey Stockton had returned from the Sandwich Islands in 1825 with Charles Stewart and his sick wife, who soon died. After caring for the Stewart children, Stockton established a missionary school for Indian children in Canada and then returned to Princeton, where for thirty-two years she conducted a school for black children. On February 14, 1840, J. W. Alexander wrote, "Yesterday I examined Betsey Stockton's school; I wish I knew of a white school where religion was so faithfully inculcated."[10] The seminary students who taught Sunday school in the black Presbyterian church grew to know and love "Aunt Betsey." When James Brookes came to Princeton, practically penniless, Betsey Stockton "forced" upon the poor seminary student "many a basket of good food, daintily prepared." But for her kindness, Brookes said, he "could hardly have lived through those few months in New Jersey."[11]

\*     \*     \*

Charles Hodge was dismayed at the severe reconstruction policies which punished the South following Lincoln's death.

He was saddened by the same attitude he saw displayed in his own church. The 1865 General Assembly in Pittsburgh took extreme measures—branding secession as an ecclesiastical crime, and requiring repentance and open confession as the condition of re-admission to the Presbyterian church. This was followed by what some—especially in the border states—saw as highhanded repression of dissent in the General Assemblies of 1866 and 1867. Separate synods were created in Kentucky and Missouri, which eventually—along with a part of the Synod of Baltimore—were received into the Southern Presbyterian Church.

The departure of the Old School southern churches in 1861, the Civil War, and the emancipation of the slaves changed the relationship between the two branches of northern Presbyterianism. In 1862, the Old School General Assembly made an unexpected move by proposing the exchange of fraternal delegates with the New School Presbyterian church. The Plan of Union of 1801, disputes concerning church government, and the question of co-operation with voluntary societies were all matters of the past; but suspicion concerning theological differences remained. New School theologian Henry B. Smith, now professor at Union Theological Seminary in New York, led the pro-union side. Smith was elected moderator of his New School church in 1863 and seized the opportunity, as he retired from that office the next May, to deliver an eloquent address on "Christian Union and Ecclesiastical Reunion." He pointed to the ongoing struggle with "infidelity" and Roman Catholicism as arguments for church union, but he insisted that the real source and center of ecclesiastical reunion was Christ. "When our theology, our preaching, and our very lives, say that Christ is our all in all," Smith declared, "then we shall meet and flow together." He set out three conditions for reunion: a spirit of mutual concession, commitment to Presbyterian polity, and acceptance of the Westminster Confession, interpreted in its "legitimate grammatical and historical sense, in the spirit of the original Adopting Act, as 'containing the system of doctrine taught in the Holy Scriptures.'"[12] Smith believed that his church was closer to its standards than it had ever been.

Most Old School Presbyterians were convinced that the New School had indeed become more conservative theologically since 1837; but some, including Samuel J. Baird (author of the *History of the New School*) and Charles Hodge, continued to oppose reunion. Some elements in the Old School— among whom Cyrus H. McCormick of Chicago and the men of Princeton Seminary were prominent—eagerly hoped that reunion might take place with the Southern Presbyterians rather than with the New School. Charles Hodge did not believe that the New School brethren were heretical but they maintained and practiced, he thought, "a principle and latitude of toleration" different from that of the Old School. While carefully repudiating a rigid confessionalism, Hodge stated that reunion with the New School would commit the Old School to "a latitudinarian principle of subscription" that required nothing more than the acceptance of the essential doctrines of Christianity.[13] Henry B. Smith angrily replied, in the *American Presbyterian and Theological Review* of October 1867, that the New School had "uniformly repudiated" the principle of subscription ascribed to it by Hodge and held a view precisely the same as Hodge's.[14]

Hodge's view of creedal subscription was set forth in a number of articles in the *Biblical Repertory*.[15] "On this subject, which is one of vital importance," he wrote in 1831, "there are, if we do not mistake, two extremes equally to be lamented. . .

On the one hand, there are some, who seem inclined to give the phrase [system of doctrines], such a latitude that any one, who holds the great fundamental doctrines of the Gospel, as they are recognised by all evangelical denominations, might adopt it; while on the other, some are disposed to interpret it so strictly as to make it not only involve the adoption of all the doctrines contained in the Confession, but to preclude all diversity in the manner of conceiving and explaining them. They are therefore disposed to regard those, who do not in this sense adopt the Confession of Faith and yet remain in the Church, as guilty of a great departure from moral honesty. This we think an extreme, and a mischievous one. Because, it tends to the impeachment of character of many upright men, and because its application would split the Church into innumerable fragments.[16]

The Presbyterian National Union Convention met in Philadelphia in November 1867 "to inaugurate measures to heal Zion's breaches, and to bring into one the divided portions of the Presbyterian family." The convention consisted of Old and New School Presbyterians and also included representatives from the smaller Presbyterian churches—United, Reformed (New Side), Cumberland, and Southern Presbyterians—and many corresponding members from other denominations. Except for a short prayer given at the request of the moderator, Charles Hodge did not speak until the third day. He then explained that he had expected a discussion of a federal union—which would allow each denomination to retain its own identity—and was surprised that "the organic union of all Presbyterian churches in the land was the object contemplated and desired." "Such being the case," Hodge said, "I have taken no part in your deliberations, but have sat in silence, waiting to see what God, in his providence and spirit, would bring to pass."[17] Henry B. Smith wrote jubilantly to his mother, "A grand meeting. . . . Some of the strongest opponents of reunion were converted on the spot. Even Dr. Hodge relented wonderfully."[18]

Even though Charles Hodge was strongly committed to Old School Presbyterianism, he was no narrow denominationalist. He had written in 1853 that it is proper to identify as a Christian any man "who professes to be a worshipper of Christ" and as a Christian church "any company of such men."[19] The annual meeting of the Protestant Episcopal Evangelical Societies, which was being held in Philadelphia at the same time (November 1867) as the Presbyterian National Union Convention, brought greetings to the Presbyterians. With about two hundred Episcopalians present, Dr. Hodge was asked by the chairman of the convention to respond. He was greeted by great applause as he rose to speak:

Gentlemen and brothers, honored and beloved: I am called upon, as you hear, to present, in the name of this Convention, their hearty greeting and salutation. You here see around you, sirs, the representatives of six Presbyterian organizations of this country, comprising in the aggregate at least five thousand ministers of Jesus, an equal number of Christian churches, and at least one million of Christians, who have been baptized in the name of Jesus

Christ. It is not only, therefore, as the organ of the Convention, but for the moment, as the mouth-piece of this vast body of ministers and public Christian men, that we, sirs, were commissioned to present to you our cordial and affectionate Christian salutations.

We wish to assure you, sirs, that your names are just as familiar to our people as to your own! That we appreciate as highly your services in the cause of our common Master, as the people of your own honored Church. And, sirs, we rejoice with them in all that God has accomplished through your instrumentality.

I hope this audience will pardon a reference that might seem too personal under any other circumstances than the present. The honored President of this Convention might easily have selected some more suitable person to be the mouth-piece of this body, but on the ground of one consideration, perhaps the choice of myself to be that organ is not altogether inappropriate.

You, Bishop McIlvaine, and Bishop Johns, whom I had hoped to see with you here today,—you and I, sir, were boys together in Princeton College, fifty odd years ago. Often at evening have we knelt together in prayer. We passed through, sir, the baptism of that wonderful revival in that institution in 1815. We sat together, year after year, side by side, in the same class-room. We were instructed through our theological course by the same venerable teachers. You, sir, have gone your way, and I have gone mine; and I will venture to say in the presence of this audience, that I do not believe you have preached one sermon on any point of doctrine or Christian experience, which I would not have rejoiced to have uttered. And I feel fully confident that I never preached a sermon, the sentiments of which, you would not have publicly and cordially endorsed.

And now, sir, after these fifty odd years, here we stand, gray-headed, side by side, for the moment representatives of these two great bodies of organized Christians. Feeling for each other the same intimate cordial love, and mutual confidence; looking not backward,—not downward to the grave beneath our very feet,—but onward to the coming glory. Brethren, pardon this personal allusion, but is there not something that may be regarded as symbolical in this? Has not your Church and our Church been rocked in the same cradle? Did they not pass through the same Red Sea, receiving the same baptism of the Spirit, and of fire? Have they not uttered from those days of the Reformation to the present time, the same great testimony for Christ and his Gospel? What difference, sir, is there between your Thirty-nine Articles, and our Confession of Faith, other than the difference between one part and another of the same great Cathedral anthem rising to the skies? Does it not seem to indicate, sir, that these Churches are coming together? We stand here, sir, to say to the whole world, that we are one in faith, one in baptism, one in life, and one in our allegiance to your Lord and to our Lord.[20]

Many in the audience were moved to tears, and cries of "amen" frequently interrupted Charles Hodge's speech!

The proposal from the joint committee of the Old School and New School was presented to their General Assemblies which met in May 1868. It stated that the usual subscription formula to the Westminster Standards should be continued with the explanation:

It being understood that this Confession is received in its proper historical, that is, Calvinistic or Reformed sense. It is also understood that various methods of viewing, stating, explaining, and illustrating the doctrines of the Confession, which do not impair the integrity of the Reformed or Calvinistic system, are to be freely allowed in the United Church, as they have hitherto been allowed in the separate Churches.

Both churches accepted the proposal and sent it down to their presbyteries for votes. Fifty-eight commissioners of the defeated minority in the Old School General Assembly (including Charles Hodge) entered a strong protest, asserting that the current proposal would allow former New School men to claim that the Presbyterian church had tolerated the New Haven views. The Old School Assembly then passed a resolution stating that it preferred to drop the qualifying statements and base the reunion on acceptance of the standards in the simple terms of the traditional formula—"the Confession of Faith shall continue to be sincerely received and adopted as containing the system of doctrine taught in Holy Scriptures." The ensuing confusion delayed the final votes for a year, but in 1869 both assemblies voted on the simple unamended formula. In the New School Assembly there was a call for a time of silent prayer; and then, by a rising vote, the adoption was declared to be unanimous. The Old School Assembly debated the issue. George W. Musgrave, pastor of the Tenth Presbyterian Church in Philadelphia, spoke in favor of the plan of reunion. He said:

Why, Sir, the change of circumstances is almost radically entire. There were causes in operation from 1828 up to 1838, which we had good reason to dread, and which were undoubtedly corrupting and revolutionizing the church of God. I have never said, because I have never felt, as some men have said and doubtless felt—I have never said that I regretted the part I took in the early conflict. . . . I will rebuke heresy now, as I did then. . . . Sir, the circumstances are different. . . . All I ask is for a man to be a good Calvinist, and a thorough Presbyterian, and a sound Christian, and I don't care from what quarter he comes.[21]

Then the vote was taken by ayes and nays, with 285 in favor of reunion and nine opposed. The news of the result, so harmoniously reached in both assemblies, was flashed by telegraph all over the land and across the ocean. The reunion—which still had to be approved by the presbyteries of the two churches—was virtually assured.

Lyman Atwater, a consistent critic of the New Divinity of New England and of the reunion, and the junior editor of the *Biblical Repertory,* now decided that the New School was indeed theologically sound; and he wrote in support of the reunion. He argued that the New School seminaries were orthodox—referring to testimony, before the last assembly, that at Lane Seminary opposition to New Divinity was so firm that "in fact, they *out-Princeton* Princeton itself." Charles Hodge, still the senior editor of the *Biblical Repertory,* quietly opposed the reunion to the end. He did not believe that the New School was unorthodox, but he held that the denomination had always tolerated questionable theological views and that this spirit of latitude could be expected to continue after the reunion. He did not believe that a united Presbyterian church of the future would take the place of the Old School church of the past. Each denomination, he believed, had "its special gift and intrusted function, and the gift and function of the Old School Presbyterian Church was one of the most precious and indispensable and one which no other could fulfill."[22] Hodge recognized his duty, however, "to bow to the will of the majority constitutionally expressed, and to unite [his] prayers with those of [his] brethren that the blessing of God in rich abundance may rest on the reunited church."[23] Charles Hodge's son A. A. Hodge, professor of

[403]

theology at Western Seminary, hailed "with pleasure" the prospect of the two great denominations uniting upon the basis of the Westminster Standards "pure and simple." All the New School presbyteries and 126 of the 129 Old School presbyteries approved the plan; and in May 1870, in Philadelphia, the Presbyterian church was reunited. To celebrate the healing of the schism, the cornerstone of Princeton College's Reunion Hall was laid on May 28, funded equally by the Old School and the New School.

\*     \*     \*

During the darkest days of the Civil War, Princeton Seminary celebrated its fiftieth anniversary. Two thousand, four hundred and twenty-two students had studied at Princeton. They had come from twenty-nine states of the United States and from Canada, Great Britain, and the continent of Europe. They represented 109 colleges and universities. The largest number, 457, were graduates of the College of New Jersey. Union College in Schenectady, New York, contributed 284 students to Princeton Seminary. Others came from Jefferson College (186), Yale (125), Lafayette (98), Williams (74), Centre (72), Washington (63), Amherst (62), Dickinson (58), Pennsylvania (53), and many other schools. Princeton students had gone out from the seminary to pastorates and other ministries: 127 had become foreign missionaries; ninety-four had served as college professors; thirty-six as college presidents; and twenty-eight were professors in theological seminaries.[24]

The Semi-Centennial Jubilee took place on a beautiful, balmy day, April 30, 1862. Linden trees were already budding and lilacs were ready to burst into flower as faculty, students, alumni and others met at First Presbyterian Church. One hundred and seventy students were enrolled at the seminary, and the directors announced with pleasure that there had been "good health generally, and much diligence in study, and unusual interest and fervor in the exercises of devotion." Henry A. Boardman reviewed the history of the seminary. He rejoiced that "our Seminary has never faltered in its maintenance of the ancient faith of the Apostolic

Church." "While keeping well abreast with the age in the general progress of Biblical science and polite literature, it has been the paramount law of this School of the Prophets to subordinate the intellectual to the spiritual, and never to exalt speculative theology at the expense of personal religious experience," he said. "This is the true glory of our Seminary, and herein, under God, lies the secret of its power and success."[25]

A call was made for Charles Hodge to address the meeting, which he did "in a very feeling and tender manner." Nine others then spoke before Dr. Gardiner Spring closed the service with prayer. Alumni and visitors were invited to the seminary gymnasium for "an abundant and elegant dinner." During the meal it was announced that Robert and Alexander Stuart had given fifty thousand dollars to the seminary.

At three o'clock in the afternoon, the alumni again gathered at First Presbyterian Church. After singing and prayer, William B. Sprague of Albany, New York, delivered an address. "This institution is a mighty power," he said— "mighty in its elements, mighty in its operations." He praised "the spirit" in which Princeton Seminary was founded and noted that "its foundations were laid by some of the master-builders in Zion." He pointed out the fortunate location of the seminary in a "lovely" and "retired spot," and near "a great literary institution." "The truth is," he claimed, "that the two institutions have, in various ways, ministered to the advantage of each other; and each of them holds a higher place to-day—the one in the world of Letters, the other in the domain of Theology—than if they had not been walking together for half a century in one another's light." Dr. Sprague stated that the "grand object" of Princeton Seminary was to make "able and faithful ministers of the Gospel." He closed his discourse by tracing the influence of the Princeton graduates:

There is not a city of any extent in the land, where the Gospel has not been sounded forth by some voice or voices that hail from this Seminary. Travel in whatever direction you will, you cannot go far, but that its influence will meet you, either in the form of the living preacher, or in the auspicious results of some ministry, upon which the grave has closed. . . . If you make your way into the wilderness, the native home of savages, where, half a century ago, the first sign of civilization had not appeared, but where now Christianity holds her well-established dominion, there, again, you will find that this Seminary has had her full share in accomplishing these blessed results. And, finally, if you cross the ocean, and explore the dark domain of Foreign Paganism or Spurious Christianity, you can scarcely pause in any country, and look around you, without finding yourself in contact with an evangelizing influence that has emanated from Princeton.[26]

\*     \*     \*

One out of every three students leaving the seminary during its first fifty years went out to preach the gospel "on missionary ground." Almost six hundred served for at least some time in "destitute places" in America. Thirty-seven went to the American Indians. Seventeen became missionaries to the slaves. One hundred and twenty-seven men went to foreign mission fields—from Turkey to the Sandwich Islands, from Brazil to Afghanistan, from West Africa to Northern China. In the words of Henry Boardman at the Semi-Centennial Jubilee service, "many a Pagan land has reason to bless God that [Princeton Seminary] has been established."[27] The Princeton missionaries "preached the gospel in many tongues. They taught the children, translated the Scriptures, prepared Christian books, trained up native ministers. The lessons learned [at Princeton] were retaught in Africa, China, and the Isles of the Sea."[28]

In 1862, Princeton graduate William Thomson was in Beirut, where he had served since 1832, preaching teaching, and organizing churches and schools. His *Land and the Book*, a commentary on the Bible and the land of Palestine, was popular in America and England and earned for Thomson the reputation of "illustrator of the fifth gospel." Levi Janvier and his cousin John Newton had completed the dictionary of the Punjabi language. In just two years, on March 24, 1864, Janvier would be clubbed to death by a fanatic Akali Sikh. Isidore Loewenthal was in Afghanistan, where he had served since 1855. Born of Jewish parents in Prussia, the dwarfed Isidore was converted through the kindness and witness of a Presbyterian minister in Wilmington,

Delaware. A brilliant student, he excelled in languages and quickly acquired a knowledge of Persian, Arabic, Kashmir, Hindustani, and Pushto—the Afghan language. His missionary career would end suddenly in 1864 when he was shot and killed by his own watchman, who claimed that he mistook Loewenthal for a robber; although some believed that he had been paid to kill the man who was becoming dangerous to the Muslims.

Walter Lowrie had done outstanding work as a scholar and linguist in China before he was drowned by pirates in the summer of 1847.[29] His fellow missionaries erected a granite monument as a testimony. The front read, "The Rev. Walter M. Lowrie, A Missionary to the Chinese. Born Feb. 18th, 1819. Died Aug. 19th, 1847. 'I am a Stranger in the Earth.'— Ps. cxix. 19." Chinese writing on the monument gave the facts about Lowrie's life and death and added, "The Holy Book says—It is appointed unto man once to die, and after this the judgment, for the hour is coming in which all that are in the graves shall hear the voice of the Son of God, and shall come forth, they that have done good unto the resurrection of life, and they that have done evil unto the resurrection of damnation."

John Nevius went to China in 1854. When he was a student at Princeton he had been moved by many compelling needs—Africa, the American Indians, "the gold-seekers" of California, and Asia, among others. He wrote to his fiancée: "Everywhere we hope to have our God with us, and everywhere we shall have as much work as we can do. The great question is, where can we do the most for our Saviour, and where would he have us go?"[30] He applied to the Presbyterian Board of Foreign Missions in April 1853, offering to go anywhere but expressing a preference for China. In 1862 he and his wife, Helen, were ministering in Tungchow in Northern China.

Stephen Mattoon went to Siam in 1846, where be became the finest Siamese scholar in the world, translating the Bible and other books into Siamese. In 1860, Samuel Johnston from Nova Scotia joined the famous Canadian missionary, John Geddie, to work in the New Hebrides. The year before he left home he wrote, "Should we not . . . be as willing to devote our lives to sending the gospel as Christ was to devote his life to providing it?"

Ashbel Green Simonton, who had been challenged to give himself to foreign missions in a sermon by Charles Hodge, went to Brazil in 1859, where in just eight years he began the first Presbyterian church, the first presbytery, the first seminary, and the first evangelical press. He died of yellow fever on December 9, 1867, with a message for his congregation in Rio de Janeiro: "God will raise up someone to fill my place. He will do his own work with his own instruments. We can only lean on the everlasting arm and be quiet."[31]  David Trumbull graduated from Yale and Princeton Seminary and, in 1845, went to Chile under the Foreign Evangelical Society, of which his fellow Princetonian Robert Baird was  secretary. In 1862 he was engaged in a thriving ministry to seamen, reaching thousands of men from over thirty different nations.

Princeton had not given up on Africa.  Robert Hamill Nassau, the college student who was converted after attending Archibald Alexander's funeral, studied at Princeton Seminary and decided to go to tropical Africa despite its deadly climate.  Nassau wrote in his journal, "Many of my acquaintances protested to me. And one said, 'What a fool you are, Nassau, to go to Africa to die!'" Nassau added: "I quietly determined not to die."  After graduating from Princeton in 1859, he studied medicine at the University of Pennsylvania, earned his M. D. degree, and sailed for Africa on July 2, 1861.

The "Fiftieth Annual Report" of the seminary directors —for the year 1862—noted the continued interest of the Princeton students in foreign missions.  "Six or seven of the Senior Class have offered themselves to be sent upon the Foreign Missionary service," it stated, "and a larger proportion than usual of the two lower classes contemplate the same destination."[32]  One of those students was Samuel Henry Kellogg.  He graduated from Princeton College and served as tutor in mathematics while studying at the seminary.  He completed his seminary training in 1864 and sailed for India on December 20.  He preached in the villages of India and in 1872 was assigned to the theological school in Allahabad.

Kellogg became an authority in the languages of North India; and his Hindi grammar, published in 1875, was widely acknowledged. He translated the Larger Catechism into Hindi and assisted in the revision of the Bible in that language. When his wife died in 1876, Samuel Kellogg returned to the United States with his two children. He became Professor of Didactic and Polemic Theology and Lecturer on Comparative Religions at Western Seminary. He was a great force for foreign missions at the seminary—with some forty students committing themselves to foreign missions as a result of his influence.[33]

# APPENDICES

# 1

The Plan of a Theological Seminary

The following Plan, which became the charter for Princeton Theological Seminary, was prepared for this purpose by a committee appointed by the General Assembly. It was signed, by order of the committee, by Ashbel Green on September 20, 1810, and published the same year by J. Seymour, New York, with the title: "Report of a Committee of the General Assembly of the Presbyterian Church Exhibiting the Plan of a Theological Seminary."

# INTRODUCTION

INASMUCH as the obtaining of salvation through Jesus Christ our Lord, to the glory of the eternal God, is the chief object which claims the attention of man; and considering, that in the attainment of this object the dispensation of the Gospel is principally instrumental; it is manifestly of the highest importance, that the best means be used to ensure the faithful preaching of the Gospel, and the pure administration of all its ordinances. With this view, therefore, institutions for the education of youth intended for the holy ministry, have been established in all Christian countries, and have been found, by long experience, most eminently conducive to the prosperity of the Church. Hence the founders of the Presbyterian Church in the United States of America did, from its very origin, exert themselves with peculiar zeal to establish and endow colleges, academies, and schools, for the education of youth for the Gospel ministry. So rapid, however, has been the extension of this Church, and so disproportionate, of late, has been the number of ministers educated, to the call which has been made for ministerial service, that some additional and vigorous efforts to increase the supply are loudly and affectingly demanded. Circumstances also do imperiously dictate, not only that the labourers in the vineyard of the Lord should be multiplied, but that they should be more thoroughly furnished than they have ordinarily been for the arduous work to which they must be called. Influenced by the views and considerations now recited, the General Assembly, after mature deliberation, have resolved, in reliance on the patronage and blessing of the Great Head of the Church, to establish a new Institution, consecrated solely to the education of men for the Gospel ministry, and to be denominated,—*The Theological Seminary of the Presbyterian Church in the United States of America.* And to the intent that the true design of the founders of this institution may be known

[415]

to the public, both now and in time to come, and especially that this design may, at all times, be distinctly viewed, and sacredly regarded, both by the teachers and the pupils of the Seminary, it is judged proper to make a summary and explicit statement of it.

It is to form men for the Gospel ministry, who shall truly believe, and cordially love, and therefore endeavour to propagate and defend, in its genuineness, simplicity, and fulness, that system of religious belief and practice which is set forth in the Confession of Faith, Catechisms, and Plan of Government and Discipline of the Presbyterian Church; and thus to perpetuate and extend the influence of true evangelical piety, and Gospel order.

It is to provide for the Church an adequate supply and succession of able and faithful ministers of the New Testament; workmen that *need not to be ashamed*, being qualified *rightly to divide the word of truth.*

It is to unite, in those who shall sustain the ministerial office, religion and literature; that piety of the heart which is the fruit only of the renewing and sanctifying grace of God, with solid learning; believing that religion without learning, or learning without religion, in the ministers of the Gospel, must ultimately prove injurious to the Church.

It is to afford more advantages than have hitherto been usually possessed by the ministers of religion in our Church, to cultivate both piety and literature in their preparatory course; piety, by placing it in circumstances favourable to its growth, and by cherishing and regulating its ardour; literature, by affording favourable opportunities for its attainment, and by making its possession indispensable.

It is to provide for the Church, men who shall be able to defend her faith against infidels, and her doctrines against heretics.

It is to furnish our congregations with enlightened, humble, zealous, laborious pastors, who shall truly watch for the good of souls, and consider it as their highest honour and happiness to win them to the Saviour, and to build up their several charges in holiness and peace.

It is to promote harmony and unity of sentiment among the ministers of our Church, by educating a large body of them under the same teachers, and in the same course of study.

It is to lay the foundation of early and lasting friendships, productive of confidence and mutual assistance in after life among the ministers of religion; which experience shows to be conducive not only to personal happiness, but to the perfecting of inquiries, researches, and publications advantageous to religion.

It is to preserve the unity of our Church, by educating her ministers in an enlightened attachment, not only to the same doctrines, but to the same plan of government.

It is to bring to the service of the Church genius and talent, when united with piety, however poor or obscure may be their possessor, by furnishing, as far as possible, the means of education and support, without expense to the student.

It is, finally, to endeavour to raise up a succession of men, at once *qualified for* and thoroughly *devoted to* the work of the Gospel ministry; who, with various endowments suiting them to different stations in the Church of Christ, may all possess a portion of the spirit of the primitive propagators of the Gospel, prepared to make every sacrifice, to endure every hardship, and to render every service which the promotion of pure and undefiled religion may require.

# PLAN OF A THEOLOGICAL SEMINARY

ARTICLE I.
Of the General Assembly.
Section 1. As this Institution derives its origin from the General Assembly, so that body is to be considered at all times as its patron, and the fountain of its powers. The Assembly shall, accordingly, ultimately sanction all its laws, direct its instructions, and appoint its principal officers.
Section 2. The General Assembly shall choose a Board of Directors, consisting of fourteen ministers, and six ruling elders, by whom the Seminary shall be inspected and conducted. This board of directors shall be chosen triennially, except that the General Assembly may, annually, when necessary, fill up the vacancies occasioned in the board by death, resignation or incapacity to serve.
Section 3. All professors of the Seminary shall be appointed by the Assembly. But in cases of necessity, the board of directors may employ a suitable person to perform the duties of a professor, till a meeting of the Assembly shall take place.
Section 4. The General Assembly shall at all times have the power of adding to the Constitutional Articles of the Seminary, and of abrogating, altering, or amending them; but in the exercise of this power, the contemplated additions, abrogations, alterations, or amendments, shall, in every case, be proposed at one Assembly, and not adopted till the Assembly of the subsequent year, except by a unanimous vote.

ARTICLE II.
Of the Board of Directors.
Section 1. The board of directors shall meet statedly, twice in each year; once in the spring, and once in the fall, and oftener on their own adjournments, if they shall judge it expedient. A majority of the board shall be a quorum; provided always, that of this majority six, at least, be ministers of the Gospel.
Section 2. The board shall choose, out of their own number, a president and secretary. In the absence of the president, the senior member present shall preside.

Section 3. The president of the board, or in the event of his death, absence, or inability to act, the senior member for the time being shall, at the request of any three members expressed to him in writing, call a special meeting of the board of directors by a circular letter addressed to each; in which letter notice shall be given, not only of the place and time of meeting, but of the business intended to be transacted at the meeting notified; and this letter shall be sent at least twenty days before the time of said meeting.

Section 4. The secretary of the board shall keep accurate records of all the proceedings of the directors; and it shall be his duty to lay these records, or a faithful transcript of the same, before the General Assembly, annually, for the unrestrained inspection of all the members.

Section 5. Every meeting of the board of directors shall be opened and closed with prayer.

Section 6. The board of directors may make by-laws, or rules and regulations for the performance of the duties assigned them, or for the preservation of order, not inconsistent with the prescriptions of this plan, or the orders of the General Assembly.

Section 7. At the commencement of each stated spring meeting, the whole plan of the Seminary shall be distinctly read before the board of directors.

Section 8. The board shall direct the professors of the Seminary, in regard to the subjects and topics on which they are severally to give instructions to the pupils, so far as the same shall not be prescribed by this plan, or by the orders of the General Assembly.

Section 9. It shall be the duty of the board of directors to inaugurate the professors of the Seminary, and to direct what forms shall be used, and what services performed, on such occasions.

Section 10. No person shall be eligible to the office of director after he shall have attained the age of seventy years.

Section 11. Every director, previously to his taking his seat as a member of the board, shall solemnly subscribe the following formula, viz.—"Approving the plan of the Theological Seminary of the Presbyterian Church in the United States of America, I solemnly declare and promise, in the presence of

God, and of this board, that I will faithfully endeavour to carry into effect all the articles and provisions of said plan, and to promote the great design of the Seminary."

Section 12. The board of directors shall inspect the fidelity of the professors, especially in regard to the doctrines actually taught; and if, after due enquiry and examination, they shall judge that any professor is either unsound in the faith, unfriendly to the principles of Presbyterian Church Government, immoral in his conduct, unfaithful to his trust, or incompetent to the discharge of his duties, they shall faithfully report him as such to the General Assembly.

Section 13. It shall be the duty of the board of directors to watch over the conduct of the students; to redress grievances; to examine into the whole course of instruction and study in the Seminary; and generally to superintend and endeavour to promote all its interests.

Section 14. The board of directors shall make, in writing, a detailed and faithful report of the state of the Seminary, to every General Assembly; and they may, at the same time, recommend such measures for the advantage of the Seminary as to them may appear proper.

Section 15. At every stated meeting of the board of directors, unless particular circumstances render it inexpedient, there shall be at least one sermon delivered in the presence of the board, the professors, and students, by a director or directors previously appointed for the purpose, calculated to impress on the minds of all, the great importance of their privileges and obligations, and the nature and extent of their duties, especially such as arise out of the ministerial character and functions.

ARTICLE III.
Of the Professors.
Section 1. The number of the professors in the Seminary shall be increased or diminished, as the Assembly may, from time to time, direct. But when the Seminary shall be completely organized, there shall not be less than three professors: one of Didactic and Polemic Divinity; one of Oriental and Biblical Literature; and one of Ecclesiastical History and Church Government.

Section 2. No professor shall be eligible to the office of professor of divinity, or of any professorship immediately connected with theology, but an ordained minister of the Presbyterian Church.

Section 3. Every professor belonging to the Seminary, whatever he may have done before, shall, on being inaugurated, solemnly subscribe the Confession of Faith, Catechisms, and Form of Government of the Presbyterian Church, agreeably to the following formula, viz.—"In the presence of God and of the directors of this Seminary, I do solemnly, and *ex animo* adopt, receive, and subscribe the Confession of Faith and Catechisms of the Presbyterian Church in the United States of America, as the confession of my faith; or, as a summary and just exhibition of that system of doctrine and religious belief which is contained in holy Scripture, and therein revealed by God to man for his salvation: and in the same manner I profess to receive the Form of Government of said Church, as most agreeable to the inspired oracles. And I do solemnly promise and engage, not to inculcate, teach, or insinuate any thing which shall appear to me to contradict or contravene, either directly or impliedly, any thing taught in the said Confession of Faith, Catechisms, or Form of Church Government, while I shall continue a professor in this Seminary."

Section 4. The salaries of the professors shall be recommended by the directors; but they shall be fixed only by a vote of the General Assembly.

Section 5. The professors may accompany their lectures and recitations with prayer, as frequently as they may judge proper, in addition to those daily seasons of prayer in which all the students will unite.

Section 6. Each professor shall lay before the board of directors, as soon as practicable after his appointment, a detailed exhibition of the system and method which he proposes to pursue, and the subjects which he proposes to discuss, in conducting the studies of the youth that shall come under his care: and in this system he shall make such alterations or additions as the board shall direct; so that, eventually, the whole course through which the pupils shall be carried, shall be no other than that which the board of directors shall have approved and sanctioned, conformably to Sect. 9. Art. II. And as often as any professor shall think that variations and additions of importance may be advantageously introduced into his course of teaching, he shall submit the same to the board of directors for their approbation or rejection.

Section 7. Every professor shall, if practicable, have at least one lecture or recitation every day, on which the pupils, in his branch of instruction shall be bound to attend; and on which the other pupils of the Seminary shall attend as often, and in such manner, as may be directed by the majority of the board of directors.

Section 8. Any professor intending to resign his office, shall give six months notice of such intention to the board of directors.

Section 9. The professors of the Institution shall be considered as a faculty. They shall meet at such seasons as they may judge proper. In every meeting, the professor of didactic and polemic divinity shall preside, if he be present. If he be absent, a president shall be chosen pro tempore. The faculty shall choose a clerk, and keep accurate records of all their proceedings, which records shall be laid before the directors at every meeting of the board. The president of the faculty shall call a meeting whenever he shall judge it expedient, and whenever he shall be requested to do so by any other member. By the faculty, regularly convened, shall be determined the hours and seasons at which the classes shall attend the professors severally, so as to prevent interference and confusion, and to afford to the pupils the best opportunities of improvement. The faculty shall attend to, and decide on all cases of discipline, and all questions of order, as they shall arise. They shall agree on the rules of order, decorum, and duty, (not inconsistent with any provision in the plan of the Seminary, nor with any order of the board of directors,) to which the students shall be subjected; and these they shall reduce to writing, and cause to be publicly and frequently read. They shall determine the hours at which the whole of the pupils shall, morning and evening, attend for social worship, and the manner in which, and the person or persons, of their own number, by whom, the exercises of devotion shall be conducted.

Section 10. The faculty shall be empowered to dismiss from the Seminary any student who shall prove unsound in his religious sentiments; immoral or disorderly in his conduct; or who may be, in their opinion, on any account whatsoever, a dangerous, unwholesome, or unprofitable member of the Institution.

Section 11. Each member of the faculty shall have an equal vote.

Section 12. It shall be the duty of the professors, under the direction of the board of directors, to supply the pupils of the Seminary and Academy with the preaching of the Gospel, and the administration of the Sacraments of the Christian Church; if this supply shall not, in the judgment of the directors, be satisfactorily furnished by a Church or Churches in the place where the Institution shall be established.

ARTICLE IV.
Of Study and Attainments.

As the particular course of study pursued in any Institution will, and perhaps ought to be modified in a considerable degree, by the views and habits of the teachers; and ought, moreover, to be varied, altered, or extended, as experience may suggest improvements; it is judged proper to specify, not so precisely the course of study, as the attainments which must be made. Therefore,

Section 1. Every student, at the close of his course, must have made the following attainments, viz. He must be well skilled in the original languages of the Holy Scriptures. He must be able to explain the principal difficulties which arise in the perusal of the Scriptures, either from erroneous translations, apparent inconsistencies, real obscurities, or objections arising from history, reason, or argument. He must be versed in Jewish and Christian antiquities, which serve to explain and illustrate Scripture. He must have an acquaintance with ancient geography, and with oriental customs, which throw light on the sacred records.—Thus he will have laid the foundation for becoming a sound biblical critic.

He must have read and digested the principal arguments and writings relative to what has been called the deistical controversy.—Thus will he be qualified to become a defender of the Christian faith.

He must be able to support the doctrines of the Confession of Faith and Catechisms, by a ready, pertinent, and abundant quotation of Scripture texts for that purpose. He must have studied carefully and correctly Natural Theology, Didactic, Polemic, and Casuistic Divinity. He must have a considerable acquaintance with General History and Chronology, and a particular acquaintance with the history of the Christian Church.—Thus he will be preparing to become an able and sound divine and casuist.

He must have read a considerable number of the best practical writers on the subject of religion. He must have learned to compose with correctness and readiness in his own language, and to deliver what he has composed to others in a natural and acceptable manner. He must be well acquainted with the several parts, and the proper structure of popular lectures and sermons. He must have composed at least two lectures and four popular sermons, that shall have been approved by the professors. He must have carefully studied the duties of the pastoral care.—Thus he will be prepared to become a useful preacher, and a faithful pastor.

He must have studied attentively the form of Church Government authorized by the Scriptures, and the administration of it as it has taken place in Protestant Churches. —Thus he will be qualified to exercise discipline, and to take part in the government of the Church in all its judicatories.

Section 2. The period of continuance in the Theological Seminary shall, in no case be less than three years, previously to an examination for a certificate of approbations.

Section 3. Those pupils who have regularly and diligently studied for three years, shall be admitted to an examination on the subjects specified in this article. The examination shall be conducted by the professors, in the presence of the board of directors, or a committee of them; and if it be passed to the satisfaction of the directors, they who so pass it, shall receive a certificate of the same, signed by the professors, with which they shall be remitted to their several presbyteries, to be disposed of as such presbyteries shall direct. Those who do not pass a satisfactory examination shall remain a longer space in the Seminary.

Section 4. It shall be the object of the professors to make such arrangements in the instruction of their pupils, as shall be best adapted to enable them, in the space of three years, to be examined with advantage on the subjects specified in this article.

ARTICLE V.
Of Devotion, and Improvement in Practical Piety.
It ought to be considered as an object of primary importance by every student in the Seminary, to be careful and vigilant not to lose that inward sense of the power of godliness which he may have attained; but, on the contrary, to grow continually in a spirit of enlightened devotion and fervent piety; deeply impressed with the recollection that without this, all his other acquisitions will be comparatively of little worth, either to himself, or to the Church of which he is to be a minister.

He must remember, too, that this is a species of improvement which must of necessity be left, in a great measure, with himself, as a concern between God and his own soul.

It is proper, however, to delineate the path of duty, to express the wishes and expectations of the founders of the Seminary, and to make such requirements as the nature of the subject will permit.
Section 1. It is expected that every student in the Theological Seminary will spend a portion of time every morning and evening in devout meditation, and self-recollection and examination; in reading the holy Scriptures solely with a view to a personal and practical application of the passage read, to his own heart, character, and circumstances; and in humble fervent prayer, and praise to God in secret.

The whole of every Lord's day is to be devoted to devotional exercises, either of a social or secret kind. Intellectual pursuits, not immediately connected with devotion or the religion of the heart, are on that day to be forborne. The books to be read are to be of a practical nature. The conversations had with each other are to be chiefly on religious subjects. Associations for prayer and praise, and for religious conference, calculated to promote a growth in grace, are also proper for this day; subject to such regulations as the professors and directors may see proper to prescribe. It is also wished and recommended, that each student should ordinarily set apart one day in a month for special prayer and self-examination in secret, accompanied with fasting.

Section 2. If any student shall exhibit, in his general deportment, a levity or indifference in regard to practical religion, though it do not amount to any overt act of irreligion or immorality, it shall be the duty of the professor who may observe it, to admonish him tenderly and faithfully in private, and endeavour to engage him to a more holy temper and a more exemplary deportment.

Section 3. If a student, after due admonition, persist in a system of conduct not exemplary in regard to religion, he shall be dismissed from the Seminary.

Section 4. The professors are particularly charged, by all the proper means in their power, to encourage, cherish, and promote devotion and personal piety among their pupils, by warning and guarding them, on the one hand, against formality and indifference, and on the other, against ostentation and enthusiasm; by inculcating practical religion in their lectures and recitations; by taking suitable occasions to converse with their pupils privately on this interesting subject; and by all other means, incapable of being minutely specified, by which they may foster true experimental religion, and unreserved devotedness to God.

ARTICLE VI.
Of the Students.

Section 1. Every student applying for admission to the Theological Seminary, shall produce satisfactory testimonials that he possesses good natural talents, and is of a prudent and discreet deportment; that he is in full communion with some regular Church: that he has passed through a regular course of academical study; or, wanting this, he shall submit himself to an examination in regard to the branches of literature taught in such a course.

Section 2. The first six months of every student in the Seminary shall be considered as probationary; and if, at the end of this period, any student shall appear to the professors not qualified to proceed in his studies, they shall so report him to

[426]

the board of directors, who, if they are of the same opinion with the professors, shall dismiss him from the Seminary.

Section 3. The hours of study and of recreation for the students shall be fixed by the professors, with the concurrence of the directors; and every student shall pay a strict regard to the rules established relative to this subject.

Section 4. Every student shall be obliged to write on such theological and other subjects, as may be prescribed to him by the professors. In the first year every student shall be obliged to produce a written composition on such subjects, at least once in every month. In the second year, once in three weeks. In the third year, once in two weeks. Once a month each student shall also commit to memory a piece of his own composition, and pronounce it in public, before the professors and students. It shall not exceed fifteen minutes in the delivery.

Section 5. Every student shall not only preserve an exemplary moral character, but shall be expected to treat his teachers with the greatest deference and respect, and all other persons with civility.

Section 6. Every student shall yield a prompt and ready obedience to all the lawful requisitions of the professors and directors.

Section 7. Diligence and industry in study shall be considered as indispensable in every student, unless the want of health shall prevent, of which the professors shall take cognizance, and make the suitable allowance.

Section 8. Strict temperance in meat and drink is expected of every student, with cleanliness and neatness in his dress and habits; while all excessive expense in clothing is strictly prohibited.

Section 9. Every student, before he takes his standing in the Seminary, shall subscribe the following declaration, viz.—
"Deeply impressed with a sense of the importance of improving in knowledge, prudence, and piety, in my preparation for the Gospel Ministry, I solemnly promise, in a reliance on divine grace, that I will faithfully and diligently attend on all the instructions of this Seminary, and that I will conscientiously and vigilantly observe all the rules and regulations specified in the plan for its instruction and government, so

far as the same relate to the students; and that I will obey all the lawful requisitions, and readily yield to all the wholesome admonitions of the professors and directors of the Seminary, while I shall continue a member of it."

Section 10. There shall be two vacations in the Seminary, of six weeks continuance each, in every year. The spring vacation shall commence on the Monday immediately preceding the third Thursday of May. The vacation in the autumn shall commence on the first Wednesday of October.

Section 11. No student shall pay any thing for instruction to any of the professors; but if any student, parent, or guardian, be disposed to contribute to the support of the Institution, it shall be thankfully accepted, and go into the general funds.

ARTICLE VII.
Of the Library.

Section 1. To obtain ultimately a complete theological Library shall be considered as a leading object of the Institution.

Section 2. It shall be the duty of the directors to present to the General Assembly, a catalogue of the most necessary books for the commencement of a library, and recommend the purchase of such a number as the state of the funds will permit.

Section 3. It shall be the duty of the professors to procure and keep a large folio, to be denominated, *The Prospectus of a Catalogue of a Theological Library*. In this folio, divided into proper heads, each professor shall, at his pleasure, enter, in its proper place, the title of such books as he shall deliberately judge to be proper for the library. The board of directors, or the members of it individually, may do the same. From this folio it shall be the duty of the directors to select such books as they think most necessary, and as the sum appropriated for the current year will purchase, and recommend their purchase to the Assembly. The Assembly shall annually decide by vote, what sum of money, for the current year, shall be laid out in the purchase of books.

Section 4. A suitable room or apartment shall be assigned for the library. The shelves for the books shall be divided into compartments or alcoves, and if any one of them be filled, or nearly so, by a donor, his name shall be conspicuously placed over it.

Section 5. A librarian shall be appointed by the Assembly.

Section 6. No book shall be permitted, on any occasion, to be carried from the Seminary.

Section 7. A book of donations shall be carefully kept by the librarian, in which shall be entered, by him, the books given to the library, the time when, and the name of the donor.

Section 8. Regulations for the use of the library, not inconsistent with the provisions of this Article, shall be detailed in a system of by-laws, for that purpose; to be draughted by the first librarian, and occasionally modified and added to, as circumstances shall require, by his successors; which regulations, after being ratified by the board of directors, shall be authoritative.

ARTICLE VIII.

Of the Funds.

Section 1. The funds of the Institution shall be kept, at all times, entirely distinct and separate from all other monies or funds whatsoever; and they shall be deposited in the hands of such corporation, or disposed of for safe keeping and improvement, in such other manner, as the General Assembly shall direct.

Section 2. The board of directors shall, from time to time, as they may see proper, lay before the Assembly plans for the improvement of the funds, and propositions for the appropriation or such sums as they may think necessary for particular purposes.

Section 3. No money shall, at any time, be drawn from the funds, but by an appropriation and order of the Assembly for the purpose.

Section 4. A fair statement shall annually be laid before the Assembly, by the proper officer, of the amount of the funds belonging to the Seminary, of the items which constitute that amount, and of the expenditures in detail for the preceding year.

Section 5. The intention and directions of testators or donors, in regard to monies or other property left or given to the Seminary, shall, at all times, be sacredly regarded. And if any individual, or any number of individuals, not greater than three, shall, by will, or during his or their lives, found or endow a professorship or professorships, a scholarship or scholarships, or a fund or funds, destined to special purposes, said professorships, scholarships, or funds, shall for ever afterwards be called and known by the name or names of those who founded or endowed them.

Section 6. After supporting the professors, and defraying the other necessary charges of the Seminary, the funds shall be applied, as far as circumstances will admit, to defray or diminish the expenses of those students who may need pecuniary aid, as well as to lessen, generally, the expense of a residence at the Seminary.

# 2

# Bibliographical Note

The only history of Princeton Theological Seminary is *Princeton Theological Seminary: A Narrative History, 1812-1992* by William K. Selden, printed by Princeton University Press in 1992. About a hundred pages cover the 1812 through 1929– period of the seminary's history. The events leading to the founding of Princeton Seminary are carefully presented by Mark A. Noll in "The Founding of Princeton Seminary," *Westminster Theological Journal* 42 (1979): 72-110. An excellent account of the early Princeton period is the book by Lefferts A. Loetscher, *Facing the Enlightenment and Pietism: Archibald Alexander and the Founding of Princeton Theological Seminary* (Westport, Conn.: Greenwood Press, 1983).

Numerous articles and books on specific aspects or periods of the Princeton Seminary history are indicated in the footnotes of the book.

For the early history of Princeton College, see Mark A. Noll, *Princeton and the Republic, 1768-1822: The Search for a Christian Enlightenment in the Era of Samuel Stanhope Smith* (Princeton: Princeton University Press, 1989).

Biographical information on the major Princetonians is summarized below. Further data on the faculty and students of Princeton Seminary can be found in the *Biographical Catalogue of the Princeton Theological Seminary, 1815-1932*, compiled by Edward Howell Roberts (Princeton: Trustees of the Theological Seminary of the Presbyterian Church, 1933). The biographical summaries of the faculty in appendix 3 are adapted from the *Biographical Catalogue.*

The biography of Archibald Alexander was prepared by his son James Waddel Alexander, *The Life of Archibald Alexander* (New York: Charles Scribner, 1854). See Charles Hodge's review of the above work, "Memoir of Dr. Alexander," *BRPR*

27 (1855): 133-59. In November 1854, Francis Wayland wrote to J. W. Alexander: "I have just completed your admirable Memoir of your father—now with God. A more charming biography I have never read. While you write as a son, it is as a son of Archibald Alexander. There is nothing filial that is not admirable, and not a word that could not be attested even more strongly by a host of witnesses. A more beautiful or noble specimen of Christian character can hardly be conceived. His gifts were great and abundant beyond the common lot of humanity; and God placed them where they shone with a radiance that illumined the whole church of Christ." *Life of Francis Wayland* 2: 174-75. See also Lefferts A. Loetscher, *Facing the Enlightenment and Pietism: Archibald Alexander and the Founding of Princeton Theological Seminary;* John DeWitt, "Archibald Alexander's Preparation for his Professorship," *PTR* 3 (1905): 573-94; John A. Mackay, "Archibald Alexander (1772-1851): Founding Father," in *Sons of the Prophets: Leaders in Protestantism from Princeton Seminary,* ed. Hugh T. Kerr (Princeton: Princeton University Press, 1963), 3-21.

The biography of Samuel Miller was prepared by his son, also named Samuel Miller, *The Life of Samuel Miller,* 2 vols. (Philadelphia: Claxton, Remsen & Haffelfinger, 1869). See also Belden C. Lane, "Democracy and the Ruling Eldership: Samuel Miller's Response to Tensions Between Clerical Power and Lay Authority in Early Nineteenth Century America" (Ph.D. diss., Princeton Theological Seminary, 1976); and John DeWitt, "The Intellectual Life of Samuel Miller," *PTR* 4 (1906): 168-90.

With Archibald Alexander and Samuel Miller, Ashbel Green was one of the major "founders" of Princeton Seminary and chairman of its board of directors from 1812 to 1848. For his life, see *The Life of Ashbel Green, V. D. M., begun to be written by himself in his eighty-second year, and continued till his eighty-fourth; prepared for the press, at the Author's request, by Joseph H. Jones, Pastor of the Sixth Presbyterian Church, Philadelphia* (New York: Robert Carter and Brothers, 1849). See also the review of the above work by J. W. Alexander, *BRPR* 21 (1849): 563-82; and the article by Robert E. Lewis, "Ashbel Green, 1742-1848—Preacher, Educator, Editor," *JPHS* 35

(1957): 141-56.

For the life of Charles Hodge, see A. A. Hodge, *The Life of Charles Hodge, D.D. LL.D., Professor in the Theological Seminary, Princeton, N. J.* (New York: Charles Scribner's Sons, 1880). Half of this volume is made up of Charles Hodge's diary and letters. Of the numerous books and dissertations on Charles Hodge's theology, two have especially good treatments of his life—Charles A. Jones, "Charles Hodge, The Keeper of Orthodoxy: The Method, Purpose and Meaning of His Apologetic" (Ph.D. diss., Drew University, 1989); and John W. Stewart, "The Tethered Theology: Biblical Criticism, Common Sense Philosophy, and the Princeton Theologians" (Ph.D. diss., University of Michigan, 1990).

Valuable information concerning the life of J. W. Alexander is found in John Hall's *Forty Years' Familiar Letters of James W. Alexander,* 2 vols. (New York: Charles Scribner, 1860). During his second year at college, J. W. Alexander began a correspondence with John Hall, a Philadelphia friend, which continued for forty years (1819-1859) and included almost 800 letters from Alexander. Charles Hodge urged Hall to publish the correspondence, saying that it "would be a unique work. It would be a literary, a theological, a religious and a conversational history of the past forty years" (Charles Hodge to John Hall, September 28, 1859).

The life of J. A. Alexander is found in *The Life of Joseph Addison Alexander,* 2 vols., by his nephew Henry Carrington Alexander (New York: Charles Scribner's, 1870). H. C. Alexander, the son of J. W. Alexander, was pastor of the same church his father served at Charlotte Court House, Virginia. He later became professor of New Testament at Union Theological Seminary in Virginia.

William Henry Green's life is sketched in John D. Davis's "William Henry Green," *PRR* 11 (1900), 377-96. See also "The Jubilee of Prof. William Henry Green," *PRR* 7 (1896): 507-21. Dwayne Davis Cox's M.A. thesis (University of Louisville, 1976), "William Henry Green: Princeton Theologian," and dissertations by John W. Stewart and Marion A. Taylor provide valuable information about Green, as well as his Princeton contemporaries. See John W. Stewart, "The Tethered Theology: Biblical Criticism, Common Sense

Philosophy, and the Princeton Theologians, 1812-1860" (Ph.D. diss., University of Michigan, 1990), and Marion A. Taylor, "The Old Testament in the Old Princeton School" (Ph.D. diss., Yale University, 1986).

An important source of information for the early Princeton Seminary history is *The Biblical Repertory and Princeton Review Index Volume from 1825 to 1868* (Philadelphia: Peter Walker, 1871). Part 1 is a "Retrospect of the History of the Princeton Review" by Charles Hodge. Part 2, an index to the authors of articles in the *Biblical Repertory*, contains brief biographies of the early Princeton figures and their contemporaries. Parts 3 and 4 are indexes to articles published in the journal between 1825 and 1868.

For helpful introductions to the thought of the major Princeton figures with selections from their writings, see Mark A. Noll, ed., *The Princeton Theology, 1812-1921: Scripture, Science, and Theological Method from Archibald Alexander to Benjamin Breckinridge Warfield* (Grand Rapids: Baker Book House, 1983). This book contains a "Selective Bibliography" which includes information on manuscripts; lists of bibliographies and indexes; books of the major Princeton theologians; secondary works about Princeton Seminary and general studies on the Princeton Theology; and a checklist of dissertations and theses on the Princeton theologians.

The history of the Princeton journals up to the year 1868 is found in Charles Hodge's "Retrospect of the History of the Princeton Review," in *The Biblical Repertory and Princeton Review Index Volume*. For more recent articles on the complete history of these journals (until 1929) see "American Calvinism Speaks" by Leslie W. Sloat in the *Westminster Theological Journal* 7 (1944-45): 1-22 and 112-35; and "The Princeton Review" by Mark Noll in the *Westminster Theological Journal* 50 (1988): 283-304.

# 3

# Biographical Summaries of Faculty

ARCHIBALD ALEXANDER, D.D., LL.D.             1812-1851

Born, near Lexington, Virginia, April 17, 1772; Timber Ridge Academy, Virginia, 1782-88; tutor, 1788-89; private study; itinerant missionary, Virginia, 1792; ordained, Hanover Presbytery, June 7, 1794; pastor, Briery and Cub Creek, Virginia, 1794-97; pastor, Briery, 1797-98; president, Hampden-Sydney College, 1797-1801, 1802-1807; pastor, Pine Street Church, Philadelphia, Pennsylvania, 1807-12; professor, Didactic and Polemic Theology, Princeton Theological Seminary, 1812-40, Pastoral and Polemic Theology, 1840-51, Pastoral and Polemic Theology and Church Government, 1851; died, Princeton, New Jersey, October 22, 1851. D.D., College of New Jersey, 1810; Moderator, General Assembly, 1807.

SAMUEL MILLER, D.D., LL.D.             1813-1849

Born, Dover, Delaware, October 30, 1769; University of Pennsylvania, 1788; theological study at home; ordained, New York Presbytery, June 5, 1793; associate pastor, First Church, New York City, 1793-1801; pastor, Wall Street Church, New York City, 1801-13; professor, Ecclesiastical History and Church Government, Princeton Theological Seminary, 1813-49, professor emeritus, 1849-50; died, Princeton, New Jersey, January 7, 1850. DD, University of Pennsylvania, 1804.

CHARLES HODGE, D.D., LL.D.             1820-1878

Born, Philadelphia, Pennsylvania, December 27, 1797; College of New Jersey, 1815; Princeton Theological Seminary,

1816-19; ordained, New Brunswick Presbytery, November 28, 1821; missionary, Falls of Schuylkill, Philadelphia, Arsenal and Woodbury, New Jersey, 1819-20; instructor, Original Languages of Scripture, Princeton Theological Seminary, 1820-22; professor, Oriental and Biblical Literature, 1822-40; study in Europe, 1826-28; professor, Exegetical and Didactic Theology, 1840-54, Exegetical, Didactic and Polemic Theology, 1854-78; died, Princeton, New Jersey, June 19, 1878. D.D., Rutgers University, 1834, LL.D., Washington College, Pennsylvania, 1864; Moderator, General Assembly, 1846.

### JOHN BRECKINRIDGE, D.D. 1836-1838

Born, Cabell's Dale, near Lexington, Kentucky, July 4, 1797; College of New Jersey, 1818; Princeton Theological Seminary, 1819-22; tutor, College of New Jersey, 1820-21; chaplain, Congress, 1822-23; ordained, West Lexington Presbytery, September 10, 1823; pastor, Second (McChord) Church, Lexington, Kentucky, 1823-26; pastor, Second Church, Baltimore, Maryland, 1826-31; corresponding secretary, Board of Education, 1831-36; professor, Pastoral Theology and Missionary Instruction, Princeton Theological Seminary, 1836-38; secretary and general agent, Board of Foreign Missions, 1838-40; stated supply, New Orleans, Louisiana; died, Cabell's Dale, Kentucky, August 4, 1841. D.D., Union College, 1835.

### JOSEPH ADDISON ALEXANDER, D.D. 1838-1860

Born, Philadelphia, Pennsylvania, April 24, 1809; College of New Jersey, 1826; private study; teacher, Edgehill School, Princeton, New Jersey, 1829-30; College of New Jersey, MA, 1829; adjunct professor, Ancient Languages and Literature, College of New Jersey, 1830-32; University of Halle and University of Berlin, 1833-34; ordained, New Brunswick Presbytery, April 24, 1839; assistant instructor, Oriental and Biblical Literature, Princeton Theological Seminary, 1833-38, associate professor, 1838-40, professor, 1840-51, Biblical and Ecclesiastical History, 1851-59, Hellenistic and New Testament Literature, 1859-60; died, Princeton, New Jersey, January 28, 1860. D.D., Franklin and Marshall College, 1845.

JAMES WADDEL ALEXANDER, D.D.                1849-1851

Born, Louisa County, Virginia, March 13, 1804; College of New Jersey, 1820; Princeton Theological Seminary, 1822-24; tutor, College of New Jersey, 1824-25; ordained, Hanover Presbytery, March 3, 1827; stated supply, Charlotte Court House, Virginia, 1826, pastor, 1827-28; pastor, First Church, Trenton, New Jersey, 1829-32; editor, *Presbyterian*, 1832-33; professor, Rhetoric and Latin Language and Literature, College of New Jersey, 1833-34; pastor, Duane Street Church, New York City, 1844-49; professor, Ecclesiastical History and Church Government, Princeton Theological Seminary, 1849-51; pastor, Fifth Avenue Church and 19th Street Church, New York City, 1851-59; died, Red Sweet Springs, Virginia, July 31, 1859.   D.D., Lafayette College, 1843, Harvard University, 1854.

WILLIAM HENRY GREEN, D.D., LL.D.       1846-1849 and
                                                          1851-1900

Born, Groveville, New Jersey, January 27, 1825; Lafayette College, 1840; tutor, Lafayette College, 1840-42; Princeton Theological Seminary, 1843-46; teacher, Mathematics, Lafayette College, 1843-44; instructor, Hebrew, Princeton Theological Seminary, 1846-49; stated supply, Second Church, Princeton, 1847-49; ordained evangelist, New Brunswick Presbytery, May 24, 1848; pastor, Central Church, Philadelphia, Pennsylvania, 1849-51; professor, Biblical and Oriental Literature, Princeton Theological Seminary, 1851-59, Oriental and Old Testament Literature, 1859-1900; died, Princeton, New Jersey, February 10, 1900. D.D., College of New Jersey, 1857 and University of Edinburgh, 1884; LL.D., Rutgers University, 1873; Moderator, General Assembly, 1891.

ALEXANDER TAGGART McGILL, D.D., LL.D.    1854-1883

Born, Canonsburg, Pennsylvania, February 24, 1807; Jefferson College, 1826; lawyer, 1826-31; Canonsburg Theological Seminary, Pennsylvania, 1831-34; ordained Associate Reformed, Carlisle Presbytery, 1835; pastor, Perry and York churches, Carlisle, 1835-38; pastor, Second Presbyterian

Church, Carlisle, 1838-42; professor, Ecclesiastical History and Church Government, Western Theological Seminary, 1842-52, 53-54; professor, Columbia Theological Seminary, 1852-53; professor, Pastoral Theology, Church Government and Homiletics, Princeton Theological Seminary, 1854-59, Church History and Practical Theology, 1859-60, Ecclesiastical History and Church Government, 1860-61, Ecclesiastical History, Homiletics and Pastoral Theology, 1861-83, professor emeritus, 1883-89; died, Princeton, New Jersey, January 13, 1889. D.D., Franklin and Marshall College, 1842; LL.D., College of New Jersey, 1868; Moderator, General Assembly, 1848.

## CASPAR WISTAR HODGE, D.D., LL.D,     1860-91

Born, Princeton, New Jersey, February 21, 1830; College of New Jersey, 1848; Princeton Theological Seminary, 1849-53; tutor, College of New Jersey, 1850-51; teacher, Princeton, New Jersey, 1852-53; ordained, New York Presbytery, Nov-ember 5, 1854; stated supply, Ainslie Street Church, Williamsburgh, New York, 1853-54, pastor, 1854-56; pastor, Oxford, Pennsylvania, 1856-60; professor, New Testament Literature and Biblical Greek, Princeton Theological Seminary, 1860-79, New Testament Literature and Exegesis, 1879-91; died, Princeton, New Jersey, September 27, 1891. D.D., College of New Jersey, 1865; LL.D., College of New Jersey, 1891.

## JAMES CLEMENT MOFFAT, D.D.     1861-1888

Born, Glencree, Scotland, May 30, 1811; College of New Jersey, 1835; tutor, New Haven, Connecticut, 1835-37; tutor, Greek, Princeton, New Jersey, 1837-39; College of New Jersey, 1838, MA; professor, Greek and Latin, Lafayette College, 1839-41; professor, Latin and Modern History, Miami University (of Ohio), 1841-52; professor, Greek and Hebrew, Cincinnati Seminary, Ohio, 1852-53; professor, Latin and History, College of New Jersey, 1854-61, lecturer, Greek Literature, 1861-77; professor, Church History, Princeton Theological Seminary, 1861-88, professor emeritus, 1888-90; died, Princeton, New Jersey, June 7, 1890. D.D., Miami University, 1853.

# NOTES

# NOTES

## Foreword

1. J. W. Alexander, *The Life of Archibald Alexander* (repr. Sprinkle Publications, Harrisonburg, Va., 1991).

## Preface

1. Archibald Alexander, *Biographical Sketches of the Founder, and Principal Alumni of the Log College, together with an account of the Revivals of Religion, under their ministry* (Princeton: J. T. Robinson, 1845; repr. The Banner of Truth Trust, 1968), 9.
2. *The Centennial Celebration of the Theological Seminary of the Presbyterian Church in the United States of America at Princeton, New Jersey* (Princeton, 1912), 558. The official name of the seminary was the Theological Seminary of the Presbyterian Church in the United States of America at Princeton, New Jersey.
3. William McLoughlin, ed., *The American Evangelicals, 1800-1900* (New York: Harper and Row, 1968), 1.
4. The only complete history of Princeton Seminary is the recent work by William K. Selden, *Princeton Theological Seminary: A Narrative History, 1812-1992* (Princeton: Princeton University Press, 1992). About one hundred pages of Selden's short history chronicles the seminary's first century.
5. Lefferts A. Loetscher, *Facing the Enlightenment and Pietism: Archibald Alexander and the Founding of Princeton Theological Seminary* (Westport, Conn.: Greenwood Press, 1983), x.
6. *LSM* 2: 147.
7. *LSM* 1: x.
8. Mark A. Noll, ed., *The Princeton Theology, 1821-1921: Scripture, Science, and Theological Method from Archibald Alexander to Benjamin Breckinridge Warfield* (Grand Rapids: Baker Book House, 1983), 11.
9. *Centennial Celebration of the Theological Seminary*, 342.

## 1. Nassau Hall

1. *George Whitefield's Journals* (The Banner of Truth Trust, 1960), 354-55.

2. Frederick S. Osborne, "Two Hundred Years of Princeton University," *JPHS* 24 (1946), 90-91.

3. Iain H. Murray, *Jonathan Edwards: A New Biography* (The Banner of Truth Trust, 1987), 405-06, 413.

4. Murray, *Jonathan Edwards*, 416.

5. Murray, *Jonathan Edwards*, 431.

6. The College of New Jersey was often called Nassau Hall or Princeton College.

7. A few months after her husband's death, twenty-six-year-old Esther died of an "acute fever," leaving her two infants, Sally and Aaron. Aaron Burr, Jr., was reared by his uncle. He graduated from Princeton in 1772 and practiced law. He became the third vice-president of the United States (1801-1805). Burr killed his political rival Alexander Hamilton in a duel in 1804. His turbulent political career ended with his arrest and trial for treason in 1807. Sadly, he lived "without God" and died, virtually friendless, in 1836, asking that he might be buried as near as possible to the *feet* of his father and grandfather in the Princeton burial ground.

8. B. B. Warfield, "Edwards and the New England Theology," in *Studies in Theology* (New York: Oxford University Press, 1932), 527.

9. Wheaton J. Lane, ed., *Pictorial History of Princeton* (Princeton: Princeton University Press, 1947), 3.

10. Allen C. Guelzo, *Edwards on the Will: A Century of American Theological Debate* (Middletown, Conn.: Wesleyan University Press, 1989), 176.

11. Seeing Samuel Davies walk through a courtyard, someone said: "He seems as an ambassador of some mighty king." Ezra Hall Gillett, *History of the Presbyterian Church in the United States of America* (Philadelphia: Presbyterian Publishing Committee, 1864), 1: 123. Dr. Martyn Lloyd-Jones considered Samuel Davies the greatest American preacher. D. M. Lloyd-Jones, *Knowing the Times: Addresses Delivered on Various Occasions 1942-1977* (The Banner of Truth Trust, 1989), 263.

12. These lectures were composed shortly after his arrival in America in 1768 and first published in John Witherspoon's collected *Works* in 1800, six years after his death. *The Works of the Rev. John Witherspoon, D.D., LL.D., Late President of the College at Princeton, New Jersey*, 4 vols. (Philadelphia: William W. Woodward, 1800-1801), 3: 268-374. See also Jack Scott, ed., *An Annotated Edition of "Lectures on Moral Philosophy" by John Witherspoon* (Newark: University of Delaware Press, 1982).

13. L. Gordon Tait, "Witherspoon: *Lectures on Moral Philosophy*," *American Presbyterians* 66 (1988): 223-28.

14. John Witherspoon, *Lectures on Moral Philosophy and Eloquence* (Philadelphia, 1810), 141-42.

15. *Works of John Witherspoon* 4: 10, 11.

16. Leonard J. Trinterud, *The Forming of an American Tradition: A Re-examination of Colonial Presbyterianism* (Philadelphia: Westminster Press, 1949), 243.

17. See John Witherspoon, *The Dominion of Providence* (Philadelphia, 1776).

18. *The Princeton Book. A Series of Sketches pertaining to the History, Organisation and Present Condition of the College of New Jersey.* By Officers and Graduates of the College (Boston: Houghton, Osgood and Company, 1879), 357.

19. William Buell Sprague, *Annals of the American Pulpit or Commemorative Notices of Distinguished American Clergymen of Various Denominations, from the Early Settlement of the Country to the Close of the Year Eighteen Hundred and Fifty-five. With Historical Introductions*, 9 vols. (New York: Robert Carter and Brothers, 1856-69; repr. New York: Arno Press, 1969), 3: 300.

20. *LAA*, 98-99.

21. Ashbel Green made this remark to the Princeton Seminary students in 1831, *BRTR* 3 (1831): 357.

22. Mark A. Noll, *Princeton and the Republic, 1768-1822: The Search for a Christian Enlightenment in the Era of Samuel Stanhope Smith* (Princeton: Princeton University Press, 1989), 53.

23. Thomas Jefferson Wertenbaker, *Princeton, 1746-1896* (Princeton: Princeton University Press, 1946), 80.

24. Noll, *Princeton and the Republic*, 83.

25. *LAG*, 126.

26. *LAG*, 127.

27. *LAG*, 130.

28. *LAG*, 143.

29. *LAG*, 146.

30. Noll, *Princeton and the Republic*, 55.

31. Edmund S. Morgan, "The American Revolution Considered as an Intellectual Movement," in *Paths of American Thought*, ed. Arthur M. Schlesinger, Jr., and Morton M. White (Boston: Houghton Mifflin Co., 1963), 11.

32. A twentieth-century Princeton Seminary president, himself a Scot, John A. Mackay, has called John Witherspoon "the most outstanding Scotsman ever to settle in the Western World." John A. Mackay, "Witherspoon of Paisley and

Princeton," in *Theology Today* 18 (1962), 475.

33. *LAA*, 267.
34. According to Mark A. Noll, Smith's *Essay* was "the most significant scientific defense of a science of morals in the early history of the United States." Noll, *Princeton and the Republic*, 196.
35. Noll, *Princeton and the Republic*, 133, 182, 247.

## 2. *The Seminary*

1. At Princeton's centennial in 1912, John Crawford Scouller, moderator of the United Presbyterian Church of North America, said: "In the early history of our branch of the Church, we built the log-cabin school alongside of the log-cabin church, and afterwards we built the log-cabin seminary," *Centennial Celebration of the Theological Seminary*, 537.
2. Kollock became pastor of the Independent Presbyterian Church in Savannah, Georgia, where he served until his death in 1819.
3. Noll, *Princeton and the Republic*, 170-71.
4. *Report of a Committee of the General Assembly of the Presbyterian Church Exhibiting the Plan of a Theological Seminary* (New York: J. Seymour, 1810). See Appendix 1. Over a hundred years later, B. B. Warfield called the "Plan" a "great document," and added that "the Seminary has been trying to grow up to it ever since." *JPHS* 9 (1918): 256.
5. *LAG*, 334.
6. Noll, *Princeton and the Republic*, 263.
7. *Plan of a Theological Seminary*, 4-5.
8. *LAA*, 327-28.
9. *LCH*, 18.
10. *The Sermon, Delivered at the Inauguration of Rev. Archibald Alexander, D. D. as Professor of Didactic and Polemic Theology, in the Theological Seminary of the Presbyterian Church, in the United States of America. To Which are Added, the Professor's Inaugural Address, and the Charge to the Professor and Students* (New York: Whiting and Watson, 1812).
11. *LSM*, 1: 357.
12. Noll, *Princeton and the Republic*, 249, 258. At Smith's death, Samuel Miller wrote the epitaph for his tomb.
13. Sprague, *Annals* 3: 481.
14. Mark A. Noll writes: "To nurture the rising generation,

Green trusted piety attended by faithful learning, Smith the reverse." Noll, *Princeton and the Republic*, 287.

15. Green edited the first edition of Witherspoon's *Works* (Philadelphia, 1800-1801) and wrote (some time after 1829) "The Life of the Rev'd John Witherspoon"—based on Green's personal recollections, unpublished manuscripts, and a collection of Witherspoon's letters.

16. Noll, *Princeton and the Republic*, 274.

17. *LAG*, 612.

## 3.  *Archibald Alexander*

1.  *LAA*, 25.
2.  Loetscher, *Archibald Alexander*, 17.
3.  *LAA*, 35-36.
4.  *LAA*, 39-41.
5.  *LAA*, 43-44.
6.  John Flavel studied at Oxford and was presbyterially ordained at Salisbury in 1650.  He was called as pastor of the church in the port city of Dartmouth during the Commonwealth.  He was ejected at the restoration of episcopacy in 1662 but continued to serve his seafaring congregation, preaching from a rock in the harbor.  The Banner of Truth Trust has reprinted *The Works of John Flavel* in six volumes.
7.  LAA, 44-45.  When Archibald Alexander was dying, the secretary in the publishing department of the American Tract Society visited him and read to him from Flavel's *Method of Grace.*  Alexander listened carefully and then commented: "All this carries me back to past scenes as if they were but yesterday.  When I was a thoughtless youth, I passed some time in a family where was a venerable, pious lady, whose sight was dim, but who was greatly attached to Flavel's works, and often requested me to read them to her.  I read to her this very work.  I would read till the truths pierced my own heart, and affected me so that I was obliged to stop, when I would excuse myself till the next day.  I would then read again, and again be obliged to stop; and those impressions never left me till I found peace in Christ."  Archibald Alexander, *Practical Truths* (New York: American Tract Society, 1857), 386.
8.  *LAA*, 44-47.
9.  *LAA*, 64.
10. *LAA*, 72.  In his "Memoir of Dr. Alexander," Charles Hodge

wrote concerning Alexander's conversion: "The narrative above given is surely adapted to teach us in matters of religion to look not at processes, but at results. If a man is led to forsake sin, to trust in Christ, to worship him and to keep his commandments, it is of small consequence how these results were brought about. The attempt, however, is constantly made to force our experience through the same steps of progress with that of others. God dealeth with souls in bringing them to Christ and holiness variously, just as the wind, the emblem of the Spirit, is sometimes scarce perceptible though all-powerful—sometimes a zephyr, and sometimes a storm—yet in every form accomplishes the same great work. Delay, suffering, and waste of strength would be prevented, if men could learn wisdom by the experience of others, and be induced to believe that Christ will accept them just as they are. . . ." *BRPR* 27 (1855): 150-51.

11. *LAA*, 16.

12. J. W. Alexander wrote on April 5, 1847: "I have recovered my father's trial sermon, preached fifty-six years ago, aet. 19. He was very boyish, and the text was Jer. 1: 7. The style is exactly that of his present writing." *LJWA* 2: 67.

13. *LAA*, 135.

14. Loetscher, *Archibald Alexander*, 364.

15. *LAA*, 116.

16. *LAA*, 525-26.

17. *LAA*, 195. In his *History of Hampden-Sydney College*, Herbert C. Bradshaw entitles the chapter on Alexander "Slow Climb Out of Doldrums: The Administration of Archibald Alexander."

18. Speece, who studied theology with William Graham at Liberty Hall, became one of the better-known Virginia preachers of his day. Rice organized the First Presbyterian Church of Richmond, Virginia, and in 1824 became president of the Theological Seminary at Hampden-Sydney (later Union Theological Seminary in Virginia). John Holt Rice's brother Benjamin married Archibald Alexander's sister.

19. *LAA*, 204.

20. *LAA*, 255.

21. *LAA*, 265.

22. There is a famous sketch of James Waddel and his preaching in William Wirt's *British Spy*. Wirt described the

dilapidated old wooden building and the feeble, blind preacher and added: "It was a day of the administration of the Sacrament; and his subject was, of course, the passion of our Saviour. I had heard the subject handled a thousand times—I thought it exhausted long ago. Little did I suppose that in the wild woods of America, I was to meet with a man, whose eloquence would give to this topic a new and more sublime pathos than I had ever before witnessed." It was in this sermon that Waddel spoke the often-quoted sentence from Rousseau, "Socrates died like a philosopher; but Jesus Christ like a God!" See Clarence Edward Macartney, "James Waddell—The Blind Preacher of Virginia," *PTR* 19 (1921): 620-29.

23. Clarence Macartney, who was himself a gifted preacher, wrote that "there is an eloquence associated with the preaching of the saving grace of God in Christ which obtains nowhere else. . . . Waddell . . . had this glowing evangelical eloquence. Paul had it; Spurgeon had it; and to a greater or less degree it has been possessed by thousands of humble preachers of the Cross of Christ. . . ." *PTR* 19 (1921): 623-24.

24. *LAA*, 227.

25. In colonial Virginia five successive generations of Harrisons compiled almost identical records as gentlemen of education and wealth, burgesses, councillors, and militia colonels. William Henry Harrison was the grandfather of Benjamin Harrison, the twenty-third president of the United States.

26. *LAA*, 275.

27. *LAA*, 104.

28. *LAA*, 403.

29. New Side Presbyterians, led by Gilbert Tennent and others of the Log College, supported the revival and forced a schism in the Presbyterian Church in 1741 which lasted until 1758.

30. The simple Georgian structure was rebuilt in 1837 and 1857 (using the original walls and roof) in the Greek Revival style popular in the new republic. It is the only colonial Presbyterian church building still standing in Philadelphia.

31. In 1560 John Calvin suggested the use of communion tokens and that same year they were used by Scottish Presbyterians. Members attended the preparatory services and were examined by the minister and elders. Those who

were judged ready to receive the sacrament were issued tokens, which were collected by the elders prior to the administration of the Lord's Supper on Sunday. Most tokens were cast or stamped in lead or pewter, but other materials—including brass, silver, ceramic, wood, and paper—were also used.

32. *LAA*, 280.
33. Hughes O. Gibbons, *A History of Old Pine Street* (Philadelphia, 1905), 145-46.
34. Charles Hodge wrote that "in some departments of learning [Dr. Alexander] was no doubt surpassed by many of his brethren; but it is believed that none of his coevals had read more extensively in the theology of the sixteenth and seventeenth centuries, including Romanist and Lutheran, as well as Reformed divines." *BRPR* 27 (1855): 140.
35. *LAA*, 295.
36. *LCH*, 48.
37. The house occupied by the Alexanders was located where the Parish House of Trinity Episcopal Church now stands. It was moved later to 134 Mercer Street, where it was greatly altered.
38. *LAA*, 375.
39. *LAA*, 353.
40. B. B. Warfield, "The Beginning of Princeton Seminary," *The Presbyterian*, May 1, 1912, 5.
41. B. B. Warfield, *The Expansion of the Seminary: A Historical Sketch* (Princeton, 1914), 4.
42. *LAA*, 376.
43. *LCH*, 26, 28.

## 4. *Samuel Miller*

1. *LSM* 1: 326.
2. *LSM* 1: 359.
3. *LSM* 1: 38.
4. *LSM* 1: 53.
5. In 1840 Miller published a life of his teacher, *Memoir of the Rev. Charles Nisbet, D.D., late President of Dickinson College, Carlisle* (New York, 1840). Nisbet rarely attended the meetings of the General Assembly and when he was present seldom took an active part in the proceedings. He sometimes came to Philadelphia during the sessions of the assembly but generally for the purpose of relaxing or seeing friends. Samuel

Miller often told the story of a conversation between Dr. John Mason of the Associate Reformed church of New York City and Dr. Nisbet. Mason: "Well, Doctor, I find you sometimes come to Philadelphia during the sessions of the General Assembly." Nisbet: "Yes, I am not a member, but I like to meet my friends, and see a little of what is going on." Mason: "But do you not sometimes go into the Assembly, and listen to its proceedings?" Nisbet: "Yes, I sometimes go in for the *benefit of hearing*, and then I come out for the *benefit of not hearing*." Mason: "Well, Doctor, which is the greater benefit?" Nisbet: "Indeed, mon, it's hard to strike the balance." Sprague, *Annals* 3: 457-58.

6. As a boy, John Rodgers once held a candle for George Whitefield as he preached in Philadelphia. He became so interested in the sermon that, much to his embarrassment, he let the candle fall. Years later, when he was a pastor in New York City, Rodgers asked Whitefield, who was preaching for him, if he remembered the incident. The great evangelist replied that he had often wondered what had become of "that earnest boy." *JPHS* 12 (1924-27): 499.

7. *LSM* 1: 85. Samuel Miller wrote the *Memoirs of the Rev. John Rodgers, D.D.* (New York, 1813).

8. *LSM* 1: 88.

9. *LSM* 1: 116-17.

10. *LSM* 2: 481.

11. *LSM* 1: 152. Sarah wrote a memoir of her life up to the year 1807. It is addressed to her husband—"my best earthly friend"—and is included in Samuel Miller's biography.

12. *LSM* 1: 163, 171, 193, 261. There would be later times of introspection, such as in 1811 when Sarah was not only doubting again her own salvation but even that of her husband! *LSM* 1: 319.

13. In New York, Samuel Miller was a member of the Masons; after his move to Princeton he never attended Masonic meetings and advised his sons not to become Masons. *LSM* 1: 99.

14. Samuel Miller, *A Brief Retrospect of the Eighteenth Century. Part the First; in Two Volumes: containing a Sketch of the Revolutions and Improvements in Science, Arts and Literature during that Period* (New York: T. and J. Swords, 1803).

15. Timothy Dwight Bozeman, *Protestants in an Age of Science: The Baconian Ideal and Antebellum American Religious Thought* (Chapel Hill: University of North Carolina Press, 1977), 49.

16. John Henry Hobart (1775-1830) came to Trinity Church in

New York City at the age of twenty-five. He became bishop of New York in 1816 and worked for the establishment of General Theological Seminary, which opened in 1819. He was, according to Sydney Ahlstrom, "perhaps the greatest religious leader the American Episcopal Church ever produced." Sydney E. Ahlstrom, *A Religious History of the American People* (New Haven: Yale University Press, 1972), 625.

17. Belden C. Lane, "Democracy and the Ruling Eldership: Samuel Miller's Response to Tensions Between Clerical Power and Lay Activity in Early Nineteenth-Century America" (Ph.D. diss., Princeton Theological Seminary, 1976), 113.

18. *LSM* 1: 273. Belden Lane surveyed Reformed history for the practice of ordaining ruling elders. It was mentioned in Knox and Gillespie, but he did not find any record of its practice. He concluded that while it is impossible to say whether Miller was the originator or not it was a "dramatic innovation" in the American nineteenth century context. Lane, "Samuel Miller," 119.

19, *LSM* 1: 358.

20. *LSM* 1: 356.

21. *LSM* 2: 10-11.

22. *LSM* 2: 12.

23. The Miller House, at 6 Mercer Street, remodeled and enlarged, is now owned by the Nassau Club of Princeton.

## 5.   *Faith and Energy*

1. R. R. Gurley, *Life and Eloquence of the Rev. Sylvester Larned* (New York: Wiley and Putnam, 1844), 37-38.

2. *Princeton Theological Seminary Alumni/ae News*, Summer 1988, 12.

3. The student was William Buell Sprague, graduate of Yale, who studied at Princeton Seminary from 1816 to 1819. *The Presbyterian Historical Almanac, and Annual Remembrance of the Church* (Philadelphia: Joseph M. Wilson, 1863), 5: 64.

4. *LAG*, 618-22.

5. *LAG*, 561.

6. Wertenbaker, *Princeton*, 165.

7. *LAG*, 624-26.

8. John Covert served as a missionary in South Carolina and Georgia until his death in 1822. Henry Weed became a pastor in New York and Virginia. He died in 1870. Halsey Wood was a pastor in Amsterdam, New York, until his death

in 1825. Leverett Huntington served as pastor of the First Presbyterian Church in New Brunswick, New Jersey. He died in 1820.

9. Mr. McComb is noted as the designer of the City Hall and other important buildings in New York City.

10. One gill and a half equalled three-eighths of a pint.

11. This building has been called by several names. In the 1865-66 catalogue it is referred to as "Seminary." By 1884 it was called "Old Seminary." In 1893 it was given the name by which it has continued to be known, "Alexander Hall." See Robert S. Beaman, "Alexander Hall at the Princeton Theological Seminary: The Construction of a Building and the Establishment of an Institution," *Princeton History* 2 (1977).

12. *LAA*, 416-17.

13. Theodore L. Cuyler, "Our Fellow-Student," in *Professor William Henry Green's Semi-Centennial Celebration, 1846-1896* (New York: Charles Scribner's Sons, 1896), 70-71. Cuyler is describing the Oratory of 1846.

14. *BRTR* 5 (1833): 18-19.

15. Archibald Alexander, *The Canon of the Old and New Testaments Ascertained; or The Bible Complete without the Apocrypha and Unwritten Traditions* (D. A. Borrenstein for G. & C. Carvill, 1826), 211-12.

16. *BRTR* 5 (1833): 9.

17. *LSM* 2: 405-6.

18. *Institutiones historiae ecclesiasticae antiquae et recentioris* (1755), of which a number of English translations were published in the nineteenth century.

19. Alexander's lectures on ethics were published in 1852 as *Outlines of Moral Science* (New York: Charles Scribner, 1852). James McCosh, professor in Queen's College in Belfast, Ireland (and later president of Princeton College) called Alexander's book "one of the very best which we have on the subject of man's moral nature." Loetscher, *Archibald Alexander*, 187. Southern Presbyterian theologian, Robert L. Dabney, praised Alexander's "beautiful course of elementary ethics." Robert L. Dabney, *Discussions: Evangelical and Theological* (The Banner of Truth Trust, 1967), 1: 458.

20. These writings were published in a volume with a "preliminary discourse" by Archibald Alexander (Philadelphia: J. Kay, 1831).

21. Isaac Watts, *A Rational Defense of the Gospel* (New York: Jonathan Leavitt, 1831), iii.

22. Archibald Alexander, *A Brief Outline of the Evidences of the Christian Religion* (Princeton: D. A. Borrenstein, 1825). Alexander's *Evidences* went through many editions and was translated into a number of foreign languages.

23. *LJWA* 1: 310.

24. Alexander, *Evidences of the Christian Religion*, 7.

25. *BR* 1 (1829): 107-8.

26. *LAA*, 367.

27. *LCH*, 47-48.

28. Loetscher, *Archibald Alexander*, 191-92.

29. Turretin's *Institutio Theologiae Elencticae* was published in Geneva (1679-85) and reissued at Edinburgh (1847-48). An English translation, a massive undertaking which came to eight thousand handwritten pages, was produced by Princeton College professor of Latin, George M. Giger, at Charles Hodge's request. It is being published in three volumes by Presbyterian and Reformed Publishing Company (1992-94).

30. John W. Beardslee III, *Reformed Dogmatics* (Grand Rapids: Baker Book House, 1965), 14.

31. D. Clair Davis writes: ". . . it is striking to notice how the apologetic concerns of Princeton, directed at the New England psychologizing of faith and its introduction of German rationalistic biblical criticism, could make so much of Turretin's response to similar issues." D. Clair Davis, "Princeton and Inerrancy: The Nineteenth-Century Philosophical Background of Contemporary Concerns," in *Inerrancy and the Church*, ed. John D. Hannah (Chicago: Moody Press, 1984), 361.

32. *LAA*, 368.

33. *LCH*, 554.

34. Elisha Swift, *Requisites to the successful cultivation of Christian theology: Address at the Inauguration of Rev. Wm. S. Plumer* (Pittsburgh: W. S. Haven, 1854), 11-12.

35. Loetscher, *Archibald Alexander*, 209-10.

36. William S. Plumer, *Hints and Helps in Pastoral Theology* (New York: Harper and Brothers, 1874), 111.

37. *LAA*, 533.

38. *BRPR* 27 (1855): 159; *LCH*, 555.

39. *LAA*, 658.

40. Theodore Ledyard Cuyler, *Recollections of a Long Life: An Autobiography* (New York: Baker and Taylor Co., 1902), 192.

41. *BRPR* 27 (1855): 153.

42. James W. Alexander, *Thoughts on Preaching: Being Contribu-*

*tions to Homiletics* (New York: Scribner, 1860; repr. The Banner of Truth Trust, 1975), 16, 18.

43. *LAA*, 410.
44. Francis Wayland, Jr., and H. L. Wayland, *A Memoir of the Life and Labors of Francis Wayland, D. D.*, 3 vols. (New York, 1868), 2: 175-76.
45. *LCH*, 556
46. Plumer, *Pastoral Theology*, 122.
47. Alexander, *Preaching*, 3.
48. In John Broadus's life of James P. Boyce, there is the story of an old man who attended a church some miles from Princeton to hear the "high larnt" young preachers who came out from the seminary. One day he looked glum on returning home, and being asked whether he had had a good sermon said, "No, sir; no, sir. There didn't none of them high larnt young gentlemen come today, but jes' a old man, and he stood up and jes' talked and talked." The preacher was Archibald Alexander. John A. Broadus, *Memoir of James Petigru Boyce, D.D., LL.D.* (New York: A. C. Armstrong and Son, 1893), 68.
49. Plumer, *Pastoral Theology*, 111.
50. Loetscher, *Archibald Alexander*, 237-38.
51. Broadus, *Boyce*, 68-69.
52. Loetscher, *Archibald Alexander*, 238-39.
53. *LSM* 2: 54.
54. Plumer, *Pastoral Theology*, 151.
55. *LSM* 2: 415.
56. *LSM* 2: 409-10.
57. *LAA*, 381.
58. *LSM* 1: 366.
59. *LSM* 2: 407-8.
60. Samuel Miller, *A Brief Account of the Rise, Progress, and Present State of the Theological Seminary of the Presbyterian Church in the United States, at Princeton* (Philadelphia, 1822), 48.
61. When J. A. Alexander went to Europe in 1833, he met Lafayette. He described the visit in the general's bedroom. "He advanced, took me by the hand, and placed me on the sofa where he sat himself, saying that he was very much pleased to see me. 'How long are you in Paris, Mr. Alexander?' . . . 'Did you leave your father and other friends at Princeton well?' I then said that I supposed that he remembered Princeton very well. 'Yes, indeed,' said he, 'many, many years before you were born. I don't know whether you

[453]

remember, but when I came to Princeton I found my diploma signed by Dr. Witherspoon: it had been waiting for me forty years; and it was publicly delivered to me.' 'Yes,' said I, 'and I was present; I was a boy at school.'" *LJAA* 1: 296.

62. Thomas Cary Johnson, *The Life and Letters of Benjamin Morgan Palmer* (Richmond: Presbyterian Committee of Publication, 1906), 176. The words quoted were written by Benjamin Palmer, who became pastor of the First Presbyterian Church in New Orleans in 1856.

63. Henry Woodward, Autobiographical and Family Notes: Addressed to his Seven Children, Speer Library, Princeton, N. J.

64. His fellow student Charles Hodge held up Newbold as an example to his seminary classes, wishing to "cause the students to see how much good can be done, by simply being good." *LCH*, 38.

65. See John A. Andrew, "Betsey Stockton: Stranger in a Strange Land," *JPH* 52 (1974): 157-66.

## 6.  *Charles Hodge*

1.  *LCH*, 44.
2.  *LCH*, 18.
3.  *LCH*, 47.
4.  *LCH*, 5.
5.  These lectures appeared later in the *Christian Advocate*, which Green edited, and in 1841 were published in two volumes by the Presbyterian Board of Publication, with the title, *Lectures on the Shorter Catechism of the Presbyterian Church in the United States of America Addressed to Youth.* See Archibald Alexander, "Dr. Green's Lectures on the Shorter Catechism," *BRTR* 2 (1830): 297-309.
6.  *LCH*, 13-14.
7.  *LCH*, 25.
8.  *LCH*, 556. Charles Hodge never forgot that statement and often repeated it. B. B. Warfield said in one of his Princeton sermons: "Dr. Charles Hodge used to startle us by declaring that no praying soul ever was lost. It seemed to us a hard saying. Our difficulty was that we did not conceive 'praying' purely enough. . . . When we really pray—we are actually in enjoyment of communion with God. And is not communion with God salvation?" B. B. Warfield, *Faith and Life:*

*"Conferences" in the Oratory of Princeton Seminary* (New York: Longmans, Green, 1916; repr. The Banner of Truth Trust, 1974), 152.

9.  *LCH*, 34.
10. *LCH*, 63.
11. *LCH*, 65.
12. *LCH*, 70.
13. *LCH*, 71.
14. *LCH*, 74; see Charles D. Cashdollar, "The Pursuit of Piety: Charles Hodge's Diary, 1819-1820," *JPH* 55 (1977): 267-74.
15. *LCH*, 65.
16. *LCH*, 66.
17. *LCH*, 77.
18. *LCH*, 79-81.
19. *LCH*, 29.
20. "List of Books Prepared for Miss Sarah Bache by Samuel Miller (Princeton, September 9, 1818)" and "Poetical Extracts and Quotations by Miss Sarah Bache" are contained in the Charles Hodge Papers, Princeton University Library.
21. *LCH*, 58-60.
22. *LCH*, 96.
23. *LCH*, 97.
24. *LJWA* 1: 13.
25. *LJWA* 1: 4. In a note written some time later he states: "I thank God for having shown me that this conviction was in some measure unfounded and hasty. Though I never can be eloquent, yet God's spirit may make me a useful preacher."
26. *LJWA* 1: 15.
27. *LJWA* 1: 30. J. W. Alexander quotes John Milton's "Paradise Lost," book 2, lines 558-61.
28. *LJWA* 1: 89; *LAA*, 417.
29. Wright graduated from Princeton in 1828 and became pastor of the First Colored Presbyterian Church of New York in 1830, which he served until his death in 1847. Looking back over his three years at the seminary and his later association with its faculty and former classmates, Wright stated: "I always feel, when at Princeton, that I am in the midst of fathers and brethren, in the holy and responsible work to which we are devoted." Theodore Wright may well have had the most thorough theological training of any African American minister in the country at the time.
30. Selden, *Princeton Theological Seminary*, 35. In his 1862

address celebrating the completion of the seminary's first half-century, William B. Sprague said that "the descendants of HAM have not been without an honorable representation here—a fact to which we appeal with confidence as proof that this Seminary has never endorsed the doctrine that, because, unhappily, a dark skin has become with us an emblem of servitude, it therefore necessarily involves the curse of ignorance and degradation." *Presbyterian Almanac* 5: 79.

31. *BR* 1 (1825): iv-v.
32. *LCH*, 99-100.
33. *LCH*, 102.
34. *LCH*, 139.
35. *LCH*, 116-17.
36. *LCH*, 118.
37. *LCH*, 189.
38. Charles Hodge, *Systematic Theology,* 3 vols. (New York: Charles Scribner and Co., 1871-73; repr. Grand Rapids: Wm. B. Eerdmans Publishing Company, 1979), 2: 452.
39. Charles Hodge, "Journal of European Travels, Feb. 1827-April 1828," Speer Library, Princeton, New Jersey.
40. *LCH*, 154.
41. Hodge was uneasy with Neander's penchant for "development"; he believed that Neander's history was scholarly and basically Christian but imprecise, *BRPR* 16 (1844): 180-83.
42. Hodge, *Systematic Theology* 2: 440.
43. *LCH*, 197.
44. *LCH*, 197, 201.
45. *LCH*, 207.
46. *BR* 1 (1829): 96, 98.

## 7. *The Sabbath Afternoon Conference*

1. John B. Adger, *My Life and Times, 1810-1899* (Richmond: Presbyterian Committee of Publication, 1899), 72.
2. Alexander, *Log College,* 182.
3. Alexander, *Preaching,* 92-93.
4. *LJWA* 1: 256.
5. Archibald Alexander, *Thoughts on Religious Experience* (Philadelphia: Presbyterian Board of Publication, 1841; repr. The Banner of Truth Trust, 1967), 43.
6. *LJWA* 1: 50.
7. *LJWA* 2: 11.
8. Broadus, *Boyce,* 76.

9.  *Memoirs of the Rev. Thomas Halyburton* (Princeton: Baker & Connolly, 1833). This edition was slightly edited by one of the Princeton Seminary students to remove Halyburton's "many Scotticisms" and "obsolete expressions."

10. Samuel Miller and Charles Hodge, "Recommendation" (iv) and Archibald Alexander, "Preface" (v-xiii) in *Memoirs of the Rev. Thomas Halyburton.*

11. This pattern persisted until 1918 when evening prayers were discontinued and the professors took turns conducting morning prayers. "In so simple a matter," B. B. Warfield commented, "the Professors have never found it convenient just to obey the 'Plan.'" B. B. Warfield, "How Princeton Seminary Got to Work," *JPHS* 6 (1918): 266.

12. *LCH*, 456-57.

13. John Frelinghuysen Hageman, *History of Princeton and Its Institutions*, 2 vols. (Philadelphia: J. B. Lippincott and Co., 1879), 1: 256.

14. *LCH*, 453; *JPHS* 6 (1918): 265.

15. LAA, 421.

16. LSM 2: 410.

17. Charles Hodge, *Conference Papers or Analyses of Discourses, Doctrinal and Practical; Delivered on Sabbath Afternoons to the Students of the Theological Seminary, Princeton, N. J.* (New York: Charles Scribner's Sons, 1879), iii. These conference talks of Charles Hodge were reprinted in 1958 by The Banner of Truth Trust as *Princeton Sermons: Outlines of Discourses, Doctrinal and Practical.*

18. *LCH*, 458.

19. In 1878 A. A. Hodge sent to Charles Spurgeon one of Charles Hodge's manuscript conference outlines. The accompanying letter stated in part: "Mr. Charles A. Salmond of Edinburgh has conveyed to me a request that I should send you a manuscript of my dear Father so recently taken from us. I send you enclosed a paper containing an analysis of a subject on experimental religion, such as he made every Sabbath day in preparation for his Sabbath afternoon talk at a religious Conference held by the Professors & Students. He left several hundred of these, which are to be published this winter." A. A. Hodge to Charles Spurgeon, September 25, 1878, The Spurgeon Collection, William Jewell College Library, Liberty, Missouri.

20. *LCH*, 459.

21. *LAA*, 462-65.

22.  Samuel Miller, *The Importance of the Gospel Ministry; an Intro-ductory Lecture, delivered at the opening of the Winter Session of the Theological Seminary at Princeton, New Jersey, Nov. 9, 1827* (Princeton: D. A. Borrenstein, 1827), 31.

23.  Samuel Miller, "The Importance of a Thorough and Ad-equate Course of Preparatory Study for the Holy Ministry," in *The Annual of the Board of Education of the General Assembly of the Presbyterian Church in the United States*, ed. John Breckinridge (Philadelphia: Russell and Martien, 1832), 85-86.

24.  Samuel Miller, "Plea for an Enlarged Ministry," *The Pres-byterian Preacher* 3 (1834): 13.

25.  Samuel Miller, *Letters on Clerical Manners and Habits, addressed to a Student in the Theological Seminary at Princeton, N. J.* (New York: G. & S. Carvill, 1827).

26.  *LCH*, 453.

27.  William B. Sprague, *A Discourse Addressed to the Alumni of Princeton Theological Seminary, April 30, 1862 on occasion of the completion of its first half century* (Albany: Van Benthuysen, 1862), 27-28.

28.  *LJWA* 2:104.

29.  Nassau, "Autobiography," Speer Library, Princeton, N. J.; Kenneth James Grant, *My Missionary Memories* (Halifax: Im-perial Publishing Company, 1923), 32.

30.  Walter Lowrie, ed., *Memoirs of the Rev. Walter M. Lowrie: Missionary to China*, 4th ed. (New York: Board of Foreign Missions of the Presbyterian Church, 1851), 451.

## 8.  *Concert for Prayer & Society of Inquiry*

1.  For Princeton Seminary's early involvement in the mission-ary movement, see David B. Calhoun, "The Last Command: Princeton Theological Seminary and Missions (1812-1862)" (Ph.D. diss., Princeton Theological Seminary, 1983).

2.  Loetscher, *Archibald Alexander*, 46.

3.  Archibald Alexander, "On the Nature of Vital Piety," intro-ductory essay in Jared Waterbury, *Advice to a Young Christian* (New York: Robert Carter, 1848).

4.  *Fourth Report of the Board of Directors of the Theological Seminary; to the General Assembly of the Presbyterian Church. Read May 22d, 1816* (Philadelphia: T. and W. Bradford, 1816).

5.  John C. Lowrie, *Princeton Theological Seminary and Foreign Missions, a paper read at the meeting of the alumni, May 25, 1876*

(Philadelphia, 1876), 10.

6. Society of Inquiry Papers, Speer Library, Princeton, N. J. These papers are the source for much of the material in this chapter.
7. *LCH*, 82.
8. Hageman, *History of Princeton*, 2: 421.
9. This statement was made by William Tennent II in 1833. See Alan Heimert, "The Great Awakening as Watershed," in *Religion in American History: Interpretive Essays*, eds. John M. Mulder and John F. Wilson (Englewood Cliffs, N.J.: Prentice-Hall, 1978), 137.
10. Kenneth Scott Latourette stated that "it was from this haystack meeting that the foreign missionary movement of the churches of the United States had an initial main impulse." Kenneth Scott Latourette, *These Sought a Country* (New York: Harper and Brothers, 1950), 46.
11. Adger, *My Life and Times*, 81.
12. American supporters commonly suggested names which were given to native children in boarding schools and missionaries' homes—such as Cotton Mather, David Brainerd, and Jonathan Edwards, as well as Archibald Alexander, Samuel Miller, and Charles Hodge!
13. In its early history Princeton Seminary observed two vacations of six weeks each (May-June and September-October); later a long summer vacation and a short Christmas holiday became the practice.

## 9. School of the Prophets

1. William Maxwell, *A Memoir of the Rev. John H. Rice, D.D.* (Philadelphia and Richmond, 1835), 233.
2. Adger, *My Life and Times*, 74.
3. Lowrie, *Princeton Theological Seminary and Foreign Missions*, 11.
4. *LJWA* 1: 207.
5. Noll, *Princeton and the Republic*, 280.
6. *LAG*, 565.
7. *LCH*, 26.
8. Wertenbaker, *Princeton*, 172.
9. Cuyler, *Recollections*, 9. Theodore Cuyler studied at the College of New Jersey in 1841.
10. After fourteen happy years at Princeton, Henry accepted a call to head the new Smithsonian Institute in Washington, D. C. Twice Princeton tried to win him back, and in 1853

actually elected him president, but, except for occasional lectures, he would not leave his work at the Institute. He was a trustee of the seminary from 1844 to 1851 and of the college from 1864 to 1878.

11.  John DeWitt, "Princeton College Administrations in the 19th Century," *PRR* 8 (1897): 649.

12.  Sprague, *Annals* 4: 739-40.

13.  *LJWA* 1: 312.

14.  *LJWA* 1: 361.

15.  *LJWA* 1: 213.

16.  Eduard N. Loring, "Charles C. Jones: Missionary to Plantation Slaves, 1831-1847" (Ph.D. diss., Vanderbilt University, 1976), 53.

17.  Hugh T. Kerr, ed., *Sons of the Prophets: Leaders in Protestantism from Princeton Seminary* (Princeton: Princeton University Press, 1963), 19.

18.  *LJWA* 1: 193.

19.  *LJWA* 1: 176.

20.  E. P. Swift, ed., *A Memoir of the Rev. Joseph W. Barr, late missionary under the direction of the Western Foreign Missionary Society* (Pittsburgh: R. Patterson, 1833), 188-89.

21.  Adger, *My Life and Times*, 74.

22.  *LAA*, 501.

23.  *LAA*, 272-73.

24.  *LAA*, 405.

25.  *LAA*, 666.

26.  *LJAA* 2: 599.

27.  *LAA*, 407. Three of the sons became ministers, two were lawyers, and one a doctor.

28.  Alexander, *Preaching*, 35.

29.  *LAA*, 406.

30.  *LJWA* 1: 228.

31.  Theodore D. Woolsey at Charles Hodge's Semi-Centennial, April 24, 1872.

32.  *LCH*, 27.

33.  *LCH*, 521.

34.  Charles Hodge, "Retrospect of the History of the Princeton Review," *The Biblical Repertory and Princeton Review, Index Volume from 1825 to 1868*, 3 vols. (Philadelphia: Peter Walker, 1871), 1: 19. And in so doing, commented Hodge, "we doubt not, he did nobly right."

35.  *LJAA* 2: 491.

36.  In his youth, Dr. Alexander wrote a religious novel which

was circulated among his friends but never published. His son described the book as the story of "a young lady of wealth and beauty, who is led through various changes and degrees, from giddy ignorance to piety and peace. The plot was engaging; there was a thread of romantic but pure love running through the whole; it abounded in graphic description and lively dialogue."

37. Archibald Alexander, *A Selection of Hymns, Adapted to the Devotions of the Closet, the Family and the Social Circle; and containing Subjects appropriate to the Monthly Concerts of Prayer for the Success of Missions and Sunday Schools; and other Special Occasions* (New York: Jonathan Leavitt, 1831), iv.

38. *LSM* 2: 388.

39. Thomas Cary Johnson, *The Life and Letters of Robert Lewis Dabney* (The Banner of Truth Trust, 1977), 100.

40. *LCH*, 379.

41. *LSM* 2: 411.

42. *LSM* 1: 304.

43. *LSM* 2: 176-77.

44. Samuel Miller, *A Sermon, Preached March 13th, 1808 for the Benefit of the Society Instituted in the City of New York for the Relief of Poor Widows with Small Children* (New York, 1808), 20. Paige P. Miller states that Samuel Miller's sermon "helped to define a restricted role for women, but at the same time he assumed the role of a genuine advocate of innovative female charity associations." Paige Putnam Miller, *A Claim to New Roles* (Metuchen, N. J.: The Scarecrow Press, 1985), 38. Samuel Miller helped to construct the parochial school proposal adopted by the 1847 General Assembly which included female secondary schools.

45. In 1866 the school, located in Chester County, Pennsylvania, became Lincoln University.

46. *LSM* 2: 179.

47. *LSM* 2: 496.

48. The lecture formed the basis of Miller's published work, *The Utility and Importance of Creeds and Confessions* (Philadelphia: Presbyterian Board of Publication, 1824). It was revised and enlarged and reprinted several times. Combined with another of Miller's work, it has been reprinted by Presbyterian Heritage Publications under the title, *Doctrinal Integrity: On the Utility and Importance of Creeds and Confessions and Adherence to our Doctrinal Standards* (1989).

49. Miller, *Doctrinal Integrity*, 3-4, 69.

50. *LSM* 2: 224-25.
51. Charles Hodge, *A Discourse delivered at the Re-opening of the Chapel, September 27, 1874* (Princeton: Chas. S. Robinson, 1874), 14.
52. Charles Beatty Alexander, *Address Delivered, By Invitation of the Directors, on the Occasion of the One Hundredth Anniversary of the Seminary in Alexander Hall, Princeton, New Jersey, May 6, 1912* (Printed for the Seminary), 5.
53. Sprague, *Annals* 3: 619.
54. Sprague, *Annals* 3: 623.
55. *BRTR* 3 (1831): 357.
56. Ashbel Green, "An Address to the Students of the Theological Seminary, at Princeton, " *BRTR* 3 (1831): 350-60.
57. Leonard Woods was in Princeton to attend the semi-annual examination of the Princeton students. Woods, a Congregationalist minister, became the professor of theology at Andover Seminary when it was organized in 1808. There he taught orthodox Calvinism for thirty-eight years.

## 10.  *The Seminary in the 1830s*

1. *LCH*, 229.
2. Never fully diagnosed, Hodge's illness was probably a chronic rheumatoid condition.
3. *LCH*, 239.
4. *LCH*, 240.
5. Adger, *My Life and Times*, 77.
6. *LCH*, 227.
7. From *The Christian Intelligencer*, and printed in the *Banner*, a church paper published by the Doylestown Presbyterian Church.
8. *LCH*, 249.
9. Hodge, "Retrospect," 2.
10. *LCH*, 248.
11. *LCH*, 260.
12. Adger, *My Life and Times*, 76.
13. *National Repository*, 65.
14. *SSW* 1: 437-40.
15. *BRTR* 5 (1833): 382.
16. *BRTR* 7 (1835): 288, 340.
17. *LCH*, 273-75.
18. Charles Hodge, *Commentary on the Epistle to the Romans* (New York: A. C. Armstrong and Son, 1900), 297.

19. The second edition (which Hodge prepared in 1864) was reprinted by William B. Eerdmans Publishing Company in 1950 and 1993 and by The Banner of Truth Trust, 1972.
20. *LCH*, 278.
21. Charles H. Spurgeon, *Commenting and Commentaries* (London: Passmore & Alabaster, 1876; repr. The Banner of Truth Trust, 1969), 171.
22. Francis L. Patton, "Charles Hodge," *PR* 6 (1881): 356-57.
23. *LJAA* 1: 323.
24. *LJAA* 1: 93.
25. His biographer lists twenty-four languages which he eventually learned. He was fluent in seven and read the others with varying ease. *LJAA* 2: 862-65.
26. Fénelon's *Télémaque* was written for the education of the grandson of Louis XIV. The *Gulistan* ("Rose Garden") was a mixture of prose and verse by the Persian poet Sadi of Shiraz, completed in 1258.
27. *LJAA* 1: 221.
28. *LJAA* 1: 222.
29. *LJAA* 1: 229.
30. *LJAA* 1: 239.
31. *LJAA* 1: 243.
32. *LJAA* 1: 263.
33. T. V. Moore entered Princeton Seminary in the fall of 1839. The faculty consisted of Archibald Alexander, Samuel Miller, Charles Hodge, and J. A. Alexander. Moore wrote: "My first sight of the latter was in the Oratory, where the four professors were seated in a row; and having never seen any of them before, I studied their faces with curious interest. The head and face of Professor Addison Alexander struck me as very much like Napoleon's in some respects—in its massive breadth, in a suggestion of prodigious strength in reserve, and a certain indication of fiery energy ready to blaze out at a moment's notice." *LJAA* 1: 478-79.
34. *LJAA* 1: 214. This was the comment of J. B. Adger.
35. Johnson, *Robert Lewis Dabney*, 100. The student was William Henry Ruffner.
36. *LJAA* 2: 584.
37. *LJAA* 1: 370.
38. *LJAA* 1: 386.
39. Johnson, *Robert Lewis Dabney*, 100.
40. *LJAA* 1: 378-79.
41. Broadus, *Boyce*, 70.

42. *LCH,* 560.
43. *LJAA* 1: 376.
44. *LJAA* 2: 571.
45. *LJAA* 1: 388.
46. *Minutes of the General Assembly of the Presbyterian Church in the United States of America,* 1830, 18-20.
47. *BRTR* 7 (1835): 458.
48. Joseph's son, and John Breckinridge's nephew, was John Cabell Breckinridge, vice-president of the United States under Buchanan and candidate for the presidency on the Southern Democratic ticket against Stephen A. Douglas and Abraham Lincoln. He became a Confederate general in October 1861.
49. *LSM* 2: 83.
50. *LSM* 2: 351.
51. *LSM* 2: 445; *Presbyterian Almanac* 5: 54-55. Samuel Miller Breckinridge, the only son of Margaret and John Breckinridge, was left in the care of his Princeton grandparents in 1841. Unruly and difficult, the boy caused the Millers much anxiety. John's brother Robert J. Breckinridge, who provided money for his nephew, eventually removed him from Dr. Miller's care and sent him to Union College. He left after a short time in order to study law and later moved to St. Louis to set up practice.
52. Adger, *My Life and Times,* 80.
53. John Adger then served as pastor of a black congregation in Charleston, South Carolina, before becoming professor of Ecclesiastical History and Church Polity at Columbia Theological Seminary in 1856.

## 11.   The Old Doctrines of Calvinism

1. *LAA,* 474, 478.
2. Ahlstrom, *Religious History of the American People,* 420.
3. Joseph Haroutunian states that Edwards's would-be disciples "used his language and ignored his piety" and consequently transformed his theology "into a farce." "Calvinism thus degenerated into a scheme of theology *plus* an independent set of 'duties.' Its holy fire was quenched, and its theological ashes lay exposed to the four winds." Haroutunian further criticizes the New England Calvinism for "focusing attention on its enemies instead of on its God." Joseph Haroutunian, *Piety versus Moralism: The Passing of the New*

*England Theology* (New York: Holt, 1932), 62, 96, 127.

4.  B. B. Warfield pointed out that Edwards's ontological specu-lations—"a complete system of Idealism, which trembled indeed on the brink of mere phenomenalism"—belonged to "his extreme youth." When he turned to theology, Warfield argued, "what he teaches is just the 'standard' Calvinism in its completeness." Warfield, "Edwards and the New England Theology," in *Studies in Theology*, 516, 519, 520, 530. Andover's Edwards Amasa Park attempted to show a continuity of theology from Edwards to Park, but Princeton was clearly more the heir of Edwards than Park. Mark Noll identifies the New School Presbyterian theologian Henry B. Smith as coming closest to being a nineteenth-century American successor to Jonathan Edwards. See Mark A. Noll, "Jonathan Edwards and Nineteenth Century Theology," in *Jonathan Edwards and the American Experience*, eds., Nathan O. Hatch and Harry S. Stout (New York: Oxford University Press, 1988): 260-87. Smith, Noll argues, drew together piety, learning, and doctrine to make the same effort that Edwards made. The same, however, can be said of the Princetonians.

5.  *BRTR* 7 (1835): 619.

6.  *LSM* 1: 298.

7.  *LSM* 2: 27.

8.  Charles Hodge, "Retrospect," 22-23; see also *BRTR* 3 (1831): 520-21 for an earlier statement of the same view.

9.  *LCH*, 289.

10. *LCH*, 290.

11. Charles Hodge, "Remarks in the Princeton Review," *BRPR* 23 (1851): 309.

12. George P. Hutchinson, *The Problem of Original Sin in American Presbyterian Theology* (Presbyterian and Reformed Publishing Company, 1972), 27-28.

13. For a competent treatment of the complex debate between Hodge, W. G. T. Shedd, James Henley Thornwell, and Robert Lewis Dabney on this doctrine, see Hutchinson, *Original Sin*.

14. Hodge, "Retrospect," 12-13.

15. For the life of Asahel Nettleton, see Bennet Tyler, *Memoir of the Life and Character of Rev. Asahel Nettleton, D. D.* (Hartford: Robbins and Smith, 1844), and John F. Thornbury, *God Sent Revival: The Story of Asahel Nettleton and the Second Great Awakening* (Grand Rapids: Evangelical, 1977). Andrew A. Bonar's

*Nettleton and His Labours* follows, with few changes, Tyler's book. The Banner of Truth Trust issued a new edition of Bonar's work in 1975, with the title *The Life and Labours of Asahel Nettleton.*

16. Ahlstrom, *Religious History of the American People,* 421.
17. Alexander, *Preaching,* 150.
18. Lyman Beecher, *The Autobiography of Lyman Beecher,* ed. B. Cross (Harvard University: Belknap, 1961) 2: 364-65.
19. *BRTR* 7 (1835): 606.
20. Keith J. Hardman, *Charles Grandison Finney (1792-1875): Revivalist and Reformer* (Syracuse: Syracuse University Press, 1987; repr. Grand Rapids: Baker Book House, 1987), 111. Nettleton never took a settled pastorate and never married. A bout with typhus fever in 1822 curtailed his activities, but he continued to preach—in New England, Virginia, and even in Britain. In 1833, with Bennet Tyler and several others, he founded the Theological Institute of Connecticut, where he taught until his death in 1844.
21. Charles G. Finney, *Memoirs of Rev. Charles G. Finney, Written by Himself* (New York: A. S. Barnes and Company, 1876), 24.
22. Finney, *Memoirs,* 14.
23. George W. Gale (1789-1861) graduated from Union College in 1814 and studied at Princeton Theological Seminary. He became minister of the Adams Presbyterian Church—the only pastorate he ever held. A distinguished educator, he directed the Oneida Institute at Whitesboro from 1827 until 1834. In 1837 he founded Knox College and the town of Galesburg, Illinois. The long-suffering Gale became a staunch supporter of Finney, although he recognized his deficiencies. In January 1826, he wrote to Samuel C. Aikin, pastor of the First Presbyterian Church in Utica, New York, that "Mr. Finney had some peculiarities, some things that were not practicable that I would alter, but many things said [against him] had little or no foundation, that he was a good man and God was with him." Hardman, *Finney,* 79.
24. In his *Memoirs,* Finney stated that some of the ministers urged him to go to Princeton to study theology, but he refused, stating "that I would not put myself under such an influence as they had been under; that I was confident they had been wrongly educated, and they were not ministers that met my ideal of what a minister of Christ should be." Finney, *Memoirs,* 45-46. It seems unlikely that he actually uttered these words to the presbytery that was taking him

under its care.

25. Finney, *Memoirs,* 46.
26. Hardman, *Finney,* 55.
27. Beecher, in so far as he was related to the revival, "for the rest of his life remained a tail to the Finney kite." Perry Miller, *The Life of the Mind in America* (New York: Harcourt, Brace and World, 1965), 24.
28. Tyler, *Nettleton,* 216-17.
29. Hardman, *Finney,* 231.
30. Hardman, *Finney,* 233.
31. Charles Hodge, "The New Divinity Tried," *BRTR* 4 (1832): 278-304.
32. *BRTR* 4 (1832): 301-2.
33. *BRTR* 7 (1835): 614.
34. *Memoirs of the Rev. Thomas Halyburton,* ix-x.
35. Samuel Miller, *Letters to Presbyterians on the Present Crisis in the Presbyterian Church in the United States* (Philadelphia: Anthony Finley, 1833), 165.
36. Charles G. Finney, *Lectures on Revivals of Religion* (New York: Fleming H. Revell, 1835), 13. Hardman comments: "The continuum was now complete; it had swung from the Puritans' astonishment at the mysterious workings of God and the awesomeness of it all, to the post-Enlightenment, sanitized and respectable cause-and-effect relationship of an efficiency principle." Hardman, *Finney,* 21.
37. Hardman, *Finney,* 279.
38. Hardman, *Finney,* 290.
39. Albert Dod, "Review of *Lectures on Revivals of Religion* and *Sermons on Various Subjects,*" *BRTR* 7 (1835): 482-527 and 626-74. William G. McLoughlin comments that Dod's "review of the *Lectures on Revivals* can and should be properly considered the official and definitive counterattack upon the theological revolution that Finney led." Finney, *Lectures on Revivals,* xxii.
40. *BRTR* 7 (1835): 504, 526-27, 656-57, 674.
41. *LJWA* 1: 186. Years later, however, when J. W. Alexander was a pastor in New York City, he wrote, "There was great interest under the Finneyitish revivals, but it was not evangelical, and I am working among its bitter fruits every day." *LJWA* 2: 62.
42. *BRTR* 4 (1832): 486.
43. Loetscher, *Archibald Alexander,* 198.
44. William B. Sprague, *Lectures on Revivals of Religion* (Albany:

Webster and Skinners, 1832). Sprague's book became the classic "Old School" statement on revivals. John Breckinridge called it "one of the most important and useful productions of the American press for the present century." See John Breckinridge, "Sprague on Revivals," BRTR 4 (October 1832): 456. Sprague's *Lectures on Revivals of Religion* was reprinted by The Banner of Truth Trust in 1959. The "Publishers' Note" states that the book was reprinted from a copy of the first American edition which had been sent by the author to the English evangelical leader, Charles Simeon of Cambridge. It is inscribed on the fly-leaf: "The Rev. C. Simeon, with great regard from W. B. Sprague." Underneath this inscription Simeon had written these words: "A most valuable book. I recommend my executor to keep it, as there are few, if any, others in this kingdom. I love the good sense of Dr. Sprague. C. S."

45. See Sprague, *Lectures on Revivals*, Appendix 1-8.
46. *BRTR* 7 (1835): 604-7.
47. *LAA*, 502.
48. *LAA*, 547.
49. This shift is brilliantly described in Nathan O. Hatch's *The Democratization of American Christianity* (New Haven: Yale University Press, 1989). Hatch credits Finney with conveying "the indigenous methods of popular culture [of the 'ignorant Methodists and Baptist exhorters'] to the middle class. As a transitional figure, he introduced democratic modifications into respectable institutions" (199).
50. *BRTR* 7 (1835): 608.
51. James W. Alexander, *The Revival and its Lessons: A Collection of Fugitive Papers, Having Reference to the Great Awakening* (New York: Anson D. F. Randolph, 1859), 14.

## 12.  *Our Beloved Zion*

1. *JPHS* 2 (1904): 287-91.
2. *LSM* 2: 444.
3. *BRPR* 11 (1839): 582.
4. *BRPR* 9 (1837): 112-14.
5. *LJWA* 1: 160.
6. *The Spruce Street Lectures: by several clergymen. Delivered during the years 1831-2* (Philadelphia: Presbyterian Board of Publication, 1841), 15.
7. *LCH*, 292. According to A. A. Hodge, the Princeton men

"desired to have the 'Plan of Union' abrogated; to have the churches organized on that basis reorganized or cut off by constitutional ecclesiastical authority; to have all ministers holding and teaching the graver errors then known as 'Taylorism' tried and excluded from office; to have new measures discouraged; and denominational Boards of Education, and of Missions, Home and Foreign, substituted in the place of Voluntary Societies. . . . They did not wish to see the church divided either by the voluntary departure of the extreme Old School wing . . . or by the forcible exclusion of the great body of the New School" *(LCH,* 290).

8. *LSM* 2: 203.

9. *LJWA* 1: 170.

10. *LJWA* 1: 177.

11. Miller, *Letters to Presbyterians;* Letters 6-8 were reprinted, under the title *Doctrinal Integrity,* by the Presbyterian Heritage Publications in 1989.

12. Miller, *Doctrinal Integrity,* 75-77, 129.

13. *LSM* 2: 222.

14. *LJWA* 1: 183.

15. A large number of Princeton Seminary alumni at the 1833 General Assembly formed an association to preserve their student friendships, promote personal piety, foster the spirit of missions, incite greater diligence in the work of the ministry, and support their beloved seminary. Selden, *Princeton Theological Seminary,* 36.

16. Archibald Alexander, *The Pastoral Office. A Sermon, Preached at Philadelphia, before the Association of the Alumni of the Theological Seminary at Princeton on Wednesday Morning, May 21, 1834* (Philadelphia: Henry Perkins, 1834), 27.

17. *LCH,* 305.

18. *BRPR* 9 (1837): 145.

19. In requesting financial help in a letter of April 28, 1840, Hodge wrote to his brother: "Only think of seven mouths, seven pair of feet, seven empty heads, and worse than all seven pairs of knees and elbows." *LCH,* 344.

20. Albert Barnes, *Notes, Explanatory and Practical, on the Epistle to the Romans* (New York, 1834). This was the first volume of Barnes's immensely popular *Notes, Explanatory and Practical, on the Scriptures.*

21. *LAA,* 478.

22. *BRTR* 8 (1836): 458.

23. *BRPR* 9 (1837): 146.

24. *LCH*, 298.
25. *BRPR* 9 (1837): 148.
26. *LCH*, 306.
27. *LSM* 2: 333.
28. *LJWA* 1: 180, 254-55.
29. Hodge, "Retrospect," 19.
30. It was reported that in the crowd the question was frequently asked, "What is the difference between the Old School and the New School?" One story is that a spectator trying to answer that question said that the Old School held that "whatever is to be will be," but broke down in trying to reverse that proposition plausibly! *Presbyterian Re-union: A Memorial Volume, 1837-1871* (New York: De-Witt C. Lent & Co., 1870), 9.
31. *LCH*, 316-18.
32. Charles Hodge, *The Constitutional History of the Presbyterian Church in the United States of America*, 2 vols. (Philadelphia: William S. Martien, 1839, 1840).
33. *LCH*, 281.
34. *LCH*, 279.
35. *LCH*, 245.
36. B. B. Warfield did not share Hodge's criticism of Jonathan Edwards. He wrote: "[Edwards] diligently sought to curb excesses, and earnestly endeavored to separate the chaff from the wheat. But no one could protest more strongly against casting out the wheat with the chaff. He subjected all the phenomena of the revivals in which he participated to the most searching analytical study; and, while sadly acknowledging that much self-deception was possible, and that the rein could only too readily be given to false 'enthusiasm,' he earnestly contended that a genuine work of grace might find expression in mental and even physical excitement." Warfield, *Studies in Theology*, 524.
37. *LCH*, 283.
38. It was subsequently copyrighted and published by the Presbyterian Board of Publication in 1851. For criticism of Charles Hodge's *Constitutional History*, see William Hill, *A History of the Rise, Progress, Genius, and Character of American Presbyterianism* (Washington: J. Gideon, Jr., 1839). See also Hodge's reply in *BRPR* 12 (1840): 322-50.
39. As a supplement to *The Log College*, Archibald Alexander compiled *Sermons and Essays by the Tennents and their Contemporaries* (Philadelphia: Presbyterian Board of Publication,

1855). Dr. Alexander donated his royalties from these books to a New Jersey orphanage, stating that God would have his ministers "attentive to the poor and afflicted."

40. Alexander, *Log College*, 176.
41. *LJWA* 2: 74.
42. *BRPR* 19 (1847): 519.
43. *Presbyterian Re-union Volume*, 11.

## 13. Old School Princeton

1. George L. Prentiss, *The Union Theological Seminary in the City of New York: Historical and Biographical Sketches of its First Fifty Years* (New York, 1889), 8.
2. Cuyler, *Recollections*, 82.
3. A. A. Hodge's preface in Hodge, *Romans*, iii-iv.
4. *SSW* 1: 473.
5. *BRPR* 16 (1844): 182.
6. An anonymous note in the *Biblical Repertory and Princeton Review* in 1845 stated that Turretin's theology bore "the tincture of scholasticism" but, nonetheless, recommended him as "the best systematic theological writer" and stated that the work was "remarkably adapted to the present state of theology in this country." *BRPR* 17 (1845): 190. In 1847 a new Latin edition of Turretin's theology—with typographical errors carefully corrected by Dr. Cunningham of Edinburgh—was published in New York. J. W. Alexander wrote an article in the July 1848 edition of the *Biblical Repertory* praising Turretin's theology, summarizing his life, and urging the purchase and use of his *Institutio*. Alexander wrote that Turretin's "adherence to the received doctrine of the Reformed church is so uniform and strict, that there is no writer who has higher claims as an authority as to what that doctrine was." The study of Turretin, Alexander stated, would do more good for theology and preaching "than cart loads of religious journals, epitomes from the German, and occasional sermons." *BRPR* 20 (1848): 461, 463.
7. *LCH*, 388.
8. Broadus, *Boyce*, 73.
9. Johnson, *Robert Lewis Dabney*, 100.
10. Broadus, *Boyce*, 78.
11. C. A. Salmond, *Princetoniana: Charles and A. A. Hodge; with Class and Table Talk of Hodge the Younger* (New York: Scribner and Welford, 1888), 46.

12. *BRPR* 18 (1846): 561-62.
13. John W. Stewart, "The Tethered Theology: Biblical Criticism, Common Sense Philosophy, and the Princeton Theologians" (Ph. D. diss., University of Michigan, 1990), 166.
14. J. A. Alexander, *The Prophecies of Isaiah* (New York: Charles Scribner, 1870), 1: 15.
15. *BRPR* 9 (1837): 199.
16. *LJAA* 2: 582.
17. *LCH*, 561.
18. Cuyler, *Recollections*, 79.
19. Francis L. Patton wrote: "Dr. Alexander was a many-sided man. He was a linguist, a critic, a theologian, a preacher, and a poet. But the wit and drollery of these 'Wistar Magazines' remind me of Lewis Carroll; and make me feel that the man who wrote the well-known hymn, and published the commentary on Isaiah, and lectured on the Canon of the New Testament, and preached the sermon on Lot's wife, could also have written 'Alice in Wonderland' if he had chosen." Francis L. Patton, *Caspar Wistar Hodge: A Memorial Address* (New York: Anson D. F. Randolph and Company, 1891), 14-15.
20. *LJAA* 2: 655.
21. Charles Hodge, *The Way of Life* (Philadelphia: American Sunday School Union, 1841; repr. The Banner of Truth Trust, 1959).
22. *LCH*, 327.
23. *Catalogue of Books and Other Publications of the American Sunday School Union* (1843).
24. *The Way of Life* has remained continuously in print. Recent English editions include The Banner of Truth (1959), Baker Book House (1977), and Paulist Press (1987). It has been translated into a number of foreign languages, including Spanish, Hindustani, and Chinese.
25. John Macleod states that "what this little book was fitted to do when it first saw the light it is fitted to do still. A more winsome presentation of cardinal truth it would be hard to find." John Macleod, *Some Favorite Books* (The Banner of Truth Trust, 1988), 99.
26. *Princeton Theological Seminary Alumni News* 22 (Summer 1982): 19.
27. His letters and counsel to them were collected and published as *Letters from a Father to his Sons in College* (Phila-

delphia, 1844).

28. *LSM* 2: 359.
29. *LJWA* 1: 384.
30. *William Henry Green's Semi-Centennial Celebration*, 69.
31. A. A. Hodge, "God, His Being, and His Attributes," *The Presbyterian*, January 30, 1886, 5.
32. Francis L. Patton in A. A. Hodge, *Evangelical Theology: Lectures on Doctrine* (The Banner of Truth Trust, 1976), xiii. Hodge's book was originally published as *Popular Lectures on Theological Themes* (Philadelphia: Presbyterian Board of Publication, 1887). Patton thought that the subject of that essay was "The Relation of God to the World." It was the same topic as A. A. Hodge's last writing, placed in Patton's hands a few weeks before Hodge's death, and published in the January 1887 issue of *The Presbyterian Review*.
33. Archibald Alexander, "Address before the Alumni Association of Washington College, June 29, 1843," in *Washington and Lee University Historical Papers*, 2 (Baltimore: John Murphy and Co., 1890), 126, 137, 139.
34. *LJWA* 1: 372, 377.
35. The Old Lenox Library (a second Lenox Library was built in 1879) was destroyed in 1956 to make way for the new Speer Library. The gates of Princeton Seminary are made with stone taken from the first Lenox Library.
36. James Lenox was born in 1800. He studied law before joining his father's "counting house." He was the donor of the Presbyterian Hospital of New York City, the First Presbyterian Church in New York City, and the New York Public Library's main building. His Fifth Avenue mansion was used for many years after his death in 1880 as the headquarters of the Presbyterian Board of Foreign Missions.
37. Selden, *Princeton Theological Seminary*, 39.
38. Cuyler, *Recollections*, 252.
39. *LJWA* 1: 383.
40. *LSM* 2: 414.
41. *LJWA* 1: 386.
42. *LCH*, 354.
43. The *Annals of the Disruption* includes this account of the meeting of Cunningham and Hodge as described by "an on-looker": "You know brother Hodge is one of the most reserved of men, nor is a first acquaintance with him generally very assuring or very attractive to strangers. But I remarked with what warmth and cordiality he met Dr.

Cunningham, as if he had met an old friend from whom he had been long separated. And it was so with Cunningham too. The two greatest theologians of the age were at once friends and brothers. They seemed at once to read and know each the other's great and noble mind." Thomas Brown, *Annals of the Disruption* (Edinburgh: Macniven and Wallace, 1893), 548.

44. Francis L. Patton claimed that Charles Hodge and William Cunningham were the ablest Calvinists of their day. He said: "Hodge proves, Cunningham disproves. Hodge shows the strength of Calvinism, Cunningham the weakness of Arminianism." *PR* 6 (1881): 373.

45. *LJWA* 1: 390.

46. *BRPR* 16 (1844): 245-47.

47. Archibald Alexander, "Rightly Dividing the Word of Truth," in *The Princeton Pulpit*, ed. John T. Duffield (New York: Charles Scribner, 1852), 31, 34-40, 42, 46. This sermon was probably the last complete discourse that Dr. Alexander prepared.

48. *LCH*, 363, 367.

49. *LJWA* 2: 42-43.

50. Charles A. Aiken, *Discourses Commemorative of the Life and Work of Charles Hodge, D.D., LL.D.* (Philadelphia: Henry B. Ashmead, 1879).

51. *Essays, Theological and Miscellaneous, reprinted from the Princeton Review, Second Series, including the contributions of the late Rev. Albert B. Dod, D. D.* (New York & London: Wiley and Putnam, 1847).

52. Hodge, "Retrospect," 206.

53. Archibald Alexander, *A Brief Compend of Bible Truth* (Philadelphia: Presbyterian Board of Publication, 1846).

54. *LJAA* 1: 414.

55. *LJAA* 2: 568.

56. J. A. Alexander, *Earlier Prophecies of Isaiah* (New York and London: Wiley and Putnam, 1846), iii, x, xliii.

57. *LJAA* 2: 599.

58. In 1865, four years after the author's death, a new edition of his Isaiah commentary appeared under the editorship of John Eadie of Edinburgh. Eadie considered Alexander's work "among the best Commentaries on Isaiah of any age or in any language." A later Old Testament professor at Princeton Seminary, John D. Davis, commented on J. A. Alexander's commentaries on Isaiah: "In copious citation

and masterful analysis they review the recorded opinion of all previous expositors on each exegetical question. They are characterized by calm, dispassionate and profound debate of the conflicting views; by the absence of dogmatism; and by willingness to leave questions open where the obtainable data do not justify a judgment. Unhurried, thorough, searching investigation, candor, fairness, insight, clear discrimination and sound judgment are in evidence on every page." John D. Davis, "Current Old Testament Discussions and Princeton Opinion," *PRR* 50 (1902): 178. Edward J. Young wrote in 1946 that "although one hundred years have passed, the reading of this commentary is a task which yields rich rewards." E. J. Young, *Westminster Theological Journal* 9 (1946): 9. In the introduction to a 1953 Zondervan edition, Old Testament scholar Merril F. Unger wrote, Alexander "was a happy combination of a thorough scholar and a skillful popularizer in whom vast learning was mellowed by true evangelical faith and piety."

59. *LCH*, 367.
60. In reviewing the work, J. W. Alexander wrote: "There is scarcely an important event in the history of our General Assembly, with which this excellent man was not in some way connected, and it would be difficult to name any one of whom it can be said that he was more devotedly attached to Presbyterian Institutions." *BRPR* 21 (1849): 563.
61. *LJWA* 1: 401.
62. Noll, *Princeton and the Republic,* 273.
63. *LAG*, 529.
64. *LAG*, 508.
65. *BRPR* 21 (1849): 582.
66. J. W. Alexander wrote: "Two things Dr. Janeway said about Dr. Green, which are too good to be lost. 1. Dr. Green, from the time of his early ministry to the close of his life, used to spend the first Monday of every month as a day of fasting and prayer. 2. In one of my visits to him in Philadelphia, he said, 'Brother, I pray for you every day, and for both branches of our Church, and for that Church of which you and I were so long collegiate pastors.'" J. W. Alexander, *Preaching,* 81.
67. *LCH*, 369.
68. *LCH*, 370.
69. *LCH*, 372-73.
70. *LJAA* 2: 554.

71. *LJAA* 2: 852.
72. *LJWA* 2: 102.
73. Alexander, *Preaching*, 69.
74. See J. A. Alexander, *Sermons*, 2 vols. (New York: Charles Scribner, 1860); also published as *The Gospel of Jesus Christ* (London: Nelson, 1861).
75. Hodge, "Retrospect," 30.
76. Cuyler, *Recollections*, 194-95.
77. Samuel Miller, *Thoughts on Public Prayer* (Philadelphia: Presbyterian Board of Publication, 1849).
78. *LJAA* 2: 665.
79. *LJWA* 1: 203. This is a rare reference to his wife in J. W. Alexander's *Familiar Letters*. Unfortunately, the recipient and editor of the letters, John Hall, "in deference to a delicacy which commands the most sacred respect . . . excluded many references to the happiness, the comfort, the spiritual benefit, which Dr. Alexander possessed and appreciated as a husband" (1: vii).
80. There are 67 different titles by J. W. Alexander in the *National Union Catalogue*. The total number of entries under his name, including multiple editions, is 132.
81. Hodge, "Retrospect," 3. J. W. Alexander commented about his literary work: "I have written a good deal and published some; it has been too much off at one side. I have not seized hold of the main things. All topics which I treat are regarded by me more historically than philosophically; more with reference to books and authors than reasons. How different my father—Dr. Hodge—Vinet—and (in error) Channing." Alexander, *Preaching*, 27.
82. *LJWA* 2: 112.
83. Broadus, *Boyce*, 77.
84. *LSM* 2: 513.

## *14. The Duty of Controversy*

1. Archibald Alexander, in Duffield, *Princeton Pulpit*, 30-31.
2. Samuel Miller, *The Primitive and Apostolical Order of the Church of Christ Vindicated* (Philadelphia: Presbyterian Board of Publication, 1840), 7, 19.
3. Charles Hodge, "Polemic Theology." Charles Hodge Papers. Speer Library, Princeton Theological Seminary, Princeton, New Jersey.
4. "Advertisement," *BR* 1 (1829); Hodge, "Retrospect," 3-4.

5. By 1825, one hundred and twenty-five churches in New England had formed themselves into the American Unitarian Association.

6. Hardman, *Finney*, 214.

7. Samuel Miller, *Letters on Unitarianism; Addressed to the Members of the First Presbyterian Church, in the City of Baltimore* (Trenton: G. Sherman, 1821).

8. *LSM* 2: 102.

9. Samuel Miller, *Letters on the Eternal Sonship of Christ: Addressed to the Rev. Prof. Stuart, of Andover* (Philadelphia, 1823).

10. Samuel Miller, *An Essay, on the Warrant, Nature and Duties of the Office of the Ruling Elder, in the Presbyterian Church* (Philadelphia: Presbyterian Board of Publication, 1821). The book was revised in 1831 and went through three American and two British editions during Miller's lifetime. He was working on another revision at the time of his death. Miller's book was reprinted by Presbyterian Heritage Publications in 1984 and 1987.

11. Miller, *Office of the Ruling Elder*, 5-6.

12. *JPH* 56 (1978): 316-17.

13. Miller, *Office of the Ruling Elder*, 339.

14. Lane, "Samuel Miller," 314-15.

15. *LSM* 2: 172.

16. Samuel Miller's and James Wilson's fathers (also Presbyterian ministers) clashed over the same issue in 1788 when Matthew Wilson complained to John Miller about the proposed establishment of a General Assembly. See Lane, "Samuel Miller," 306.

17. Lane, "Samuel Miller," 276.

18. Samuel Miller, *Letters to Presbyterians*, 283.

19. *LSM* 2: 172.

20. Lane, "Samuel Miller," 352.

21. Robert Jefferson Breckinridge, *Spirit of the Nineteenth Century* (1843): 316

22. For a study of this debate, see Iain Murray, "Ruling Elders—A Sketch of a Controversy," *The Banner of Truth* 235 (1983): 1-9; and Edgar Mayse, "Robert Jefferson Breckinridge and the 'Elder Question,'" *Affirmation: Union Theological Seminary in Virginia* 6 (1993): 73-87. Robert S. Rayburn comments, "This debate was concluded long before a satisfactory outcome was achieved and this fact explains the confusion and the many ambiguities of practice observable today." Robert S. Rayburn, "Three Offices: Minister, Elder, Deacon,"

*Presbyterion: Covenant Seminary Review* 12 (1986): 105. For some of the material in the above section, I am indebted to the paper by George W. Robertson, "Fencing God's Garden: Samuel Miller and the Ruling Eldership" (Covenant Theological Seminary, 1993).

23. Samuel Miller, *Letters Concerning the Constitution and Order of the Christian Ministry: Addressed to the Members of the Presbyterian Churches in the City of New York. To which is prefixed a letter on the present aspect and bearing of the Episcopal controversy* (Philadelphia: Towar, J. & D. M. Hogan, 1830).

24. Samuel Miller, *Presbyterianism the Truly Primitive and Apostolical Constitution of the Church of Christ* (Philadelphia: Presbyterian Board of Publication, 1835), 6-8. There were at least nine different editions of Miller's *Presbyterianism* published by 1855, including two editions published in Edinburgh and London and an Italian translation published in Genoa in 1855.

25. Miller, *Presbyterianism,* 7.

26. John DeWitt, *PTR* 4 (1906): 182.

27. *LSM* 2: 491.

28. *LSM* 2: 507. The quotation is from Leroy J. Halsey, student at Princeton Seminary from 1837 to 1840 and professor at McCormick Theological Seminary from 1859 until 1892.

29. I am indebted to Patrick S. Allen and his paper "Charles Hodge and the 1845 Romish Baptism Question" (Covenant Theological Seminary, 1993) for some of the material for this section.

30. In his 1843 lectures on pastoral theology, Archibald Alexander stated that converts from Roman Catholicism should not be rebaptized but added that "each is to form his own opinion."

31. *LSM* 2: 198-200.

32. The practice continued until the 1852 General Assembly, when after nominations for the preacher of the sermon for the next year considerable debate ensued and the matter was "postponed indefinitely" and seems never to have been taken up again. *Minutes of the General Assembly of the Presbyterian Church in the United States of America (1852),* 209.

33. *BRPR* 17 (1845): 444-71.

34. *BRPR* 17 (1845): 445, 450, 464-65, 467.

35. *BRPR* 18 (1846): 320. James Henley Thornwell responded to Hodge in a series of articles in *The Watchman and Observer*—which totaled some one hundred and thirty pages.

36. *BRPR* 18 (1846): 321-45.
37. *LCH*, 340.
38. In 1852, J. W. Alexander wrote: "I find it very hard to swallow the tenet, that the existing church of Rome is incapable of being improved, and is to be looked at only as for hellfire." *LJWA* 2: 168.
39. Charles Hodge, "Finney's Lectures on Theology," *BRPR* 19 (1847): 237-77. For a competent survey of Hodge's critique of Finney's revivalism and theology, Darwinism, the Mercersburg movement, and various expressions of romanticism in American religion, see Charles A. Jones, "Charles Hodge, The Keeper of Orthodoxy: The Method, Purpose and Meaning of His Apologetic" (Ph. D. diss., Drew University, 1989).
40. *BRPR* 19 (1847): 237.
41. *BRPR* 19 (1847): 275.
42. Charles Finney, *Views of Sanctification* (Oberlin: Steele, 1840), 59.
43. Hardman, *Finney*, 377.
44. *BRPR* 19 (1847): 276. "For forty pages Charles Hodge made the definitive Old School review of Finney's theology in a surprisingly mild tone," according to historian Keith J. Hardman; "there is hardly any vitriol spilled anywhere, and not one approximation to Finney's favorite phrase for his opponents, 'it is absurd.'" Hardman, *Finney*, 393. In 1921 B. B. Warfield subjected the "Oberlin Perfectionism" to over two hundred pages of careful analysis and refutation in *The Princeton Theological Review* 19 (1921): 1-63, 225-88, 451-93, and 568-619. These articles are reprinted in Benjamin Breckinridge Warfield, *Studies in Perfectionism* (New York: Oxford University Press, 1932): 2: 3-215. Warfield wrote: "It is quite clear that what Finney gives us is less a theology than a system of morals. God might be eliminated from it entirely without essentially changing its character" (193).
45. Charles Finney, *The Oberlin Quarterly Review* 3 (1847), 23-81.
46. Hodge summarized his critique of Finney's theology in his *Systematic Theology* 3: 8-22, 255-58.
47. David W. Lotz, "Philip Schaff and the Idea of Church History," in *A Century of Church History: The Legacy of Philip Schaff*, ed. Henry W. Bowden (Carbondale: Southern Illinois University Press, 1988), 4.
48. Ahlstrom, *Religious History of the American People*, 615.
49. Ahlstrom, *Religious History of the American People*, 618.

50. Charles Hodge, "Schaff's Protestantism," *BRPR* 17 (1845): 626-36

51. *BRPR* 17 (1845): 626.

52. *BRPR* 17 (1845): 631-32.

53. *BRPR* 20 (1848): 227-77.

54. Timothy George judges that in the connection between the Lord's Supper and the doctrine of election "the *Consensus* tilts a bit toward Hodge." Timothy George, "John Calvin and the Agreement of Zurich," in *John Calvin and the Church: A Prism of Reform,* ed. Timothy George (Louisville: Westminster/John Knox Press, 1990), 52.

55. James H. Nichols, "John Williamson Nevin (1803-1886) —Evangelical Catholicism," in Kerr, ed., *Sons of the Prophets,* 80.

56. *BRPR* 26 (1854): 149, 151.

57. Ahlstrom, *Religious History of the American People,* 618.

58. *LJWA* 2: 54.

59. *LJAA* 2: 740. Dr. Schaff appreciated the ability of J. A. Alexander and asked him to assist him in preparing a history of the church—an invitation which Alexander declined.

60. *LJAA* 2: 814. Charles Hodge said that J. A. Alexander completely ignored philosophical matters as of no interest to him. "When Dr. Schaff's work on *The Apostolic Age* came out, he was greatly delighted with it. The theory of historical development which it broached, he took no notice of. He did not even know it was there." *LCH,* 558.

61. *BRPR* 26 (1854): 149, 151.

62. B. B. Warfield criticized Schaff's "comprehension," stating that Schaff had represented himself as occupying "a position in which not only Arminianism, Lutheranism, and Calvinism, but also Rationalism and Supranaturalism, are reconciled." Warfield describes this "concessive" method as "a neat device by which one may appear to conquer while really yielding the citadel." Warfield, *Studies in Theology,* 588-89.

63. Jonathan Sinclair Carey, "'For God or Against Him': Princeton Orthodoxy and Transcendentalists," *JPH* 64 (1986), 246. Here Carey quotes Perry Miller.

64. *BRPR* 11 (1839): 95, 97.

65. *BRPR* 12 (1840): 63.

66. *BRPR* 19 (1847): 307. See Hodge's views on this subject in *The Faithful Mother's Reward,* published in 1855 by the Presbyterian Board of Publication. The book contains "A

Narrative of the Conversion and Happy Death of J. B." by an anonymous mother. Hodge wrote the introductory essay in which he developed both the obligations of parents to train their children and the responsibility of children to keep God's covenant. Paige P. Miller explains that accountability for children's religious training shifted during the early part of the nineteenth century from ministers and fathers to mothers. Charles Hodge was one of the few who examined the theological implications of making mothers "the distributors of salvation." He by no means downplayed the role of mothers as spiritual guides but insisted on the participation of both parents in the training of the child and stated that proper Christian instruction "does not preclude the possibility of any well educated child going astray." Hodge's message, Miller states, "may well have come as words of liberation from real or potential guilt." Miller, *A Claim to New Roles*, 70-71.

67. *LCH*, 98.
68. *BRPR* 19 (1847): 533, 536.
69. Ahlstrom, *Religious History of the American People*, 611.
70. Horace Bushnell, *God in Christ: Three discourses, delivered at New Haven, Cambridge, and Andover, with a preliminary dissertation on language* (Hartford: Brown and Parsons, 1849), 73.
71. *Bibliotheca Sacra* 7 (1850): 542.
72. Charles Hodge, "The Theology of the Intellect and That of the Feelings," *BRPR* 22 (1850): 642-74. Mark Noll calls this article "a virtual recapitulation" of Hodge's contribution to the Princeton theology. Noll, *The Princeton Theology*, 186.
73. *BRPR* 22 (1850): 543, 565.
74. *BRPR* 21 (1849): 436, 469.
75. *BRPR* 38 (1866): 161-94.
76. *Theological Essays: Reprinted from the Princeton Review* (Edinburgh: T. & T. Clark, 1856), iii-iv.
77. During Princeton Seminary's first fifty years, forty-nine scholarships were established by persons giving $2500 for each scholarship. The first two were provided by Mrs. Martha Le Roy of New York City. The third was given by Robert Lenox, also of New York City. The fourth came from John Whitehead of Burke County, Georgia, and the fifth was given by the Congregational and Presbyterian Female Association of Charleston, South Carolina. Robert and Alexander Stuart of New York City gave eight scholarships.
78. *Presbyterian Magazine* 7 (1857): 24-25.

## 15. The Church and the Country

1. *LSM* 2: 132, 135.
2. *LCH*, 346.
3. Society of Inquiry to the American missionaries at Bombay, July 30, 1831, Speer Library, Princeton, N. J.
4. Society of Inquiry to missionaries in Beirut, September 1, 1831, Speer Library, Princeton, N. J.
5. *LCH*, 230-31.
6. Archibald Alexander, "The Duty of Christians in Relation to the Existing War," Speer Library, Princeton, N. J.
7. *LJWA* 2: 51.
8. *LJWA* 2: 68.
9. *LSM* 1: 91.
10. *LSM* 1: 94.
11. George Marsden shows how this strongly-worded statement was actually a compromise, conceding "hasty emancipation to be a greater curse" than slavery. George M. Marsden, *The Evangelical Mind and the New School Presbyterian Experience: A Case Study of Thought and Theology in Nineteenth-Century America* (New Haven: Yale University Press, 1970), 91.
12. *LSM* 2: 292-93.
13. *BRTR* 8 (1836): 268-305; *BRPR* 16 (1844): 545-81; and *BRPR* 21 (1849): 583-607. For several points in the discussion of this topic I am indebted to the paper by Paige Benton, "Charles Hodge on Slavery: Abstraction and Accommodation" (Covenant Theological Seminary, 1993).
14. *BRPR* 36 (1864): 548.
15. *LCH*, 336.
16. *LSM* 2: 312.
17. See Joseph C. and Owen Lovejoy, *Memoir of the Rev. Elijah P. Lovejoy* (New York: John S. Taylor, 1838).
18. *LJWA* 2: 65.
19. *BRTR* 8 (1836): 286.
20. Timothy Dwight Bozeman, "Inductive and Deductive Politics: Science and Society in Antebellum Presbyterian Thought," *Journal of American History* 64 (1977).
21. William S. Barker, "The Social Views of Charles Hodge (1797-1878): A Study in 19th-Century Calvinism and Conservatism," *Presbyterion: Covenant Seminary Review* 1 (1975): 11. Barker writes that Hodge "was ready to welcome and support emancipation when the tortuous course of providence finally did produce it" (14).

22. Albert Barnes, a graduate of Princeton Seminary (1823), who was often at odds with his former teachers, criticized the Princeton position on slavery and called for stronger measures in his *Inquiry into the Scriptural Views of Slavery* (Philadelphia: Parry and McMillan, 1846).

23. *BRPR* 21 (1849): 40.

24. *BRPR* 16 (1844): 580.

25. *LJWA* 1: 297.

26. *LAA*, 451.

27. Archibald Alexander, *A History of Colonization on the Western Coast of Africa* (Philadelphia: William S. Martien, 1846), 11. Alexander's book is the most thorough early study of African colonization.

28. Ahlstrom, *Religious History of the American People*, 651.

29. *LJWA* 1: 319.

30. Loetscher, *Archibald Alexander*, 246.

31. *BRPR* 15 (1843): 22.

32. For the life of C. C. Jones, see the remarkable family correspondence edited by Robert M. Myers, *The Children of Pride: A True Story of Georgia and the Civil War* (New Haven: Yale University Press, 1972) and *A Georgian at Princeton* (New York: Harcourt Brace Jovanovich, 1976). See also Eduard N. Loring, "Charles C. Jones: Missionary to Plantation Slaves, 1831-1847" (Ph. D. diss., Vanderbilt University, 1976), and Erskine Clarke, *Wrestlin' Jacob: A Portrait of Religion in the Old South* (Atlanta: John Knox Press, 1979).

33. Kenneth Scott Latourette has written: "All the extensive Protestant missionary effort of Europeans and Americans in Asia and Africa in the century between 1815 and 1914 had resulted in no greater numerical gains than had been achieved among the Negroes of the United States in the same period." Kenneth Scott Latourette, *A History of the Expansion of Christianity* (Grand Rapids: Zondervan, 1970) 4: 327.

34. *LJWA* 1: 260.

35. Hageman, *History of Princeton* 1: 269.

36. Alexander, *Sermons* 1: 280.

## 16. Two Great Lights

1. Helen S. Coan Nevius, *The Life of John Livingstone Nevius: for Forty Years a Missionary in China* (New York: Fleming H. Revell Co., 1895), 68. At Princeton, Nevius adopted twenty-

four rules for himself—he would not sleep more than seven hours; he would keep in mind that he was was living for God and heaven; he would make it the object of his studies to become a useful rather than merely a learned man; and in many other ways he determined to profit from his time at the seminary.

2. *PSB* 28 (1934): 10.
3. Broadus, *Boyce*, 70.
4. *LJWA* 2: 104. One of these Baptist students was a young South Carolinian, James Petigru Boyce. After serving as pastor of the First Baptist Church of Columbia, South Carolina, and as professor of theology at Furman University, Boyce helped found the Southern Baptist Theological Seminary in Greenville, South Carolina, in 1859. The seminary moved to Louisville, Kentucky, in 1877.
5. Sprague, *Annals* 3: 611.
6. *LJWA* 2: 109-10.
7. *LSM* 2: 534.
8. *LJWA* 2: 110.
9. *LJAA* 2: 671.
10. *LSM* 2: 539.
11. "Thus parted for a little time, at the brink of the river, these veteran soldiers of the cross," Samuel Miller's son wrote, *LSM* 2: 539-40.
12. *LSM* 2: 538.
13. *LAA*, 582; *LSM* 2: 42-44.
14. *LSM* 2: 548.
15. Sprague, *Annals* 3: 624.
16. Horace G. Hinsdale, *An Historical Discourse, commemorating the Centenary of the Completed Organization of the First Presbyterian Church, Princeton, New Jersey, Preached December Twenty-Sixth 1886* (Princeton: Princeton Press, 1888), 64.
17. Loetscher, *Archibald Alexander*, 238.
18. Sprague, *Annals* 3: 624.
19. Myers, ed., *A Georgian at Princeton*, 72.
20. Myers, ed., *A Georgian at Princeton*, 76.
21. Archibald Alexander, *Practical Sermons: to be read in families and social meetings* (Philadelphia: Presbyterian Board of Publication, 1850), 6.
22. *LAA*, 596-97.
23. *LJWA* 2: 163.
24. Sprague, *Annals* 3: 625.
25. *LAA*, 606.

26. *LAA*, 605-6; *LCH*, 382. The walking stick is now in the archives of Princeton Theological Seminary. The small cane measures only a few feet, more the size of a baton than a staff. It was carved from a whale's tusk by a tribal chief of one of the Hawaiian Islands and sent to America with Princeton missionary Charles Stewart, to Stewart's "chief"— Archibald Alexander. After Charles Hodge's visit with Dr. Alexander on the evening of October 12, he went home and wrote a "memorandum" to himself concluding with these words: "This record of this solemn interview with my spiritual father, to whom I am more indebted in every respect than to any man or to all other men, was made that I may never forget it or lose the humbling impression of it, immediately after its occurrence." Stewart, "The Tethered Theology," 124-25.
27. *LCH*, 382.
28. Alexander, *Practical Truths*, 386.
29. Noll, *The Princeton Theology*, 13. A president of Princeton Seminary described Archibald Alexander as a "plain man, true saint and scholar, great preacher, professor and ecumenical Churchman." John A. Mackay, "Founding Father" in Kerr, ed., *Sons of the Prophets*, 21.
30. Sprague, *Annals* 3: 620.
31. *LAA*, 416; John Oliver Nelson, "Archibald Alexander, Winsome Conservative (1772-1851)," *JPHS* 35 (1957): 15-32.
32. *LCH*, 456.
33. Alexander, *Address . . . 1912*, 14.
34. Cuyler, *Recollections*, 192.
35. Johnson, *Robert Lewis Dabney*, 100.
36. Lovejoy, *Memoir*, 54.
37. *LSM* 2: 416; *LCH*, 454.
38. *LSM* 2: 398.
39. Bruce M. Stephens, "Watchmen on the Walls of Zion: Samuel Miller and the Christian Ministry," *JPH* 56 (1978): 305.
40. *LCH*, 551-53.

## 17. *Our Elisha*

1. *LCH*, 514.
2. John Macleod, *Scottish Theology in Relation to Church History Since the Reformation* (The Banner of Truth Trust, 1974), 271; *LCH*, 429.

3. *LJWA* 2: 107.
4. Alexander, *Preaching*, 27.
5. Francis Wayland wrote to J. W. Alexander in November 1854: "I have just completed your admirable Memoir of your father—now with God. A more charming biography I have never read. While you write as a son, it is as a son of Archibald Alexander. There is nothing filial that is not admirable, and not a word that could not be attested even more strongly by a host of witnesses. A more beautiful or noble specimen of Christian character can hardly be conceived. His gifts were great and abundant beyond the common lot of humanity; and God placed them where they shone with a radiance that illumined the whole church of Christ." Wayland, *Francis Wayland* 2: 174-75.
6. *LJWA* 2: 165.
7. *LJAA* 2: 663.
8. *PSB* 15 (1921): 8.
9. Frederick W. Loetscher, "John DeWitt," *PTR* 22 (1924): 212.
10. J. A. Alexander's lecture notes on church history were published posthumously. See Joseph Addison Alexander, *Notes on New Testament Literature and Ecclesiastical History* (New York: C. Scribner's Sons, 1860). The preface by J. A. Alexander's brother, Samuel Davies Alexander, states that the book contains all that J. A. Alexander left "fit for the press of his remarkable Biblical and historical lectures."
11. *LJAA* 2: 732.
12. *LJAA* 2: 801.
13. Broadus, *Boyce*, 71. Boyce added: "These lectures. . . are the earliest known instance of making the English Bible the text-book in a large scale in a theological seminary."
14. *LJAA* 1: 393.
15. J. A. Alexander's commentary on the Psalms went through six editions in twenty-five years. Charles Spurgeon wrote that Alexander's *Psalms* "occupies a first place among expositions. It is a clear and judicious explanation of the text, and cannot be dispensed with." Spurgeon, *Commenting and Commentaries*, 81. In preparing his famous *Treasury of David*, Spurgeon made more use of Alexander's commentary on the Psalms than that of any other single writer. Spurgeon also greatly valued Alexander's New Testament commentaries, considering them works "of the highest merit" (162). Concerning Hodge's commentaries on I and II Corinthians and Ephesians, Spurgeon wrote that "the more we use

Hodge, the more we value him" (174) and "with no writer do we more fully agree" (178). Alexander's *Mark* and *Acts* and Hodge's *Romans* and *First and Second Corinthians* have been reprinted by The Banner of Truth Trust.

16. These New Testament commentaries give further proof of J. A. Alexander's scholarship, exegetical ability, and critical judgment. The *Sunday School Times* wrote in 1897 concerning his Acts commentary: "Though printed in 1857, it anticipates more than half the changes made in the Revised Version." John Stott in the preface to his commentary on Acts expresses his appreciation for "the godly and clearheaded insights of J. A. Alexander, the brilliant Princeton linguist of the nineteenth century." John R. W. Stott, *The Spirit, the Church and the World* (Downers Grove, Ill.: InterVarsity Press, 1990), 6.

17. *LJAA* 2: 824-25.

18. John Cleve Green was a trustee of the seminary for twenty-one years (1853-74), attending all but nine of the forty-four meetings held during that period—three of these absences coming during his final illness. Among his gifts to the seminary were the following: endowment of a professorship in memory of a deceased child of the Greens—the Helena Professorship of Old Testament Language and Exegesis (1861); house for occupancy by a professor (1861); completion of the endowment for the Archibald Alexander professorship (1872); renovation of the chapel (1874); and renovation of the Old Seminary Building (1875). John C. Green was the largest single donor that the College of New Jersey had ever had. He gave more than a third of the college's endowment, the first library building (named the Chancellor Green Library for his brother), and the School of Science building. A memorial presented shortly after his death in 1875, at a meeting of the Chamber of Commerce of the State of New York, stated that John Cleve Green was "a true Christian gentleman—who was the master, not the slave of his wealth—holding his possessions as a faithful steward, and, in the sight of God." Selden, *Princeton Theological Seminary*, 42.

19. *William Henry Green's Semi-Centennial Celebration*, 67.

20. *LJAA* 2: 645.

21. John D. Davis, *The Life and Work of William Henry Green: A Commemorative Address. Delivered in the Chapel of Princeton Theological Seminary. Tuesday, March 27, 1900* (Philadelphia:

MacCalla and Co., 1900), 8.

22. *William Henry Green's Semi-Centennial Celebration,* 160.

23. *Discourses at the Inauguration of the Rev. William Henry Green as Professor of Biblical and Oriental Literature in the Theological Seminary at Princeton, N. J.* (Philadelphia, 1851), 41.

24. John D. Davis, "William Henry Green," *PRR* 11 (1900): 380.

25. Davis, *William Henry Green,* 33.

26. James M. Boice, ed., *Making God's Word Plain: One Hundred and Fifty Years in the History of Tenth Presbyterian Church of Philadelphia* (Philadelphia: Tenth Presbyterian Church, 1979), 44-45, 54.

27. Robert Hamill Nassau Ms. Speer Library, Princeton Theological Seminary, Princeton, N. J.

28. David Riddle Williams, *James H. Brookes: A Memoir* (St. Louis: Presbyterian Board of Publication, 1897), 53-62. Brookes served churches in St. Louis from 1858 until his death in 1897. He was editor of *The Truth* and became a powerful figure in the Presbyterian church.

29. Carnahan spent his last years in Newark, New Jersey, where he died March 3, 1859. He remained a member of the board of trustees of the college until his death, at which time he was also president of the board of trustees of the seminary.

30. Thomas Wertenbaker stated that the college reached its "nadir" under Ashbel Green, but Mark Noll argues that the lowest point came in the two administrations after Green— James Carnahan (1823-54) and John Maclean (1854-68). Noll, *Princeton and the Republic,* 289. In important aspects, however, the years of Carnahan and Maclean represented greater success than the later history of the college. The tendency toward secularization was delayed by their single-minded commitment to the historic Christian purpose of Princeton College.

31. *PRR* 8 (1897): 655.

32. *PRR* 8 (1897): 647.

33. Myers, ed., *A Georgian at Princeton,* 327.

34. *PRR* 8 (1897): 662.

35. *LCH,* 392.

36. *LJAA* 2: 735.

37. *LCH,* 396.

38. Daniel McGilvary, *A half century among the Siamese and the Lao; an Autobiography* (New York: Fleming H. Revell Co., 1912), 36.

39. Cuyler, *Recollections*, 188-89.
40. Ashbel Green Simonton, Journal, Nov. 5, 1852-Dec. 31, 1866. Speer Library, Princeton, N. J., 83-84.
41. The fifth son of Dr. and Mrs. Archibald Alexander, Samuel Davies Alexander was born at Princeton, New Jersey, May 3, 1819. He graduated from the College of New Jersey in 1838. After studying civil engineering for a time, he entered Princeton Seminary. He was ordained in 1847, and served churches in Philadelphia and Freehold, New Jersey, before being called to the Fifteenth Street Church, New York City, in 1856. He retired from the pastorate of that church (renamed Phillips Presbyterian Church) in 1889, remaining pastor emeritus until his death in 1894.
42. *LJAA* 2: 797.
43. *LJAA* 2: 798-99.
44. Alexander, *The Revival*, 6.
45. Samuel I. Prime, *The Power of Prayer: Illustrated in the Wonderful Displays of Divine Grace at the Fulton Street and Other Meetings in New York and Elsewhere, in 1857 and 1858* (New York: Sheldon, Blakeman and Co., 1859; repr. The Banner of Truth Trust, 1991), 2-3.
46. Alexander, *The Revival*, 9-10.
47. *New York Times*, March 20, 1858, 4.
48. *LJWA* 2: 237. The titles of the tracts are: The Revival; Seek to Save Souls; Pray for the Spirit; The Unawakened; Harden not your Hearts; Varieties in Anxious Inquiry; Looking unto Jesus; God be Merciful to me a Sinner!; O for more Feeling!; Have I come to Christ?; My Teacher—My Master; My Brother; Sing Praises; The Harvest of New York; Compel them to Come in; Help the Seamen; To Firemen.
49. Prime, *The Power of Prayer*, 1.
50. *LJAA* 2: 826.
51. Wayland, *Francis Wayland* 2: 175, 177.
52. Dwayne Davis Cox, "William Henry Green: Princeton Theologian" (M. A. thesis, University of Louisville, 1976), 26.
53. Princeton, and many others, were convinced that "the American pulpit has had few superiors to Dr. [James Waddel] Alexander." *The Princeton Book*, 116. Charles Hodge said that it was the combination of natural ability, wide scholarship, eloquence, and Christian devotion that made J. W. Alexander, "not the first of orators to hear on rare occasions, but the first of preachers to sit under, month after month and year after year." *LJWA* 2: 302. J. W.

Alexander's *Thoughts on Preaching* was published posthumously in 1864 and reprinted by the Banner of Truth Trust in 1975. His brother Samuel Davies Alexander edited the volume, bringing together James's writings on preaching—homiletical paragraphs in his private journals, several articles in the *Biblical Repertory*, and a series of letters to young ministers published in *The Presbyterian*. Collections of his sermons appeared in books entitled *Consolation: in discourses on select topics, addressed to the suffering people of God* (New York: C. Scribner, 1852); *Faith; treated in a series of discourses* (New York: Charles Scribner, 1862); and *Sacramental Discourses* (New York: Randolph, 1859). *Sacramental Discourses* was reprinted as *God is Love: Communion Addresses* by The Banner of Truth Trust in 1985. Alexander's *Thoughts on Family-Worship* (Philadelphia: Presbyterian Board of Publication, 1847) was reprinted in 1990 by Soli Deo Gloria Publications.

54. *LJWA* 1: 291; *LJWA* 2: 62. J. W. Alexander admired the style and manner of preaching in the Free Church of Scotland.
55. Wayland, *Francis Wayland* 2: 175-76.
56. Robert J. Breckinridge, *The Christian Pastor, One of the Ascension Gifts of Christ* (Baltimore: D. Owen & Son, 1844).
57. Gardiner Spring, *The Power of the Pulpit; or, Thoughts Addressed to Christian Ministers and Those who Hear Them* (New York: Baker and Scribner, 1848), 379-83.
58. *BRPR* 20 (1848): 464.

## 18. Transitions

1. *LJAA* 2: 876.
2. *LJAA* 2: 736.
3. *LJAA* 2: 850.
4. John DeWitt wrote of his Princeton predecessor: "Had he continued in the chair, he would probably have produced in part, at least, one of the most vivid, graphic and dramatic of Church Histories." *PTR* 1 (1903): 626.
5. *LJAA* 1: 217-19.
6. *LJAA* 2: 870.
7. *LJWA* 2: 295; *Presbyterian Almanac* 3: 72.
8. During the Civil War, Elizabeth Cabell Alexander lived in the Isle of Wight, England. After the war she returned to America and lived with her sons. In 1885 she died at the home of her brother in Charlottesville, Virginia. Her body

was taken to Princeton and buried next to the grave of her husband. The Alexanders had seven children, four of whom died in infancy. James Waddel Alexander (born 1839) became a lawyer and officer of The Equitable Life Assurance Society of New York City. William Alexander (born 1848) joined his brother in The Equitable Life Assurance Society. Henry Carrington Alexander (born 1835) graduated from the College of New Jersey and from Princeton Seminary. After a short ministry in New York City, he was called to the church at Charlotte Court House, Virginia, where his father and grandfather had served before him. In 1870, he became professor of Biblical Literature and New Testament Interpretation in Union Theological Seminary in Virginia. He resigned in 1891 and served churches in Maryland and West Virginia until his death in 1894. His grave is in the Princeton cemetery, adjoining those of his grandfather, father, mother, and uncles.

9.   *Presbyterian Almanac* 3: 73-74.
10.  Hodge, *Discourse. . . 1874*, 26.
11.  *LJAA* 2: 890.
12.  *LCH*, 438.
13.  *Presbyterian Almanac* 3: 76.
14.  *LJAA* 2: 895-96.
15.  *LCH*, 438.
16.  *LCH*, 444-45. Hodge later wrote: "I believe that I was rash enough to say on the floor of the General Assembly of 1860, that I thought Dr. Addison Alexander the greatest man whom I had ever seen. This was unwise: both because there are so many different kinds of greatness; and because I was no competent judge. I feel free to say now, however, that I never saw a man who so constantly impressed me with a sense of his mental superiority—with his power to acquire knowledge and his power to communicate it. He seemed able to learn and to teach anything he pleased." *LCH*, 557. A more recent tribute to J. A. Alexander came from Merrill F. Unger who wrote in 1953, "Joseph Addison Alexander represents the finest in the spiritual and scholastic attainments of the Presbyterian Church in America." Preface to J. A. Alexander, *Commentary on the Prophecies of Isaiah* (Grand Rapids: Zondervan Publishing House, 1953).
17.  Hodge, *Discourse. . . 1874*, 28.
18.  Theodore L. Cuyler, *Thoughts for Heart and Life* (London, 1890), 100.

19. Thomas V. Moore, *Zechariah, Haggai and Malachi* (New York: Robert Carter, 1856). This book was reprinted by The Banner of Truth Trust in 1958. Moore served churches in Carlisle, Pennsylvania, Greencastle and Richmond, Virginia, and Nashville Tennessee. In 1867 he was elected moderator of the Presbyterian Church in the United States.
20. *SSW* 1: 486.
21. For a summary of Charles Hodge's views, see his article on "Presbyterianism," *BRPR* 32 (1860): 546-67.
22. *LJAA* 2: 551-52.
23. *LJWA* 2: 118.
24. *LCH*, 441.
25. *LCH*, 441-42. The *Presbyterian Banner* of January 12, 1898, states: "Several times we have heard the late Rev. Archibald Alexander Hodge, D.D., say that he regarded Dr. Dabney as the best teacher of theology in the United States, if not in the world." Johnson, *Robert Lewis Dabney*, 534.
26. Johnson, *Robert Lewis Dabney*, 313.
27. Johnson, *Robert Lewis Dabney*, 200, 202-3, 210.
28. Patton, *Caspar Wistar Hodge*, 18-19.
29. *LJWA* 1: 264.

## *19.  War and Peace*

1. Wertenbaker, *Princeton*, 268.
2. *Presbyterian Almanac* 5: 78-79.
3. *BRPR* 36 (1864): 562.
4. Charles Hodge wrote this article before the secession of South Carolina but it did not appear in print until January 1861. Mark Noll considers Charles Hodge's articles on the great affairs of the country "one of the most intriguing series of theological reflections on national matters since the Puritans." Mark Noll, "The *Princeton Review*," *Westminster Theological Journal* 50 (1988): 295.
5. *BRPR* 33 (1861): 322-76.
6. *BRPR* 33 (1861): 543-44.
7. *BRPR* 34 (1862): 177, 523.
8. *LCH*, 475.
9. The student was Henry Branch. He had been captured early in the Civil War and released on his word of honor not to fight again. Alone in the North, he requested admission to Princeton Seminary and was promptly welcomed. He graduated in 1865 and served churches in Maryland, Con-

necticut, and Virginia. He died in 1931 at the age of ninety-one.

10. *LJWA* 1: 294.

11. Williams, *James H. Brookes*, 54.

12. Robert T. Handy, *A History of Union Theological Seminary in New York* (New York: Columbia University Press, 1987), 42-43.

13. *BRPR* 39 (1867): 505.

14. A. A. Hodge's *Commentary on the Confession of Faith* (1885 edition) included an appendix with statements from Charles Hodge and Henry Smith "as to the sense in which the historical Presbyterian Church understands intrants into her ministry to accept the 'Confession of Faith as containing the system of doctrine taught in the Holy Scriptures.'" These quotations showed, A. A. Hodge stated, that "the two branches of the Presbyterian Church are thus shown to have been perfectly agreed" on the matter of subscription. A. A. Hodge, *A Commentary on the Confession of Faith* (Philadelphia: Presbyterian Board of Christian Education, 1940 [1885]), 539-43.

15. For Hodge's views on subscription, see "Remarks on Dr. Cox's Communication" (*BRTR* 3 [1831] ), "Adoption of the Confession of Faith" (*BRPR* 30 [1858]: 669-92), and "The General Assembly—Reunion" (*BRPR* 39 [1867]: 440-522).

16. *BRTR* 3 (1831): 520-21. Hodge believed that he was one of about a dozen ministers in the Presbyterian church who actually held to every proposition of the Confession, and so he would have been able to subscribe under the strict view; but most ministers, he claimed, not even Ashbel Green, could have done so. *BRPR* 30 (1858): 686. Hodge's statements in his *Constitutional History* which appear to demand a stricter position than he advocates elsewhere must be interpreted in the context of his polemic against what he saw as the New School view of subscription to the essential doctrines of the gospel only. Hodge, *Constitutional History*, 172. I am indebted to Kevin Twit's paper, "Old Princeton and Subscription" (Covenant Theological Seminary, 1993) for several points in this section. He correctly identifies the Old Princeton theologians as "moderates in their view of the strictness of subscription." They saw both the Old School every-proposition-view and the New School substance-of-doctrine view as innovations.

17. *Presbyterian Re-union Volume*, 263-64.

18. *Henry Boynton Smith: His Life and Work,* edited by his wife (New York: A. C. Armstrong, 1881), 280.

19. *BRPR* 25 (1853): 680.

20. *LCH,* 505-7.

21. *BRPR* 41 (1869): 457-59.

22. *LCH,* 503. See Charles Hodge, "Principles of Church Union, and the Re-union of Old and New School Presbyterians," *BRPR* 37 (1865): 271-313. According to Dr. Ward, editor of the *Independent,* Charles Hodge "at first . . . opposed the ultra Old School men in 1836 who were bent on the division of the Church because the New School brethren were too bad to live with. Again, he opposed the same men and their successors in 1866 and '8, who would precipitate the re-union of the two branches because the same New School brethren were too good to live without." Mark Noll writes that Hodge's deliberations on the issue of reunion "were particularly moving, perhaps because he so clearly felt the tension between the equally worthy goals of ecclesiastical catholicity and confessional integrity." Mark Noll, "The *Princeton Review,*" *Westminster Theological Journal* 50 (1988): 295.

23. Hodge, "Retrospect," 38.

24. *Presbyterian Almanac* 5: 59-60.

25. *Presbyterian Almanac* 5: 46, 59-60.

26. *Presbyterian Almanac* 5: 61, 63-64, 73, 79-80.

27. Sprague, *Discourse . . . 1862,* 54-55, 64.

28. Lowrie, *Princeton Theological Seminary and Foreign Missions,* 12.

29. Charles Hodge wrote in 1850 that "the American Churches have probably sent out no missionary to the foreign field of higher qualifications or greater promise than Walter M. Lowrie." See Charles Hodge, "Memoirs of the Rev. Walter M. Lowrie," *BRPR* 22 (1850): 280-312.

30. Nevius, *John Livingstone Nevius,* 96.

31. Robert Leonard McIntyre, "Portrait of Half a Century: Fifty Years of Presbyterianism in Brazil (1859-1910) (Th. D. diss., Princeton Theological Seminary, 1959), 146.

32. *Presbyterian Almanac* 5: 46.

33. Kellogg was also a noted author. His book *The Light of Asia and the Light of the World* was described by Robert Speer as "the best statement of our Christian faith as contrasted with Buddhism." A convinced premillennialist, Kellogg often wrote and lectured on eschatology. In 1886 he became pastor of the St. James Square Presbyterian Church of Toronto,

Canada. In 1892 he returned to India to accept the appointment of the North India and British and Foreign Bible Societies, as one of the committee of three to translate the Old Testament into Hindi. In 1899 in India he died as a result of a fall from his bicycle. A memorial service was conducted on August 13, 1899, and Kellogg was buried at Landour, India. The marker over his grave has the words "Until He Come."

The Index to both volumes of this work
will be found at the end of Volume 2.

SOME OTHER
BANNER OF TRUTH
TITLES

# BIBLICAL THEOLOGY
## Old and New Testaments
### *Geerhardus Vos*

The aim of this book is no less than to provide an account of
the unfolding of the mind of God in history, through the
successive agents of his special revelation. Vos handles this
under three main divisions: the Mosaic epoch of revelation,
the prophetic epoch of revelation, and the New Testament.

Such an historical approach is not meant to supplant the
work of the systematic theologian; nevertheless, the Christian gospel is inextricably bound up with history, and the
biblical theologian thus seeks to highlight the uniqueness of
each biblical document in that succession. The rich variety
of Scripture is discovered anew as the progressive development of biblical themes is explicated.

To read these pages—the fruit of Vos' 39 years of teaching
biblical theology at Princeton—is to appreciate the late
John Murray's suggestion that Geerhardus Vos was the
most incisive exegete in the English-speaking world of the
twentieth century.

*Geerhardus Vos was born in the Netherlands, emigrating to the
United States in 1881 at the age of 19. In 1893 he was invited
to Princeton Seminary, where he had studied, to teach biblical
theology. He remained there until his retirement in 1932. He died
in 1949. His* Pauline Eschatology *is also available in a paperback edition from Eerdmans.*

*ISBN 0 85151 458 8*
*440pp. Large Paperback*

# REVIVAL AND REVIVALISM
The Making and Marring of American
Evangelicalism 1750–1858
*Iain H. Murray*

Marrying careful historical research to popular and relevant presentation, *Revival and Revivalism* traces the spiritually epoch-making events of the eighteenth and nineteenth centuries through the eyes of those who lived at their centre.

Fundamental to the book's thesis is a rejection of the frequent identification of "revival" with "revivalism". The author demonstrates that a common understanding of the New Testament idea of revival was prevalent in most denominations throughout the period 1750–1858. Reviva*lism*, on the other hand, is different both in its origin and in its tendencies. Its ethos is man-centred and its methods too close to the manipulative to require a supernatural explanation.

Iain Murray argues that an inability to recognise this distinction has led many to ignore the new and different teaching on evangelism and revival which began to be popularised in the 1820s. While the case against that teaching was argued almost universally by the leaders of the Second Great Awakening, their testimony was submerged beneath propaganda which promised a "new era" if only the churches would abandon the older ways.

Today, when that propaganda is largely discredited, there is a great need to rediscover the earlier understanding of revival possessed by those who most intimately experience it. *Revival and Revivalism* will do much to aid this rediscovery. Powerfully presented, it contains a message of major importance for contemporary Christians.

*ISBN 0 85151 660 2*
*480pp. Cloth-bound. Illustrated*

# PREACHERS WITH POWER
## Four Stalwarts of the South
### *Douglas Kelly*

Douglas Kelly here reintroduces one of the richest periods of evangelical history, spanning the years 1791–1902, and captures its ethos in the lives of four of its most influential men: *Daniel Baker*, who spent his life as a missionary and itinerant evangelist though sought by a church and two US presidents for Washington; *James Henley Thornwell*, equally able as a pastor and professor but best remembered as a preacher 'wrapt in wonder at the love, humiliation and condescension of the Trinity'; *Benjamin M. Palmer*, who, in the words of a Jewish rabbi, 'got the heart as well as the ear of New Orleans'; and *John L. Girardeau*, 'the Spurgeon of America', who was so remarkably used among the black people of South Carolina.

In addition to these moving lives, Dr Kelly gives us many illuminating sidelights on Christians of the South, such as those of the Midway Church, Georgia, for whom 'religion was a matter of their brightest hopes, their warmest feelings, their deepest convictions.'

*Douglas Kelly is well-qualified to write on 'the old South'. A native of North Carolina, he is currently Professor of Theology at Reformed Theological Seminary, Jackson, Mississippi, USA.*

*ISBN 0 85151 628 9*
*224pp. Cloth-bound.*

*For further details and a free illustrated catalogue please write to:*
THE BANNER OF TRUTH TRUST
3 Murrayfield Road, Edinburgh EH12 6EL
P.O. Box 621, Carlisle, Pennsylvania, 17013, U.S.A.